David Young Comstock

A first Latin book

David Young Comstock
A first Latin book
ISBN/EAN: 9783337278182
Printed in Europe, USA, Canada, Australia, Japan
Cover: Foto ©Paul-Georg Meister /pixelio.de

More available books at **www.hansebooks.com**

A

FIRST LATIN BOOK

DESIGNED AS A

MANUAL OF PROGRESSIVE EXERCISES AND SYSTEMATIC
DRILL IN THE ELEMENTS OF LATIN

AND INTRODUCTORY TO

CÆSAR'S COMMENTARIES ON THE GALLIC WAR

BY

D. Y. COMSTOCK, M.A.
PRINCIPAL OF ST. JOHNSBURY ACADEMY, VERMONT.

ALLYN AND BACON
Boston and Chicago

UNIVERSITY PRESS:
JOHN WILSON AND SON, CAMBRIDGE.

PREFACE.

THE design of this book is to afford a thorough preparation for the reading of Caesar's Commentaries on the Gallic War. It is a very common experience on the part of teachers to find, after several months or a year have been spent in the study of the elements of Latin, that, on beginning to read some Latin author, certain difficulties present themselves at the very outset and increase with every onward step. Some of the sources of these difficulties are : —

1. In nine cases out of ten, the pupil begins the study of Latin with no definite knowledge of his own language, even in the simplest points of sentence structure. As has been said, " he does not appreciate the relations of things."

2. The beginner has been taught to translate isolated sentences, which are never combined into connected narrative. Fragments of sentences, phrases, oblique cases of nouns and pronouns, all absolutely meaningless in themselves, have constituted a large portion of his fundamental work.

3. His elementary book has lacked logical method. Many peculiarities of the Latin language, which, in their proper place, would be shorn of all difficulty, and would appear as reasonable constructions, are presented to the beginner too early in his Latin study. These not only demand a needless amount of time and labor, but also tend to discourage the young student.

iv PREFACE.

A teacher of experience has said: "By a strange inversion we supply an advanced student with all the light he can have, but give a beginner, at best, a meagre abridgment of the same information." In this manual an attempt has been made to present solutions of some of the difficulties which beset the young student of Latin, and to prepare him for an intelligent study of Caesar.

The general plan of the book is as follows: —

1. It opens with a short and simply worded **review of English Etymology and Analysis**. This may be taken at the outset as a preparation for the Latin Lessons, or left for consultation and comparison as constructions are presented in Latin which have parallels in English. At the end of this review are placed such English idioms and peculiarities in the use of Cases as have similar or analogous uses in Latin.

2. **Elementary principles and definitions** of Latin Etymology form the next chapter. These cover all essential points from the Alphabet to the First Declension of Nouns. They are briefly and clearly stated, with an explanation of every topic (such as Quantity) which might present a difficulty to the beginner. All statements are excluded which do not have a direct bearing upon the end in view, — the mastery of the essentials.

3. **The Latin Lessons**, beginning with the First Declension, follow. These contain references to Grammars, notes (explained below), test-questions, and a double exercise, — first, of translation from Latin into English; and secondly, from English into Latin. There is no vocabulary printed on the same page as the Lesson, thus removing from the pupil the temptation to make in the recitation-room the preparation that should have been made beforehand. To avoid, however, any possible difficulty or confusion arising from the necessity of consulting a general vocabulary at the outset, a special vocabulary for each of the first twenty-nine Lessons is placed at the end of the book.

The **Simple Sentence** is introduced as early as possible, the Present Indicative of a few simple verbs being employed. A special attempt has been made to present the various uses of the Cases, Verb, etc., in the order in which their force and peculiarities will be best appreciated by the young student.

The **uses of the Subjunctive** have been presented in a simple and natural order of development. Particular attention has been bestowed on the constructions of **Indirect Discourse**, and carefully graded material has been given for translation and drill.

The final Lessons contain a variety of selections for translation into Latin, including a large number of sentences of different degrees of difficulty, English translations from Caesar, etc.

4. Several pages of **Latin Narrative** for translation, taken from the Commentaries on the Gallic War, are then given. These are accompanied by notes and explanations.

5. The **Notes** follow. These have been prepared with great care, and give a compact and complete outline of all essential principles of Latin Etymology and Syntax, with explanation of difficult constructions, useful hints on translation, and illustrative examples when necessary. References are made to these Notes in every Lesson; and as they are arranged in the usual grammatical order, they will form a convenient outline for frequent review.

6. An **Appendix**, containing all the **essential forms of Inflection**, is added, that the book may serve as a complete manual for the beginner; if, however, the instructor prefer that these forms should be learned from a Grammar, the references to the Latin Grammars of Allen and Greenough, Bennett, and Harkness, given in connection with the Lessons, will furnish the same information.

7. At the end of the book are given **Special Vocabularies and Examples** for the first twenty-nine Lessons (already re-

PREFACE.

ferred to) and a complete **General Vocabulary**, Latin-English and English-Latin.

In the preparation of this manual, the author has been greatly aided by the advice and suggestions of many friends, whose experience in the same and kindred departments of instruction has made them welcome counsellors; to all such he desires to return sincere thanks.

DAVID Y. COMSTOCK.

PHILLIPS ACADEMY, ANDOVER, MASS.,
June 30, 1883.

TABLE OF CONTENTS.

	PAGE
REVIEW OF ENGLISH GRAMMAR	1
INTRODUCTION TO THE LATIN LESSONS	17

LATIN LESSONS.

LESSON
- I. NOUNS: FIRST DECLENSION 27
- II. VERBS; THE SIMPLE SENTENCE; SUBJECT NOMINATIVE 28
- III. NOUNS: SECOND DECLENSION 29
   Direct Object.
- IV. NOUNS: SECOND DECLENSION (*continued*); ADJECTIVES: FIRST AND SECOND DECLENSIONS 30
   Agreement of Adjectives.
- V. APPOSITION; GENITIVE CASE 31
   Genitive denoting Possession.
- VI. PREDICATE NOUN AND ADJECTIVE 32
   Sum: Present Indicative.
- VII. VERBS: DEFINITIONS; FIRST CONJUGATION (*continued*) . 33
- VIII. VERBS: PRINCIPAL PARTS AND STEMS 35
   Declension of dea and filia.
- IX. VERBS (*continued*); DATIVE CASE 36
   Dative of Indirect Object.
- X. VERBS: FIRST CONJUGATION; SUBJUNCTIVE MODE . . 37
- XI. FIRST CONJUGATION: IMPERATIVE MODE; VOCATIVE CASE 38
   Second Declension: filius and Proper Names in ius.
- XII. FIRST CONJUGATION: INFINITIVES, PARTICIPLES, GERUND, SUPINE 39
- XIII. DECLENSION OF **Deus**; IRREGULAR ADJECTIVES: GENITIVE IN ĭus, DATIVE IN ī 41
- XIV. NOUNS: THIRD DECLENSION; ELEMENTARY PRACTICE . 42

TABLE OF CONTENTS.

LESSON		PAGE
XV.	Nouns: Third Declension; General Principles; Gender	43
XVI.	Nouns: Third Declension; Consonant-Stems	44
XVII.	Nouns: Third Declension; Vowel-Stems	46
XVIII.	The Verb **Sum**: General Practice	47
XIX.	The Verb **Possum**; Use of the Infinitive. Infinitive as Complement.	48
XX.	The Infinitive with a Subject Accusative	49
XXI.	Use of the Subjunctive Mode	50
XXII.	First Conjugation: Passive Voice; Ablative Case. Ablative of Means and Agent.	52
XXIII.	First Conjugation: Passive Voice; Ablative Case. Ablative of Separation.	53
XXIV.	First Conjugation: Subjunctive Passive	55
XXV.	First Conjugation: Passive Voice: Imperative, Infinitives, Participles	56
XXVI.	Adjectives: Third Declension	57
XXVII.	Adjectives: Third Declension (continued). Subjunctive expressing a Command.	58
XXVIII.	Adjectives: Regular Comparison. Declension of Comparatives.	60
XXIX.	Adjectives: Irregular Comparison; Adverbs	61
XXX.	Verbs: Second Conjugation	62
XXXI.	General Review	64
XXXII.	Deponent Verbs: First and Second Conjugations	65
XXXIII.	Two Accusatives	66
XXXIV.	Adjectives: Irregular Comparison. Dative with Adjectives.	67
XXXV.	Nouns: Fourth Declension. Declension of **domus**.	69
XXXVI.	Nouns: Fifth Declension. Compound Nouns.	70
XXXVII.	Verbs: Third Conjugation: Active Voice	71
XXXVIII.	Verbs: Third Conjugation: Passive Voice	72
XXXIX.	Prepositions; Place	74
XL.	Deponent Verbs: Third Conjugation. Ablative of Cause; Subjunctive of Purpose.	75
XLI.	Verbs: Fourth Conjugation. Adjectives used as Nouns.	77
XLII.	Deponent Verbs: Fourth Conjugation. Ablative with Deponent Verbs.	78

TABLE OF CONTENTS.

LESSON		PAGE
XLIII.	THIRD CONJUGATION: VERBS IN iō.	79
	Tenses of the Infinitive.	
XLIV.	PARTICIPLES	81
XLV.	NUMERAL ADJECTIVES	82
	Accusative of Time; Ablative of Time.	
XLVI.	ACCUSATIVE OF EXTENT; PARTITIVE GENITIVE	84
XLVII.	ACCUSATIVE: ADVERBIAL USES	85
XLVIII.	SUBJUNCTIVE MODE: PURPOSE, COMMAND, EXHORTATION	87
	Correlatives.	
XLIX.	ABLATIVE OF MANNER, ACCOMPANIMENT, SPECIFICATION	88
L.	PRONOUNS: PERSONAL, REFLEXIVE, POSSESSIVE	90
LI.	PRONOUNS: DEMONSTRATIVE	91
LII.	PRONOUNS: RELATIVE	92
LIII.	PRONOUNS: INTERROGATIVE; INTERROGATIVE SENTENCES	94
	Single Questions.	
LIV.	PRONOUNS: INDEFINITE	95
	Double Questions.	
LV.	PLACE: EXCEPTIONS	97
LVI.	IRREGULAR VERBS: Ferō.	98
	Genitive after sum; Infinitive as Subject.	
LVII.	DATIVE WITH COMPOUND VERBS	100
LVIII.	IRREGULAR VERBS: Eō.	101
	Conditional Sentences.	
LIX.	ABLATIVE ABSOLUTE.	103
LX.	PERIPHRASTIC CONJUGATIONS	104
	Dative of Agent.	
LXI.	IRREGULAR VERBS: Fīō	106
	Subjunctive expressing a Wish.	
LXII.	IRREGULAR VERBS: Volō AND ITS COMPOUNDS.	107
LXIII.	DEFECTIVE VERBS	109
	Objective Genitive.	
LXIV.	IMPERSONAL VERBS	110
LXV.	SUBJUNCTIVE OF RESULT; SUBSTANTIVE CLAUSES	111
LXVI.	DATIVE WITH INTRANSITIVE VERBS; INTRANSITIVE VERBS USED IN THE PASSIVE.	113
	Historical Present; Sequence of Tenses.	
LXVII.	DATIVE OF POSSESSION; TWO DATIVES.	114
	Semi-Deponent Verbs.	
LXVIII.	ABLATIVE WITH COMPARATIVES; ABLATIVE DENOTING MEASURE OF DIFFERENCE	116

TABLE OF CONTENTS.

LESSON		PAGE
LXIX.	CAUSAL CLAUSES	117
	Relative Pronoun used for a Demonstrative.	
LXX.	USES OF THE ABLATIVE CASE	119
	(1) Denoting Quality; (2) with Adjectives; (3) denoting Price.	
LXXI.	CONCESSIVE CLAUSES	120
	Historical Infinitive.	
LXXII.	TEMPORAL CLAUSES	121
LXXIII.	GERUND AND GERUNDIVE	123
LXXIV.	SUPINE	125
LXXV.	INDIRECT DISCOURSE: QUESTIONS	126
LXXVI.	INDIRECT DISCOURSE: COMMANDS	128
	General Laws of Modes and Tenses.	
LXXVII.	INDIRECT DISCOURSE: GENERAL PRACTICE . . .	129
LXXVIII.	INDIRECT DISCOURSE: GENERAL PRACTICE. . . .	130

MISCELLANEOUS SENTENCES FOR TRANSLATION INTO LATIN . . 132

CAESAR'S HISTORY OF THE GALLIC WAR: BOOK I. — CHAPTERS 1-13 136

REFERENCES AND EXPLANATIONS ON THE HISTORY OF THE GALLIC WAR 143

NOTES.—THE ESSENTIALS OF LATIN GRAMMAR:—

Etymology 149
Syntax 188
Order of Words in a Latin Sentence . . 229
General Facts and Useful Hints 230
Hints on Translation 232

APPENDIX, — FORMS OF DECLENSION, CONJUGATION, ETC. . . . 235

SPECIAL VOCABULARIES AND EXAMPLES 259

GENERAL VOCABULARY:—

Latin-English 269
English-Latin 295

INDEX 302

REVIEW OF ENGLISH GRAMMAR.

THE NUMBERS IN PARENTHESES REFER TO SECTIONS OF THIS REVIEW.

ETYMOLOGY.

1. *Etymology* treats of the Parts of Speech and their changes of form and meaning.

2. There are eight Parts of Speech: *Noun* (or *Substantive*), *Adjective, Pronoun, Verb, Adverb, Preposition, Conjunction, Interjection.*

3. A *Noun* (Latin *nomen, name*), or *Substantive*, is the name of a person or object.

   a. A *Common Noun* is the name of any person or object of a general class; as, *city, man.*

   b. A *Proper Noun* is the name of a particular person or object; as, *Rome, Caesar.*

   c. A *Verbal Noun* has the general use of a noun, but a verbal form and force; as, *Seeing* is *believing*; *To be* is better than *to seem*; He gained his promotion by *doing* his duty faithfully.

   d. A *Collective Noun*, though singular in form, denotes a *group* of persons or objects; as, *crowd, army, society, legion.*

4. To nouns belong *Gender, Person, Number, Case.*

5. *Gender* distinguishes sex. Names of males are *Masculine*; of females, *Feminine*; of objects neither male nor female, *Neuter.*

Some nouns may denote either sex; as, *pupil, child.* These are said to be of the *Common Gender.*

6. Nouns have three *Persons.* The First Person denotes the speaker; as, *I*, your *general*, command you. The Second Person denotes the person or thing addressed; as, *Boys*, be attentive. The Third Person denotes the person or thing spoken of; as, *Haste* makes *waste*.

7. *Number* shows how many are meant. The Singular Number denotes but one; the Plural, more than one.

8. *Case* shows the *relation* of a Noun or Pronoun to other words. A change of relation requires a change of case. There are four cases, — the *Nominative,* the *Possessive,* the *Objective,* and the *Independent.*

 a. The *Nominative Case* denotes the relation of a Subject to its Verb, and answers the question *Who?* or *What?*

 b. The *Possessive Case* denotes the relation of possession, and answers the question *Whose?*

 c. The *Objective Case* * denotes the relation of a Direct Object (39, *a*) to the Transitive Verb which governs it, and answers the question *Whom?* or *What?* It is also used with a Preposition to form a Phrase (43); as, Men gain *wealth by industry.*

 d. The *Independent Case,* or, as it is sometimes called, the *Case Absolute,* has no dependence on any other word. Its most common uses are: (1) as the Case of Address; † as, *Soldiers, we have conquered;* (2) with Participles, forming a contracted clause; as, The *guard* having been killed, the prisoner escaped (that is, *since,* or *when he had been killed*).

9. An *Adjective* limits or describes a Noun or the equivalent of a Noun; as, *Honest* men prosper; To err (error) is *human,* to forgive (forgiveness) is *divine;* That he should come was *strange.*

 a. Adjectives are sometimes used as Nouns, the words with which they agree being understood. When thus used, they are called *Pronominal Adjectives,* that is, used *for a Noun* (11); as, The *wise* grow in wisdom; The *first* is my friend, but the *second* I never saw before.

 b. Adjectives denoting number are called *Numeral Adjectives.* They are either *Cardinal,* telling *how many* (as, *one, twenty*), or *Ordinal,* telling *which one in order* (as, *sixth, third*).

10. *Comparison* of Adjectives is a change in form by which they express different degrees of quality.

There are three degrees of comparison: the *Positive,* denoting a quality in its simple state; as, *wise, good;* the *Comparative,* denoting a higher or lower degree than the Positive; as, *wiser, better, less;* the *Superlative,* denoting the highest or lowest degree of the quality; as, *wisest, best, least.*

Adjectives are compared in three ways: (1) Regularly, by adding *r* or *er* to the Positive for the Comparative, and *st* or *est* for the

---

* The peculiar uses of the Objective Case are given in section 54.
† In Latin, the Vocative Case (from *voco,* I call).

Superlative, as, *tall, taller, tallest;* (2) Irregularly, as, *good, better, best;* (3) By using the Adverbs *more* and *most,* or *less* and *least,* with the Positive.

11. A *Pronoun* (Latin *pro, for,* and *nomen, name*) is a word used *for a noun,* and, like a noun, has *Gender, Person, Number, Case.* Pronouns are either *Personal, Relative,* or *Interrogative.*

 a. A *Personal Pronoun* indicates, by its form, the person speaking, the person addressed, and the person spoken of. The Personal Pronouns are *I, you* (sometimes *thou*), *he, she, it,* and their plural forms, *we, you* (sometimes *ye*), *they.*

 b. A *Relative Pronoun* refers to a preceding substantive (or its equivalent), called the *Antecedent,* and connects clauses. The Antecedent may be a Noun, or any word, or collection of words, used as a Noun; as, The *man who* (Pronoun and connective) came to see me was my friend; *We climbed the mountain, which* was a dangerous feat. In the last example, *We climbed the mountain* is the antecedent of *which,* the Relative Pronoun. The Relative Pronouns are *who, which, what, that.* After *such* and *same, as* is often used as a Relative Pronoun.

 c. An *Interrogative Pronoun* asks a question; as, *What* did you say? The list is *who, which, what.*

12. A *Verb* expresses *being, action,* or *state;* as, *am, run, sleep.* A Verb is either *Transitive,* acting on a Direct Object (39, *a*); as, Brutus *killed* his friend; or *Intransitive,* not acting on a Direct Object. The word *transitive* means *passing over;* that is, the action *passes over* from the actor to the object receiving the action.

13. To verbs belong *Voice, Mode, Tense, Number, Person.*

14. There are two *Voices, Active* and *Passive.* The *Active* represents some person or thing as existing or acting; as, He *is praising.* The *Passive* represents some person or thing as acted upon; as, We *are praised;* They *are loved;* He *is conquered.*

15. *Mode* (Latin *modus, manner*) shows *how* a person regards an action, etc., and therefore *how* he states it.

"The *Mode* of a verb shows the *mood* of the speaker."

 a. The *Indicative Mode* states a *fact,* or asks a *question;* as, He *comes; Has* he *come?*

 b. The *Potential Mode* expresses *liberty, ability,* or *necessity.* It employs, as Auxiliary verbs (25), *may, can, must, might, could, would, should;* as, I *may go;* We *must obey.*

c. The ***Subjunctive Mode*** states something as *possible* (or *uncertain*) or *impossible;* as, If I *were* general; If he *should come.* More will be said of this mode when the subject of ***Tense*** is reached (19).

d. The ***Imperative Mode*** *commands, exhorts,* or *entreats;* as, Soldiers, *advance;* Friend, *renounce* your evil habits; *Help* me.

e. The ***Infinitive Mode*** is not limited, as the other modes are, in respect to person or number; hence its name (*infinite, unlimited*). The other modes are called *finite* (i. e. *limited* in person and number). The Infinitive Mode does not state anything. It is often used as a Verbal Noun; as, *To be* is better than *to seem.*

16. ***Tense*** is a distinction of *time.*

Time is *present, past,* or *future.*

An act may be thought of, in *any* time, as

I. Indefinite; as, I *wrote* (whenever I wished).
II. Imperfect; as, I *was writing* (action not completed).
III. Completed; as, I *have written* (the writing is *now* finished).

17. The Indicative Mode is the only one in which the tenses denote proper distinctions of *time.* In the other modes, the same *names* are applied to the tenses, but, in most instances, these names give no idea of the real time thought of. That this fact may be more clearly understood, the tenses of each mode will be described separately.

a. The following table shows for the ***Indicative Mode***, (1) The divisions of time; (2) How the action may be stated in connection with each; (3) Examples; (4) Names which we usually give to the tenses: —

TIME.	ACTION STATED AS	EXAMPLES.	COMMON NAMES.
Present.	Indefinite,	I give (whenever I please).	Present.
	Imperfect,	I am giving (action *not completed*).	
	Completed,	I have given (action *now completed*).	Present Perfect.
Past.	Indefinite,	I gave (whenever I pleased).	Past.
	Imperfect,	I was giving (action *not completed*).	
	Completed,	I had given (action *completed* in past time).	Past Perfect.
Future.	Indefinite,	I shall give (at any time).	Future.
	Imperfect,	I shall be giving (action *not completed*).	
	Completed,	I shall have given (action *completed* in the future).	Future Perfect.

b. The Imperfect forms (present, past, and future) are often called *progressive,* because they denote the act or state as *going on.* The Indefinite forms (present and past) are often expressed in *statements,* with *do* and *did,* and these are called *emphatic,* because they state more positively than do the ordinary forms. In *questions,* these words do not give this force; as, *Did* you not visit the sick man? Yes, I *did* visit him.

NOTE. We often use forms which might be misleading if not studied in connection with another thought. In the sentence, "When he *comes,* I shall welcome him," *comes* represents *future time.* Also, in the sentence, "If I *do not find* my trunk before Tuesday, I shall go without it," *do find* is equivalent to *shall have found.* The knowledge of this fact is of great value in expressing many English sentences in Latin, since in that language the distinctions of tense are more carefully observed.

18. The tenses of the *Potential Mode* are four, — the *Present, Past, Present Perfect, Past Perfect.*

These *names,* however, are of little value in indicating distinction of *time,* which, in very many cases, can be decided only by the *sense.* Some of these peculiar uses arise from the lack of a *Future* and *Future Perfect.* The *Past Perfect* is more accurate in its use than any of the others.

These tenses employ the following Auxiliary Verbs (25) : —

a. May, can, must, to form the Present.

b. Might, could, would, should, to form the Past.

c. May (can, must) have, to form the Present Perfect.

d. Might (could, would, should) have, to form the Past Perfect.

The following examples show what has already been stated, — that the *sense,* and not the *name* of the tense, must often decide the time denoted by the tenses of the Potential Mode : —

He *may be* here (*now,* or *to-morrow*); I *must go* (next year); We *can do* that (*to-day,* or *next week*); The general said that the town *must be taken* (at that time); He *may have been* here yesterday; The soldiers *may have taken* the town before we *can reach* it.

REMARK. The above examples show that the Potential Mode has, in *sense* if not in *form,* six tenses; the *Present* being used when a *Future* is required, and the *Present Perfect* when a *Future Perfect* is needed.

19. The *Subjunctive Mode* * has only one form, in common use, that is unlike the tense-forms of the Indicative and Potential. That form is *were*, in the First and Third Persons Singular, where the Indicative has *was;* as, If I *were* you; If he *were* industrious. It borrows its other tense-forms from the Indicative and Potential.

In the Subjunctive, as in the Potential, the *sense*, and not the *name* of the tense, must often decide the time (18).

According to the definition given in section 15, *c*, the Subjunctive states something as *possible* (or *doubtful*) or *impossible*.

Four Subjunctive tense-forms will be described, a thorough knowledge of which will be of very great value to the student when he shall translate Latin sentences containing the same thoughts. These forms denote action as : (1) Future; (2) Future Perfect; (3) Present; (4) Past. These are chosen, not because they are the *only* tenses of the Subjunctive, but because they best illustrate the *mode*, or *way*, of expressing a thought in the Subjunctive Mode. The following will make this clear : —

a. Future *Possibility* (or *Doubt*). 1. If he *should come* to-morrow, I *would be* glad. 2. If he *should* (*have*) *come* before next Thursday, he *could* and *would save* the prisoner's life.

b. Impossibility.
{ Present. 1. If I *were* richer, I *should be* contented. 2. If you *loved* your country, you *would be* fighting for it. 3. If he *saw* the snake, he *would be* afraid.
Past. If he *had been* general, he *would have managed* affairs more wisely.

REMARK. The student will notice that (under *b*) a tense *past* in form is used to state something as impossible in *present* time.

In the following sentences, tell, — (1) What *time* is thought of; (2) What

---

* TO TEACHERS. No attempt has here been made to follow the system ordinarily adopted in school grammars. An excellent authority remarks, "The Subjunctive is evidently passing out of use" (i. e. as a *form* of the language), and it is important that a student should be so trained in the use of language that he may be able to recognize in the Subjunctive a medium of *thought;* and this is the only purpose that the author has in presenting this view of the mode. The teacher may prefer to omit this section until the Latin Subjunctive is studied. It will aid the student greatly to study the illustrative sentences given here; and the teacher should emphasize the fact that correct speech in English requires certain forms to express certain thoughts.

each sentence *means* (that is, whether something is stated as *possible* or *impossible*). Some of these sentences may require to be changed in form before the thought can be clearly seen : —
1. Were he to confess his fault, he would be forgiven. 2. Were he here, he would be among friends. 3. If thy brother trespass against thee, rebuke him; and if he repent, forgive him. 4. If we should not find the house, I'd be in despair. 5. If the doctor had come yesterday, the sick man would be better to-day. 6. If thou hadst been here, my brother had not died. 7. Were he more diligent, he would be more successful.

20. The *Imperative Mode* has but one tense-form (the Present), and one person (the Second). This tense denotes the time of *giving* a command; the time of *obeying* is future; as, Soldiers, when you attack (shall attack) the enemy to-morrow, *advance* fearlessly. A *direct* command can be expressed in the Second Person only. Such forms as "Let me go," "Let him beware," express an *entreaty, exhortation, warning*, etc. Really, *let* is in the Imperative, and *go* in the Infinitive (56, REMARK); but, by constant use, *let* has become a mere sign of an *exhortation, warning*, etc.

21. The *Infinitive Mode* has two tenses, the *Present* and the *Perfect* ; as, *to see, to have seen, to be struck, to have been struck*.

Notice that the *time* of these tenses depends on the *time of the principal verb*. The Present represents an event as *taking place* at the time of the principal verb; as, I wish (shall wish, had wished) *to go*. The Perfect represents an event as *completed* at, or before, the time of the principal verb; as, He is said (was said, will have been said) *to have heard*.

22. The *Number* and *Person* of a Verb are the same as those of its Subject.

23. A *Participle* is a *Verbal Adjective;* that is, it has the general meaning of a Verb, but, like an Adjective, it modifies a Noun or a Pronoun. Participles are used in both voices, and in three tenses.

Active Participles: —
  a. The Present Participle ends in *ing;* as, The boy, *seeing* the danger, flees; He, *hearing* the sound, arose.
  b. The Past Participle differs from the others in that it has no strictly adjective use, but is only used in forming compound tenses in the Active; as, I have *seen;* He had *heard*.
  c. The Perfect Participle; as, *Having seen* his friends, he returned; *Having learned* the lesson, he will recite.

Passive Participles: —

d. The Present Participle, ending in *d* or *ed,* unless the verb is *irregular* (24). Sometimes, however, it is preceded by *being;* as, The soldier falls (or fell), (*being*) severely *wounded.*

e. The Past Participle, used in the Passive as the same participle is employed in the Active, but with more *adjective* force; as, He has been *injured.*

f. The Perfect Participle; as, *Having been wounded,* he must be (will be, was) carried home.

REMARK. Notice that, as in the Infinitive Mode, the *time* of a participle depends on the time of some other verb. This will be seen from the preceding examples. The Present Participle, therefore, represents an action as *going on* (Active) or *received* (Passive) at the time expressed by the principal verb.*
Also, notice that the Perfect Participle represents an action as *completed* at the time of the principal verb.

24. Verbs are called *regular,* when they form their *past tense* and *past participle* by the addition of *d* or *ed* to the simple form; as, *help, helped.* Verbs are called *irregular,* when they do not follow this law; as, *am, was, been.*

25. An *Auxiliary Verb* (Latin *auxilium, aid*) is one used to *aid* in the conjugation of other verbs; as, He *does* not think that you *will* tell me what he *has* done and *can* do, if the opportunity *is* offered.

26. Some Verbs are found only in the Third Person Singular. They never have a *personal* subject (*I, you, he*), and hence are called *Impersonal Verbs.* They are also called *Unipersonal* (one person), because used only in the Third Person.

This subject (*it*) is very indefinite in its meaning, and if, when we say, "*It* rains," "*It* snows," some one were to ask, "*What* rains (or snows)?" the question would not be easy to answer.

It stands for the *thought,* or general *idea,* of the verb; or, as we should say in Latin, for the *stem* of the verb. "*It* rains," "*It* snows," mean "*Rain* is falling," "*Snow* is falling," etc.

27. A *Defective Verb* lacks some of its modes or tenses; as, *may, can, ought, quoth, shall.*

---

* Therefore some grammarians call this tense of the Participle, in both voices, the Imperfect Participle, because its action is represented as *not completed.* The Present Infinitive is often called the Imperfect Infinitive, for a like reason.

28. An ***Adverb*** is used to modify a Verb, Adjective, or another Adverb.

An adverb may express: —

Time; as, *lately;* ***Place;*** as, *here;* ***Cause;*** as, *why;* ***Degree;*** as, *very, wholly;* ***Manner;*** as, *well, earnestly;* ***Affirmation;*** as, *yes, certainly;* ***Negation;*** as, *no, not.*

29. A ***Preposition*** (meaning *placed before*) connects a Noun or Pronoun with some other word; as, He lived *in* Rome. This Noun or Pronoun must be in the Objective Case (8, *c*).

REMARK. When the Noun or Pronoun is omitted, the Preposition becomes an Adverb;* as, He ran *down* the hill (Preposition); He ran *down* (Adverb).

30. A ***Conjunction*** (Latin ***con,*** *together,* and ***jungo,*** *join*) is a word used to connect words, phrases (43), and clauses (41).

Conjunctions are: —

a. Co-ordinate, when they connect elements of equal importance; as, *and, but.*

b. Subordinate, when they connect elements of unequal importance; as, *if, because.*

Adverbs used as Subordinate Conjunctions are called *Conjunctive Adverbs;* as, *when, while, before.*

31. An ***Interjection*** (meaning *thrown in,* or *between*) is a word *thrown into* a sentence, not dependent on any other word, and not affecting the construction of the sentence. It expresses some strong or sudden emotion; as, *alas! ah!* Many other parts of speech are sometimes used as Interjections; as, *What!* don't you remember me? *Nonsense!*

SYNTAX.

32. ***Syntax*** treats of the construction of sentences, and the relation of their different parts to each other.

33. A ***Sentence*** is a collection of words expressing a complete thought; as, The brave soldier received a reward from his general.

34. ***Analysis*** is the separation of a sentence into the elements, or parts, that compose it, in order to discover their relation to each other.

---

* Really, Prepositions are Adverbs used as *connectives.*

35. Every complete sentence must contain: —

a. A **Subject,** telling the person or thing that *is,* or *acts,* or *is acted upon.* It answers the question *Who?* or *What?*

b. A **Predicate,** telling what is said of the Subject. In the sentence, "Brave soldiers fight with no thought of fear," *soldiers* is the Subject, and *fight with no thought of fear* is the Predicate.

36. The Subject must be a **Noun,** or the equivalent of a Noun. In place of a Noun, as Subject, may be used: —

a. A **Pronoun;** as, The man said that *he* would come.

b. An **Adjective;** as, The *good* are happy.

c. An **Infinitive** (3, c); as, *To err* is human.

d. A **Clause** (41); as, *That he is my friend* is true; *Why he killed his friend* will always be a problem.

e. **Any word or collection of words,** not a Noun, but of which something can be stated; as, *A* is a letter; *To* is a preposition; + is the sign of addition.

REMARK. Of course the *gender* of such subjects as those mentioned in c, d, e, must be *neuter.*

37. The Predicate must contain a **Verb,** since this is the only part of speech that can make a *statement.* The Imperative Mode may form a complete sentence, the Subject being understood. Verbs in other modes may form complete Predicates; as, Dogs *bark;* Birds *fly;* It *rains.*

a. The verb *to be,* however, cannot (in its ordinary use) form a complete Predicate, as it does not *state* anything. *Snow is, Cæsar was, The boy will be,* are not sentences, since each requires some word to complete its meaning. Such a word is called a *Complement.* A Complement of the first example would be the word *white;* of the second, *general* or *victorious;* of the third, *studious.* The forms *is, was, will be,* simply *connect* the subjects and the words which describe them. *To be* is therefore called a **Copula** (meaning *link, coupler*).

b. Other verbs, besides *to be,* are used as Copulative Verbs. **To become, to appear, to seem,** are the most common of these; as, He *became* a hero; The boy *appeared* (*seemed*) honest.

c. The Passive Voice of the verbs **to make, to choose, to call, to think,** and others of like meaning, has the same use (as Copulative Verbs); as, I *have been made* (*chosen, called, considered*) leader.

REMARK. An Adjective used after one of the verbs mentioned in *a, b, c,* modifies the Subject; and as the Copulative Verb has no more effect on the case after it than the sign =, a Noun following such a verb, defining or describing the subject, will be in the Nominative. As both the Adjective and Noun help to form the Predicate, they are called the **Predicate Adjective** and **Predicate Noun** (or **Nominative**).

d. The principles stated above will apply to any Noun or Adjective standing after an Intransitive Verb, but describing the Subject; as, He returned a *friend*, who came a *foe* (*friend* and *foe* being in the Nominative Case).

38. The principal elements (the Subject and Predicate) may be modified: —

a. By an **Adjective element;** that is, a word, phrase (43), or clause (41), which performs the office of an Adjective; as, A *wise* man (man *of wisdom,* man *who is wise*) will care for his health.

Under this head should be included any word, or collection of words, which may modify a Substantive; for example: —

A *Possessive Case;* as, The *boy's* book has been found.

An *Appositive* (46); as, We, the *people* of these United States, are free; The saying, "*Honesty is the best policy,*" is an old proverb.

A *Predicate Noun* or *Adjective* (37, REMARK).

b. By an **Objective element;** that is, a word, phrase, or clause, used as an Object; as, He wishes *food* (or *to eat*); He says *that he must go ;* They asked *what I had said.*

c. By an **Adverbial element;** that is, a word, phrase, or clause, that performs the duty of an Adverb; as, He runs *swiftly* (or *at full speed*); He will come *when he can* (or *to-morrow*).

39. An **Object** may be: —

a. Direct; that is, receiving the full effect of the action expressed by a Transitive Verb; as, He struck *me.*

b. Indirect; that is, showing the person or thing *to* (or *for*) *whom* (or *which*) anything is done, or happens; as, They told *him* (*to him*, Indirect Object) the *story* (Direct Object); Give *me* (*to me*) the *book.*

40. Sentences are divided, with respect to their *form,* into three classes: **Simple, Compound,** and **Complex.**

a. A *Simple Sentence* expresses a single complete thought; that is, it contains but one Subject and one Predicate; as, Caesar wrote a history of his campaigns in Gaul.

b. A *Compound Sentence* contains two or more Simple Sentences, each expressing an independent thought; as, Put not your trust in money, but put your money in trust; He exercises, therefore he is well.

c. A *Complex Sentence* contains one Simple Sentence and one or more thoughts that are dependent upon it; as, Milton, who wrote "Paradise Lost," said that he did not educate his daughters in the languages, because one tongue was enough for a woman.

41. In Compound and Complex Sentences, each separate thought is called a *Clause*. A Compound Sentence, therefore, consists of two *Independent*, or *Principal*, Clauses; and a Complex Sentence contains one *Principal*, and one or more *Dependent* (or *Subordinate*) Clauses.

42. Dependent Clauses are either *Substantive, Adjective,* or *Adverbial*.

a. A *Substantive Clause* is one that takes the place of a Substantive; that is, of a Noun or Pronoun. The use of such a clause, as *Direct Object*, is seen in the example (40, c), where *that he did not educate his daughters in the languages*, etc., is the Direct Object of *said*.

b. An *Adjective Clause* performs the office of an Adjective. In 40, c, *who wrote "Paradise Lost,"* describes *Milton*, and is an Adjective Clause.

c. An *Adverbial Clause* takes the place of an Adverb. The clause, *because one tongue*, etc. (40, c), is an Adverbial Clause expressing *cause*, and answering the question *Why?*

43. A *Phrase* is a collection of words, without Subject or Predicate, which may be used as an Adjective or Adverb; as, She had a voice *of* wonderful *power*, and sang *with* great *expression*. Phrases are of several forms; that most common is called a *Prepositional Phrase*, and consists of a Noun or Pronoun and a Preposition, which connects it with the word which is modified by the phrase; as, in the example under this section, in which *of power* is an Adjective Phrase (= *powerful*) modifying *voice*, and *with expression* (= *expressively*) is an Adverbial Phrase, modifying *sang*.

44. A Sentence, according to its *meaning*, may be:—
a. *Declaratory,* when it makes a *statement;* as, It rains.
b. *Interrogative,* when it asks a *question;* as, Does it rain?
c. *Imperative,* when it expresses a *command;* as, Let it rain; Go.
d. *Exclamatory,* when it has the form of an *exclamation;* as, How it rains!

SOME ELEMENTARY RULES OF SYNTAX.

Nominative as Subject.

45. A Noun or Pronoun, used as the Subject of a Finite Verb, must be in the Nominative Case.

Apposition.

46. A Noun or Pronoun, used to explain another Noun or Pronoun, and meaning *the same* person or thing, is put in the same case. This is called *Apposition* (meaning *near position*); as, Caesar, the *general,* addressed his soldiers, *men* tried in many conflicts.

Predicate Nominative and Adjective.

a. A Noun or Pronoun, used as the Complement of *to be* or any other Copulative Verb (37, *a, b, c*), describes the subject and must be in the Nominative Case. This principle is the same as Apposition, except that the descriptive Noun or Pronoun requires a Copulative Verb to connect it with the word which it modifies.

b. An Adjective, used as the Complement of *to be* or any other Copulative Verb, modifies the Subject.

REMARK. In general, it may be stated that—

c. *An Intransitive Verb or a Passive form takes the same case after as before it.*

Adjectives and Participles.

47. An Adjective or Participle (Verbal Adjective) must describe or limit some Noun or Pronoun.

Possession.

48. Possession must be expressed by the Possessive Case or by the Preposition *of* with a Substantive.

Direct Object.

49. The Direct Object of a Transitive Verb must be in the Objective Case; as, He obeyed the *law*.

This rule applies to Participles and Verbal Nouns (from Transitive Verbs), as well as to all ordinary forms of the verb; as, The man, seeing his *friend*, ran after him, shouting his *name ;* Obeying the *law* is a citizen's duty; To preach *honesty* is one thing; to practise *it* is another.

Relative Pronouns.

50. A Relative Pronoun agrees with its Antecedent in Gender, Number, and Person; but its Case depends upon the form of its own clause; as, You have injured me, *who am* your friend.

Verb.

51. A Finite Verb agrees with its subject in Person and Number.

a. If there are several subjects, of different persons, the verb will be in the First Person, rather than the Second or Third, and the Second, rather than the Third; as, John, you, and I (that is, *we*) have finished *our* lessons; This gentleman and yourself (that is, *you*) have cast *your* votes.

b. A Collective Noun may take a verb in the Singular, when the body (or group) *as a whole* is spoken of; but when the *separate individuals* (or *objects*) are thought of, the verb must be Plural; as, A regiment of nine hundred men *was ordered* to charge; The council (that is, the members of it) *were* in doubt.

c. When a verb has two or more subjects in the Singular number, it will be: —

(1) Plural, if it agrees with them taken *together ;* as, The master and his servant *have come*.

(2) Singular, if it agrees with them *separately ;* as, Neither (either) the man nor (or) his servant *has come*.

The Independent Case.

52. The Independent Case has no grammatical dependence upon any word in the sentence; as, *Citizens*, behold your king; The *time* having arrived, we started.

The Infinitive as a Verbal Noun.

53. The Infinitive is often used as a Verbal Noun in the Nominative or Objective Case; as, *To die* for one's country is noble; He wishes *to see* you.

Some Peculiar Uses of the Objective Case.*

54. The Objective Case is used to express: —
1. The object *directly* affected by an action (39, *a*).
2. The object *indirectly* affected by an action (39, *b*).
3. The *space over which* the action, etc., extends; as, He drove the horse *twenty miles;* The house is *fifty feet* high.
4. The *time during which* the action or state continues; as, He lived *fifty years;* She was *nineteen years* old.
5. The *time when* (or *at which*) an event takes place; as, He arrived (on) *the next day*.
6. The *amount* (or *degree*) *to which* the action or state is exerted; as, He was injured *a great deal*.
7. The *amount* (or *degree*) *of difference* between two objects or actions; as, He is *five years* older than I (that is, older *by* that difference); He is *a head* taller than John; He ran *a great deal* faster than his brother; He is not *one cent* richer.
8. The *place toward which* motion is directed; as, I went *home;* They desire to go *West*.
9. *Price;* as, The book cost *two dollars*.

REMARK. The Objective Case, in Examples 3, 4, 5, 6, 7, has the force of an Adverb of Degree or Time, answering the question *How? How much? When? How long?* it is, therefore, often called, in such uses, the *Adverbial Objective*.

"It" and "There" as Introductory Subjects.

55. *It* and *There* are often used as *introductory subjects* (the real subjects following the verb) to give variety to the form of the sentence; as, *It* is a law of war that might makes right (= *that might makes right* is a law of war).

The sentence, "*There* are five men there," means "Five *men* are there," and the first *there* has no particular value as a part of the sen-

* The remaining sections of this English Review may be omitted for the present, and employed for comparison of idioms when the Syntax of Latin cases is studied. They will be of service to the beginner in his study of the Accusative with the Infinitive, Accusative of Extent, etc.

tence. As they help to fill out the sentence, they are called *Expletives* (from a Latin word meaning *to fill out*). As they stand in the place of Substautives, they might be called *Expletive Pronouns*.

The Objective Case as Subject of the Infinitive.

56. The Infinitive Mode is often used to denote an *act*, and the Objective Case to denote the *actor;* as, He ordered *me to go*. Therefore the laws regulating the relations of Subject and Verb are these: —

a. The Subject of a Finite Verb (15, *e*) must be in the Nominative Case.

b. The Subject of an Infinitive must be in the Objective Case; as, I knew *him to be* a thief. Let *him (to) come*. Whom (predicate Pronoun) do you suppose *him to be?* I wish *him to go*. I heard the *bell (to) ring*.

REMARK. After *bid, dare, feel, see, let, make, need, hear,* the sign *to* is generally omitted with the Infinitive ; as in the examples above.

INTRODUCTION

TO THE

LATIN LESSONS.

---

1. "The Latin Language was the language of *Latium* (a district in Italy), of which Rome was the chief city. The conquests of the Romans caused it to spread over the rest of Italy, and over the greater part of France and Spain. The Latin Language is no longer spoken; but the French, Italian, Spanish, and Portuguese languages are mainly derived from it."

Alphabet.

2. The Latin Alphabet is the same as the English, except that it has no **w**. **K** occurs only in a very few words. **Q**, as in English, is always followed by **u**.

3. The letters are divided into Vowels (**a, e, i, o, u, y**) and Consonants. **J** and **v** are consonant forms of **i** and **u**.

4. There are several classes of Consonants, of which these are the most important: —

a. *Liquids* (**l, m, n, r**). They are called *Liquids* because they unite easily in sound with a preceding consonant, or *flow* smoothly after it. This is especially true of **l** and **r**, and these letters are therefore frequently called *semi-vowels*. The English words *able, betray, snow, small*, are examples of Liquids pronounced with other consonants.

b. **H** is not a consonant, but an *Aspirate* (that is, a *rough breathing* of the vowel following it).

c. *Double Consonants* (**x, z**). **x** = cs, gs; **z** = ds.

d. *Mutes;* so called because they are uttered without opening the vocal passage, therefore they are *voiceless*.

18 INTRODUCTION TO THE LATIN LESSONS.

REMARK.* Mutes may be divided, (1) according to the organ by which their pronunciation is effected; (2) according to the degree of breathing employed; that is, they may have a *light* (or *sharp*) sound, an *intermediate* sound, or a *rough* sound.

According to the first division, they are called *Labials* (or *lip-letters*), *Palatals* (or *palate-letters*), and *Linguals* (or *tongue-letters*). According to the second division, they are called *Smooth*, *Middle*, and *Rough*. The table here given shows these two divisions: —

	LABIALS.	PALATALS.	LINGUALS.
Smooth Mutes,	p,	c (k, qu),	t.
Middle Mutes,	b,	g,	d.
Rough Mutes,	ph,	ch,	th.

5. A *Diphthong* (meaning "double sound") is the union of two vowel sounds in one syllable; as, **cau-sae** (Eng. *causes*). The most common Diphthongs in Latin are **ae, oe, au**; the least common are **eu, ei, ui**.

6. There are as many Syllables in a Latin word as there are single vowels or diphthongs. The English words *separate, accurate, miles, crates, more, persuade,* would be pronounced, as Latin words, **se-pa-ra'-te, ac-cu-ra'-te, mi'-les, cra'-tes, mo'-re, per-sua'-de**.

Pronunciation.

7. The Pronunciation of Latin differs in different countries. The two methods which are most commonly employed in American schools are the Roman and the English. These are presented in the next two sections.

Roman Method.

8. By the Roman Method, the letters have the following sounds: —

LONG. SHORT.

VOWELS.
- ā as in *father*.   ă as in *idea*.
- ē as *ey* in *they*.   ĕ as in *net*.
- ī as in *machine*.   ĭ as in *verily*.
- ō as in *old*.   ŏ as in *obey*.
- ū as *oo* in *moon*. ŭ as in *full*.

Y has a sound between that of **i** and **u**.

* The Teacher may omit this for the present, employing the statements here made concerning the Mutes for reference in the future. The Table will be very

INTRODUCTION TO THE LATIN LESSONS. 19

REMARK. In a syllable long *by position* (11, I, *b*) a short vowel is pronounced short; but, before **nf, ns, gn,** and **j,** the vowel becomes *long*, and must be pronounced as a long vowel (11, I, *b*, NOTE).

DIPHTHONGS: ae like English *ay* (*yes*).   ei as in *eight*.
oe like *oi* in *coin*.   eu as *ew* in *few*.
au like *ow* in *how*.   ui like English *we*.

CONSONANTS: c, g, always hard, as in *car, gun*.
j like *y* in *yet*; s sharp, as in *sale*.
t as in *tent*; v like *w* in *went*; qu as in *quart*.
bs, bt, like *ps, pt*; ch as *k*; ph as *f*.

English Method.

9. The letters have their ordinary English sounds. Notice, however, these Special Rules: —

1. Final **a**, in words of more than one syllable, sounds like final *a* in *America*; but in monosyllables (as ā, dā, quā) the long sound is usually given.

2. In **tibi** and **sibi**, the **i** in both syllables sounds like *i* and *y* in *fitly*.

3. **Es** final sounds like *ease*.

4. **Os** final (in the *plural*) sounds like *ose* in *dose*.

REMARK. In **post** and its compounds, **os** sounds like *ose;* but in *derivatives*, o is sounded *short;* as, **pos'-te-rus.**

5. **Ae** and **oe** have the same sound as **e;** **au** is like *aw* in *saw;* in **huic** and **cuī, ui** = *ī* (as though these words were spelled *hike, kī*).

6. In such words as **Cāius, Pompēius, Aquilēia, i** sounds like *y;* as, *Pom-pē'-yus, A-qui-lē'-ya*.

7. **C** has the sound of *s*, and **g** the sound of *j*, before **e, i, y, ae, oe, eu.**

8. **Ch** is always hard (like *k*); as, **mach'-i-na**.

9. **T** and **c** (before **i**) often have, as in English, the sound of *sh ;* as, ra'-ti-o (= *ra'-shǐ-o*). The hard sound is retained after **s, t,** and **x;** as, **jus-ti-or, Met'-ti-us**.

useful to the student in his study of the Verb, as showing that most of the consonant changes made result from interchange between mutes of the *same family;* as, **scriptus** (from **scribo**), **rectus** (from **rego**), etc.

20   INTRODUCTION TO THE LATIN LESSONS.

Quantity.

10. In pronouncing the English word *quantity*, the second and third syllables are more hastily pronounced than the first; in other words, it takes more *time* to pronounce the first. This difference in the length or *quantity* of time required to pronounce different syllables was far more carefully observed by the Romans than it is by us.

In Latin, syllables are *long* (-) or *short* (◡). A long syllable requires twice as much *time* for pronunciation as a short one.

Rules of Quantity.

11. The quantity of most Latin syllables is decided by the following Rules: —

I. LONG SYLLABLES. A syllable is said to be

(a) *Long by nature*, if it contains a *long vowel* or a *diphthong;* as in **māter, rēs, Rōma, Caesar, aurum, poena.**

NOTE. Vowels, in Latin, are *long* or *short*, not according to fixed rules, but *by nature* (that is, because the Romans made them so), and therefore their quantity can be learned only by observation and practice.

REMARK. The vowel of a syllable formed by contraction is *long;* as in **nīl** (for **nihil**), **currūs** (for **curruis**

(b) *Long by position*, if its vowel (short by nature) is followed by two consonants (but see II, *b*), or a double consonant (**x, z**); as in **quantus** (Eng. *quantity*), **index, sunt.** This is owing to the distinct pronunciation of *both* consonants. A careless speaker might pronounce the English word given above *quan'ity*, and thus shorten the *time* of the first syllable by not sounding both consonants.

REMARK. If, however, the second consonant is **h**, the syllable is *not* made long (II, *a*, REMARK). For example, the quantity of the negative particle **in** (Eng. *un*) remains short before **h** in the compound **inhonestus** (Eng. *dis-* (*h*)*onorable*).

NOTE. Before **nf, ns, gn**, and **j**, a short vowel itself becomes *long* (8, REMARK); as in **inferō, cōnsul, rēgnum, hūjus.**

II. SHORT SYLLABLES. A syllable is said to be *short* (*a*) If its vowel is followed by another vowel or by a diphthong; as in **via, diēs.** This is because, in Latin as in English, the first vowel naturally "runs into" the second, and loses its value as a separate letter; as in **impius** (Eng. *impious*), **victōria** (Eng. *victorious*).

REMARK. This same law applies to a vowel before **h**, which is only a *breathing* (4, *b*); as in **prohibeō** (so also, Eng. *pro*(*h*)*ibition*), **vehō** (Eng. *ve*(*h*)*icle*), **nihil** (Eng. *ni*(*h*)*ilist*).

INTRODUCTION TO THE LATIN LESSONS. 21

b.* If its vowel (naturally short) is followed by a mute (4, *d*) with l or r (that is, the mute must stand *before* l or r); as in **agrī** (from **ager**), **patris** (from **pater**); but **ācris** (from **ācer**), **mātris** (from **māter**). This is because l and r blend so easily with the preceding mute that the short vowel is really followed by one consonant *and a half*, i. e. a *semi-vowel* (4, *a*), and not by two full consonants.

REMARK. If, however, l or r is preceded by another l or r, the syllable is *long;* as in **carrus**.

NOTE. Syllables whose quantity is decided by the foregoing rules will not be marked in this book. *All other syllables are to be considered short, unless they are marked long.*

12. Decide, by the rules given in section 11, and also by the NOTE at the end of that section, the quantity of every syllable in the following list of words: —

tempestās	via	Caesar
patria	index	aurō
nihil	mansisset	pervius
trahō	dux	prohibeās

Accent.

13. Accent is the special emphasis which a particular syllable of a word receives in pronunciation; as in the English *hap'py, secure', qual'ity*. English accent is largely a matter of memory; for example, the following words of two syllables are derived from the same Latin Verb (**ferō,** *I bear*), yet some are accented on the first syllable, and some on the second: *suf'fer, infer', dif'fer, defer'*. In Latin, Accent is determined by these simple laws: † —

a. In words of two syllables, always accent the *first;* as, **stel'la, de'us.**

b. In words of more than two syllables, always accent the *last but one*, if it is *long;* if *short*, accent the *last but two;* as, **amī'cus, prŏprae'tor, dīlex'it, tur'rĭbus, Jū'pĭter, ingĕ'nĭum.**

---

* To TEACHERS. The author is convinced that the term *Common*, as usually applied to the quantity of a vowel thus placed, conveys little if any meaning to the mind of a beginner; it should not be used in connection with his study of prose, but left for his consideration when he shall take up Latin poetry. The same remark will apply to final **o**, which will be marked *long*, except in the few instances where it is short.

† The accent as affected by an Enclitic is explained later; also that of Vocatives like **Mercuri.**

22 INTRODUCTION TO THE LATIN LESSONS.

REMARKS. 1. The last syllable of a word is called the *ultima* (Eng. *ultimate = final*).

2. The last syllable but one is called the *penult* (meaning "almost the last." Compare Eng. *peninsula*, "almost an island").

3. The syllable before the *penult* is called the *antepenult* (i. e. *before the penult*).

Parts of Speech.

14. The Parts of Speech are the same in Latin as in English (2, page 1).

Inflection.

15. Inflection is a change made in the form of a word to show its different relations to other words.

a. In English, Nouns and Pronouns are inflected to show relations of *possession*, etc. This is called *Declension*. English Verbs are inflected to show different relations of *voice, mode, person*, etc. This is called *Conjugation*. English Nouns and Pronouns have very few changes of form. The Possessive Case is the only one that *always* has a special form. For instance, the words *fish, sheep*, may be Nominative or Objective, Singular or Plural. In the sentence "The king the slave in silence viewed," we cannot tell whether the king viewed the slave, or the slave viewed the king.

b. In Latin, there are *six* cases. Each has its own uses and meanings; so that, while the case of an English Noun or Pronoun can very often be decided only by the *sense* of the sentence, the case of these same parts of speech in Latin is almost always shown by its *ending*. Adjectives are inflected (that is, *declined*) in Latin, as well as Nouns and Pronouns. Latin Verbs are *conjugated;* their *endings* indicate *voice, person, number*, etc.

Stem.

16. The Stem of a word is that part from which its different cases, modes, tenses, persons, etc., are formed by inflection. It is the *trunk*, and the various forms are the *branches*.

Properties of Nouns.

17. In Latin, as in English, Nouns have Gender, Person, Number, and Case; but the laws of Gender and the number of Cases are somewhat different.

INTRODUCTION TO THE LATIN LESSONS. 23

Gender.

18. The Gender of English nouns is decided by their meaning. So it is in Latin nouns, in the case of human beings and animals; that is, names of males are Masculine, and names of females, Feminine.

In many respects, however, the rules for the gender of Latin nouns denoting *things without life* are very different from the English rule.

The Gender of Latin nouns is decided in two ways, — by their *meaning* and by their *endings*.

The Rules that decide Gender by *meaning* are general, and apply to nouns of *all* Declensions.

The Rules that decide Gender by *endings* are special, and will be given with each Declension separately.

Rules for Gender according to Meaning.*

19. *These Rules apply to Nouns of all Declensions.*

a. Names of *males, rivers, winds,* and *mountains,* are Masculine; as, **agricola** (*a farmer*), **Septentriō** (*the north wind*), **Arar** (*name of a river*), **Jūra** (*name of a mountain-chain*)..

b. Names of *females, countries, towns, islands,* and *trees* are Feminine; as, **mulier** (*a woman*), **Gallia** (*Gaul*), **Rōma** (*Rome*), **Dēlos** (*an island*), **Corinthus** (*a city in Greece*), **pirus** (*a pear-tree*), **Cyprus** (*an island*).

REMARK. There are exceptions to the above laws, which must be decided by the Special Rules for Endings. They can be learned only by observation and practice.

c. These are Neuter : —

1. Indeclinable Nouns (as, **nihil, fās**).

2. Infinitives, Phrases, Clauses, and other parts of speech used as Nouns. These are, of course, *indeclinable*, and would be regarded as Neuter in English, when used as Nouns (36, REM., page 10) ; as, *To err* is human (that is, a human *thing*). In the Latin for this sentence,

---

* This section may be omitted until the beginner shall have acquired a familiarity with the forms of Nouns and the use of the Cases. In the earlier lessons of this book, only those nouns are used whose gender is decided by the *English sense* (as **nauta, agricola**) and by the Special Rules (for gender *by endings*) given in connection with each Declension. Later, the General Rules will be required, and reference will be made to this section as well as to NOTE 3.

24 INTRODUCTION TO THE LATIN LESSONS.

Errāre est hūmānum, the Adjective hūmānum is in the neuter gender, agreeing with the Subject errāre.

Cases.

20. Latin nouns have six Cases: *Nominative, Genitive, Dative, Accusative, Vocative, Ablative.* The following table tells: (1) The relation of each to other words in a sentence; (2) Its English equivalent; (3) What question it answers. Notice that what we express in English by a Preposition is very often indicated in Latin merely by a change in the ending of a word (Inflection).

Latin Case.	Relation to other Words.	Like what English Case.	Answers what Question.
NOMINATIVE.	Subject.	Nominative.	Who? or What?
GENITIVE.	Possession, or *Of.*	Possessive, or *Of* with Objective.	Whose? Of { Whom? What?
DATIVE.	Indirect Object.	Objective with *To* or *For.*	To { Whom? For { What?
ACCUSATIVE.	Direct Object.	Objective.	Whom? or What?
VOCATIVE.	Case of Address.	Independent.	Used in addressing a person or thing.
ABLATIVE.	Adverbial Phrases.	Objective with *By, From, In, With.*	With From { Whom? By In { What?

REMARK. Besides these there was a Locative Case, answering the question *Where?* Its form and use will be described hereafter.

N. B. It will be found very helpful to the class if the teacher will apply the above principles to the following sentences, showing what Latin case should be used to represent each Noun and Pronoun. The use of the Cases will be more clearly understood by such a practical application.

Exercise.

1. The troops of the enemy were overcome in one battle. 2. John's companion will not tell him the name of the farmer. 3. My friend, will

INTRODUCTION TO THE LATIN LESSONS.

you give a tired man some supper and a room in which he can rest with comfort? 4. "Boys," said the teacher, "you have recited the morning's lesson well." 5. The man died from the effects of sunstroke. 6. This district is bounded by the river Garonne, the Atlantic, and the country of the Belgae. 7. I will keep these facts in mind. 8. He was treated with great kindness.

Declension of Nouns.

21. Latin Nouns have five Declensions. They are distinguished: —

1. By the final letter (or *characteristic*) of the Stem (16).
2. By the ending of the Genitive Singular.

The Declensions will be presented separately, beginning with the First.

TO TEACHERS.

In the following Lessons the author has not attempted to prescribe the exact amount to be assigned for each day's recitation. Classes differ so much in maturity and general preparation, that the individual teacher must use his own judgment as to the length of the daily lesson.

If any Lesson seems too long for a single exercise, it may, of course, be assigned in two or more portions, or some of the sentences may be omitted.

Various uses may be made of the "English into Latin" exercises: —

I. They may be assigned, one each day, as a regular part of the next recitation.

II. A few sentences only from each may be required.

III. The English exercises of two successive Lessons may form the material for the third day's recitation.

IV. The writing of these sentences may be made *work at sight*, to be performed in the class-room, allowing the pupil to consult the English-Latin Vocabulary for needed Latin theme-forms.

LATIN LESSONS.

EXPLANATION OF REFERENCES.

In this book, References are made: —
1. To sections of the Latin Grammars of Allen and Greenough, Bennett, and Harkness, and to the Appendix (at the end of this book): for example, A. 25; B. 20; H. 37; App. 5.
2. To the NOTES (beginning on page 149 of this book). These, in the *headings* of the Lessons, are indicated thus: N. 35. In the Exercises, N. is omitted.
3. To other portions of the book (Lessons, etc.). These will explain themselves.

LESSON I.

FIRST DECLENSION OF NOUNS.

Learn N. 9, *a, b, c, d* (page 153); also N. 8 (1), (2), (5), (6), (8).

Learn the Declension (with English meanings) of **stella**, A. 35; or **porta**, B. 20; or **mensa**, H. 48; or **silva**, App. 1.

Remember that all syllables for whose Quantity rules have not been given (11, page 20), *and not marked long, are short.*

Study each Latin word in the following Exercise so as to be able to give: —

1. Its Pronunciation. 2. The Quantity of syllables for which rules have been given. 3. Its Accent. 4. Its Stem and Gender. 5. Its Case and Number. 6. Its Meaning. If any form, as **viae**, can be found in more than one Case or Number, tell what these are, and give its meaning for each. 7. All the Case Endings of **stella** (6).

EXERCISE.

Special Vocabularies for the first 29 Lessons are given on pages 259 – 265. The Special Vocabularies must be so thoroughly learned by the student that, when questioned by the teacher, the English meaning can be given at once, when the Latin equivalent is stated, or the Latin word, when the English meaning is given.

1. Glōriārum. 2. Causa.* 3. Linguā. 4. Nautīs. 5. Viae. 6. Silvās. 7. Mensam. 8. Pecūniae. 9. Agricolīs. 10. Stellae. 11. Viā. 12. Victōriārum.

In each of the following English sentences, give the exact Latin equivalent for the words printed in *italics;* for example, *farmer's* = agricolae, Genitive Singular.

1. The *farmer's* garden contained a bed *of roses*. 2. That *sailor* has a good *memory*. 3. *Sailors*, you have won many *victories*. 4. We intrust many facts *to the memory*. 5. The *sailors* will win a *victory*. 6. The *farmers' tables* were bought *with money*. 7. He brought the *money from Rome*. 8. *Rome's glory* was great. 9. The *sailors' language* seems strange *to the farmers*.

LESSON II.

VERBS; THE SIMPLE SENTENCE; SUBJECT NOMINATIVE.

First Conjugation of Verbs: Present Indicative Active.
Learn: (1) N. **54** (entire), **56, 57,** *a.* (2) The Conjugation of **amō,** in the Present Indicative Active, and the English meanings. A. **128;** B. **101;** H. **205;** APP. **28.**

The Simple Sentence. Learn N. **100, 102, 105.**
Subject Nominative. Learn N. **118.**
Agreement of the Verb with its Subject. Learn N. **117** (*the simple Rule only*).

* There is no Article (*a, an, the*) in Latin. **Causa** may mean *cause, a cause,* or *the cause.*

EXERCISE.

Translate these sentences, and apply all the principles given in the NOTES *on this Lesson.*

1. Vocāmus. 2. Puellae vocant. 3. Amat. 4. Pugnās. 5. Nauta pugnat. 6. Laudātis. 7. Vocō. 8. Agricola vocat. 9. Laudāmus. 10. Vocās.

Give the Latin for —

1. They are calling. 2. You (*plural*) fight. 3. The girl loves. 4. We praise. 5. You (*singular*) love. 6. The sailors fight. 7. He praises. 8. The girls call. 9. You (*singular*) praise. 10. The farmers are praising. 11. He does call. 12. The girl's memory.

General Questions.

What is the Stem of **mensa?** **via?** What is the Present Stem of **amō?** **vocō?** **laudō?** **pugnō?** What are the Personal Endings of the Present Tense? What Person does each represent? Is **vocāmus** a complete sentence? Why? Name the Present Stem and Personal Ending of each Latin Verb-form used in this Exercise (**54, 3**). In how many ways can you translate **amant?** What is a Simple Sentence? What must every Sentence contain? Decline **via.**

LESSON III.

SECOND DECLENSION OF NOUNS; DIRECT OBJECT.

Second Declension of Nouns (*Masculine*). Learn N. **10,** *a, b, c.* Learn the Declension (with English meanings) of **servus, puer, ager, vir.** A. **38;** B. **23;** H. **51** & **4;** APP. **2.**
Direct Object. Learn N. **139.**

EXERCISE.

Translate. Apply all the principles given in the NOTES *on this Lesson and on Lesson II.*

1. Magister puerōs laudat.* 2. Servī pugnant. 3. Puerī equōs

---

* In Latin, the Subject regularly stands first, and the Verb last (see **192**).

amant. 4. Dant agrōs. 5. Puerōs vocātis. 6. Servum līberās. 7. Puer puellās vocat. 8. Amīcī amīcōs amant. 9. Agrīs. 10. Equōrum. 11. Serve. 12. Librō. 13. Virī. 14. Puer.

Give the Latin for —
1. The man frees the slaves. 2. The Romans fight. 3. O friend! 4. Of books. 5. I praise the boys' friends (120). 6. To the man. 7. The man's slave calls the boys. 8. Of a book. 9. With money. 10. For the slaves. 11. To the Romans' horses. 12. We praise the boy.

General Questions.

What is the Stem of **vir**? **servus**? **ager**? **puer**? Is this a true statement: "The Nominative and Vocative are always alike" (10, *c*)? What are the Case Endings of **equus**? **liber**? What Verbs can take a Direct Object in the Accusative? What are the Personal Endings of **līberō**? Decline, side by side, **equus, stella**; also, **ager, causa**. What Nouns of the Second Declension are Masculine? Name the Present Stem and Personal Ending of each Verb-form used in this Exercise.

LESSON IV.

SECOND DECLENSION OF NOUNS; FIRST AND SECOND DECLENSIONS OF ADJECTIVES.

Second Declension of Nouns (*Neuter*). Learn N. **10**, *a, b*; 8 (3). Learn the Declension of **bellum**, A. **38**; B. **23**; or **templum**, H. **51**; or **dōnum**, APP. **2**.

Adjectives of the First and Second Declensions. Learn N. **24** & *a*. Learn the Declension of **bonus, miser, niger**, A. **81, 82**; or **bonus, tener, sacer**, B. **63, 64, 65**; or **bonus, līber, aeger**, H. **148, 149, 150**; or **magnus, līber, niger**, APP. **10** & *a*.
Agreement of Adjectives. Learn N. **108**.

EXERCISE.

Translate. Decline the Nouns and Adjectives. Give the Rule for the agreement of each Adjective. Some of the Adjectives are not

in the proper form and must be corrected, with reasons for the corrections.
1. Puerī bonī.* 2. Equus nigrī. 3. Praemia parvum. 4. Virīs līberīs. 5. Servōrum miserōrum. 6. Dōnō magnā. 7. Silvae magnae. 8. Puellās magnōs. 9. Templa magna Rōmānōrum. 10. Nautae aegrae. 11. Templī magnī. 12. Glōriam magnam amās.

Give the Latin for —
1. With small rewards. 2. Of good friends. 3. Of a great forest. 4. Large temples (*Accusative*). 5. Good friend (*Vocative*). 6. Sick farmers (*Nominative*). 7. By a great war. 8. The wretched slaves fight. 9. We call the black horses. 10. For the small boys.

General Questions.

What are the Stems of **miser? parvus?** Is final a ever *long?* Where? What Cases are always alike in Neuter Nouns? Decline, side by side, **equus, stella, bellum**; also, **ager, causa, dōnum**; also, **vir bonus**; also, **agricola bonus**; also, **bellum magnum**. Give the Latin for: *You praise; We fight; He gives.*

LESSON V.
APPOSITION; GENITIVE CASE.

Apposition. Learn N. **106.**
Genitive Case. Learn N. **119** and CAUTION. *Genitive denoting Possession.* Learn N. **120.**

EXERCISE.

Translate.† Decline the Nouns and Adjectives, and give the Rules for their Case and Gender. Conjugate the Verbs; give the Stem and Personal Endings of each; give the Rule for their agreement.

---

* The Adjective regularly follows its Noun (**193**, 1).
† Read carefully N. **200.**

1. Genēvam, oppidum magnum, occupant. 2. Germānī agrōs Gallōrum * vastant. 3. Sabīnus lēgātus Gallōs superat. 4. Oppida magna occupās. 5. Titum, amīcum Sabīnī, laudātis. 6. Agrum agricolae vastāmus. 7. Puer gladium Titī lēgātī portat. 8. Titus et Sabīnus oppidum Genēvam occupant (**117,** *a*). 9. Librōs magistrī portās. 10. Virī equōs agricolārum laudant. 11. Gallī et Germānī oppida et agrōs Rōmānōrum occupant. 12. Lēgātī praemia magna dant. 13. Servus virī puerum amat. 14. Sabīnus, amīcus Titī, servōs miserōs līberat. 15. Cōpiae Titī et Sabīnī lēgātōrum oppida Germānōrum occupant.

Give the Latin for —

1. Rome's glory. 2. With the sword of Titus, the lieutenant. 3. A great abundance of good books. 4. We seize Geneva; the lieutenant's forces fight. 5. O wretched slave. 6. The man's friends love good books. 7. The farmers' slaves praise the lieutenants, Titus and Sabīnus.

General Questions.

What is the difference between an Appositive and a Genitive? What is the regular position of an Adjective? Give the Rules for the Gender of Nouns of the First and Second Declensions.

LESSON VI.

PREDICATE NOUN AND ADJECTIVE.

Predicate Noun and Adjective. Learn section **37** & *a*, page 10; also section **46** & *a, b, c*, page 13.

Learn N. **107**; **108** & 1, 3, 4.

Sum: *Present Indicative.* Learn N. **55**.

---

* The regular position for a Genitive (unless it is emphatic) is after the Noun on which it depends (**193,** 2).

EXERCISE.

Translate. Analyze (**194**, *a*). *Give the Rule for the form and agreement of each word.*

1. Stellae clārae sunt. 2. Virī multī agricolae sunt. 3. Rosa alba est. 4. Beātī estis. 5. Attentus es. 6. Gladius lēgātī acūtus est. 7. Exemplum virī bonī bonum est. 8. Numerus puerōrum et puellārum magnus est. 9. Portae oppidī Genēvae multae et magnae sunt. 10. Līber sum; līberī sumus. 11. Regna Germānōrum parva sunt. 12. Amīcus Sabīnī es. 13. Servōs timidōs vocat. 14. Perīculum magnum est. 15. Victōriae Titī multae sunt. 16. Insula longa et lāta est. 17. Genēva est oppidum magnum; oppidum Genēvam occupātis. 18. Via longa est; nautae timidī sunt.

Give the Latin for —

1. The sailor's danger is great. 2. We (*feminine*) are wretched. 3. Titus's friend is sick: 4. The wars of the Gauls are long. 5. The man's horses are black. 6. You (*singular*) are small and timid. 7. The boy's book is large. 8. The man is a teacher; the men are teachers. 9. The lieutenant is the sailor's friend. 10. The temples of the Romans are long and high.

General Questions.

What is the difference between an Appositive and a Predicate Noun? Pronounce these words, and give the reason for the *accent* of each: **agricolae, mensam, servōrum, magister, praemia, stellārum, amīcōs, victōriīs.**

LESSON VII.

VERBS: DEFINITIONS; FIRST CONJUGATION (*continued*).

Transitive and Intransitive; Voice; Number; Person; Mode, — *Indicative; Tense,* — *Present, Imperfect, Future; Personal Endings; Conjugation and Present Stem; Formation of Tenses.* Learn N. **56**; **57** & *a*; **60, 61**, 1, 2; **63**, *a*; **64** & *a* (*Active Endings*); **65**; **68**, *a, b, c*; **117** & *a*.

LATIN LESSONS.

Learn the Conjugation (and English meanings) of the *Present, Imperfect,* and *Future Indicative, Active,* of **amō.** A. **128**; B. **101**; H. **205**; App. **28**.

EXERCISE.

Translate. Analyze * *each Verb-form. Conjugate the Tense in which each is found.*

1. Servum vocās; servōs vocātis. 2. Puerum laudābās; puerōs laudābātis. 3. Pugnābis; pugnābitis. 4. Vir vocat; virī vocābant. 5. Oppidum occupābimus. 6. Amābit; amāmus; amābat. 7. Amātis; amābis; amābāmus. 8. Portābō; portābitis; portābam. 9. Titus agrōs Germānōrum vastābat. 10. Occupābitis oppida. 11. Bonus est, et virōs bonōs amābit. 12. Titus et Sabīnus lēgātī pugnābunt. 13. Cōpiās Gallōrum superābās. 14. Amīcōs virī vocābit.

Give the Latin for —

1. He calls; he will call; we call; they used to call. 2. You (*plural*) were carrying; they will carry; we carry; he is carrying. 3. You (*singular*) fight; you (*plural*) will fight; you (*singular*) do fight; we shall fight. 4. The dangers are many and great. 5. The temple is small. 6. We are free. 7. You (*singular*) are a lieutenant. 8. You (*plural*) are slaves.

General Questions.

What is Mode, and what does it show? (15 & *a*, page 3.) What is Tense, and what are the three divisions of time? (16, page 4.)

---

* In the First and Second Conjugations, any form in the
Present Indicative = Present Stem + Personal Ending (**54**, 3).
Imperfect Indicative = Present Stem + Tense Sign (**ba**) + Personal Ending.
Future Indicative = Present Stem + Tense Sign (**bi**) + Personal Ending (**68** *c*).

LESSON VIII.

VERBS: PRINCIPAL PARTS AND STEMS. NOUNS: DECLENSION OF FĪLIA AND DEA.

Principal Parts and *Stems*. Learn N. **65, 66, 67**, so far as they apply to the *First Conjugation*.
Declension of fīlia and dea. Learn N. 9, *e*.

General Questions and Practice.

How many *Principal Parts* has a Regular Verb? Why are they so called? What name is given to each? How many Stems has a Regular Verb? What are they called? How is the Present Stem found? The Perfect Stem? The Supine Stem? From which Stem is the Imperfect Indicative formed? The Future Indicative? Give the Principal Parts of the Verbs contained in the Special Vocabulary for this Lesson. Give the Stems of the same Verbs. Conjugate the Present, Imperfect, and Future Tenses of each.

Decline fīlia; dea. How do they differ from other Nouns of the First Declension?

Analyze these forms, and *prove* the Tense, Person, and Number: amābitis; narrās; vastābant; vocātis; dabimus; līberābās; servābunt; monstrābāmus; pugnābō; dās; portābis.

Give the Latin for —
1. O goddesses; of goddesses. 2. To a daughter; to the daughters. 3. The daughter's book is large. 4. The girls love the lieutenant's daughters. 5. For the goddesses; the temples of the goddess. 6. The man's daughter calls the boys. 7. The goddesses' gifts are many. 8. You (*plural*) will call the goddess. 9. The forces of the Romans will lay waste many fields. 10. The wall is high; the walls are long.

General Review.

What Nouns of the first Declension are Masculine? Of what gender are the others? What Nouns of the second Declension are Masculine? Neuter? Give the stem of dōnum; via; puer; magister; vir. Decline together: **puer, silva, dōnum**; also, **vir magnus**; also, **equus niger**. What is the regular position of an Adjective? of a Subject? of a Genitive? of a Verb? Why is **sum** called a *Copula*? Can **sum** take an Accusative as Object? What is the Noun or Adjective after **sum** called? Why? Review the Vocabularies of Lessons I., II., III., IV., V., VI.

LESSON IX.

VERBS (continued); DATIVE CASE.

Learn N. 61, entire; 64, b; 67; 68, d, e, f. (N. 62 may be learned or omitted, as the teacher may desire.)
Learn the Conjugation of the *Perfect, Pluperfect*, and *Future Perfect Indicative, Active*, of ·amō. A. 128; B. 101; H. 205; APP. 28.
Dative of Indirect Object. Learn N. 129.

EXERCISE.

Translate. Analyze each Sentence. Analyze* each Verb-form; conjugate its Tense. Give a Synopsis (78) *of each Verb, in the Indicative Mode. Give the Principal Parts and Stems of each Verb.*

Notice that dō *is unlike other Verbs of this Conjugation, as it has* ă (*not* ā) *when it takes an additional syllable; as,* dămus, dăbis (*but* amāmus, amābis).

1. Servum vocāvistis. 2. Oppidum servāverat. 3. Oppida occupāverimus. 4. Cōpiae Titī Gallōs superāvēre. 5. Viam monstrāvit. 6. Fābulam narrāverās. 7. Puerō librum dedistī. 8. Virīs frūmentum dederit. 9. Servō gladium dedit. 10. Puer nautīs fābulam narrābit. 11. Puerīs attentīs fābulās narrāvērunt. 12. Amīcus praemium magnum nōn dederat. 13. Puellīs viam monstrāvimus. 14. Cōpiīs pecūniam nōn dabātis. 15. Injūriae Gallōrum multae sunt.

Give the Latin for —

1. The teacher will give the attentive boy a book. 2. He has told his (*omit*) friend a good story. 3. Many Germans overcome

---

* In the Indicative Mode, of *all Conjugations*, the
Perfect Tense = Perfect Stem + the Personal Endings (of the Perfect Indicative; **64**, b).
Pluperfect Tense = Perfect Stem + the Tense Sign (**era**) + the Personal Endings.
Future Perfect Tense = Perfect Stem + the Tense Sign (**eri**) + the Personal Endings (**68**, f.)

large forces of the Gauls. 4. The lieutenants, Titus and the friend of Sabinus, will have seized the town of Geneva. 5. He had carried; we were carrying; you (*plural*) have carried. 6. He has given; he gave; you (*singular*) had given; we shall have given. 7. We called the boy; the boys called the man; the girls were calling.

LESSON X.

VERBS : FIRST CONJUGATION ; SUBJUNCTIVE MODE.

Learn N. 63, *b ;* 69, *a* (1), *b, c, d.*
Learn the Conjugation of the *Subjunctive Mode, Active Voice,* of amō. A. 128; B. 101; H. 205; App. 28.

REMARK. In this Lesson the meanings of the Subjunctive Mode are not required; but numerous Latin forms are given for practice in analysis of the verb. The *use* of the Subjunctive is presented later (Lesson XXI.).

EXERCISE.

Tell the Mode, Tense, Number, and Person of each word. Prove your answers by analyzing * *each Latin form.*

1. Dēs; dederis; dedissētis; darent. 2. Amāverit; amētis; amāvissēs; amārēmus. 3. Portās; portēs; portārēs; portābis. 4. Pugnēmus; pugnābās; pugnāvissēmus; pugnāverimus. 5. Narret; narrāret; narrābat; narrāverit. 6. Laudārēmus; laudābimus; laudāvissent; laudāvistis. 7. Servāverās; servāvēre; servēs; servārētis. 8. Vocāvit; vocāvisset; vocābunt; vocāverint.

* In the Subjunctive Mode of the First Conjugation, the Tenses contain these elements : —
Present Subjunctive = Present Stem (a changed to e) + Personal Endings.
Imperfect Subjunctive = Present Stem + Tense Sign (re) + Personal Endings.
Perfect Subjunctive = Perfect Stem + Tense Sign (eri) + Personal Endings.
Pluperfect Subjunctive = Perfect Stem + Tense Sign (isse) + Personal Endings.

General Questions.

What questions does the Direct Object answer? the Indirect Object? What Tenses does the Subjunctive lack? Name the Tenses of the Indicative. How does the Imperfect Indicative differ in meaning from the Perfect? Translate **vocābās ; vocāvistī**. What two meanings may **vocāvistī** have? What names are given to the Perfect Tense? How many Tenses are there in the Indicative differing in *form*? How many differing in *meaning*? How do the forms of the Perfect Subjunctive differ from those of the Future Perfect Indicative? Give a Synopsis of the Indicative and Subjunctive, Active, of **narrō ; dō**.

LESSON XI.

FIRST CONJUGATION: IMPERATIVE MODE; VOCATIVE CASE. SECOND DECLENSION: **FĪLIUS** AND PROPER NAMES IN **IUS**.

Learn N. **57**, *c ;* **63**, *c ;* **64**, *c* (Active Endings); **70** ; **100**.
Learn the Conjugation of the *Imperative Active* of **amō**.
A. **128**; B. **101**; H. **205**; App. **28**.
Vocative Case. Learn N. **145**.
Learn the Declension of **fīlius**, and also of Proper Names in **ius**; as, **Cassius, Manlius**. N. **10**, *d, e.*

EXERCISE.

Translate. Analyze each Sentence. Analyze each Verb-form (**64**, *c*). *Give Rule for the use and form of each word.*

1. Virōs bonōs amāte. 2. Tite, oppidum occupā. 3. Mī * fīlī, agricolam vocā. 4. Fīlius meus servum vocat. 5. Concilium, Cāī, magnum est. 6. Proelium, Sabīne, nuntiā. 7. Pugnātō ; pugnantō ; pugnātōte. 8. Proelia, mī amīce, multa et magna sunt. 9. Auxilium deārum nōn parvum est. 10. Cōpiae Cassī (**10**, *e*) magnae sunt. 11. Cōpia frūmentī parva est. 12. Date, virī,

---

* **Meus** has **mī** (not **mee**) in the Voc. Sing. Masc. In the other forms it is like **bonus**.

LATIN LESSONS. 39

frūmentum equīs. 13. Meam patriam, Jūlī, servā. 14. Equī Jūlī albī sunt. 15. Conciliō, puerī, fābulam narrāte. 16. Amātō; laudantō; vocātōte.

Give the Latin for —
1. Fight, my men. 2. My men fight. 3. O Pompey, save the towns. 4. My son, give the money to the daughters of Cassius. 5. Marcus and Caius are good men. 6. Call the slaves, Marcus. 7. The lieutenants, Cāius and Cassius, have seized the town of the Germans. 8. Sabīnus, my friend, the rewards of the battle are great.

General Questions.

What Stem does the Imperative contain? What can you say of the use of the Future Imperative? How does **Cassius** differ in declension from **servus**? How does **meus** differ from **bonus**? Give the Vocative of **Marcus Tullius**; **Lūcius Cotta**.

LESSON XII.

FIRST CONJUGATION: INFINITIVES, PARTICIPLES, GERUND, AND SUPINE.

Learn N. **57,** *d;* **58,** *a* & REMARK; **59,** *a, b;* **63,** *d;* **71;** **72.**

Learn the *Active Infinitives, Participles,* also the *Gerund* and *Supine,* of amō. A. **128;** B. **101;** H. **205;** APP. **28.**

General Questions and Practice.

Give the Stem and Ending of the Present Infinitive, also of the Perfect Infinitive. Do Infinitives have Personal Endings? Give the reason for your answer (**15,** *e,* page 4). Of what forms is the Future Infinitive composed? What Stem does it contain? Give the Stem and Ending of the Present Participle of **amō; līberō; vocō**. The same Participle in English ends in what letters? What Active Participle is found in English, but not in Latin? (*Ans.* The Perfect; as, *having loved.*) What Stem does the Future Participle contain? Give its ending. What is a Participle (**189**)? To what Declension of Adjectives does the Future Participle belong? Does the Present Participle belong to that Declension? Why not? Describe the Gerund; the Supine.*

---

* The meaning and use of the Supine are taken up later.

In the following sentences, give the exact Latin equivalents for words printed in *italics:* —

He fell, *fighting* bravely. He wishes *to seize* the *town*. We are said *to have praised* the *slave*. He is thought *to be about to fight*. *You* (plural) *are desirous* (**cupidus**) *of fighting*. *Titus will overcome by fighting*. *He pays* (**dō**) *attention* (**opera**) *to fighting*.

Give a *complete* Synopsis (**78**) of **vastō; vocō; dō; līberō**, in the Active Voice.

The following Verbs belong to the First, Second, Third, and Fourth Conjugations. The Roman Numeral at the left of each indicates its Conjugation. Their Principal Parts are given, and, in answering the questions below, precisely *the same Rules* for Stems, Formation of Tenses, etc., are to be applied, as for **amō**. (See N. **67, 68, 69, 70, 71, 72**.)

	Present Indicative.	Present Infinitive.	Perfect Indicative.	Supine.
I.	servō,	servāre,	servāvī,	servātum.
II.	moneō,	monēre,	monuī,	monitum.
III.	regō,	regere,	rexī,	rectum.
IV.	audiō,	audīre,	audīvī,	audītum.

Questions and Application of Principles.

Give all the Stems of these Verbs (**65, 67**). Conjugate the Imperfect Subjunctive of each; the Perfect Indicative; the Perfect Subjunctive; the Pluperfect Subjunctive; the Pluperfect Indicative; the Future Perfect Indicative. Give all the Infinitives of each.

Conjugate the Present Indicative of **moneō**; the Imperfect Indicative; the Imperative; the Future Indicative.

What is the Present Imperative, Second Person Singular, of **regō? audiō?** What is the Present Participle of **servō? moneō? regō?** Give the Gerund of **servō; moneō; regō.**

Give the Supine forms of the four Verbs.

How may the Imperfect Subjunctive Active of all Conjugations be found? (**69,** *b.*)

LESSON XIII.

DECLENSION OF **DEUS**; IRREGULAR ADJECTIVES; GENITIVE IN **Ius**, DATIVE IN **ī**.

Learn the Declension of **deus**, N. 10, *f*.
Learn the list of Adjectives having **ius** in the Genitive, and **ī** in the Dative, N. 43, *a, b*. Decline them. A. 83, *a, b*; B. 66; H. 151; App. 11.

General Questions.

What is the Vocative Singular of **servus**? **deus**? What is the Nominative Singular Neuter of **malus**? **alius**? Decline together the Masculine of **bonus** and **alius**; the Feminine; the Neuter. How does **alter** differ from the others in declension? (*Ans.* The i is *short* in the Genitive; as, **alte′rīus**, but **utrīus**, **alīus**.) How does **alter** differ in meaning from **alius**? (*Ans.* Alius means *another*, of several; alter, *the other*, of two.) Decline together the Latin for *no god ; any boy ; another gift ; the other sailor ; one daughter* (in the singular); *the other son ; no way ; the whole town* (in the singular). What is a Diphthong? Pronounce **deae**; **neuter**; **coelum**.

EXERCISE.

Translate. Decline the Nouns and Adjectives. Conjugate the Verbs.

1. Aliī virī templa aedificant. 2. Injūriae alterius virī multae sunt. 3. Victōriae ūnīus lēgātī nōn multae sunt. 4. Nullī agrī. Germānōrum vacant. 5. Nātūra amīcō meō vītam longam nōn dedit. 6. Equī neutrīus servī nigrī sunt. 7. Occupāte, virī, tōtum oppidum. 8. Nullī poëtae * Cāium laudābunt. 9. Aliud templum altum est. 10. Laudā, Cassī, servōs sōlōs. 11. Nuntiā, Marce, proelium Cāiō sōlī. 12. Amīcī meī, poëtae fābulam narrābimus.

---

* The mark (¨) is called a *Diaeresis*, and shows that the vowel over which it is placed does *not* form a Diphthong with the preceding vowel. **Poëta** is pronounced **po-ĕ′-ta.**

Give the Latin for —
1. Of other gods; to one god. 2. For the goddesses alone.
3. Of any aid; for no aid. 4. The life of the other horse is long.
5. The Romans alone give aid to the Gauls. 6. Julius, the Germans·will seize the whole town of Geneva. 7. The glory alone of the war is great. 8. The stars alone are bright. 9. Other forces will fight. 10. We show (point out) the dangers of one battle.

LESSON XIV.

NOUNS: THIRD DECLENSION; ELEMENTARY PRACTICE.

REMARK. Nouns of the Third Declension have a great variety of forms in the Nominative Singular; but their Case-endings follow the same law (N. 6). These nouns are Masculine, Feminine, and Neuter; but as their gender depends ·largely upon their Nominative *endings,* and as there are over *twenty* different endings in the Nominative, the Gender of nouns in the Third Declension is not so easily distinguished as in the other Declensions.

The Stems of nouns in the Third Declension have various endings; and this fact is apt to present some· difficulty to the beginner.

In this Lesson, eight nouns are given for practice: three Masculine, two Feminine, three Neuter. Their Gender can be easily remembered by their *meaning*. The Stem of each can be found by cutting off the ending is from the Genitive Singular; as, **mīlit-, nōmin-, rēg-** (stems of **mīles, nōmen, rex**). English words derived from the Latin are given to show that *the Latin Stem is often found in the English word,* and so to aid the pupil's memory.

Learn the REMARK at the head of this Lesson.
Learn N. 6 (for the Third Declension); 8 (1), (2), (3), (4), (5), (6).
Learn the Declension of **consul, mīles, rex, virgō, soror, caput, nōmen, corpus.** A. **46, 49**; B. **31, 32, 33, 34, 35, 36**; H. **58, 59, 60, 61**; APP. **3, 4**.

EXERCISE.

Translate. Decline the Nouns and give their Stems. Conjugate the Verbs.

1. Lēgātus mīlitēs consulis laudāvit. 2. Soror rēgis virginem

laudābit. 3. Caput equī magnum est. 4. Corpora virōrum magna sunt. 5. Mīles rēgī proelium nuntiāverat. 6. Fīliī rēgum malī sunt. 7. Fīliae Titī lēgātī virginem timidam vocāvēre. 8. Amāte, puerī, sorōrēs.* 9. Consulēs oppidīs nōmina dederint.

Give the Latin for —
1. To the kings; the king's; the kings' horses. 2. For the consul's sisters. 3. With the bodies of the soldiers. 4. The maiden's sister's name. 5. O sister; the consuls' soldiers. 6. For the body of the horse. 7. The boy's head is small. 8. My friend's sisters are praising the consul's daughters.

General Questions.

What is the Stem of **mīles**? **caput**? **virgō**? **rex**? **soror**? **consul**? **corpus**? **nōmen**? What are the Case-endings of a Masculine or Feminine noun? of a Neuter noun? In what Cases will the endings vary with different nouns? (*Ans.* Nominative and Vocative Singular.) What Cases are always alike in Neuter nouns of all Declensions?

LESSON XV.

NOUNS: THIRD DECLENSION; GENERAL PRINCIPLES; GENDER.

General Principles. Learn N. **1** & (2), (3), (4), *a;* **2** (1), (2), (3), (4); **11** (entire); **12** (entire); **13** (entire); **14**.

Rules of Gender. Learn the Nominative Gender Endings of Nouns of the Third Declension. N. **4** (3).

Questions and Practice.

The answers to these questions are given in the NOTES *on this Lesson, and in the Examples under them.*

Into what two classes are nouns of the Third Declension divided (11)? What is the Genitive Plural of the nouns whose stems are **mīlit-, nāvi-,**

---

* The possessive words, *my, your, their,* etc., are not expressed in Latin when they can be readily supplied from the general meaning of the sentence.

jūdic-, rēg-, aetāt-, custōd-, lapid-, turri-, virgin-, capit-, nōmin-, corpor-? Give the Nominative Singular of each. What changes of consonants or vowels appear in them? Why is not the Genitive Singular of **corpus, corporis**? What is meant by "increasing in the Genitive" (15)? What is an *abstract* noun? a *collective* noun?*

In the following list of nouns, the Nominative and Genitive Singular of each are given; tell the Gender of each noun, and give the reason: —

Acstās (aestātis), opus (operis), lux (lūcis), ōrātiō (ōrātiōnis, *a speech* or *speaking*), honor (honōris), animal (animālis), turris (turris), leō (leōnis), calcar (calcāris), mōs (mōris), virtūs (virtūtis), tempus (temporis), agger (aggeris), nūbēs (nūbis), obses (obsidis), mare (maris), legiō (legiōnis, *a legion*), pater (patris), palūs (palūdis), trāmes (trāmitis), pax (pācis), rex (rēgis), onus (oneris), cīvitās (cīvitātis), altitūdō (altitūdinis, *height*), caput (capitis), urbs (urbis), nōmen (nōminis), rūpēs (rūpis), flōs (flōris), genus (generis), consul (consulis), custōs (custōdis), soror (sorōris), nox (noctis), hostis (hostis, *an enemy*), vectīgal (vectīgālis).

Decline the nouns whose stems are: aetāt-, lūc-, custōd-, virtūt-, lapid-.

LESSON XVI.

NOUNS: THIRD DECLENSION; CONSONANT-STEMS.

Review all the NOTES at the head of Lesson XV.
Learn Section **4**, *a, d* (omitting the REMARK), page 17. Learn, also, N. **15** & *a, b*, REMARK.
Learn the Declension of all the Nouns given in A. **46, 49**; or B. **31, 32, 33, 34, 35, 36**; or H. **57, 58, 59, 60, 61**; or APP. **3, 4**.

---

* An *abstract* noun is the name of a *quality* (as, *height, bravery, greatness, goodness*, etc.), or of an *action* (as, *siege, running*). A *collective* noun is defined in section 3, *d*, page 1.

LATIN LESSONS.

To the Student. Remember that, to inflect a noun of the Third Declension, two things must be known: 1. its *Genitive Singular* (which will show the *Stem*); 2. its *Gender*. Remember, also, that the Stems of Latin words are very often found in English words derived from them; this fact is of great value as a means of aiding the memory, as has already been said. Many such may be found in the Latin words used in this Lesson and Lesson XIV.; as, FLOR-AL (flōr-; stem of flōs); CAPIT-AL (capit-, stem of caput); PRINCIP-AL (princip-, stem of princeps).

General Questions and Practice.

Decline each of the following nouns side by side with the proper form of the adjective. First decide the gender of the noun, and make the adjective agree with it in gender. The Genitive forms of the nouns are given in Lesson XV. and in the Vocabulary for this Lesson.

Aestās longus. Opus magna. Lux clārum. Honor magnus. Leō parva. Mōs bonum. Longitūdō magna. Virtūs magnus. Tempus longa. Legiō nullus. Pater bona. Rex misera. Cīvitās ulla. Caput alius. Nōmen sōlus. Flōs alba. Consul aegrum. Custōs ūnus (*in singular*). Soror beātus.

What Consonants are called *Liquids*? Why? What Mutes suffer some change before **s**? Do nouns having *consonant-stems* increase in the Genitive? How do **pater, mater, frater** differ from the other nouns of this class?

EXERCISE.

Translate. Decline the Nouns and Adjectives. Conjugate the Verbs. Give the Stem of each Noun. Tell how the Nominative Singular is formed from the Stem.

1. Flōrēs albī sunt. 2. Altitūdō mūrī magna est. 3. Patrī puerī librum dedit. 4. Consulēs opus mīlitum laudāverant. 5. Mōrem malum nōn laudābimus. 6. Soror rēgis fīliābus consulum flōrēs dat. 7. Virtūs rēgum nōn parva est. 8. Nōmina flōrum multa sunt. 9. Principēs * beātī sunt.

Give the Latin for —

1. To the guards of the gates. 2. In width of fields. 3. Of

---

* * The Gender is often decided by the *sense*, without regard to the Nominative ending.

the king's soldiers. 4. By the great height of the wall. 5. To my brothers' bravery. 6. The honors of a good man are great. 7. The light of the stars is bright. 8. The king praised my father; he will not praise my mother. 9. The leaders of the Gauls will have laid waste the whole town.

LESSON XVII.

NOUNS: THIRD DECLENSION; VOWEL-STEMS.

Learn N. 16, entire; 17, entire.

Learn the Declension of the Nouns given under one of these References: A. 52; B. 38, 39; H. 62, 63; App. 5.

Mixed Stems (*consonant-stems* in the Singular, *vowel-stems* in the Plural). Learn N. 18. Learn the Declension of urbs and nox, A. 54; or of arx, B. 40: or of urbs and arx, H. 64; or of urbs, mons, nox, App. 6.

Questions.

Do nouns having i-*stems* increase in the Genitive? Do those having *consonant-stems*? How do nouns (*vowel-stems*) usually form the Nominative Singular from the Stem? What nouns do not? What vowel change is very common? Give the Nominative Singular endings of nouns of this class. What nouns have i as the *regular* ending in the Ablative Singular? What nouns have e or i? What nouns *seem* to increase in the Genitive? Explain this? What is the Genitive Plural of pars, nox, mons, urbs? Why? What name may be given to the stems of these nouns? What three classes of stems may nouns of the Third Declension have? [*Ans.* I. *Consonant* (Mute or Liquid); as, mīlit-, rēg-, virgin-, corpor-: II. *Vowel* (i); as, nāvi-, nūbi-, animāli-: III. *Mixed;* as, urb-, mont- (Singular); urbi-, monti- (Plural)]. What nouns, in common use, are Masculine, contrary to the Rules of Gender (19, *a*)?

EXERCISE.

Translate. Decline the Nouns and Adjectives. Analyze the complete Sentences.

1. Custōdēs leōnum timidī sunt. 2. Principēs et ducēs Gallōrum pugnāvērunt. 3. Montēs et colles Galliae altī sunt. 4.

Nautae mare et nāvēs amant. 5. Numerus hostium magnus est. 6. Dux hostium fīnēs rēgis vastāverat. 7. Calcāria ducis acūta sunt. 8. Partem urbis occupant. 9. Multa animālia pulchra sunt. 10. Custōs turris amīcus meus est. 11. Monstrā, Tite, montem. 12. Altitūdine montium. 13. Animālium magnōrum. 14. Pars nāvium; nāvēs multae. 15. Montēs altōs; maris altī. 16. Vectīgālī magnō; noctium longārum.

Give the Latin for —
1. Of taxes; by towers; of the hills; to the leaders of the enemy. 2. Soldiers, lay waste the Germans' territory. 3. By fire; of fires; for a part of the city. 4. By the sea; of many seas; O beautiful city; O lofty mountains. 5. By a great cloud; O my father; by a bad custom. 6. The bodies of many animals. 7. Save the city, Cāius.

Decline, side by side, the Latin words meaning —
The deep sea; a great tax; a lofty mountain; a great citadel; a good custom; a small body.

LESSON XVIII.

THE VERB SUM: GENERAL PRACTICE.

Learn N. 55, 83, 84 & *a, b, c*.
Learn the entire Conjugation of **sum.** A. 119; B. 100; H. 204; App. 40.

Questions and Practice.

How many stems has **sum**? What are they? What forms are lacking in its conjugation? Give a complete Synopsis of **sum.** Why is not the Imperfect Indicative **esam,** and not **eram**? What is Mode? Tense? How many meanings has **fuī**? By what two names is this tense-form called? Why is **sum** called a *Copula*? What is the Noun or Adjective after it called? Why? Tell where these forms are found: **este; fuerātis; sītis; estis; fuissēmus; fuerit; fuisti; essēs; futūrus; erātis; sīs; es; fuēre; suntō.**

Give the Latin for —
1. The cities were great. 2. Caius and Marcus will be good leaders. 3. The forces of Pompey, the leader of the enemy, are great. 4. You are a good man, Marcus. 5. My brother had been a teacher. 6. Father, show the boy (129) the beautiful gifts. 7. Boys, be attentive. 8. The flowers are white and beautiful. 9. The example of the consul was bad. 10. The mountain is high. 11. The legions of the enemy will have seized the city of Rome. 12. The number of states will be great. 13. We have been good lieutenants of good soldiers. 14. Men, give corn to the horses. 15. You (*plural*) will have been timid. 16. The leaders have praised and will praise the legion. 17. My son, be good.

LESSON XIX.

THE VERB POSSUM; USE OF THE INFINITIVE.

Learn N. 1 (4) *b*; 85, 1.
Learn the Conjugation of **possum**. A. 120; B. 126; H. 290, II.; App. 41.
Infinitive as Complement. Learn N. 165, *b;* 173, CAUTION.

TO THE STUDENT. *Can* and *could* must always be expressed by **possum**.

EXERCISE.

Translate. Apply Rule for the use of each word. Examples on Page 262.

1. Urbēs Gallōrum expugnāre nōn poterimus. 2. Caesar castra servāre nōn potuit. 3. Mīlitibus arma dare potuerīs. 4. Jūdex injustus esse potest. 5. Mīlitēs ducis bonī ignāvī esse nōn possunt. 6. Servus virō frūmentum dare poterat. 7. Noctēs longae esse nōn possunt. 8. Arcem expugnāre potuerātis. 9. Castra Caesaris longa et lāta sunt. 10. Partem hostium superāre potuistī. 11. Date, ducēs, arma virīs.

Give the Latin for —
1. We can fight; you (*singular*) could fight. 2. You (*plural*) could have overcome Titus, the leader. 3. He will not be able to seize the mountain. 4. The keepers could not free the animals. 5. The width of the camp cannot be great. 6. We consuls (**106**) had not been able to overcome Caesar's forces. 7. No soldiers of the king can be cowardly. 8. The leaders' arms were many and great.

Questions and Practice.

How are these forms obtained: **possum ? possim ? possem ? potui ? possunt ?** What forms of Conjugation does **possum** lack ? How is **potens** used ? Translate **rex potens est; consulēs potentēs sumus.** Give a complete Synopsis of **possum.** Tell how these Nominatives are formed from their stems : **jūdex; virtūs; custōs; civitās.** Decline, side by side, the Latin for : *a large spur; a long night; a good work; a cowardly legion; no battle; a bad name.*
Why is the *Complementary Infinitive* so called ?

LESSON XX.

THE INFINITIVE WITH A SUBJECT ACCUSATIVE.

Learn N. **143, 166, 189** (*the heading only*) ; also **56**, page 16.

CAUTION. Remember that a Participle is *always* a Participle, even in a compound tense, as the Future Infinitive Active, and must agree with its Noun in Gender, Number, and Case.

EXERCISE.

Translate. Give Rules for the form and use of all words. Examples on Page 262. *The Accusative with the Infinitive should be translated precisely like a clause ; that is, as though the Accusative were Nominative, and the Infinitive in the Third Person, Singular or Plural.*

1. "Urbēs magnae sunt." 2. Dīcit urbēs magnās esse. 3. Nuntiābit Rōmānōs cōpiās Gallōrum superāvisse. 4. Negat (**199, 5**)

Caesarem oppidum expugnātūrum esse. 5. "Dux castra servābit." 6. Lēgātus dīcit ducem castra servātūrum esse. 7. Putat legiōnēs pugnāre nōn posse. 8. Putō cōpiās Sabīnī ignāvās esse. 9. Spērāmus mīlitēs consulis Genēvam occupātūrōs esse. 10. Putābitis consulēs injustōs fuisse. 11. Dīcit iter longum futūrum esse. 12. Dīcit nullōs agrōs vacāre. 13. Putās nautam Caesarī proelium nuntiāre potuisse. 14. Dīcit maria lāta et alta esse. 15. Putātis rēgem urbī Rōmae (106) nōmen dedisse. 16. Custōdēs nuntiant hostēs arcem occupāvisse. 17. Spērās bella longa futūra esse. 18. Nuntiū, Pompēī, consulī mīlitēs castra servātūrōs esse.

Give the Latin for —
1. He says that the teacher praised the boy. 2. The men think that the mountains are high. 3. You (*plural*) hope that the soldiers can protect the city and the citizens. 4. They will deny that the bodies of animals are small. 5. He hopes that the marches will not be long. 6. "The rewards of bravery will be great." 7. The king says that the rewards of bravery will be great.

Questions.

What is a *Direct Quotation* ? an *Indirect Quotation* ? What verbs are followed by the Infinitive with a Subject Accusative ? Why can **putō** and **spērō** be followed by the same construction as **dīcō**, **negō**, and **nuntiō** (166, II.) ? What Conjunction is omitted in Latin after verbs of *saying*, etc. ?

LESSON XXI.

USE OF THE SUBJUNCTIVE MODE.*

Learn N. **57**, *b*; **170**; **174** & *a*, *b*; **175** & *a*, *b*, *c*, REMARK 1. Read carefully section **19**, page 6.

* To TEACHERS. Although the Subjunctive presents some difficulties to a beginner, yet it seems best to give him an insight into that mode at an early period of his study, that he may not be compelled to memorize the Subjunctive forms of all the Conjugations, and yet not make a practical application of them. If the principles stated in this Lesson are emphasized when it is

LATIN LESSONS.   51

Review the Conjugation of the Subjunctive, Active, of **amō, sum, possum**.

Study these References in connection with the Examples for this Lesson (page 263), *and also the following* —

HINTS FOR THE STUDENT. The Subjunctive Mode has a great variety of uses; this Lesson deals with one which is very common, and which illustrates the *whole* mode better than any other use. The Indicative states something as a *fact;* the Subjunctive states something, not as a *fact*, but as *possible* or *impossible*. The sentences of this Lesson contain the Conjunction **sī** (*if*), and are called *Conditional Sentences*. They are Complex (section **40**, *c*, page 12). Of course, the Conjunction **sī** introduces the Subordinate Clause. The *statement*, or more important thought, will always be found in the Principal Clause. In these sentences, both the Indicative and Subjunctive are used.

Remember, it is not **sī** that requires the Subjunctive, but the *thought* to be expressed. *Remember*, that the Subjunctive has no Future or Future Perfect Tense; in such sentences as these, the Present must be used as a Future, and the Perfect as a Future Perfect. *Notice* that, as in English, *were* (as, *if I were rich*) indicates that something is *not true* at the *present* time; such a meaning must not be decided by the *if* clause altogether, but by the *Principal* clause.
STUDY THE EXAMPLES.

EXERCISE.

Translate. Tell what TIME *each Verb denotes, and* WHAT KIND *of a statement it makes. Study the* EXAMPLES, *page* 263.

1. Sī puellās laudārētis, beātae essent. 2. Sī jūdex jūstus fuisset, servum līberāvisset. 3. Sī Caesar pugnāvit, hostēs superāvit. 4. Sī pugnāre potuisset, cōpiās Gallōrum superāvisset. 5. Sī lēgātī oppida expugnāverint, servī līberī sint. 6. Sī Caesar mīlitēs laudāvisset, pugnāvissent. 7. Sī Titus ignāvus sit, urbem nōn occupet. 8. Sī hostēs urbem expugnārent, perīculum cīvium magnum esset. 9. Sī servus pugnāre posset, pugnāret. 10. Sī hostēs superāverimus, oppidum occupēmus. 11. Sī pugnant, superant. 12. Sī mīlitēs timidī fuissent, Germānī agrōs vastāvissent. 13. Sī timidī fuērunt, nōn pugnāvērunt. 14. Sī Titus perīculum nuntiet, urbem servāre possīmus.

assigned, the difficulties referred to can be very greatly lessened. Section **19**, page 6, if it can be read in the class-room and the Examples under it briefly explained, will make the expression of a *possible* (or *impossible*) statement comparatively easy.

Give the Latin for —
1. If Caesar should be judge, he would be just. 2. If the fathers were good, the sons would be good. 3. If the mothers are bad, the daughters are bad. 4. If they were judges, they were just. 5. If he should storm (should have stormed) the cities, he would free the slaves. 6. If he fights (shall have fought), he will overcome the enemy. 7. If we are slaves, we are not citizens. 8. If he praises (shall praise) the sailors, they will fight.

LESSON XXII.

FIRST CONJUGATION: PASSIVE VOICE; ABLATIVE OF MEANS AND AGENT.

Learn the Personal Endings of the Passive Voice. N. **64,** *a*. Learn, also, N. **73,** *a, b, c*.

Learn the Conjugation of the *Present, Imperfect,* and *Future Indicative, Passive,* of amō. A. **129**; B. **102**; H. **206**; App. **29**.

Ablative of Means or Instrument. Learn N. **146; 151; 193,** 5.

Ablative of Agent. Learn N. **151,** Caution; also, N. **95,** *a,* and section **4,** *b,* page 17.

EXERCISE.

Translate. Apply Rules for Case, Number, etc. Analyze each Verb-form, giving its Stem, Tense Sign (if it have one), and Personal Ending.

1. Urbs expugnātur; oppida expugnantur. 2. Cōpiae Caesaris superābuntur. 3. Servus līberābitur; servī līberābimur. 4. Amāberis; amāminī; amāris; amābāminī. 5. Tite, vulnerāberis. 6. Laudāmur; laudābitur; laudātis; laudābunt; laudābimur. 7. Dīcit ducem signum tubā datūrum esse. 8. Signum ā Caesare

tubā datur. 9. Mīles gladiō vulnerābitur. 10. Equī ab hostibus vulnerantur. 11. Lapidibus vulnerābiminī. 12. Montēs altī ā Titō lēgātō occupantur. 13. Proelium Caesarī ā mīlite decimae legiōnis nuntiābitur. 14. Urbēs hostium dōnīs magnīs servantur. 15. Sī perīculum ducī ā servō nuntiābitur, urbs servābitur. 16. Equus puerō ab agricolā dabitur.

Give the Latin for —
1. The tenth legion is praised by Caesar. 2. You (*plural*) will be wounded by the large stone. 3. The signals are given with a trumpet. 4. You (*singular*) will be freed by the consul. 5. They will not be able to lay waste the fields of the enemy. 6. He thinks that the tenth legion was able to storm the great city. 7. If they had been able to fight, they would have given the signal. 8. Fight, soldiers; overcome the enemy's forces. 9. He hopes that the leaders will give arms to the tenth legion. 10. If they are (**168,** *a*) wounded by the weapons, they will not be able to fight.

Questions.

What kind of ideas does the Ablative usually express ? What is the proper position of an adverb or word (or phrase) used adverbially ? What is the difference between a *means* and an *agent ?* When should **ā** be used, and when **ab ?** What tenses does the Subjunctive lack ? How may this lack be supplied ? How does the Subjunctive differ (in *thought*) from the Indicative ?

LESSON XXIII.

FIRST CONJUGATION : PASSIVE VOICE ; ABLATIVE OF SEPARATION.

Learn N. **73,** *d.*

Learn the Conjugation of the *Perfect, Pluperfect,* and *Future Perfect Indicative, Passive,* of amō. A. **129**; B. **102**; H. **206**; App. **29.**

Ablative of Separation. Learn N. **147.**

LATIN LESSONS.

EXERCISE.

Translate. Analyze. Apply Rule for the form and use of each word.

Read the CAUTION, Lesson XX.

1. Amātī sunt; amātus erō; amābiminī; amātī estis; amāvērunt. 2. Mīlitēs laudātī erant; puellae laudātae erunt. 3. Dux ā mīlite vocātus est. 4. Virī tēlīs lapidibusque * vulnerābuntur. 5. Pater amātus est ā fīliīs fīliābusque.* 6. Cīvēs servitūte līberābit. 7. Urbs custōdibus nūdāta est. 8. Rex perīculō magnō līberātur. 9. Consulēs suspiciōne timōris līberābuntur. 10. Collēs multī virīs nūdātī erunt. 11. Castra dēfensōribus nūdantur. 12. Mūrum custōdibus dēfensōribusque * nūdāvērunt. 13. Nautae timōre servitūtis līberātī sunt. 14. Oppidum ā mīlitibus servātum est. 15. Dīcit rēgem fīliōs fīliāsque * Titī servitūte līberātūrum esse.

Give the Latin for —

1. You (*singular*) have been wounded; we were wounded. 2. He was called; he used to be called. 3. I shall have been freed; you (*plural*) had been freed. 4. They will have been called by the boys. 5. The judges cannot free the slaves from fear. 6. He hopes that the forces of the king will overcome the enemy. 7. If he has been wounded, he is wretched. 8. If he should seize the town, he would free the tenth legion from great fear.

Questions.

What part of the verb is **amātus**? What decides its *form* in a sentence? What stems are found in the Passive Voice? What is **-que** called? Why? How does it differ in use from **et**? Pronounce **lapidibusque**; **fīliābusque**; **dēfensōribusque**; **fīliāsque**. Decline, side by side, the Latin for *no small animal; another great danger.*

---

* Learn **96**, *a*, 1, 2; **195**, 3, 4.

LESSON XXIV.

FIRST CONJUGATION: SUBJUNCTIVE PASSIVE.

Learn N. 74, *a*, *b*.
Learn the Conjugation of the *Subjunctive Passive* of amō.
A. 129; B. 102; H. 206; APP. 29.

EXERCISE.

Translate. Analyze* each sentence according to **194,** *c. Tell the time and thought expressed by each verb. Study the Special Examples.*
1. Sī vīta longa rēgibus darētur, beātī essent. 2. Sī castra ab hostibus occupāta sint, dēfensōribus nūdentur. 3. Sī laudātus es, beātus fuistī. 4. Sī servus līberētur, pugnet. 5. Sī puerī bonī fuissent, laudātī essent. 6. Sī urbēs expugnātae sint, perīculum cīvium magnum sit. 7. Sī pugnētis, laudēminī. 8. Sī pugnābunt, laudābuntur. 9. Sī virtūs mīlitum magna esset, laudārentur. 10. Sī exemplum amīcī meī malum est, nōn amātur. 11. Sī arx expugnāta sit, sorōrēs fīliaeque rēgis timidae sint. 12. Sī signum tubā datum esset, pugnāvissēmus. 13. Sī pecūnia servīs ā rēge bonō data sit, līberentur. 14. Fīlia agricolae silvās multās magnāsque esse dīcit.

Questions.

What is mode? How does the Subjunctive differ from the Indicative in making a statement? Does **sī** "take the Subjunctive"? Give a synopsis of the Indicative and Subjunctive, Active and Passive, of **amō; laudō; vocō.** Which tenses of these modes are compound? Which are simple? What is the *tense-sign* of the Imperfect Indicative? Imperfect Subjunctive? Future

---

* In general, special directions concerning the analysis of sentences are not given with the Exercises. The teacher can use his own judgment as to the extent to which he desires this to be practised. The directions for analysis (**194**) and the "Hints on Translation" (**200**) will be found useful by the beginner.

Indicative ? Pluperfect Subjunctive Active ? Pluperfect Indicative Active ? Give the stems of laudō; dō; vulnerō. Conjugate the Imperative Active of occupō; līberō. Tell where these forms are found: amēris; amātis; amātī essētis; amātus erās; amārēris; amābiminī; amēs; amātae sint; amāvissēs; amentur; laudātī estis; laudēminī; laudābere.

LESSON XXV.

FIRST CONJUGATION: PASSIVE VOICE: IMPERATIVE, INFINITIVE, PARTICIPLES.

Learn N. 75, 76, 77.

Learn the *Imperative, Infinitive,* and *Participles, Passive,* of amō. A. 129; B. 102; H. 206; App. 29.

TO THE STUDENT. *In future Lessons, no special directions will be given with each Exercise. It is expected that the student will prepare himself thoroughly on each. The proper preparation of an Exercise includes Translation; Conjugation of Verbs; Declension of Nouns and Adjectives; Rules for Gender, Number, and Case of Nouns and Adjectives; Rules for Agreement of Verbs; Reason for use of Modes.*

EXERCISE.

1. Līberātor; līberāre; līberāminī; līberantor. 2. Vocā; vocantō; vocātō; vocāte; vocātōte. 3. Putat puerōs attentōs esse. 4. Dīcit mīlitēs ā duce laudātōs (108) esse. 5. Mons ā Titō lēgātō occupārī (165, b) potest. 6. Dīcit urbem ā decimā legiōne expugnārī posse. 7. Consul opus servī laudāvisse putātur. 8. Negat animālia līberāta esse. 9. Dīcit puellās attentās ā magistrō laudārī. 10. Putat rēgem suspiciōne timōris līberātum esse. 11. Mīlitēs Sabīnī urbēs hostium occupātās esse nuntiāvērunt. 12. Negat agrōs vastārī. 13. Nuntiā, Cassī, hostēs superātōs esse. 14. Putāmus jūdicēs justōs fuisse. 15. Sī urbs expugnārī possit, expugnētur.

Give the Latin for —
1. We think that the gifts were great. 2. He will deny that the towers of the citadel are high. 3. The mountains can be seized by the lieutenant. 4. The leader says that the Gauls have been overcome by the soldiers. 5. You (*plural*) think that many cities have been stormed by Cassius.

General Questions and Drill.

What names are given to the Active Participles? to the Passive? Give a complete synopsis, Active and Passive, of **vocō**. Decline **alius**; **ūnus**. Decline, side by side, the Latin for *no night; a high mountain; a free state; a large head*. Decline, side by side, **pater, nāvis, mare**.

LESSON XXVI.

ADJECTIVES: THIRD DECLENSION.

Learn N. **24,** *b*; **25** & *a, b*; **26,** *a, b*.
Learn the Declension of the Adjectives mentioned under one of these References: **ācer, levis**, A. **84**; **ācer, fortis**, B. **68, 69**; **ācer, tristis**, H. **153, 154**; **ācer, fortis**, App. **12, 13**.

EXERCISE.

1. Aestātēs brevēs sunt. 2. Onera servōrum miserōrum gravia fuērunt. 3. Dīcit hominēs omnēs mortālēs esse. 4. Mīlitēs alacrēs fortēsque erunt. 5. Putat deōs inmortālēs esse. 6. Dīcit sociōs celerēs futūrōs esse. 7. Itinere longō difficilīque vēnit (*he came*). 8. Putat onus grave portārī posse. 9. Sī sociī omnēs fortēs sint, hostēs urbis superēmus. 10. Sī Caesar vulnerātus esset, tristēs fuissēmus. 11. Onus leve ā puerō parvō portārī potest. 12. Omnia bella nōn ūtilia sunt. 13. Templa diīs (**131**) immortālibus ab hominibus mortālibus aedificāta sunt. 14. Ars longa est; tempus breve est. 15. Dīcit aestātēs brevēs futūrās

esse. 16. Sī dux fortis esset, mīlitēs fortēs alacrēsque essent. 17. Poētae fīliās deārum immortālēs esse putant.

Give the Latin for —

1. The leaders' sons are brave. 2. The gods are friends and allies of the Romans. 3. The gift is large and heavy. 4. You (*plural*) are sad; he is sad. 5. He says that the journey will be easy. 6. Useful gifts were given to the brave allies. 7. O allies, be brave. 8. My friend, you can be a good and useful man. 9. All men (mankind) are mortal. 10. He says that light burdens can be carried by small boys. 11. All animals are not swift.

Questions.

How do **pater, nāvis, mare,** when declined side by side, differ from **ācer**? Tell the Stem, Genitive Singular Neuter, Ablative Singular Feminine, Dative Singular Masculine, Genitive Plural Neuter, of these Adjectives: **ācer; brevis; sōlus; celer; omnis; alius; alacer.** What is meant by *three terminations* (or *endings*) ? by *two endings*? How does **homō** differ in meaning from **vir**? (See General Vocabulary, vir.)

LESSON XXVII.

ADJECTIVES: THIRD DECLENSION; SUBJUNCTIVE EXPRESSING A COMMAND.

Learn N. **25,** *c ;* **26,** *c* & CAUTION.

Learn the Declension of **atrox, egens, pār, vetus, dīves,** A. **85,** *a, b ;* or that of Adjectives given in B. **70**; or in H. **156, 157, 158**; or in APP. **14** & *a* (omitting **praeceps, iens**).

Subjunctive expressing Command, Exhortation, etc. Learn N. **164,** *c* & REMARK. Learn, also, section **20,** page 7.

EXERCISE.

1. Corpora Germānōrum ingentia fuērunt. 2. Dīcit Caesarem dīvitem potentemque esse. 3. Putat urbēs flōrentēs futūrās esse.

4. Oppida vetera sunt. 5. Dīcit sociōs infēlīcēs fuisse. 6. Sī ducēs nōn fortēs essent, infēlīcēs essēmus. 7. Mīlitēs Rōmānī audācēs erunt. 8. Perīculum ducis et mīlitum pār fuit. 9. Victōriae recentēs rēgis fuērunt multae. 10. Dīcit iter breve facileque futūrum esse. 11. Amīcī hominum sapientium fēlīcēs sunt. 12. Virī fortēs ā rēgibus nōbilibus laudābuntur. 13. Sī infēlix sīs, miser sim. 14. Glōria urbium veterum magna fuit. 15. Mīles fortis ā servō ignāvō superārī nōn potest. 16. Fortēs sīmus; audācēs este; bonī sint. 17. Dux sociōs laudet; ducem laudēmus. 18. Laudā, consul, mīlitēs. 19. Cīvēs rēgem bonum ament. 20. Servōs līberēmus; fēlīcēs sint. 21. Nautae nāvēs aedificent. 22. Nāvēs ā nautīs aedificentur.

Give the Latin for —

1. By the recent victories of the Roman forces. 2. Of the equal dangers. 3. To the noble kings and consuls. 4. O unhappy legions, be brave. 5. Of huge bodies. 6. By a wide sea. 7. He will have announced the recent dangers. 8. He says that the city is flourishing. 9. The lion and horse are large. 10. Wise men are happy. 11. Let us storm the cities and towns. 12. Friends, be wise. 13. Let the king be just. 14. Boys and girls, love your (*omit*) father and mother. 15. Let us love (our) country.

Questions.

What is an adjective *of one ending*? What adjectives of the Third Declension have *three endings*? Which have *two*? Which have *one*? How many endings have **brevis**? **ingens**? **celer**? **vetus**? What Persons has the Present Imperative? How is the lack supplied? Show how an Imperative thought may be expressed in *all* the Persons of **sum** and **amō**. Which of these forms expresses a *direct* command? Decline, side by side, the Latin for *a noble name*.

LESSON XXVIII.

ADJECTIVES: REGULAR COMPARISON; DECLENSION OF COMPARATIVES.

Learn N. 29; 30 (entire); **40,** *b.*
Declension of Comparatives. Learn N. **26,** *d,* & CAUTION.
Learn the Declension of **melior,** A. **86**; or **fortior,** B. **69**; or **tristior,** H. **154**; or **fortior,** APP. **15.**

Questions and General Drill.

Compare **acūtus, audax, altus, ingens, attentus, fēlix, clārus, lātus, potens, longus, sapiens, amīcus, amans.** Decline the Comparative of **altus, nōbilis, potens.** In how many ways are adjectives compared, both in English and Latin? Decline, side by side, the Latin for *a higher temple; a more wretched daughter; the dearest son; a deeper sea.* To what Declension of Adjectives does the Superlative always belong?

EXERCISE.

1. Dīcit hostēs fortissimōs esse. 2. Putat frātrēs amantiōrēs futūrōs esse. 3. Aeduī amīcissimī erunt. 4. Sī equitēs fortiōrēs fuissent, Ariovistum superāvissēmus. 5. Dīcit lēgēs ūtilissimās esse. 6. Sī Ariovistus, rex Germānōrum, amīcus esset, fēlīcēs essēmus. 7. Peditēs audācissimī ab equitibus superārī nōn possunt. 8. Dīcit lēgem brevem esse ūtiliōrem. 9. Putat urbēs Rōmānās amīcissimās fuisse. 10. Corpora leōnum ingentia erant. 11. Nuntiat equitēs audāciōrēs esse. 12. Opus frātris meī ūtilius est. 13. Sī aestās longior fuisset, Ariovistus ā Caesare superātus esset. 14. Dīcit onus levius esse. 15. Templa altiōra aedificāta erunt. 16. Sī lēgēs bonae essent, cīvitās flōrentior esset. 17. Cīvēs perīculīs recentibus līberātī sunt. 18. Dīcit insulās longissimās lātissimāsque esse. 19. Sī bellum brevius sit, urbs expugnārī nōn possit. 20. Puerī, amantiōrēs este. 21. Jūdex justior sit. 22. Nuntiābit dōna Aeduīs ab Ariovistō, rēge potentissimō, data esse. 23. Dīcit mūrum dēfensōribus ab hostibus nūdātum esse.

Give the Latin for —
1. Let the forces be very brave. 2. He says that the rich cities are very flourishing. 3. Let the battle be brief. 4. Life is dear to cowardly soldiers. 5. Friends, let us free the city from slavery.

LESSON XXIX.

ADJECTIVES: IRREGULAR COMPARISON;* ADVERBS.

Adjectives having Irregular Superlatives. Learn N. 31, *a, b* (learn the list).
Adjectives having Irregular Comparatives and Superlatives. Learn N. 33. Learn the Comparison (and meanings) of bonus, malus, magnus, parvus, multus, multa, multum. A. 90; B. 72; H. 165; APP. 17, *a*.
Adverbs. Learn N. 38 (entire); 94 & *a;* 193, 5. Learn, also, section 28, page 9.

Questions and Practice.

Compare miser, bonus, facilis, ûtilis, âcer, malus, celer, audax, magnus, similis, parvus, fortis, multus, multa, multum, sapiens. Which of these have no peculiarities of comparison? Which have but one, and what is that? What is the rule for the use of an adverb? Give the Latin adverbs meaning *attentively, bravely.* State the rule for forming each. How may the Comparative and Superlative of an adverb be found? Form and compare adverbs derived from cârus, audax, diligens (38, *b,* last part), liber, malus, longus, félix, facilis (39), sapiens, celer, fortis, nôbilis, lâtus. What adjectives are compared like âcer? like facilis? Where does an adverb regularly stand in a sentence? What ideas may adverbs express?

EXERCISE.

1. Dīcit lēgātum oppidum mājus expugnāre. 2. Nāvēs minimae (40, *b*) sunt. 3. Putat mīlitēs plūrimōs pugnātūrōs esse. 4. Dīcit iter difficillimum fuisse. 5. Corpora equōrum mājōra

---

* The comparison of citerior, superior, etc., is presented later.

quam leōnum sunt. 6. Putat frātrēs Titī dissimillimōs esse. 7. Sī perīculum minus esset, audācius pugnārēmus. 8. Veterēs urbēs mājōrēs fuērunt. 9. Cōpiae Sabīnī ducis ācerrimē pugnābunt. 10. Dīcit oppidum Genēvam celeriter expugnārī posse. 11. Mīlitēs, audacter pugnēmus. 12. Turrēs facile servāre poterimus. 13. Dīcit castra dīligentissimē servāta esse. 14. Virtūs Cassī mājor est quam Titī. 15. Putat Germānōs omnēs inimīcissimōs esse. 16. Urbem dīligentius servēmus. 17. Sī fortius ācriusque pugnēmus, ab Gallīs nōn superēmur. 18. Plūrima templa minōra sunt. 19. Glōria praemium melius est.

Give the Latin for these sentences and phrases (English words in parentheses not to be translated into Latin) —

1. Many (men) think that the war was very great. 2. They had fought very boldly. 3. If the battle had been announced more quickly, the city would have been saved. 4. Of very bad kings; to worse poets. 5. Of a greater camp; to a smaller body. 6. He easily freed the very wretched slaves. 7. The number of small animals is very great. 8. Of better sons; to very many daughters. 9. Let us be friendly and useful. 10. The ships of the Gauls are longer and wider than (those) of the Romans. 11. Let us be better citizens. 12. He says that the infantry and cavalry were praised by Caesar.

LESSON XXX.

VERBS: SECOND CONJUGATION.

In the Second Conjugation there are the same rules for the formation of tenses from stems as in the First Conjugation. There is only one exception: the *Present Subjunctive* [N. 69, *a* (2)].

Learn N. 69, *a* (2); 79, 1. Review N. 65, 66, 67, 68; 69, *b, c, d;* and from 70 to 77.

Learn the entire Conjugation, Active and Passive, of **moneō**. A. 130; B. 103, 104; H. 207, 208; App. 30, 31.

LATIN LESSONS.   63

General Questions.

No Special Vocabularies will be given for the remaining Lessons. Hereafter the meanings of all Latin words must be obtained from the General Vocabulary.

What are the Principal Parts of **moneō** and **habeō**? What are the stems of each? If the Perfect and Supine were formed like those of **amō**, what would they be? (*Ans.* **monēvī, monētum; habēvī, habētum.**) How are **monuī, monitum; habuī, habitum,** formed from these? What is **v** (see 3, page 17)? Are there any verbs in the Second Conjugation having **ēvī, ētum**, in the Perfect and Supine (79, 1)? Give the Principal Parts (in both Voices) and stems of **compleō**.* Give the Present Subjunctive, Active and Passive, of **amō, moneō.** Give a complete synopsis of **moneō**, in both Voices (78).

EXERCISE.

Notice carefully the Tense-signs.

1. Monuerātis; monētis; monēbis; monuerit.   2. Monuistis; monēs; monēbātis; monēbunt.   3. Monēberis; monitus es; monēbātur; monēbiminī.   4. Monēris; monitī erāmus; monēminī; monitī erunt.   5. Monē puerōs; monēte ducem.   6. Sī puerum moneās, fēlix sit.   7. Sī equōs habērēmus, fortiter pugnārēmus.   8. Sī Titum monuerit, oppidum expugnet.   9. Sī nāvēs multās habuissent, fēlīcēs fuissent.   10. Dīcit consulem ducem monēre.   11. Dīcit ducem ā consule monērī.   12. Putat Gallōs nāvēs plūrimās habuisse.   13. Nuntiat nāvēs mīlitibus ā Caesare complētās esse.   14. Dīcit consulēs sapientēs ducēs fortēs monitūrōs esse.   15. Putat lēgātum ā rēge monitum esse.   16. Nāvēs complērī nōn potuērunt.   17. Sī monērētur, melior esset.   18. Sī moneāminī, fēlīciōrēs sītis.   19. Sī virī ūtiliōrēs cīvēs sint, laudentur.   20. Mīlitēs ā ducibus monitī erunt.   21. Gallī templa altiōra latiōraque habuērunt.   22. Fīliam Marcī moneāmus.   23. Cīvem bonum sapientemque laudēmus.

Give the Latin for —

1. The ditches (**fossa**) were filled.   2. The ships were being filled.   3. We (*feminine*) shall have been advised.   4. Let us

---

* **Compleō,** *I fill, fill up,* is the verb from which we get the word *Complement* (that which *fills out* the Predicate); also, *Complementary* (that use of the Infinitive which *completes* the meaning of another verb).

advise the king's sons. 5. Let us have peace. 6. He will advise the man very well (adverb of *good*). 7. You (*plural*) had filled the ships with men and boys. 8. He says that the ditches have been filled. 9. He thinks that the sailors can build a larger ship. 10. If he had had very many soldiers, he would have laid waste the enemy's fields.

LESSON XXXI.

General Review.

(1) Decline the Latin for *another danger; a wider sea; a greater animal; a very small state; a worse son; a better daughter; a wise citizen; an easy journey; a heavy body.*

(2) Give the Gender Endings of the Third Declension; of the Second; of the First. What nouns of the Third Declension (in common use) are Masculine, contrary to the Rule (19, *a*)?

What classes of stems has the Third Declension? Name the stems of **caput, mare, corpus, rex, leō, virgō, animal, magnitūdō, flōs, miles, iter, ignis, mons, mōs, nūbēs.** Give the Ablative Singular and the Genitive Plural of these same words. Give the Vocative Singular of **deus, Cāius Jūlius Caesar, filius;** the Dative Plural of **dea, filia.**

(3) What adjectives have **ius** in the Genitive Singular? Do any have **īus**? What adjectives have **rimus** in the Superlative? What ones have **limus**? Into what classes are adjectives of the Third Declension divided? How are they distinguished? What is the Ablative Singular of **brevis? ācer? prūdens? major?**

(4) Compare the adjectives meaning: *easy, attentive, high, wise, bad, good, wretched, much, many, like, happy, small, bold, difficult, eager.*

Compare the adverbs meaning: *easily, badly, fiercely, wisely, happily, dearly, boldly, carefully, timidly.*

(5) Translate these sentences and tell : —
I. *What* TIME *each denotes.* II. *What* THOUGHT *each expresses.*

1. Sī puerum monēre possem, fēlix essem. 2. Sī pugnāvit, superāvit. 3. Sī dux mīlitēs moneat, sapiens sit. 4. Sī nāvēs aedificātae essent, minimae fuissent. 5. Sī sapientēs sunt, fēlīcēs sunt. 6. Sī urbem servāre potuerim, cīvēs serventur.

(6) Give the *tense-signs* of the following : —
Imperfect Subjunctive; Future Indicative; Future Perfect Indicative (*Active*); Perfect Subjunctive (*Active*); Imperfect Indicative; Pluperfect Subjunctive (*Active*); Pluperfect Indicative (*Active*). How is the Present Sub-

junctive (*Active* and *Passive*) formed in the First Conjugation? in the Second? Illustrate by **superō** and **habeō**. What Participles has the Active Voice? the Passive? Give all the Participles of **līberō, moneō, dō, habeō, spērō, compleō**.

(7) Translate these sentences, and give the Rule for the *case* and *gender* of each noun and adjective: —
Rēgēs Gallōrum sapientiōrēs quam Germānōrum fuērunt. Equī animālia celerrima sunt. Titus lēgātus Caesaris oppidum Genēvam expugnābit. Equitēs fortissimī sunt. Dux decimae legiōnī frūmentum dedit.

LESSON XXXII.

DEPONENT VERBS: FIRST AND SECOND CONJUGATIONS.

Learn N. **80**, entire.

Learn the Conjugation of **hortor** and **vereor** (see General Vocabulary). The Conjugation of these or similar verbs is given in A. **135**; B. **113**; H. **232**, and Note; App. **37**.

NOTICE that these verbs are conjugated exactly like the Passive of **amō** and **moneō**, with these exceptions: (1) The Future Infinitive is *Active* in form; (2) After the Infinitive Mode, Deponent Verbs have *all the forms of both Voices*.

Questions.

What does *Deponent* mean? Why are these verbs so called? Give a complete synopsis of **cōnor, doceō, polliceor**. What stems does a Deponent Verb have? Give the stems of **doceō** and **terreō**. Give the Latin for *less widely, more widely, very widely*.

EXERCISE.

1. Cōnātus est; cōnans; cōnāre; cōnābuntur. 2. Verētur; veritī sumus; veritī eritis; verēbāminī; verēberis. 3. Opus magnum cōnātī sumus. 4. Puerum parvum docēre cōnābitur. 5. Puellās doceāmus. 6. Laudem magnam mereāmur. 7. Sī puerōs puellāsque docuissent, laetātī essēmus. 8. Hostēs agrōs sociōrum fortium populābuntur. 9. Īnsulam minōrem populārī cōnantur. 10. Hostēs itinere prohibēre cōnābimur. 11. Dīcit

virōs fortēs praemia maxima meritōs esse. 12. Putat mīlitem laudem meritūrum esse. 13. Honōrem merēbimur. 14. Lactēmur; mīlitēs hortēmur. 15. Dīcit ducēs cōpiās hortārī et hortātūrōs esse. 16. Dīcit leōnem magnum servōs timidōs terruisse. 17. Cōpiae hostium lātius vagābantur. 18. Minus lātē vagābiminī. 19. Putat equitēs minus audacter pugnātūrōs esse. 20. Mīlitēs, minus lātē vagāminī. 21. Ducī pecūniam pollicitī sunt. 22. Rēgibus dōna magna polliceāmur. 23. Verēbimur magnitūdinem silvārum. 24. Dīcit hominēs pessimōs praemia nōn merērī.

Give the Latin for —

1. He thinks that the tenth legion can keep the enemy from the city. 2. We can try to teach the boys. 3. He says that Caius and Marcus have been taught by Julius. 4. The leaders, who (quī) have not feared danger, deserve praise. 5. If he should be terrified by the danger of death, he would not be a Roman. 6. Consuls could not be terrified by bad men.

LESSON XXXIII.

TWO ACCUSATIVES.

Two Accusatives:

(1) *Both denoting the same Person or Thing.* · Learn N. **141**, *a.* Learn, also, **37**, *c*, page 10, and N. **103**, *a.*

(2) *One denoting the Person, the other denoting the Thing.* Learn N. **141**, *b*, & REMARK 1.

Questions.

What verbs take two Accusatives denoting the *same* person or thing? What verbs take one Accusative of the *person*, and another of the *thing*? What happens when these verbs are changed to the Passive? Are these strictly *Latin* idioms? What two meanings may the plural of **littera** have?

EXERCISE.

1. Puerōs docēbimus litterās. 2. Consulem amīcum appellāvērunt. 3. Titus amīcus appellātus est. 4. Pompēium, virum

fortissimum, imperātōrem creābant. 5. Cīvēs, mātūrāte Caesarem consulem creāre. 6. Ducem sententiam consulis rogāvimus. 7. Consul sententiam rogātur. 8. Puellae litterās ā sorōre meā doctae erant. 9. Prōvinciam flōrentem occupāre mātūrābimus. 10. Jūlium rēgem creēmus. 11. Rōmānōs frūmentum flāgitāvistī. 12. Gallōs cōpiam frūmentī flāgitēmus. 13. Puerī magistrum sermōnem cēlābunt. 14. Dīcit flūmina altissima lātissimaque esse. 15. Virōs artēs multās docuerit. 16. Titus et Sabīnus mīlitēs fortissimī appellātī sunt. 17. Imperātōrem sermōnem sociōrum cēlāre nōn potuimus. 18. Mīlitem nōmen imperātōris rogēmus. 19. Urbem, quam (*which*) vidēs, Rōmam appellant. 20. Urbs Rōma appellābitur. 21. Spērat puellās servōs miserōs litterās docēre cōnātūrās esse. 22. Litterās scrībit (*writes*), quās (*which*) puerō dat. 23. Litterae Caesaris longae sunt.

Give the Latin for —

1. If I had called the man (my) friend, he would have rejoiced. 2. You (*plural*) can ask the teacher (his) opinion. 3. He says that the soldiers will demand corn of the general. 4. Let us call the town Geneva. 5. The large island was called a province. 6. He denies that other islands are larger. 7. If the enemy should wander about less widely, we should not be frightened. 8. We shall see the men whom (**quōs**) you tried to terrify. 9. The rich men will promise money, but will not give (it). 10. We think that the best and wisest citizens will elect Ariovistus king.

LESSON XXXIV.

ADJECTIVES: IRREGULAR COMPARISON; DATIVE WITH ADJECTIVES.

Learn N. **34, 35**; also the Comparison (and English meanings) of the Adjectives described in those Notes. A. **91** & *a*; B. **73**; H. **163**, 3; **166**; App. **17**, *b*, *c*.

Comparison by Adverbs (magis and maximē). Learn N. 37.
Dative with Adjectives:
(1) To denote Advantage or Disadvantage. Learn N. 131 & *b*.
(2) With Adjectives meaning *like* (or *unlike*), *equal* (or *unequal*), and *near*. Learn N. 132. *Notice how similar this is to the English construction.*

EXERCISE.

Examples for this Lesson are given on page 265.

1. Negat urbēs Galliae citeriōris mājōrēs quam Galliae ulteriōris esse. 2. Maria ultima altissima sunt. 3. Putat urbem fīnibus Belgārum proximam fuisse. 4. Aestātēs priōrēs longae erant. 5. Superiōrem partem collis castrīs complēverant. 6. Belgae proximī sunt Germānīs. 7. Dīcit summum (110, *b*) montem ā Titō tenērī. 8. Ducī servī fidēlēs erunt. 9. Virī puerīs īrātī (*angry*) fuērunt. 10. Dōna Caesaris cīvibus grāta sunt. 11. Dīcit Aeduōs Rōmānīs amīcōs fuisse. 12. Urbs Genēva Helvētiīs cārissima fuit. 13. Gallīs inimīcī sīmus. 14. Nuntiat locum castrīs idōneum esse. 15. Urbī ūtilēs sīmus. 16. Titus Caesarī similis est. 17. Locus magis idōneus castrīs quam urbī fuit. 18. Patrī meō simillimus es. 19. Imperātor mīlitibus fortibus cārus est. 20. Putat fīliōs patribus dissimilēs esse. 21. Sī Caesar Pompēiō inimīcus sit, laudem nōn mereātur. 22. Puerī, quōs (*whom*) litterās docēre cōnātus es, fidēlēs erunt. 23. Animālia, quae (*which*) vīdistī, leōnibus simillima fuērunt. 24. Hostibus parēs esse poterimus. 25. Oppidum propius Rhēnō quam Rhodanō est.

Give the Latin for —

1. The lower part of the river Rhine. 2. We are a match for (equal to) the Belgae. 3. You (*plural*) are very dear to all Romans. 4. He says that the general cannot be friendly to the consuls. 5. The towns of hither Gaul are very small. 6. The girls are very like (their) mothers. 7. You (*singular*) can be more useful to the city than to the camp. 8. The friends of Marcus are very unfriendly to Sabinus. 9. The width of the upper part of the temple was very great.

LESSON XXXV.

NOUNS: FOURTH DECLENSION.

Learn N. 20 (entire); 21 & *a;* also the Case-Endings of the Fourth Declension, N. 6. Learn the Declension of the Nouns given in A. 68; or B. 48; or H. 116; or APP. 8. **Domus.** Learn N. 21, *b;* also its Declension. A. 70, *f;* B. 49, 4; H. 119, 1; APP. 8, *a*.

Questions.

What is the stem of **magistrātus**? **cornū**? **manus**? State the laws of gender for the Fourth Declension, and give two exceptions. Give a synopsis, Active and Passive, of **moveō**. Decline **sinister**. Decline **locus**.

EXERCISE.

Study the Examples for this Lesson, page 265.

1. Adventum Ariovistī Germānōrumque verentur. 2. Ā dextrō cornū proelium commīsit (*began*). 3. Currūs Germānōrum maximī fuērunt. 4. Fīliae imperātōris infēlīcissimae sunt. 5. Pollicēbimur dōnum mājus magistrātuī. 6. Equitātus oppida omnia dēlēvit. 7. Consul domī erit. 8. Exercitūs populī Rōmānī maximī fortissimīque fuērunt. 9. Dīcit exercitūs impetūs omnēs Germānōrum fortissimē sustentūrōs esse. 10. Mens manum movet. 11. Castra movēbunt. 12. Oppidum quam (**40,** *c*) fortissimē oppugnēmus. 13. Putat impetum hostium ā dextrō cornū sustinērī posse. 14. Dīcit Belgās Galliae fīnitimōs esse. 15. Domum consulis deleāmus. 16. Sī adventū Caesaris hostēs terreantur, āb exercitū Rōmānō superentur. 17. Manūs meae magnae sunt. 18. Impetūs Belgārum sustineāmus. 19. Castra mōta erunt. 20. Superiōra loca occupāvistis. 21. Equitātus summum collem occupet. 22. Templa pulcherrima āb exercitū dēlēta sunt. 23. Quam plūrimōs currūs pollicēmur.

Give the Latin for —

1. By the hands of the enemy; to the braver cavalry. 2. Of a better army; by very many attacks. 3. As many hands as possi-

ble. 4. For smaller houses; of wise magistrates. 5. We wept; you (*plural*) had wept; let him weep. 6. Let's break up camp. 7. You (*plural*) were at home.

LESSON XXXVI.

NOUNS: FIFTH DECLENSION; COMPOUND NOUNS.

Learn N. 22 (entire); also the Case-Endings of the Fifth Declension. N. 6.
Learn the Declension of the Nouns given in A. 72; or B. 51; or H. 120; or App. 9.
Compound Nouns. Learn the Declension of **respublica** and **jusjūrandum**. N. 23, *a*, *b*.

Questions.

What is the stem of **diēs**? **plānitiēs**? **spēs**? **aciēs**? What nouns of this Declension are complete? State the laws of gender, and give exceptions. Pronounce the Genitive of **aciēs**; **fidēs**. State the law respecting the quantity of **e** in the Genitive and Dative Singular.

EXERCISE.

1. Aciēs longissima est. 2. Dīcit aciem impetum Gallōrum sustinēre posse. 3. Spēs magnās habuit. 4. Rem Rōmānīs nuntiant. 5. Nuntiāte, amīcī, rēs omnēs consulī. 6. Caesar jūra populō dedit. 7. Jūra sociōrum servābit. 8. Jusjūrandum cīvibus dederat. 9. Jūrejūrandō nōn tenēbantur. 10. Dīcit cīvēs rempublicam servātūrōs esse. 11. Respublica virtūte mīlitum servāta est. 12. Prīma aciēs impetūs omnēs fortissimē sustinēbit. 13. Maximam spem habēbō. 14. Spēs victōriae magna fuit. 15. Suspicātur senātum Rōmānum fidem Gallīs dedisse. 16. Fidem servēmus. 17. Servus fidem servābit. 18. Fidēs hostibus ā senātū data est. 19. Negat ducem fidem violāvisse (*break*). 20. Rōma

caput Italiae est. 21. Lātitūdō plānitiēī mājor quam castrōrum fuit. 22. Sī suspicātī essent bellum longum fore (**84,** *d*), Cacsarem imperātōrem creāvissent. 23. Consulēs senātuī inimīcī sunt.

Give the Latin for —
1. By the hope of victory. 2. For the senate of the Roman people. 3. We are held by (our) oath. 4. The commonwealth is dear to all good men. 5. Let us have as great hope as possible. 6. Let the army fight as boldly as possible. 7. We suspect that the line of battle has not been able to sustain the attack. 8. The attacks could not be sustained by the cavalry.

LESSON XXXVII.

VERBS: THIRD CONJUGATION: ACTIVE VOICE.

Review such portions of N. **65** to **72** as have already been referred to in connection with the First and Second Conjugations.

Learn the Conjugation of the Active Voice of **regō** or **tegō**. A. **131**, page 82; B. **105**; H. **209**; App. **32**.

CAUTION. The peculiarities of the Active Voice are found in the Present Indicative; Future Indicative; Present Subjunctive; Imperative. Therefore study with special care N. **68,** *a, c;* **69,** *a* (3); **70.**

Questions and Applications.

Give the principal parts of **regō**; **dicō**; **dūcō**; **mittō**. Give the stems of these verbs. Explain the form of the Perfect Indicative for each (**79,** 2, *a*). Conjugate the Present Indicative, the Future Indicative, the Present Subjunctive, and the Imperative, of **amō**; **moneō**; **mittō**. What are the personal endings of the Active Voice? of the Passive? Give a synopsis, in the Active Voice, of **mittō**.

EXERCISE.

1. Imperātor auxilia omnia dīmīsit (**99,** 2). 2. Rempublicam sapienter regent. 3. Dīcitis lēgātum proelium nōn commissūrum

esse. 4. Sī Caesar cōpiās dūceret, fortiōrēs essent. 5. Sī proelium ā dextrō cornū commīsissent, exercitus nōn superātus esset. 6. Gallīs obsidēs polliceāmur. 7. Proelium quam audācissimē committāmus. 8. Sī summum montem ab hostibus tenērī dīcat, castra moveāmus. 9. Dīcunt Titum prīmam legiōnem duxisse. 10. Dixistis Belgās obsidēs nōn missūrōs esse. 11. Senātus dōna mājōra nōn mittet. 12. Suspicāris locum castrīs nōn idōneum fore. 13. Obsidēs Germānīs ā magistrātibus datī erant. 14. Extrēmum oppidum Allobrogum proximumque Helvētiōrum fīnibus Genēva est.

Give the Latin for —
1. We shall send hostages. 2. Let him join battle on the right wing. 3. Let the magistrates rule the Commonwealth. 4. He says that the leaders will dismiss the council. 5. They will have led the troops. 6. They are very near the Allobroges.

LESSON XXXVIII.

VERBS: THIRD CONJUGATION: PASSIVE VOICE.

Review such portions of N. 73 to 77 as have been referred to in connection with the First and Second Conjugations.

Learn the Conjugation of **regō** or **tegō** in the Passive Voice. A. 131, p. 82; B. 106; H. 210; App. 33.

CAUTION. The peculiarities of the Passive Voice are found in the Present Indicative; Future Indicative; Present Subjunctive; Imperative; Present Infinitive. Study carefully N. 73, *a, c;* 75; 76, *a;* also NOTES in Lesson XXXVII.

Questions and Practice.

What are the principal parts of these verbs in the Passive: **regō? mittō? moneō? superō?** Conjugate these verbs in the following tenses, Active and Passive: Present Indicative; Future Indicative; Present Subjunctive. Conjugate their Imperative, Active and Passive. Give their Infinitives and Participles, Active and Passive.

EXERCISE.

Study N. 79, 2. *The principal parts of the verbs employed in the last Lesson were simple and very similar; as stated in* N. 79, 2, *however, verbs of the Third Conjugation have a great variety of forms in the Perfect and Supine (as in this Lesson). Learn these principal parts thoroughly.*

1. Omnēs portae urbis ā mīlitibus clausae sunt. 2. Consul portās oppidī claudī jubet. 3. Dīcit imperātōrem castra posuisse. 4. Litterae āb amīcō meō scriptae erant. 5. Victōrēs oppidum dēlērī jusserint. 6. Jubēbimus litterās scrībī. 7. Nuntiant mīlitēs decimae legiōnis victōrēs esse. 8. Equōs currūsque relīquerat. 9. Dīcitur hostēs vīcisse. 10. Sī Helvētiōs vincāmus, obsidēs dent. 11. Dīcit legiōnēs Marcī Titīque āb exercitū maximō victās esse. 12. Reīpublicae ūtilissimus esse potes. 13. Equitātus impetum Belgārum nōn verētur. 14. Vincite, sociī; proelium breve erit. 15. Sī ā Caesare ductī essēmus, urbem fortius oppugnāvissēmus. 16. Dīcit auxilia castra relictūra esse. 17. Putat exercitum vincī nōn posse. 18. Prōvincia Gallīs propior est quam Belgīs. 19. Castra pōnere jussī erant. 20. Vince; vincāmus; vincat.

Give the Latin for —
1. Let's write a letter. 2. We victors will destroy the town. 3. They cannot conquer the auxiliaries. 4. He says that the legion is not held by the oath. 5. If we should be as friendly as possible to the senate, we would be called good citizens. 6. The general is said to have been frightened by a slave. 7. We shall be dismissed by the judge. 8. We are at home.

LESSON XXXIX.

PREPOSITIONS; PLACE.*

Learn N. 95 (entire); commit to memory the list of Prepositions which *always* require the Ablative.
Place. Learn N. 158.

Questions and Practice.

What prepositions, in common use, are *always* used with the Ablative? When do **in** and **sub** require the Accusative? the Ablative? What prepositions have double forms? How are they used? How does **ā (ab)** differ in meaning from **ē (ex)**? What does **sub monte** mean? When is *to* a sign of the Dative? When must it be translated by **ad**? (129, *a*.) What meaning have these syllables in a compound word (see **99**, 1, 2): **con**? **dī**? **prae** (as in **praemittō**)? **dē** (as in **dēdūcō**)? Decline **diēs longior; senātus jūstus; cornū dextrum.**

EXERCISE.

Tell which sentences answer the question Where? the question Whither? the question Whence? Notice carefully the meaning of the prepositions used in this Lesson (see General Vocabulary).

1. Cōpiās trans Rhēnum duxit. 2. Inter Rhēnum et Rhodanum sunt. 3. Ad oppidum contendērunt. 4. Urbī nōmen dat. 5. Bellum circum Rōmam gerit. 6. Sine spē victōriae pugnant. 7. Mīlitēs sub jugum missī sunt. 8. Sub monte castra posuit. 9. Ab urbe ad castra contendit. 10. Ex oppidō venit (*comes*). 11. Prō castrīs stetit. 12. Virōs in templum convocātis. 13. Agricolae in agrīs sunt. 14. Contrā populum Rōmānum conjūrāvistī. 15. In fīnibus Belgārum vagātī sumus. 16. In fīnēs Germānōrum exercitum dūcit. 17. Equitātum in hīberna dēdūcet. 18. Dē montibus ad mare contendunt. 19. Equitēs ad flūmen praemīsit. 20. Erat (**193**, 6) plānitiēs magna. 21. In Galliā vīvit; in castrīs est. 22. Servī sine praemiīs magnīs nōn pugnā-

---

* The *regular* construction is presented first. The Locative Case is taken up later.

bunt. 23. Legiōnem novam in Galliā citeriōre conscripsit. 24. Legiō, quae (*which*) in Galliā ulteriōre conscripta erat, in Galliam citeriōrem contendit. 25. Dīcit cīvēs plūrimōs contrā rempublicam conjūrāre. 26. Post castra sunt loca superiōra. 27. Trans flūmen auxilia ē castrīs et ā colle duximus.

Give the Latin for —
1. Let us call together the boys into one place. 2. There can be no victory without arms. 3. Let us send ahead the troops. 4. We shall easily lead the brave army across the wide river. 5. If we should be conquered, the city would be in great danger. 6. The lieutenant's troops have been conquered by the brave slaves. 7. We will hasten to the camp as quickly as possible. 8. He comes (**venit**) into the city; out of the town; away from the camp. 9. There is a temple at the foot of the hill. 10. Between hope and fear. 11. The army will be sent under the yoke.

LESSON XL.

DEPONENT VERBS: THIRD CONJUGATION; ABLATIVE OF CAUSE; SUBJUNCTIVE OF PURPOSE.

Review N. **80** & *a, b*. Learn the Conjugation of the Deponent Verb **sequor**. A. **135**; B. **113**; H. **232** & NOTE; APP. **37**.

Ablative denoting Cause. Learn N. **149** (entire).

Subjunctive denoting Purpose.* Learn N. **179** (*Simple Rule*).

Sequence of Tenses. Learn N. **171, 172** (omitting the REMARKS). Study the special Examples (and the explanations) for this Lesson, on page **265**.

NOTICE that the Ablative of Cause and the Subjunctive of Purpose both answer the question *Why?*

---

* The more technical constructions of Purpose are taken up later.

Questions and Practice.

Give a complete synopsis of **sequor**. What Active forms have Deponent verbs? What does *sequence* mean? What tenses are *Primary*? *Secondary*? State the law for the "Sequence of Tenses." Give the Latin for *to see* in this sentence: *He is sent to see Marcus*. What conjunction introduces a *positive* purpose? a *negative* purpose?

EXERCISE.

1. Ducem amīcitiae causā sequuntur. 2. Adventū amīcī meī laetābar. 3. Victōriīs multīs glōriātī erant. 4. Lēgātōs servitūte līberābit. 5. Dīcit proelium ab equitātū commissum esse. 6. Propter virtūtem laudor. 7. Nuntiant castra dēfensōribus nūdāta esse. 8. Virī glōriae causā pugnant. 9. Pugnāmus ut rempublicam servēmus. 10. Hostēs audācissimē sequāmur. 11. Cāius servusque ab urbe profectī sunt. 12. Portās claudāmus, nē urbs dēleātur. 13. Puerōs servum sequī jussit. 14. Cōpiās in Galliam citeriōrem mittunt ut Gallōs terreant. 15. Auxilia ut oppidum expugnent mittentur. 16. In Galliā morābimur ut urbēs hostium videāmus. 17. In urbe Rōmā nātus es. 18. Lēgātiōnēs ad Marcum ut pācem peterent mīsimus. 19. Circum Genēvam morābuntur. 20. Sī ad castra profectus esset, laetātī essēmus. 21. Hostēs sequēris, nē in fīnibus Helvētiōrum morentur. 22. Custōdēs cīvēs malōs sequī nōn potuērunt. 23. Dīcit consulem līberē loquī. 24. Lēgātiōnēs plūrimae ā cīvitātibus multīs ad Caesarem missae sunt. 25. Sequiminī, sociī, ducem fortem. 26. Profectus eram, ut ad flūmen contenderem. 27. Sī in oppidō Genēvā nōn nātus essēs, cīvis Rōmānus appellārēris. 28. Cōpiās trans Rhēnum dūcēmus, ut summum montem occupēmus. 29. Litterās scrībēbat, nē novum mājusque perīculum amīcum terrēret. 30. Timōre Gallōs nōn secūtus es.

Give the Latin for these sentences, bearing in mind the fact that the Infinitive cannot be used to denote a Purpose; that is, to answer the question Why?

1. The ambassadors will be sent to see the city. 2. We had followed the enemy from the river to the town. 3. He had left soldiers to protect the town. 4. Let us fight lest we be slaves.

5. Let us set out for the river. 6. He says that a large animal followed the boys in the forest. 7. You (*plural*) say that the ambassadors were not born in Gaul. 8. We will fight for the sake of glory.

LESSON XLI.

VERBS: FOURTH CONJUGATION; ADJECTIVES USED AS NOUNS.

Learn N. 67; 68, *a, c*; 69, *a* (4).
Learn the Conjugation of **audiō**, Active and Passive. A. **132**, page 86; B. **107, 108**; H. **211, 212**; APP. **35, 36**.
Adjectives used as Nouns. Learn N. **109** & *c*.

Questions and Practice.

What are the stems of **audiō**? **sciō**? Give a complete synopsis of **audiō**. In what two ways can "all things" be expressed? (*Ans.* **rēs omnēs; omnia.**)
What does **fēlīcēs esse vidēbantur** mean?

EXERCISE.

Notice that, with **videor** (*meaning* seem), **esse** *may be expressed or omitted, as in English. Study the Examples for this Lesson, on page* 266.

1. Audīvistī castra mūnīta esse. 2. Scīmus Cāium urbem mūnītūrum esse. 3. Dīcit imperium populī Rōmānī Rhēnō fīnīrī. 4. Cīvēs sciunt consulem mīlitem ignāvum pūnīvisse. 5. Profectiō fugae (**132**) simillima vidētur. 6. Bona mea ad urbem mittam. 7. Nuntiābunt flūmen agrōs sociōrum fīnīre. 8. Omnēs audient ducēs fugā (**149**) legiōnem pūnītūrōs esse. 9. Mūnīte, sociī, oppida Rōmānōrum. 10. Vīta omnibus cārissima est. 11. Dīcit profectiōnem fugae similem fuisse. 12. Omnēs fortēs nōbilēsque fuērunt. 13. Sciant imperium populī Rōmānī maximum esse. 14. Castra mūniāmus. 15. Fīnitimī omnēs servum pūnītum esse scient. 16. Cōpiae fortissimae esse videntur. 17. Exercitus

hostium minor quam Cāiī vidētur. 18. Iter facillimum vidēbitur.
19. Puerī patrī quam mātrī similiōrēs sunt. 20. Hominēs ignāvī
inimīcī virōrum bonōrum sunt. 21. Malī pūnientur; bonī laudābuntur. 22. Multās rēs audīverāmus. 23. Aliud audiēmus.
24. Lēgātus multa Caesarī nuntiat. 25. Dīcit jūdicem multa
dixisse. 26. Magnam urbem magnīs (virīs) aedificābit. 27.
Urbem mūniāmus nē cīvēs timidī sint. 28. Puerīs dōna dedit,
ut amīcus putārētur. 29. Multī hostēs veritī sunt. 30. Rex
plūrimīs amīcus est. 31. Nōn omnibus omnia facilia sunt. 32.
Consul multa dixit.

Give the Latin for —
1. We will fortify the camp. 2. Let us hear many things (*express in two ways*). 3. The citizens say that the judge will punish the slave. 4. The towns have not been fortified by Caesar. 5. Let us punish the soldier. 6. The empire of the Gauls is limited by the river Rhine. 7. We will set out from the camp. 8. We have seemed very wise. 9. He says that the town has been fortified.

LESSON XLII.

DEPONENT VERBS: FOURTH CONJUGATION; ABLATIVE WITH DEPONENTS.

Review N. 80 & *a, b.* Learn the Conjugation of **potior.** A. 135; B. 113 (**largior**); H. 232 & NOTE; APP. 37.

Ablative of Means with Five Deponent Verbs, and also with **vīvō.** Learn N. 151, *a.*

REMARK. **Vescor** means *I feed on;* **vīvō,** *I live on.* Of the Deponent Verbs given in the NOTE, **ūtor** and **potior** are most frequently used.

Questions and Practice.

What Deponent Verbs take the Ablative? Why? Give a synopsis of **potior; ūtor.** Give the stems of **veniō; conscrībō; praemittō; vīvō.** Decline together the Latin for *a shorter time; a longer sword.*

LATIN LESSONS. 79

EXERCISE.

1. Trans Rhēnum incolēbant; citrā flūmen incolunt. 2. Impedīmentīs castrīsque potiēmur. 3. Nāvibus ūtī nōn possumus. 4. Multa animālia frūmentō vīvunt. 5. Armīs bene (39) ūtiminī. 6. Gladiīs ūtāmur. 7. Dīcit Germānōs equīs nōn ūsōs esse. 8. Hostēs nāvibus omnibus potītī sunt. 9. Cīvēs lēgibus ūtēbantur. 10. Putat Rōmānōs tōtīus Galliae imperiō potītūrōs esse. 11. Oppidō facile potīrī potuimus. 12. Vēnimus ut rēgem videāmus. 13. Nē impedīmentīs potīrēminī, pugnābant. 14. Equitēs curribus ūsī erunt. 15. Dux cōpiās ab oppidō profectās esse nuntiat. 16. Gladiō, mī fīlī, ūtī nōn potes. 17. Tōtō imperiō potiāmur. 18. Helvētiī trans Rhodanum incoluerant. 19. Sī ad castra venīret, fēlīcissimus essem. 20. Dīcit Caesarem vēnisse, vīdisse, vīcisse. 21. Hostēs sequēmur, nē in fīnibus Belgārum morentur. 22. Domus urbī proxima fuit.

Give the Latin for —
1. They had obtained possession of Gaul. 2. Let him use the arms. 3. They will not be able to get possession of Caesar's camp. 4. We hope that the general will get possession of the enemy's winter-quarters. 5. You (*plural*) had come into the winter-quarters as quickly as possible. 6. The good were praised; the bad were punished. 7. The neighbors were unfriendly to my brothers. 8. The winter-quarters of Sabinus were smaller than Caesar's.

LESSON XLIII.

THIRD CONJUGATION: VERBS IN IO; TENSES OF THE INFINITIVE.

Learn N. **79**, 3. Learn the Conjugation, Active and Passive, of **capiō**. A. **131**; B. **110, 111**; H. **218, 219**; APP. **34**.

Tenses of the Infinitive. Learn N. **173**. This Note gives Examples, showing the *time* expressed by the Infinitive tenses; they should be carefully studied.

LATIN LESSONS.

Questions and Practice.

When does a "Verb in *iō*" keep the *i*? Give a complete synopsis, Active and Passive, of *capiō*. What tenses has the Infinitive? To what may the Present be equivalent? the Perfect? What is a Direct Quotation? an Indirect Quotation? What is a *Copula*? a *Complement*? the *Complementary Infinitive*?

EXERCISE.

1. Dīcit Helvētiōs agricultūrā prohibērī. 2. Dixērunt hostēs itinere prohibitōs esse. 3. Putat oppida ā Jūliō capta esse. 4. Dixit legiōnem fugere. 5. Spērāveram Rōmānōs Genēvam occupātūrōs esse. 6. Spērātis magistrātūs cīvēs venīre passūrōs esse. 7. Consul hostēs pācem factūrōs esse nuntiāvit. 8. Urbēs ā lēgātō fortī legiōneque captae erunt. 9. Scīmus agricolās agrōs colere. 10. Tēla multa in mīlitēs conjicient. 11. Dixistī lapidēs magnōs jactōs esse. 12. Nāvis, quam (*which*) vidētis, ā fīliō meō facta est. 13. Helvētiōs per fīnēs Gallōrum venīre nōn passī sunt. 14. Capite, mīlitēs fortēs, loca superiōra. 15. Sī omnēs tēla conjiciant, urbs capiātur. 16. Fugiāmus; castra oppugnēmus; proficiscāmur. 17. Sī gladiīs ūsī essent, castrīs potītī essent. 18. Colite, agricolae, agrōs, quī (*which*) longī lātīque sunt. 19. Patiminī, jūdicēs, cīvem dīvitem dīcere. 20. Hostēs fugient; nōn morābimur; vincēmus.

Give the Latin for —

1. We cannot allow the man to come. 2. They will not till the fields. 3. He said that the slaves would not fight bravely. 4. They thought that the town could be taken. 5. The weapons cannot be hurled. 6. Let us throw stones and weapons. 7. Let them follow the cavalry. 8. We know that the line of battle can sustain the attacks. 9. They seem to be powerful and rich. 10. We were dwelling across the river Rhine.

LESSON XLIV.

PARTICIPLES.

Learn N. 189 & *a, c* (first sentence), *d.*
Learn the Declension of the Present and Future Active, and the Perfect Passive, Participles of **audiō.**

Study these NOTES *in connection with the Examples for this Lesson, on page* 266.

NOTICE that only Deponent Verbs have Perfect Participles with an *Active* meaning. To express *having seen, having conquered*, etc., a special construction is used, which will be explained in a future Lesson.

NOTICE, also, the *vowel changes* in compound words; as, **rējiciō, interficiō, accipiō** (from **jaciō, faciō, capiō**). See N. 2 (5).

Questions and Practice.

Decline the Present Participle of **sequor.** How many Participles have Deponent Verbs? What is the difference in meaning between **vocō** and **convocō? veniō** and **conveniō?** How may Participles be often best translated? What is a Participle? What, therefore, is the rule for its use? To what Declensions do the Participles, Active and Passive, belong? What *time* does the Present Participle denote? the Perfect?

EXERCISE.

Compare these sentences carefully with the Examples.

1. Equitēs ā Caesare praemissī revertuntur. 2. Obsidēs reductōs in numerō hostium habuit. 3. Tēla in mūrum conjecta rējicient. 4. Ad Cāium litterās ā duce scriptās mittit. 5. Lēgātum dē adventū legiōnis certiōrem fēcī. 6. Imperātor dē proeliō certior factus est. 7. Consulēs certiōrēs facit exercitum vēnisse. 8. Titus hostēs fugientēs secūtus magnum numerum peditum interfēcit. 9. Mīlitēs ā flūmine prōgressī ab hostibus captī sunt. 10. Caesar suspicātus perīculum maximum fore (**84,** *d*) decimam legiōnem sequī jussit. 11. Fortissimē pugnans interficitur. 12. Servī fortiter pugnantēs interfectī sunt. 13. Adventum Ariovistī veritī, cōpiās in castra dēdūcent. 14. Obsidēs multīs ā cīvitātibus missōs

accēpērunt. 15. Dōna pulcherrima ā frātre meō missa accipiam. 16. Iter per prōvinciam fēcimus, ut Genēvam oppugnārēmus. 17. Iter per fīnēs Gallōrum faciens interfectus erat. 18. Rēgem certiōrem fēcistis legiōnēs ā Galliā reductās esse. 19. Belgae superātī in oppidum rējectī sunt. 20. Cīvis, quī (*who*) ad urbem vēnit, ducem fortem audacter pugnantem interfectum esse dixit. 21. Caesar ab Galliā discēdens Gallīs obsidēs reddidit. 22. Dixerat cīvēs magnō dē perīculō certiōrēs factōs esse. 23. Iter in Galliam quam celerrimē faciāmus. 24. Nuntiābant auxilia superāta in castra rējicī. 25. Multī virōs ab Italiā proficiscentēs laudāverant. 26. Servōs in Galliam transductōs interfēcērunt. 27. Vōcem consulis mīlitēs laudantis audītis. 28. Senātum in templum convocāvit. 29. Dīcit senātum ā Caesare vocātum convēnisse. 30. Consul ab hībernīs in Italiam discēdens servum interficī jussit.

Give the Latin for these sentences (those numbered 2, 3, 4, are to be written as Simple sentences) —

1. Having promised many gifts to the brave soldiers, the king returns to the city. 2. The troops, that had been sent forward by the leader, could not storm the town. 3. After they had attempted to obtain possession of the camp, they were ordered to return. 4. He will follow the enemy as they depart from the town. 5. The guards killed the slaves attempting to seize the temple. 6. Having followed the army of the Gauls to the Rhone, he was unable to lead across (his) infantry. 7. Having been conquered by the allies, the legion was driven back into the city.

LESSON XLV.

NUMERAL ADJECTIVES; ACCUSATIVE OF TIME; ABLATIVE OF TIME.

Learn section **9**, *b*, page 2; also, N. **41**; **42** (entire); **43**, *a, c, d*.

Learn the Cardinals (to **30**), the Ordinals (to **12th**), and the answers to Questions given below. A. **94**; B. **79**; H. **174**; APP. **19**.

LATIN LESSONS. 83

Learn the Declension of ūnus, duo, trēs. A. 83, *a ;* 94, *b, c ;*
B. 66, 80; H. 175; APP. 11, *a ;* 20, *b.*
Accusative of Time. Learn N. 142 & *a ;* also 54, 4, page 15.
Ablative of Time. Learn N. 160; also 54, 5, page 15.

Questions.

The Numerals are given in the Grammars and Appendix ; they are not given in the Vocabulary.

What is the Latin for 25, 18, 100, 1000, 5, 300, 278, 130, 19, 15th, 3d, 9th, 7th, 2d, 8th ? What question is answered by the Accusative of Time? by the Ablative of Time? What Cardinals are declined?

EXERCISE.

1. Septem hōrās pugnāvērunt. 2. Diē quintō ad castra revertitur. 3. Mediā nocte oppidum oppugnābimus. 4. Sōlis occāsū exercitum trans flūmen duxit. 5. Quattuor diēs in fīnibus hostium morātus est. 6. Frūmentō multōs annōs vixerat. 7. Tertiō diē in fīnēs Sequanōrum perveniēmus. 8. Duōs mensēs trans Rhēnum incoluī. 9. Septendecim annōs bellum gerēbant. 10. Mille virī ab Ariovistō missī erant, ut castra oppugnārent. 11. Quartā hōrā ē castrīs proficiscēmur. 12. Tōtam noctem cōpiae Rōmānae iter fēcērunt. 13. Sōlis occāsū castrīs impedīmentīsque potītus es. 14. Domī quinque mensēs fuerās. 15. Novendecim diēs commeātūs causā morābiminī. 16. Quam celerrimē iter faciāmus nē Sēquanī nāvibus potiantur. 17. Unō annō oppida trīgintā capta sunt. 18. Aestāte ad urbem Rōmam veniētis. 19. Decima legiō hostēs sex diēs secūta partem maximam impedīmentōrum cēpit. 20. Tertiō diē Titum equitēs peditēsque Germānōrum vīcisse audīvimus. 21. In Italiā centum urbēs magnae fuērunt. 22. Castra quartā hōrā pōnet.

English into Latin.

1. We shall use the horses all (**tōtus**) day. 2. Let him come at sunset. 3. We shall break up camp at midnight. 4. Let us delay two days for the sake of supplies. 5. Let the king praise

the soldiers (as they are) setting out for (in) battle. 6. For two hours the cavalry fought very bravely. 7. He seems to deserve great praise.

LESSON XLVI.

ACCUSATIVE: DENOTING EXTENT OF SPACE; PARTITIVE GENITIVE.

Accusative denoting Extent of Space. Learn N. 142 & *b*; also 54, 3, page 15.
Declension of Mille. Learn N. 43, *e*; App. 20, *c*.
Partitive Genitive. Learn N. 122, & *a*; 123, *c*.

CAUTION. Cardinal numbers require a peculiar construction. N. 123, *a*.
Notice that the Accusative of Extent (either of *time* or *space*) has an Adverbial force of Degree (telling *How far* or *How much*), as in English: *the tree is* very *high; the tree is* sixty feet *high.*

Questions.

When should mille, the noun, be used? (*Ans.* When more than *one* thousand are spoken of.) What is the Latin for *three miles? five thousand men? a thousand horses?* What is the difference in meaning between perterreō, permoveō, and terreō, moveō? (99, 1.) Give the Latin for *a part of the soldiers; five of the boys.* What part of speech does the Accusative of *time* and *extent* most resemble?

EXERCISE.

1. Domum pedēs trīgintā septem lātam aedificāvit. 2. Quinque millia passuum iter fēcērunt. 3. Castra millia passuum octo in lātitūdinem patēbant. 4. Equum mille quingentōs passūs sequitur. 5. Collis ducentōs pedēs altus fuit. 6. Mare mille pedēs altum est. 7. Dīcit mūrum decem millia pedum longum esse. 8. Ūnus ex mīlitibus iter difficillimum fore dixit. 9. Millia hominum quattuor ut urbem oppugnārent missa sunt. 10. Turris vīgintī quinque pedēs alta est. 11. Servōs fugientēs millia passuum novem secūtus, ad oppidum revertitur. 12. Agrī Helvētiōrum in longi-

LATIN LESSONS. 85

tūdinem millia passuum ducenta et quadrāgintā, in lātitūdinem centum et octōgintā patēbant. 13. Magnam partem auxiliōrum dīmīsit. 14. Centum ex cīvibus contrā rēgem conjūrāvērunt. 15. Domus mea altior lātiorque quam Marcī est.

English into Latin.

1. The horse is sixteen hands high. 2. Let us follow the enemy for three hours. 3. We will pitch the camp on the higher ground (places). 4. They say that the legion marched fifteen miles. 5. The forests extend eight miles in width. 6. The temple is two hundred feet long and eighty feet wide. 7. Pompey's camp is larger than Caesar's.

LESSON XLVII.

ADVERBIAL ACCUSATIVE; CERTAIN PHRASES OF TIME, PLACE, ETC.

Adverbial Accusative, denoting Degree. Learn N. **94**, *d*, 1; **142** & *c*. Compare the English: *He was hurt* a very little; They were injured *a great deal* (**54**, 6, page 15).

How to express such Phrases as: the rest of the Gauls; half-way up the hill; at day-break, etc. Learn N. **110**, *b*; **123**, *e*.
Plūs: Learn its Use. N. **27, 122**, *b*. Learn its Declension. A. **86**; B. **70**; H. **165**, N. 1; APP. **15**, *a*.

Study carefully the Examples under the NOTES *for this Lesson; also Special Examples, p.* 266. *The Accusative in many of the sentences of this Lesson denotes Extent of Space.*

Questions.

What is the difference in meaning between **exercitus, aciēs**, and **agmen**? Express in Latin: *at day-break; at midnight; for the most part; in the last part of winter; the rest of the Belgae; at noon.* What part of speech is **plūs** in the Singular? in the Plural? Give the Latin for *more wisdom* (**sapientia**).

EXERCISE.

1. Merīdiē veniet. 2. Castra tantum spatiī patēbant. 3. Nullam partem noctis iter fēcimus. 4. Exercitum prīmā lūce ēduxit. 5. Prīmā nocte servōs ēmīsērunt. 6. Multō diē portās claudī jussī. 7. Frūmentō (**151,** *a*) maximam partem vīvēbant. 8. Ariovistus in Galliā plūrimum potuerat. 9. Impetūs hostium paulum tardantur. 10. Reliquī Belgae fortissimī sunt. 11. Extrēmā hieme ad urbem vēnērunt. 12. Mediō in colle templum fuit. 13. Dīcit summum montem ā tertiā legiōne occupārī. 14. Spērō ducem in Italiā bellum gestūrum esse. 15. In Galliā hiemēs longissimae sunt. 16. Princeps plūs auctōritātis habuit. 17. Dē secundā vigiliā castra dēfensōribus nūdābuntur. 18. Circum Rōmam tōtam hiemem mansērunt. 19. Dīcit reliquōs Suēvōs ēductōs esse. 20. Nihil impetus legiōnis Rōmānōs terrēre potuit. 21. Arma reliquōrum mīlitum āmissa erant. 22. Reliquī (**109**) ad castra sine vulnere revertentur. 23. Bellō servīlī (**110,** *c*) plūs imperiī habuī. 24. Rempublicam metū maximō līberābis. 25. Suēvī, reliquōs millia passuum multa secūtī, in fīnēs Helvētiōrum sub vesperum pervēnērunt. 26. Magnam partem diēī iter faciēmus. 27. Nihil perīculō mortis territus sum. 28. Dīcit urbem magnam esse, et decem millia passuum in lātitūdinem patēre. 29. Putāverat agmen longius futūrum esse.

English into Latin.

1. Let us pass the winter in the territory of the Suevi. 2. They will set out in the fourth watch. 3. They say that the chief is very powerful at home. 4. More (men) will be led out by the general. 5. The rest of the ships are very small. 6. Let us march all (**tōtus**) night. 7. If he should lose (his) arms, he would be killed. 8. He says (**199,** 5) that the gate is not twenty feet wide. 9. They can set out at day-break.

LESSON XLVIII.

SUBJUNCTIVE MODE: PURPOSE, COMMAND, AND
EXHORTATION (*continued*).

Purpose. Learn N. 179 & CAUTION 1, *d*.
Command and Exhortation. Learn N. 178 & CAUTION 1.
Correlatives. N. 195, 8. Learn the meaning of these Correlatives: alius ... alius; alter ... alter; aliī ... aliī; alterī ... alterī; et ... et; neque ... neque; nōn sōlum ... sed etiam.
Study the Special Examples for this Lesson, page 267.

NOTICE that hortor, nītor, rogō, do not *state* anything, and cannot take the Accusative and Infinitive, like dīcō. *I ask, strive,* or *exhort* for a *Purpose*.
REMEMBER, the Infinitive Mode cannot express a *Purpose*.

Questions.

What are *Correlatives?* What conjunction is required for a *positive* Purpose? for a *negative* Purpose? Where must **nōn** NEVER be used? (*Ans.* In Imperative sentences.) If this Latin is not correct, make it so: **Hortātur puerōs bonōs esse.**

EXERCISE.

1. Nē vereāmur. 2. Vēnit ut vinceret. 3. Nītimur ut sapientēs sīmus. 4. Mīlitēs hortābimur ut fortiter pugnent. 5. Aliī pugnābant, aliī fugiēbant. 6. Alter consulum justus fuit, alter injustus. 7. Caesarem rogāverant ut mīlitibus arma daret. 8. Nē castra dē tertiā vigiliā oppugnent. 9. Lēgātus imperātōrem rogat nē per Galliam iter faciat. 10. Et puerī et puellae nītuntur ut ā magistrō laudentur. 11. Neque consul neque jūdex oppida dēlēta esse dixit. 12. Alterī laudātī sunt, alterī pūnientur. 13. Dīcit legiōnēs ā Pompēiō conscriptās per prōvinciam iter facere, ut oppidum ab Ariovistō mūnītum occupent. 14. Nē servīs malīs dōna polliceāmur. 15. Audīvī imperātōrem decimam legiōnem nē hostēs sequerētur hortātum esse. 16. Hortāminī custōdēs ut quam dīli-

gentissimī sint. 17. Venī ut virum fortem et videās et laudēs. 18. Jūdicēs nītantur nē injustī appellentur. 19. Nōn sōlum mīlitēs sed etiam agricolae reīpublicae ūtilissimī fuērunt. 20. Cōpiās hortātī erant nē ex urbe proficiscerentur. 21. Cāium hortābantur ut contrā rempublicam conjūrāret.

English into Latin.

1. Let us not set out at day-break. 2. Let them not pass the winter in the forest. 3. The Suevi are very near the Helvetii. 4. He exhorted the soldiers to march ten miles. 5. I will ask the consul not to punish the slave. 6. Some are good, others bad. 7. Of the two men, one was a judge, the other a lieutenant. 8. We will not only lead out the legion in the fourth hour, but also seize the mountain-top before noon.

LESSON XLIX.

ABLATIVE OF MANNER, ACCOMPANIMENT, AND SPECIFICATION.

Ablative expressing Manner. Learn N. **150**.
Ablative denoting Accompaniment. Learn N. **150,** *a.*
Ablative denoting In what Respect (Specification). Learn N. **153; 36,** *b.*
Learn the Declension of **vīs.** A. **61**; B. **41**; H. **66**; APP. **7**.

Questions and Practice.

When must **cum** be used? What question does the Ablative of Manner answer? the Ablative of Specification? Decline **mille** (the noun). Decline together the Latin for *great strength*. Give a complete synopsis of **vereor; jubeō.** What prepositions *always* take the Ablative? What prepositions take the Ablative *or* the Accusative? What adjectives have **limus** in the Superlative? Give the Latin for *He is older; We are younger* (**36,** *b*).

EXERCISE.

1. Consul clārā vōce dixit. 2. Mīles ducem cum tribus legiōnibus ā Galliā vēnisse audīverat. 3. Omnēs sciunt rēgem cīvitātem sapienter et bene rexisse. 4. Et sociī et auxilia magnā vī contendēbant. 5. Auxilium ā Caesare magnō flētū petunt. 6. Posterō diē castra movit et per fīnēs Suēvōrum iter fēcit. 7. Dixit Titum cum equitibus atque (96, a, 3) auxiliīs ut loca superiōra occupāret missum esse. 8. Gallī reliquōs virtūte praecēdunt. 9. Legiōnem proximē conscriptam et magnam partem equitātūs mīsit nē castra ab hostibus occupārentur. 10. Magistrātūs modō servīlī obsidēs pūniēbant. 11. Imperātor nōmine fuit. 12. Frātrēs mājōrēs nātu sunt. 13. Locus omnibus rēbus castrīs idōneus est. 14. Bellō Gallicō nāvibus atque oppidīs hostium potītī sumus. 15. Mediō in colle aciem triplicem quattuor legiōnum instruxit. 16. Dīcit Germānōs bellum cum Gallīs multōs annōs gessisse. 17. Dītior (36, a) agrīs et equīs fuit. 18. Puerī patrī omnibus rēbus similēs sunt. 19. Mīles magnā vī (149) et animī et corporis laudābātur. 20. Dīcit labōrem omnia victūrum esse. 21. Agmen quinque millibus peditum claudēbant. 22. Hortēmur servōs ut fidēlēs sint.

English into Latin.

1. Let us surpass all in strength of body. 2. He will pitch (his) camp at the foot of a very high mountain. 3. They broke up camp on the following day. 4. Let us not march with Cassius. 5. The line of battle was drawn up at the fifth hour. 6. The goddesses' temples are larger than (those) of the gods. 7. With a flood of tears (great weeping) he promised that the leader should send back the hostages. 8. The allies bring up the rear (close the line of march) with two thousand horsemen.

LESSON L.

PRONOUNS: PERSONAL, REFLEXIVE, POSSESSIVE.

Learn N. 45, 46, 47 & CAUTION; 48 & CAUTION; 108 & REMARK; 111, 112, 113 & a.
Learn the Declension of ego, tū, suī, meus, tuus, suus, noster, vester. A. 98, a, c; 99, a; B. 84, 85, 86; H. 184, 185. APP. 21, 22, 23.

Questions and Practice.

Why are *Reflexive* Pronouns so called? Give the Latin for these sentences, expressing a *subject* in each: *let us teach ourselves; the man teaches himself; you teach yourself; I taught myself; the leaders praise themselves; the girl taught herself; the auxiliaries will save themselves; soldiers, save yourselves.* Name the Personal Pronouns. Why cannot **suī** be used as a Personal Pronoun of the Third Person? How is the lack of the Third Personal Pronoun supplied? In the sentence, "The general called his lieutenant and praised him for his bravery," can *his, him,* and *his* be expressed by **suī** and **suus**? Give the reason for your answer. Give the rule for the use of a Possessive Pronoun (**108 & REMARK**). How can you tell whether (after a transitive verb, as *give*) **praemium suum** means *his, her, its,* or *their reward?* Express in Latin (in the shortest form): *our men are brave; he encouraged his soldiers.*

EXERCISE.

1. Nōs laudātī sumus; tū pūnītus es. 2. Vōs nōbīs inimīcī fuistis. 3. Imperātor dixit sē * Aeduīs auxilium pollicitum esse. 4. Mīlitēs sē * neque ā vōbīs neque ab imperātōre laudārī dīcunt. 5. Vōbīs dōna mājōra pollicēmur. 6. Servī tuī sē ventūrōs esse ut castra nostra mūnīrent dixērunt. 7. Urbs vestra fīnibus Aeduōrum proxima est. 8. Nostrī castra mūrō altissimō mūnient. 9. Tū mihi amīcus atque ūtilis fuistī. 10. Mājōrēs cōpiae ā ducibus nostrīs missae esse dīcēbantur. 11. Nē tuī hostēs vereantur. 12. Germānī nulla arma sibi ab Ariovistō, duce suō, data esse dixērunt. 13. Sē suaque omnia rēgī dēdidērunt (*from* dēdō). 14. Dēdite,

* Translate **sē** like a Personal Pronoun (that is, *he, they*).

cīvēs, vōs vestraque omnia consulī. 15. Nōs (**123**, *d*) omnēs tibi cārissimī sumus. 16. Alter consulum Cāius, alter amīcus meus fuit. 17. Duodecim ex cīvibus (**123**, *a*) commeātūs causā ad urbem missī erant. 18. Et tū et Marcus Caesarī amīcissimī eritis (**117**, *d*). 19. Tē amīcum, mē hostem appellant. 20. Diximus proelium vōbīs omnibus perīculōsum fore. 21. Sibi sapientissimus esse vidētur.

English into Latin.

1. All of us are Romans. 2. He says that your friends are very brave soldiers. 3. All things (*express in two ways*) have been said by us. 4. Surrender yourself and all your goods (things) to the brave leader. 5. We think the bad have been punished by the consuls. 6. The best (men) fight best. 7. He says that you (*singular*) deserve well of (**dē**) the state. 8. Some are happy, others most wretched. 9. The men have lost their swords. 10. Soldiers, you have conquered your enemies.

LESSON LI.

PRONOUNS: DEMONSTRATIVE.

Learn N. **49** (entire) ; **114**, 1, 2, *a;* **48**, CAUTION.
Learn the Declension of **hīc, ille, is, īdem, ipse, iste**. A. **101** & *a;* B. **87, 88**; H. **186**; App. **24**.

Questions and Practice.

Why are *Demonstrative* Pronouns so called? In what two ways may they be used? Which is very commonly employed as the *Third Personal Pronoun*? Why not use **suī** instead?. Decline **is** in the Masculine (*he*); in the Feminine (*she*); in the Neuter (*it*). What are **hīc, ille, iste** often called, and why? Decline the Latin meaning: *this temple; that boy* (yonder); *that door* (by you); *the citizen himself; the same fact* (**rēs**). When must *his* and *their* be expressed by **ējus** and **eōrum**? When by **suus**?

EXERCISE.

Tell which Demonstratives are used as Adjectives, and which as Substantives (that is, as Personal Pronouns).

1. Hīc vir deōs immortālēs esse negat. 2. Illa oppida ā Caesare dēlēta sunt. 3. Nōs ipsī eum pugnāre vīdimus. 4. Haec (109) ā consule dicta sunt. 5. Dīcit hās legiōnēs laudem maximam meritās esse. 6. Hī tibi inimīcī erunt; illī nōbīs amīcī sunt. 7. Eadem dōna ad Ariovistum missa erunt. 8. Is servum suum vocāvit, et opus ējus laudāvit. 9. Virtūs eōrum magna fuit. 10. Pollicētur sē iīs arma datūrum esse. 11. Hōs fortiter pugnantēs vīdit. 12. Dixit eōs hostēs millia passuum quinque secūtōs impedīmentīs potītōs esse. 13. Sī illī vōs nōn sequantur, urbem nōn expugnōtis. 14. Centum mīlitēs eō tempore habuit. 15. Hīc puer idem dīcet. 16. Dixistis aciem ipsam impetum sustinēre nōn potuisse. 17. Tū ipse, ut rēgem vidērēs, in illā urbe quattuor diēs mansistī. 18. Hōrum omnium fortissimī sunt Belgae. 19. Ipsī in eōrum fīnibus bellum gerunt. 20. Suīs fīnibus eōs prohibent. 21. Dīcunt eundem virum bella multa in Italiā gessisse et patriam suam servitūte līberāvisse.

English into Latin.

1. These books are heavy; those burdens are light. 2. They sent those soldiers under the yoke. 3. At day-break, these things (*express in two ways*) will be announced. 4. That house is one hundred feet long. 5. The same camp was taken by them. 6. These (men) marched from the deep river to the lofty mountain. 7. The temple is very beautiful; we ourselves have seen it.

LESSON LII.

PRONOUNS: RELATIVE.

Learn N. **50, 115** & *a, c*. Learn the Declension of **Quī**. A. **103**; B. **89**; H. **187**; App. **25**.

Quī (= ut ego, tū, is, etc.) in Clauses of Purpose. Learn
N. 179, a ; 193, 4.

NOTICE *that the Relative Pronoun, both in English and Latin, is equivalent to a Personal Pronoun + a connective.*

EXERCISE.

Directions for the analysis of Complex Sentences, 194, c.
1. Urbs, quam vidēs, Rōma est. 2. Ego, quī tē laudāvī, rex sum. 3. Mīlitēs, ā quibus oppidum captum erat, fortēs fuērunt. 4. Cōpiās, quae arcem expugnārent, praemīsit. 5. Imperātor, dē quō scripsī, servōs omnēs sēcum (53, *a*) transduxerat. 6. Mīlitēs, quōrum virtūs magna fuit, ut summum montem occupārent ā Caesare missī sunt. 7. In Galliam decimam legiōnem mittāmus, quae oppida omnia hostium dēleat. 8. Gallia est omnis dīvīsa (189, *b*) in partēs trēs, quārum ūnam incolunt Belgae, aliam Aquītānī, tertiam (iī incolunt), quī ipsōrum linguā Celtae, nostrā Gallī appellantur. 9. Proximī sunt Germānīs, quī trans Rhēnum incolunt, quibuscum bellum gerunt. 10. Eōrum ūna pars initium capit ā flūmine Rhodanō. 11. Aquītānī ab hōc flūmine ad Pȳrēnaeōs montēs et eam partem Oceanī, quae est ad Hispāniam, pertinent. 12. Prō multitūdine hominum angustōs sē fīnēs habēre arbitrābantur, quī in longitūdinem millia passuum ducenta et quadrāgintā, in lātitūdinem centum et octōgintā patēbant. 13. Eum hortātus est ut regnum in cīvitāte suā (112, *a*) occupāret, quod pater ante habuerat. 14. Dux legiōnēs, quārum virtūte urbs servāta erat, laudāvit. 15. Puellae, quās tē vīdisse dixistī, fīliae meae sunt. 16. Dē secundā vigiliā equitēs eōdem itinere, quō hostēs fūgerant, profectī sunt.

English into Latin.

1. That house (115, *c*) you see is mine. 2. The man who came to see you was my friend. 3. They had come to ask me my opinion about peace. 4. I informed him concerning the enemy's attack. 5. Let us not say these things. 6. We will send Caius to get possession of the heavy baggage. 7. He has brought (dūcō) with him the hostages which he has received from the Aquitani.

LESSON LIII.

PRONOUNS: INTERROGATIVE; INTERROGATIVE SENTENCES.

Learn N. 51 (entire). Learn the Declension of the Interrogatives **Quis** (*Substantive*) and **Quī** (*Adjective*). A. 104 & *a*; B. 90; H. 188; APP. 26.
Single Questions. Learn N. 100, 101 & *a*, REMARK.
Study the Examples given under the NOTES *for this Lesson.*

Questions.

What is the Latin for: *who praises me? what man praises me?* What is the difference in meaning between **quis** (**quī**) and **uter**? (43, *b*; 51, CAUTION.) How many words are spelled **ne**? how is each used? (197, 4.) What words are *always* Enclitics? (195, 3.) When is **cum** an Enclitic? (53, *a*.) What effect has an Enclitic upon accent? Pronounce **imperātōribusque; cōnsulēsne**. How are *yes* and *no* usually expressed? Is this correct: **quisne vēnit?** Give the Rule for the use of the Relative Pronoun.

EXERCISE.

Tell which of these sentences are Declaratory; Interrogative; Imperative. Analyze each. An Interrogative or Imperative sentence should be analyzed as though it were Declaratory; as, "What did that man say?" = *"That man said what?"*

1. Quō (*adverb*) mīlitēs dūcentur? 2. Quis hostēs fugientēs verētur? 3. Unde vēnistis? 4. Quod templum vidēs? 5. Quam urbem cēperātis? 6. Utram in partem flūmen fluit? 7. Nonne sōlem orientem vidētis? 8. Quid ille, quem vīdistis, dīxit? 9. Quod perīculum vītābis? 10. Mīlitēsne ut fortēs essent hortātī sunt? 11. Ubi hae cōpiae victae erant? 12. Uter consulum amīcus vester est? 13. Num servus fēlix esse potest? 14. Cūr haec dīxistī? 15. Quamobrem (*or* quam ob rem) urbem nōn oppugnāvit? 16. Cur hōc difficile est? 17. Quae cīvitātēs ut pācem peterent ad tē veniēbant? 18. Dīcit hostēs perterritōs fūgisse.

19. Spērat equitēs exercitum fugientem secūtōs numerum magnum hostium interfectūrōs esse. 20. Nonne hostēs castrīs nostrīs potītī nōs interficient? 21. Servus, cuī arma data erant, sē nōn pugnātūrum esse dixit. 22. Estne sapiens? Nōn est. 23. Hostēsne vīcistis? Vīcimus. 24. Nonne imperātor vōs nōmina vestra rogāvit? 25. Nē fugiāmus; et multī et fortēs sumus. 26. Duxne legiōnem nē fugeret hortātus erat? 27. Sequiminī, sociī, agmen fugiens, quod neque magnum neque forte est. 28. Quemadmodum (*or* quem ad modum) castrīs Ariovistī potīrī possumus? 29. Quem ad modum mē tibi amīcum facere potes? 30. Germānī Rōmānōs sibi obsidēs pollicitōs fidem nōn servāre dīcunt.

English into Latin.

1. Who is that man? 2. What boy is this? 3. Is he at home? 4. Is n't Caesar brave? 5. This town cannot be stormed, can it? 6. Why have the men not come? 7. Which of the (two) boys is more like his father? 8. Which (of several) is most unlike her mother? 9. Those boys have taught themselves (their) letters. 10. Let's ask the farmer the horse's name.

LESSON LIV.

PRONOUNS: INDEFINITE; DOUBLE QUESTIONS.

Learn N. **52** (entire). Learn the Declension of **aliquis, sī quis, nē quis** (both as *Substantives* and *Adjectives*). A. **105,** d; B. **91**; H. **190,** 1, 2; APP. **27.** Learn, also, the Declension of **quisque, quīdam,** N. **52,** d; **53,** c.

Double Questions. Learn N. **101,** b.

NOTICE *that the simple forms of the-Indefinite Pronouns* (**quis, quī**) *are not used in this Lesson.* (See N. **52.**)

Questions and Practice.

How does the declension of **aliquis** and **aliqui** differ from that of **quis** and **qui**? What other Indefinite Pronouns have the same peculiarity? Which may be written as separate words, and why? Give the exact meaning of **aliquis**. What does **quisque ditissimus** mean? (**53**, *b.*) Decline the Latin meaning: *each soldier ; a certain animal.* Why is **utrum** a suitable particle to introduce a Double Question? Give the Latin for: *are we brave, or not?* Also for these sentences (expressing the subject in each): *each loves himself; he teaches him; she praises herself; they conquer them; they* (feminine) *teach themselves; you praise yourself; they themselves praise you.*

EXERCISE.

1. Inter sē (**53**, *d*) cohortātī sunt. 2. Aliquis Cāium laudābit. 3. Sī quem pugnantem videat, eum laudet. 4. Hortātus est mīlitēs nē quod tēlum rējicerent. 5. Ad puerum, cūjus pater interfectus erat, aliquod dōnum mīsit. 6. Sī quī fugiant, eōs interficite. 7. Quīdam dixit nātūram hominibus vītam breviōrem quam permultīs animālibus dedisse. 8. Quisque nōbilissimus patriam suam servābit. 9. Sī quod templum aedificātum esset, dēlētum esset. 10. Cūjus virtūs magna fuit? 11. Sī quibus inimīcus sit, consul nōn creētur. 12. Aliqua castra ā nostrīs capta sunt. 13. Eōs cohortātur, nē quis vereātur. 14. Sī quis perīculō perterritus domī mansisset, eum pūnīvissēmus. 15. Quendam dēlēgit, quem ad exercitum mitteret (**179**, *a*). 16. Nāvem metū relinquēbant. 17. Lēgātī ā senātū Rōmānō missī interficiuntur. 18. Omnēs virtūtem cīvium, ā quibus patria servāta est, et laudant et mīrantur. 19. Utrum domī an in Galliā est? 20. Utrum Rōmānus es, annōn? 21. Num mihi inimīcī erunt? 22. Utrum rex dōna accēpit, an ea remīsit? 23. Dixit sē neque fidē neque jūrejūrandō tenērī posse. 24. Plūs imperiī quam virtūtis habēre dīcitur. 25. Summā vī proelium ā dextrō cornū commissum est ab equitibus, quī ā locīs superiōribus vēnerant. 26. Putāvistī quemque dītissimum mīlitī pecūniam datūrum esse. 27. Nuntiat mīlitēs permultōs ā manū parvā superātōs esse. 28. Lēgātiō ab cīvitāte vēnit, quae eum nē bellum gereret hortārētur. 29. Quī sunt virī, quōs sēcum habuit?

LATIN LESSONS. 97

English into Latin.

1. Whom did you send to the camp? 2. Some one has given a sword to each soldier. 3. If he had said anything, he would have been punished. 4. He has stormed a town, fortified both by nature and by art (hand). 5. Did n't they say those things, which were not true (vĕrus)? 6. Every man said that he would come at sunset. 7. Let us not choose any commander. 8. Having followed the line of march for three miles, they are not able to get possession of the baggage which they have lost.

LESSON LV.

PLACE: EXCEPTIONS.

Learn N. **159** & *a, b, c,* REMARK 1.

REMEMBER that, to express Place *where, whence,* and *whither,* Prepositions are *required,* as in Lesson XXXIX. The *exceptions* are those classes of nouns mentioned in the NOTES on this Lesson. Study the RULE (**159,** *c*), in connection with the Examples under it, so as to be able to apply it without hesitation.

Questions and Practice.

Many of the proper nouns used are not in the Vocabulary, but under **159.** *Notice that many names of towns have no Singular.*
What is meant by the *Locative* case? In what Declensions is it found? What cases does it resemble in form? What nouns omit the preposition to express place? Do they illustrate the regular, or the exceptional, use? When *must* prepositions be used with **Rōma, Capua,** etc.? Give the Latin for: *he is at home; we are in Gaul; they set out from the camp; he came from Rome; there is a temple in the city; he is in Capua; they marched from the river to Lyons; he will be at Veii; they have come to Carthage; we will march from Veii to the camp; he passed the winter in the neighborhood of Rome; we have come from the vicinity of Athens; let us march into the country.*

EXERCISE.

1. In ulteriōre Galliā duās legiōnēs, quae in prōvinciā citeriōre proximē conscriptae erant, relīquit. 2. Dixit sē cum tribus cohortibus Vēiōs profectūrum (**199**, 2) dē secundā vigiliā. 3. Dīcit exercitum Londīnium urbem Britanniae maximam prīmā lūce iter factūrum. 4. Ex Cisalpīnā Galliā ad Caesarem, quī eō tempore Vesontiōne fuit, lēgātī missī sunt. 5. Venīte, amīcī, Bibracte. 6. Noviodūnō, oppidō Aeduōrum, Lugdūnum vēnit. 7. Utrum Sardibus an Rōmae mortuī sunt? 8. Capuaene nātus es? 9. Nonne flūmina Galliae Transalpīnae longiōra quam Britanniae sunt? 10. Quot cohortēs in legiōne sunt? 11. Utrum Caesar ad Noviodūnum hiemābit, annōn? 12. Utrum domum an rūs proficiscēmur? 13. Quis mēcum Athēnās ībit (*will go*)? 14. Num Bibracte ūnā legiōne expugnāre potes? 15. Karthāgine extrēmā (**110**, *b*) hieme Rōmam vēnit. 16. Locī nātūrā Helvētiī continentur; ūnā ex parte flūmine Rhēnō, lātissimō atque altissimō, quī agrum Helvētium ā Germānīs dīvidit; alterā ex parte, monte Jūrā (**3**, & REMARK 1) altissimō, quī est inter Sēquanōs et Helvētiōs; tertiā, lacū Lemannō et flūmine Rhodanō, quī prōvinciam nostram ab Helvētiīs dīvidit.

LESSON LVI.

IRREGULAR VERBS: **FERŌ**; GENITIVE AFTER **SUM**.

Learn N. **83, 86**. Learn the Conjugation of **Ferō**, Active and Passive. A. **139**; B. **129**; H. **292**; APP. **42**.

Genitive after **Sum.** Learn N. **126**, entire.

Infinitive as Subject. Learn **36**, *c*, REMARK, page 10; also N. **109**, *b*; **165**, *a*. Read carefully **53**, **55**, page 15.

Study the Examples under the NOTES *for this Lesson.*

LATIN LESSONS. 99

Questions and Practice.

To what Conjugation (in general) does **ferō** belong? How would the Present Indicative (Active and Passive) be conjugated, if **ferō** were like **regō**? What is the chief irregularity of **ferō**? (86, a.) What would these forms be, if regular: **ferre**? **fer**? **ferrem**? **fertor**? **ferrer**? **ferrī**? What is the Latin for: *this horse is Caesar's*? What relation does *Caesar's* express? Analyze this English sentence : *to die for one's country is noble*. What would be the gender of *noble* in Latin? Why?

EXERCISE.

1. Onus grave ā servō timidō fertur. 2. Dīcit injūriās lātās esse. 3. Nōs omnēs scīmus arma ā servīs ferrī. 4. Sociī sē castrīs auxilium nōn lātūrōs esse dīxērunt. 5. Equī armaque conferentur. 6. Hostēs ūnum impetum nostrōrum ferre nōn poterant. 7. Dōna atque praemia ad imperātōrem lāta sunt. 8. Fer, puer, hās litterās ad Caesarem. 9. Ferre injūriās est virī fortis. 10. Haec domus Caesaris fuit. 11. Putat eōs impedīmenta in ūnum locum contulisse. 12. Omnia sunt victōris. 13. Imperātōris est jubēre. 14. Mīlitis Rōmānī est aut vincere aut morī. 15. Onera ferāmus. 16. Sī suīs auxilium tulissent, laudātī essent. 17. Haec legiō Marcī est. 18. Iter longum facere nōn facile est. 19. Utrum rēgem malum ferēmus, annōn? 20. Dīcit jūdicium dē bellō ducis esse. 21. Hīc dixit hōs agrōs agricolārum fuisse. 22. Dē hīs duōbus generibus alterum est servōrum, alterum cīvium. 23. Fortiter pugnāre ducis bonī est. 24. Consulem pējōrem tulerātis. 25. Conferte, cīvēs, arma in hunc locum. 26. Esse melius quam vidērī est.

English into Latin.

1. It is the duty of a good king to rule wisely. 2. We have borne the gift to the city. 3. He bears the injury that he may be thought brave. 4. Let us carry weapons. 5. He says that the general has ordered the baggage to be collected. 6. To call together the men was difficult. 7. To free the camp from danger was very easy. 8. These arms are mine. 9. That house is yours.

10. To fight as bravely as possible is the legion's duty. 11. These arms cannot be carried by a small man. 12. To send corn to the army was more useful than to promise auxiliaries.

LESSON LVII.

DATIVE WITH COMPOUND VERBS.

Learn N. 133. Notice that the Dative thus used is the *Indirect Object*.

Learn the Principal Parts of these Compounds of **ferō**, which are the ones most commonly used: **afferō; cōnferō; differō; inferō; referō;** also of **tollō**. Notice that the Perfect and Supine of **tollō** are taken from **sufferō**, but used with a different meaning.

Learn N. 1 (6), and apply it to the compounds of **ferō**.

General Questions.

What cases do prepositions (used alone) take ? What prepositions are used in compound verbs taking the Dative ? What is the meaning of *assimilation* ? How does it appear in **afferō** ? **cōnferō** ? **inferō** ? **possum** ? How did the Romans express *you and I* ? *Caius and I* ? (193, 8.) Give a synopsis, Active and Passive, of **ferō**.

EXERCISE.

1. Et ego et tū Galliae bellum intulimus (**117,** *d*). 2. Caesar exercituī praefuit. 3. Omnibus virtūte praestant. 4. Sī quid mihi accidat, Rōma expugnētur. 5. Legiōnī, quam conscripserat, Cāium praefēcit. 6. Hī omnēs linguā lēgibusque inter sē differunt. 7. Bellum patriae nostrae ā cīvibus pessimīs infertur. 8. Galliae bellum infer. 9. Dīcunt sē bellum nōbīscum gestūrōs esse. 10. Nāvibus eum praeficiēmus. 11. Litterae mihi allātae sunt. 12. Ego et Cāius rēgī haec nuntiābimus. 13. Utrum oppidō an castrīs lēgātus praeest ? 14. Sī tū et amīcus meus vulnerātī essētis, ego et frāter tuus īnfēlīcissimī fuissēmus. 15. Spēs fugae sublāta

erat. 16. Dīcit spem victōriae ab imperātōre sublātam esse. 17. Equī omnium ut spēs fugae tollerētur remōtī sunt. 18. Dōna rēgis ab urbe referent. 19. Genēvā profectī estis ut per prōvinciam nostram iter facerētis, atque bellum sociīs nostrīs inferre possētis. 20. Nē spem fugae tollāmus.

English into Latin.

1. This (thing) seems to be easier. 2. Let us make war upon the enemies of the state. 3. These messages were brought to Caesar. 4. We will send the tenth legion home, lest anything should happen to the city. 5. Are you in command of this camp, or not? 6. We differ from each other in many respects (rēs). 7. We used to be in command of the ships. 8. The leader and I have sent the cohort to Rome.

LESSON LVIII.

IRREGULAR VERBS: Eō; CONDITIONAL SENTENCES.

Learn N. 87. Learn the Conjugation of Eō. A. 141; B. 132; H. 295; App. 43.

Compounds of Eō. Learn N. 87, REMARK.

Conditional Sentences. The general principles have been given in Lesson XXI., and should now be reviewed. Learn N. 174, 175 (entire).

Questions.

Eō: When does i become e? What *would* the Future be, if not **ībō**? Decline the Present Participle. Tell the quantity of i in: ībunt; itūrus; itū; ībam; īrem. Give the principal parts of adeō; ineō; trānseō; subeō.

What tenses does the Subjunctive lack? How is this lack supplied in Conditional Sentences? Is the Conclusion a *principal*, or *subordinate*, clause? Tell what *time* and *kind of statement* is expressed in each of the following sentences; also what mode and tense would be required in Latin to express each

LATIN LESSONS.

verb: *if he were now here, he would be happy ; he would have been successful, if he had been diligent ; if he called, he found him ; if the bell should ring (before you start), you would be late ; if he saw the danger (now), we should be glad ; if he had worked, he would now be rich.*

EXERCISE.

1. Jūre (149) bellī stīpendium capit, quod victōrēs victīs impōnere consuērunt (79, 4).* 2. Dīcit sē mēcum itūrum esse. 3. Vōbīscum ībimus; quibuscum ībat? 4. Rōmamne iērunt (= īvērunt)? 5. Profectus est ut domum īret. 6. Eāmus; īte; ībitis; eunt; iit. 7. Utrum ībātis an veniēbātis? 8. Sī Karthāginem īvissent, interfectī essent. 9. Sī perīcula omnia subeant, laudem mereantur. 10. Sī Galliam vīcit, Gallīs victīs stīpendium jūre bellī imposuit. 11. Titum urbī praeficiāmus. 12. Consilia dē summīs rēbus saepissimē ineunt. 13. Sī insulam adeat, barbarī cum interficiant. 14. Flūmen transīre difficillimum fuit. 15. Dixit eōs cum millibus hominum quinque Rhēnum transitūrōs. 16. Dīcit Helvētiōs obsidēs accipere, nōn dare, consuesse (79, 4). 17. Sī nuntius Caesarī nōn allātus sit, cum decimā legiōne sōlā ad castra eat. 18. Sī flūmen cum omnibus cōpiīs transīrent, maximō in perīculō essēmus. 19. Omnēs impetūs barbarōrum diūtissimē sustinuērunt. 20. Sī injūriās diūtius tulissētis, nunc servī essētis.

English into Latin.

1. Let him go; boy, go; boys, go. 2. If he had come, he would have seen and conquered. 3. Let us undergo all perils. 4. We will cross the river Rhone with the infantry. 5. If he should come to Rome as often as possible, he would be a wiser man. 6. The conquered do not impose tribute on the conquerors. 7. War has been made on Gaul, and carried on with the Gauls. 8. If any one should go to see the consul, he would receive a gift. 9. This soldier is very like that (one). 10. Peace is very unlike war in all respects (rēs).

* See also **91**, REMARK; **98**, *d.*

LESSON LIX.

ABLATIVE ABSOLUTE.

Learn N. 157, entire. Study carefully the Examples.

Questions and Practice.

What does *absolute* mean? What three uses has the English Independent Case (8, *d*, page 2), with Participles? In what three ways may the Ablative Absolute be expressed? Give the Latin for: *the camp having been fortified, he came to Rome; the soldiers being brave, the enemy were conquered; Caesar being the judge, you will be punished.* How do these sentences (when expressed in Latin) differ from the English? Why? *When* MUST *the Ablative Absolute be used?* [Ans. (REMARK 1.) To express the Perfect Active Participle of any verb, *not* Deponent; as, *having seen, having heard.*] To what is the Ablative Absolute usually equivalent? (REMARK 2.) Translate, in at least three ways: **hostibus victis, castris potīti sumus.**

EXERCISE.

Translate these sentences in as many ways as you can. Remember that the Ablative Absolute can generally be best translated by a clause.

1. Cnēiō Pompēiō et Marcō Crassō consulibus, mortuus est. 2. Obsidibus trāditīs, Caesar in fīnēs Aeduōrum contendit. 3. Nullō hoste prohibente, legiōnem in prōvinciam perduxit. 4. Caesar, locō castrīs idōneō captō, Crassum ad flūmen Rhēnum praemīsit. 5. Hostēs apud oppidum morātī, agrōsque Rēmōrum populātī, omnibus vīcīs aedificiīsque incensīs, ad castra Caesaris contendērunt. 6. Hīs verbīs audītīs, lēgātī sē pācem cum populō Rōmānō nōn confirmātūrōs dixērunt. 7. Praesidiō relictō castrīs, dē tertiā vigiliā mēcum profectus est. 8. Nuntiīs acceptīs, consulēs cuique praemium mājus pollicentur. 9. Prīmā legiōne superātā, impedīmentīsque ab hostibus captīs, aliae legiōnēs fūgērunt. 10. Aeduīs petentibus, victōrēs sē victīs agrōs datūrōs dixērunt. 11. Oppidō captō, castra sub monte pōnit. 12. Imperātor, exercitū trāductō,

ad Genēvam quinque diēs morābitur. 13. Audīverat barbarōs, millia passuum tria nostrōs secūtōs, ab equitibus pulsōs esse. 14. Mīlitibus in ūnum locum convocātīs, ōrātiōnem longam habuistī. 15. Hōc conciliō dīmissō, iīdem principēs, quī ad Caesarem ante (95) vēnerant, sē haec ad suōs relātūrōs dixērunt. 16. Tempore brevissimō, nōn mansimus.

English into Latin.

1. Having seen the city, he went to the camp. 2. Having heard the voice of the general, he fled as quickly as possible. 3. Having promised corn to the legion, he did not give it. 4. Having fortified that place, they sent legates to seek peace. 5. Having set-fire-to the city, the barbarians crossed the Rhone.

Translate these sentences into Latin, as Simple sentences: —

6. When this speech had been heard, all praised the consul. 7. After the city had been freed from the fear of slavery, we all said that Pompey deserved a great reward. 8. When the cities have been destroyed, we shall go home. 9. After the king had been killed, the citizens elected Caius consul.

LESSON LX.

PERIPHRASTIC CONJUGATIONS; DATIVE OF AGENT.

Learn N. 82 (omitting REMARK). Learn the synopsis of the Periphrastic Conjugations (Active and Passive) of **amō**. A. **129**; B. **115**; H. **233, 234**; APP. **39**, *a*, *b*.

Dative of Agent. Learn N. **136**.

Questions and Practice.

What does *Periphrastic* mean? Give the synopsis of the Periphrastic Conjugations, Active and Passive, of **ferō**; **faciō**. How is the *real* agent expressed? What does the Dative of Agent express, that the Ablative does not?

Express, in Latin: *we must carry these burdens.* What name is given to Perfect tenses formed like **dedī, stetī, pepulī**? (79, 6.) Translate: **vereor nē interficiātur; verētur ut veniat** (179, *e*). Explain the meaning of **nē** and **ut** in these sentences. How do **impedīmenta** and **sarcinae** differ in meaning?

EXERCISE.

(*Special Examples, page 267.*)

1. Hīc liber mihi legendus est. 2. Litterās ad frātrem missūrus eram. 3. Quam celerrimē iter vōbīs faciendum erit. 4. Dīcit flūmen sibi transeundum esse. 5. Dē secundā vigiliā Genēvam profectūrī sumus. 6. Equitēs, quī in fīnēs Aeduōrum commeātūs causā īvērunt, exspectandī sunt. 7. Hīs rēbus cognitīs, Caesarem sibi certiōrem faciendum esse dē adventū hostium dīxit. 8. Nonne castra oppugnātūrī fuistis? 9. Utrum hī servī imperātōrī interficiendī an līberandī sunt? 10. Num Rhēnum transitūrī estis? 11. Quid faciendum fuit? 12. Mīlitēs ducī cohortandī erant (**80, REMARK 2**). 13. Existimat, agrīs Rēmōrum vastātīs, Titum, quī oppidum expugnet, cum tertiā legiōne mittendum esse. 14. Helvētiī populō Rōmānō bellum illātūrī sunt. 15. Veritī estis nē hostēs nostrōs vincerent. 16. Quis verētur nē urbs nostra ā cīvibus dēleātur? 17. Dēlenda est Karthāgō. 18. Dixitne sē verērī ut Crassus consul creārētur? 19. Domum itūrus es; domus aedificanda fuit.

•

English into Latin.

1. I am going to follow the fleeing enemy. 2. They intended to find out these things. 3. We were about to carry on war with you. 4. He says that he must make war on the state. 5. We must carry on many wars in Gaul. 6. They will have to march through Italy. 7. Crassus must inform Caesar about these matters (**rēs**). 8. The tenth legion must be sent to get possession of the light-baggage. 9. Were they not going to set fire to all the buildings? 10. Having read the book through (**perlegō**), the boy wrote a letter to his friend about it.

LESSON LXI.

IRREGULAR VERBS: FĪŌ; SUBJUNCTIVE EXPRESSING A WISH.

Learn N. 88 (entire). Learn the Conjugation of FĪŌ. A. 142; B. 131; H. 294; App. 44.

Subjunctive expressing a Wish. Learn N. 176 (entire).

NOTICE: (1) That *compounds* of faciō are formed and conjugated in two different ways (REMARK under N. 88); (2) That a clause containing a *wish* expresses something *impossible* (past or present) or *possible* (future).

The general principles of *Indirect Command* have already been given. Review N. 164, c & REMARK; also learn N. 178 & CAUTION 1.

Questions and Practice.

What are the principal parts of faciō, Active and Passive; also of these compounds (in both Voices): con + faciō; bene + faciō; inter + faciō? Conjugate the Imperative, Active and Passive, of ferō. What verbs form the Second Person Singular, of the Present Imperative Active, like ferō? (79, 5.) Give the Second Person Singular of the Present Imperative and the Future Indicative (both Voices) of faciō and the compounds mentioned in the first question. When must nē the *adverb* be used? (*Ans.* In negative *commands* and *wishes.*) When must nē the *conjunction* be used? (*Ans.* In negative *purposes.*) When must nĕ the *enclitic* be used? What two meanings may fīō have?

EXERCISE.

1. Haec nullō modō fierī possunt. 2. Hī virī consulēs fīent. 3. Cōpiās, Cāī, ēdūc et cum hostibus pugnā. 4. Imperātor fīs; nāvēs fīēbant. 5. Rogāvit ut illa quam prīmum fierent. 6. Nē impetus in hostēs fīat. 7. Utinam consul factus esset! 8. Nē moriāmur; utinam Caesar vīveret! 9. Ferte, servī, haec arma ad rēgem vestrum. 10. Dīc, puer, haec patrī tuō. 11. Sī Gallī Rōmānōs vīcissent, nunc in servitūte tenērēmur. 12. Nē Belgīs bellum īnferant, nē vincantur. 13. Belgās plūrimōs manū minimā victūrī sumus. 14. Nonne Marcus verētur nē barbarī urbe poti-

LATIN LESSONS.   107

antur? 15. Utinam vōs ipsī amīcī Caesaris essētis! 16. Nuntius, quem ducēs praemīserant, nōs certiōrēs fēcit Belgās, omnibus portīs oppidī clausīs, inter sē cohortārī nē arma trāderent.

English into Latin.

1. Let nothing (nē quis) be done without the aid of Caesar. 2. In the consulship of Cicero and Antonius, these men made war upon the state. 3. Bring (afferō) me the books, Antonius, that I may read. 4. Let the messages be carried from Geneva to the camp. 5. Would that they were better citizens! 6. Let us not order the camp to be broken up. 7. He says that this happens very often. 8. Let (there) be (193, 6) light; (there) was light. 9. Go, slave; tell these things to your king. 10. Having overcome the forces of the Gauls, he received the hostages that they had promised.

LESSON LXII.

IRREGULAR VERBS: VOLŌ AND ITS COMPOUNDS. Learn N. 89; 90. Learn the Conjugation of Volō; Nōlō; Mālō. A. 138; B. 130; H. 293; App. 45.

Questions and Practice.

Tell what these forms would be, if volō and its compounds were conjugated like regō: vīs; vult; nōlle; velim; vellet; mālle; volumus; velle; vultis. Of what are mālō and nōlō compounded? Conjugate the Imperative of faciō (Active and Passive); ferō (Active and Passive); cōnficiō (Active and Passive); sum; eō; nōlō.

EXERCISE.

1. Mons, quem Caesar ā Crassō tenērī voluerat, ab hostibus tenēbātur. 2. Ad oppidum redībō; vōs omnēs flūmen transīre vultis. 3. Is regnum, quod pater multōs annōs obtinuerat, occu-

pāre voluit. 4. Vīsne ut mē videās venīre? 5. Dixit sē velle eum rēgem illīus cīvitātis facere. 6. Trēs mīlitēs ferentēs lēgātum suum, quī vulnerātus erat, vīdī. 7. Nonne ex oppidō ēgredī vultis? 8. Tū mē, quī laudārī nōlēbam, laudastī (79, 4). 9. Helvētiī agrōs fīnitimōrum vastāre nōlunt. 10. Caesar sē ab ulteriōre prōvinciā discēdere nōlle dixit. 11. Rēgem bonum ferre nōluistis; nunc pējōrem ferte. 12. Barbarī nōs, quī pugnāre nōlumus, oppugnābunt. 13. Germānī spērābant sē Caesarem ipsum victūrōs esse. 14. Utrum pugnāre an fugere māvīs? 15. Sī signa sequī nōlint, pūniantur. 16. Nōlīte (**178**, 2 & *b*) longius (**40**, *a*) prōcēdere, nē ā barbarīs capiāminī. 17. Sī Rōmae manēre mālit, ignāvus appellētur. 18. Helvētiī, equitātū nostrō rējectō, peditēs flūmen transīre audācissimē cōnantēs repulērunt. 19. Nonne domī esse quam in urbe hostium mālētis? 20. Barbarī omnibus in collibus instructī exercitum ējus itinere prohibēre cōnātī sunt. 21. Num bellum populō (**133**) Rōmānō suō nōmine indixit? 22. Ēgredere, Cāī, ex urbe; līberā rem publicam metū; proficiscere.

English into Latin.

1. Are you not unwilling to advance too far? 2. Let us go back to our friends, whose buildings are in great danger. 3. Were they unwilling to surrender (**trādō**) their arms to you, Caesar? 4. Caesar ascertained that the higher places were held by his men, and that the Gauls had moved their camp. 5. Do you (*plural*) wish to hear the words which I, the consul, speak? 6. The soldiers, returning from that battle, found a certain slave, who had been left near the heavy baggage. 7. Having been made consul, he led his forces across the sea and conquered the general whom all had feared. 8. He drew up two cohorts behind the camp; he sent forward five others, with all the auxiliaries, to storm the town.

LESSON LXIII.

DEFECTIVE VERBS; OBJECTIVE GENITIVE.

Learn N. 91 & 1, 2. Learn the Conjugation of **Coepī**; **Ōdī**; **Meminī**. A. 143 (entire); B. 133; H. 297; App. 46, & Remark 1.
Genitive as Object:
a. *With Nouns and Adjectives.* Learn N. 124.
b. *With Verbs of Remembering and Forgetting.* Learn N. 125.
Study very carefully the Examples under N. **124, 125**.

EXERCISE.

Tell which Genitives denote the Subject, and which the Object, of an Action or Feeling.

1. Hōs cīvēs esse fortēs crēdere incipiunt. 2. Castra Rōmānōrum summā vī oppugnāre coepit. 3. Oppidum aedificārī coeptum est. 4. Omnēs legiōnēs ē castrīs ēgredī coeperant. 5. Caesarem et Rōmānōs ōdit, quod adventū eōrum spēs victōriae sublāta est. 6. Nōs omnēs ōderimus illōs hominēs, quī patriam suam dēlēre cōnantur. 7. Meministīne? nōn meminī. 8. Dixit sē omnēsque cīvēs meminisse. 9. Habētis ducem memorem vestrī (**123**, *b*), oblītum suī. 10. Helvētiī, quod bellandī (**190**) cupidissimī sunt, in fīnēs Gallōrum iter facient. 11. Dīcit Rēmōs rērum novārum cupidiōrēs quam pācis futūrōs esse. 12. Ariovistus sē nōn imperītum rērum esse dixit. 13. Hūjusne reī ignārī fuērunt? 14. Scīmus Helvētiōrum injūriās Gallōrum maximās fuisse. 15. Oblīviscimini, sociī, veterum injūriārum. 16. Ejus timor mortis magnus fuit. 17. Is, Marcō Messālā et Marcō Pīsōne consulibus, rēgnī cupiditāte inductus conjūrātiōnem nōbilitātis fēcit. 18. Dīxērunt mīlitum amōrem bellī magnum esse. 19. Num illīus conjūrātiōnis, quam malī fēcērunt, unquam oblīviscēmur? 20. Dīcit hominēs suae patriae oblītōs consulī pūniendōs (esse). 21. Semper mortis Caesaris meminerō. 22. Nunquam illīus noctis

obliviscar. 23. Reminiscātur veteris incommodī populī Rōmānī. 24. Hanc esse patriam meam atque mē consulem hōrum oblīviscī nōn possum.

LESSON LXIV.

IMPERSONAL VERBS.

Learn N. 92 (entire), 93 & 1, *a, c,* 2. Learn the synopsis of licet and **pugnātur.** A. **145**; B. **138**; H. **298, 299, 301,** 1; APP. **47.** *Study the Examples under* N. **92, 93, 198.** Remember that *every* verb has a subject, which answers the question *Who?* or *What?* Study the special Examples, page 267; the subjects are printed in *italics.* The subject may be an Infinitive Clause (N. **188,** *b,* 1).

Questions and Practice.

What value has *it* in the sentence: *it is wrong to steal?* (**55,** page 15.) What is the actual subject of *is?* Translate: **pugnātur; pugnātum est; pugnandum est; nōbīs mātūrandum est; optimum vīsum est mīlitēs mittere.** What is the gender of **vīsum** and **optimum?** Why? (**109,** *b.*) What case must be used with **licet? oportet?** (**197,** 2.) How do you express *may* and *can?* (**197,** 3.) In what two ways can *must* be expressed? (*Ans.* By the Passive Periphrastic Conjugation and by **oportet.**)

EXERCISE.

These sentences should be analyzed. If the Infinitive, or a Clause, is used as Subject, then it must have a Case. Tell which verbs are Impersonal, and which are USED *impersonally.*

1. Licet nōbīs bellum cum iīs gerere. 2. Licuit iīs nōbīscum bella multa gerere. 3. Oportet mē omnia fortiter ferre. 4. Eum ad mortem dūcī oportuit. 5. Is ad mortem dūcendus fuit. 6. Dīcit sē frūmentō ūtī oportēre. 7. Pugnābātur diū et ācriter ad impedīmenta. 8. Pugnābitur ā septimā hōrā ad occāsum sōlis. 9. Optimum vidētur Marcum ad eum mittere. 10. Dīxistī iter per Galliam facere tibi licēre. 11. Oportet vōs Rhēnum trānsīre;

Rhēnus vōbīs transeundus est. 12. Nōbīs nōn exspectandum (esse) existimātis. 13. Lēgibus bonīs ūtendum est. 14. Mihi contendendum est; Caesarī eundum est. 15. Liceat mihi ex urbe ēgredī. 16. Audīvit mīlitēs flūmen transīre nōn dubitā(vi)sse. 17. Moenia ā nōbīs dēfensa sunt et vōbīs dēfendenda erunt. 18. Consulis sapientis est bonōs circum sē semper habēre. 19. Virōs ut fortēs atque veteris incommodī suī memorēs sint hortātur. 20. Mē certiōrem faciunt apud Helvētiōs longē nōbilissimum et dītissimum Orgetorigem fuisse. 21. (Eum) damnātum poenam sequī oportēbat.

English into Latin.

1. It is very difficult to undergo perils. 2. We must fight as boldly as possible. 3. We must not forget the death of our leader. 4. They had begun to set out from Rome. 5. They ought to have been sent with the cavalry. 6. We may teach the boys (their) letters. 7. He could have marched twenty miles. 8. We must inform the citizens about the revolution.

LESSON LXV.

SUBJUNCTIVE OF RESULT; SUBSTANTIVE CLAUSES.

Subjunctive of Result. Learn N. 181 (entire).
Substantive Clauses. Learn N. 188 & *a, b,* 1, 2 (*b*).

REMEMBER that *any word, clause, or group of words* answering the question WHAT? may be the subject or object of a verb. NOTICE, in the sentences of the Exercise, that a clause may express a *result*, and be, at the same time, the *subject* of a verb. Study carefully the Examples under the NOTES for this Lesson.

Questions and Practice.

What is the *gender* of an Infinitive or a Clause? Why? (*Ans.* Because it is indeclinable.) What is regularly used instead of the Future Infinitive Passive? (181, *a*, REMARK.) Give the principal parts and synopsis (as *Impersonal Verbs*) of accidit, sequitur, fit. Analyze this English sentence: *that he is my friend is true.*

EXERCISE.

Special Examples for this Lesson are given on page 267.

1. Ita ācriter impetus factus est, ut nostrī fugerent. 2. Tantus timor omnēs occupāvit, ut sē flūmen nōn transitūrōs (esse) dīcerent. 3. Vir ējusmodī (121) est, ut eum terrēre nōn possīmus. 4. Nēmō tam multa scripsit, ut plūra scrībere nōlit. 5. Cicerō sīc ab omnibus amātus est, ut consul fieret. 6. Accidit, ut lūna plēna esset. 7. Sequitur, ut ignāvus sīs. 8. Restat, ut dē illō proeliō dīcam. 9. Hīs rēbus fīēbat, ut et minus lātē vagārentur et minus facile fīnitimīs bellum inferre possent. 10. Fēcērunt ut profectiō simillima fugae vidērētur. 11. Dixit fore ut omnēs Helvētiī Rhēnum transīrent. 12. Spērat fore ut hostēs vincantur (*not* hostēs victum īrī). 13. Quis tam ignāvus est, quī sē suaque omnia Ariovistō dēdere velit? 14. Ego nōn is sum, quī mortis perīculō terrērī possim. 15. Imperātor mīlitēs sīc hortātus est, ut ā decimā legiōne ad occāsum sōlis pugnārētur. 16. Nostrī retinērī nōn potuērunt, quīn tēla in hostēs venientēs conjicerent. 17. Nōn est dubium, quīn tōtīus Galliae (122, *b*) plūrimum (142, *c*) possint. 18. Nōn dubitō quīn hīc fortissimus sit. 19. Castra Rēmōrum quam prīmum oppugnāre nōn dubitābimus. 20. Nē faciāmus ut haec urbs ab Helvētiīs dēleātur. 21. Quis vestrum oblītus nostrī (123, *b*) esse potest? 22. Nostrī virtūte maximā, quod (115, *b*) in spē victōriae saepe accidit, pugnāre coepērunt. 23. Oppida sua omnia numerō (153) ad duodecim, vīcōs ad quadringentōs, reliqua aedificia incendunt. 24. Hāc ōrātiōne adductī inter sē fidem et jusjūrandum dant et, regnō occupātō, per trēs potentissimōs populōs imperiō tōtīus Galliae sēsē potīrī posse spērant.

English into Latin.

1. It very often happens that slaves fight more bravely than soldiers. 2. He was so just that he was unwilling to punish you. 3. He says that the towns will not be taken. 4. The enemy are so many in number that we cannot conquer them. 5. His speech was of-such-a-sort that we were all influenced by it. 6. Let us

LATIN LESSONS. 113

always be mindful of praise and glory. 7. They cannot be restrained from following the enemy. 8. He said that there was no doubt that the Belgae were the bravest.

LESSON LXVI.

DATIVE WITH INTRANSITIVE VERBS; INTRANSITIVE VERBS USED IN THE PASSIVE.

Dative with Intransitive Verbs (Advantage or Disadvantage). Learn N. **131** & *a*. For the Dative of Advantage or Disadvantage with Adjectives, see Lesson XXXIV.

Intransitive Verbs used in the Passive. Learn N. **131**, *a*, CAUTION; **134**. Study the Examples under N. **198**.

Historical Present. Learn N. **168**, *b;* **172**, REMARK 2.

Sequence of Tenses. Learn N. **171, 172** (entire). This subject has been partially presented in Lesson XL.

Questions.

What verbs are followed by the Dative of Advantage or Disadvantage? What case follows **imperō? jubeō?** (**197,** 1.) What mode follows **imperō? jubeō?** (**179,** *d.*) Name the Primary tenses of the Indicative; the Secondary tenses. Why is the *Historical Present* so called? Is it a Primary or Secondary tense? What Deponent verbs require the Ablative? (**151,** *a.*) Verbs compounded with what Prepositions require the Dative? (**133.**)

EXERCISE.

The classes of Substantive Clauses employed in this Exercise are described in **188,** *b,* 1, 2.

1. Haec amīcīs nostrīs nocēbunt. 2. Omnia nōn omnibus placent. 3. Hī imperātōrī nōn pāritūrī erant. 4. Verēbāmur nē cīvēs Ariovistō rēgī Germānōrum servīrent. 5. Mihi crēdite, sociī; hostēs vōbīs nōn resistent. 6. Lēgātī Caesarem Rēmīs ignōvisse et eōs nōn pūnīvisse dixērunt. 7. Per eōs, nē causam dīceret, sē

ēripuit. 8. Cōpiīs, quās sēcum habuit, ut in fīnēs Sēquanōrum iter facerent, imperāvit. 9. Dīcit sē obsidēs Aeduīs ā Rēmīs darī jussisse. 10. Sciunt fore ut dē tertiā vigiliā castra moveantur. 11. Crēdidērunt Cāium ipsum imperātōrem creārī oportuisse. 12. Sī haec ita essent, tēcum īre nōllem. 13. Helvētiī lēgātōs ad eum mittunt, quī pācem peterent. 14. Dum haec geruntur, imperātor cōpiās suās flūmen (**141,** *c*) transdūcēbat. 15. Cīvitātī persuāsit, ut dē fīnibus suīs cum omnibus cōpiīs exīrent (**117,** *c*). 16. Nōn est dubium quīn urbem expugnātūrī sint. 17. Nāvibus nocērī nōn poterat. 18. Vōbīs lēgibus pārendum esse intelligitis. 19. Nōbīs hostibus resistendum est. 20. Mihi persuādētur; dīcit sibi persuāsum esse. 21. Legiōnibus ā Caesare imperātum est.

English into Latin.

1. The slaves were ordered (**jubeō**) to go. 2. The soldiers are ordered (**imperō**) to march. 3. The states are persuaded to go. 4. The consul is not believed. 5. The cavalry will be resisted. 6. They say that they have obeyed the general. 7. These men ought to be resisted. 8. We shall persuade the troops to go (**179,** *d*) home. 9. The city cannot be harmed.

LESSON LXVII.

DATIVE OF POSSESSOR; TWO DATIVES; SEMI-DEPONENT VERBS.

Dative denoting the Possessor. Learn N. **135.** This use is sometimes seen in English; as, "*To him* that overcometh, a crown of life *shall be.*"

Two Datives. Learn N. **137.**

Semi-Deponent Verbs. Learn N. **81.**

NOTICE that both the Dative of *Possessor* and the Dative of the *Person* (two Datives) are Datives of Advantage (or Disadvantage).

LATIN LESSONS.

Questions and Practice.

Give the principal parts of audeō, fīdō, gaudeō, soleō. Give the synopsis of audeō. What is the meaning of *Deponent*? *Semi-Deponent*? When *must* the Ablative Absolute be used? Can Intransitive verbs be used in the Passive? Translate: **Caesarī persuādērī nōn potest; ducī ab omnibus pārētur.**

EXERCISE.

1. Virō quinque equī sunt. 2. Ducī maximus mīlitum numerus fuit. 3. Dīcit sibi in animō esse per prōvinciam iter facere. 4. Utrum hīs cīvibus virtūs est, annōn? 5. Mihi spēs magna fuit. 6. Illīs oppida numerō (153) circiter (*or* ad) vīgintī sunt. 7. Certiōrēs factī sunt permultōs servōs Germānīs esse. 8. Mīlitēs legiōnum duārum, quae in' novissimō agmine praesidiō impedīmentīs fuerant,* proeliō nuntiātō, cursū incitātō, in summō colle ab hostibus conspiciēbantur. 9. Decimam legiōnem subsidiō nostrīs (*or* urbī, nōbīs, castrīs) mīserat. 10. Caesar ab secundā legiōne ad dextrum cornū profectus, suōs urgērī signīsque in ūnum locum collātīs † duodecimae legiōnis confertōs mīlitēs sibi esse impedīmentō vīdit. 11. Hīs difficultātibus duae rēs erant subsidiō. 12. Partem suārum cōpiārum transdūcere cōnātī sunt, eō consiliō, ut castellum, cuī pracerat Quintus Titurius lēgātus, expugnārent. 13. Veritī sumus nē agrōs Rēmōrum populārentur, quī magnō nōbīs ūsuī erant, commeātūque nostrōs prohibērent. 14. Illī, ut (**197**, 5) erat imperātum, ēductīs quattuor cohortibus, quae praesidiō castrīs relictae erant, et longiōre itinere (**159**, REMARK 3) circumductīs, nē ex hostium castrīs conspicī possent, omnium oculīs mentibusque ad pugnam intentīs,† celeriter ad eās, quās dīximus, mūnītiōnēs pervēnērunt. 15. Caesar haec sibi cūrae esse dixit. 16. Audīverat hōs flūmen lātissimum transīre ausōs esse. 17. Verētur ut exercitus dictō audiēns futūrus sit (**82**, REMARK). 18. Num in hunc locum venīre audēs? 19. Aestāte rūs īre solet. 20. Nonne Ariovistus Galliae bellum inferre audēbit?

* **Esse**, with two Datives, is usually best translated *to serve* (*as*).
† **157**, REM. 2.

LESSON LXVIII.

ABLATIVE WITH COMPARATIVES; ABLATIVE DENOTING MEASURE OF DIFFERENCE.

Ablative with Comparatives (**Quam** omitted).* Learn N. 154.

Ablative denoting the Measure (or *Degree*) *of Difference.* Learn N. 155 (entire). This may express: —
a. *Difference in Length, Height, Width, etc.*
b. *Difference in Time.*
c. *Difference in Distance.*
d. *Various ideas of Difference in Amount or Degree.*

All these forms have equivalents in the use of the English Objective Case; as, *a.* He is *a head* taller; *b.* He has lived here *two years* longer than I; *c.* We are *three miles* distant from home; *d.* He is *a great deal* richer.

REMARK. **Longē,** *by far* (really an old Ablative), expresses Degree of Difference.

EXERCISE.

1. Omnia consilia tua nōbīs clāriōra lūce sunt. 2. Nēmō Rōmae Crassō fuit dītior. 3. Quis nōbilior Caesare esse potest? 4. Dixit Rhēnum altiōrem Rhodanō esse. 5. Castra amplius millibus passuum octo in lātitūdinem patēbant. 6. Hiems longior aestāte erit. 7. Patria mihi multō cārior vītā meā est. 8. Hīc puer bienniō mājor est quam illa puella. 9. Castra ā Rōmā millibus passuum quinque aberant. 10. Aliud aedificium suprā pontem spàtiō aequō est. 11. Flūmen trīgintā millibus passuum infrā eum locum fuit. 12. Annum longiōrem duōbus mensibus fēcērunt. 13. In senātum paulō ante vēnistī. 14. Mīles, dē quō paulō ante diximus, vir longē fortissimus fuit in exercitū. 15. Eō opere per-

---

* Of course, if **quam** is *expressed*, the noun or pronoun after it will be in the same case as that preceding; as, **Caesar fortior est quam Pompēius** (est).

fectō, castella commūnit, quō (179, b) facilius eōs, sē invītō, transīre cōnantēs prohibēre possit. 16. Lēgem brevem esse oportet, quō facilius intelligātur. 17. Dixit exercitum dictō audientem nōn fore. 18. Portīs (159, REMARK 3) omnibus ēruptiōnem faciunt. 19. Relinquēbātur ūna per Sēquanōs via, quā, Sēquanīs invītīs, propter angustiās īre nōn poterant. 20. Quantō (155, b) gravior oppugnātiō fuit, tantō crēbriōrēs nuntiī ad Caesarem mittēbantur. 21. Post ējus mortem nihilō minus Helvētiī id, quod constituerant, facere cōnantur, ut ē fīnibus suīs excant (181, e). 22. Erant omnīnō itinera duo, quibus itineribus domō exīre possent (181, c): ūnum per Sēquanōs, angustum et difficile, inter montem Jūram et flūmen Rhodanum, vix quā (94, 2) singulī (41, a) carrī dūcerentur; mons autem altissimus impendēbat, ut facile perpaucī (eōs) prohibēre possent: alterum per prōvinciam nostram, multō facilius atque expedītius, proptereā quod inter fīnēs Helvētiōrum et Allobrogum Rhodanus fluit, isque nonnullīs (195, 1) locīs vadō transītur.

English into Latin.

1. The tower is ten feet higher than the wall. 2. The boy is a whole head taller than his father. 3. Did the messenger come a little while ago? 4. This temple is much wider than that. 5. They are twenty miles from the camp. 6. Friends, be brave, that you may the more easily encounter dangers. 7. He commands (**imperō**) me to go to Bibracte. 8. The consul is much wiser than the judge.

LESSON LXIX.

CAUSAL CLAUSES.

Clauses expressing a Cause. Learn N. 182, a, b, c.
The Relative Pronoun used for a Demonstrative. Learn N. 115, d.

EXERCISE.

1. Dumnorix grātiā apud Sēquanōs plūrimum poterat, et Helvētiīs erat amīcus, quod ex eā cīvitāte Orgetorigis fīliam in mātrimōnium duxerat; et cupiditāte regnī adductus novīs rēbus (131, a) studēbat, et quam plūrimās cīvitātēs suō sibi beneficiō habēre obstrictās volēbat. 2. Quae quum ita sint, domum contendēmus. 3. Quō factō, quum alius aliī (195, 9) subsidium ferrent, neque timērent nē ab hostibus circumvenīrentur, audācius resistere ac fortius pugnāre coepērunt. 4. Quibus rēbus cognitīs, Caesar trēs cohortēs, quae Rōmā vēnerant, subsidiō legiōnī praemīsit. 5. In prīmam aciem prōcessit centuriōnibusque nōminātim appellātīs, reliquōs cohortātus mīlitēs, signa inferre et manipulōs laxāre jussit, quō facilius gladiīs ūtī possent. Cūjus adventū spē illātā mīlitibus, quum quisque in conspectū imperātōris etiam in extrēmīs suīs rēbus* quam fortissimē pugnāre cuperet, paulum hostium impetus tardātus est. 6. Quum tē fortiōrem Titō esse dīcās, cōpiās tuās ēdūc et impetum in hostēs fac. 7. Condemnātus est, quī amīcum suum interfēcerit. 8. Magnam Caesar injūriam facit, quum lībertātem nostram ēripiat. 9. Equitātuī (133), quem auxiliō (137) Caesarī Aeduī mīserant, Dumnorix praeerat. 10. Diūtius quum nostrōrum impetūs sustinēre nōn possent, alterī (195, 8) sē, ut (197, 5) coeperant, in montem recēpērunt, alterī ad impedīmenta et carrōs suōs sē contulērunt. Ad multam noctem pugnātum est, proptereā quod prō vallō carrōs objēcerant, et ē locō superiōre in nostrōs venientēs tēla conjiciēbant. 11. Ex eō proeliō circiter millia hominum centum et trīgintā superfuērunt, eāque tōtā nocte continenter iērunt; nullam partem noctis itinere (157) intermissō in fīnēs Lingonum diē quartō pervēnērunt, quum propter vulnera mīlitum nostrī trīduum morātī eōs sequī nōn potuissent.

* Equivalent to in extrēmō suō perīculō.

LATIN LESSONS. 119

LESSON LXX.

USES OF THE ABLATIVE CASE.

Ablative denoting Quality. Learn N. 152.
When should the Genitive of Quality be used ? (N. 152, a.)
Ablative with Adjectives:
a. *With* Frētus, Contentus (denoting *Means*). Learn N. 151, b.
b. *With* Dignus, Indignus. Learn N. 156.
Ablative denoting Price. Learn N. 151, c.

EXERCISE.

1. Germānōs corporum ingentī magnitūdine esse dixērunt. 2. Audīverat turrēs magnā altitūdine esse. 3. Quod cīvitās erat magnā inter Belgās auctōritāte atque hominum multitūdine praestābat, sexcentōs obsidēs poposcit. 4. Iter quinque diērum fēcit, et ad flūmen pervēnit. Ejus flūminis altitūdō quindecim pedum erat. 5. Dīcit frātrem suum magnā vī et animī et corporis fuisse. 6. Frētī diīs immortālibus audācissimē resistēbant. 7. Puer dōnīs, quae dedistī, contentus erit. 8. Pugnātum est diū atque ācriter, quum hostēs superiōribus victōriīs frētī in suā virtūte tōtīus Aquītāniae salūtem positam putārent (182, b). 9. Hīc praemiō, quod tē datūrum (esse) dixistī, dignus fuit. 10. Consul tantō honōre indignus est. 11. Num iī, quī urbem servāre nōluērunt, amīcitiā nostrā dignī sunt? 12. Putat sē librum vīgintī sestertiīs venditūrum esse. 13. Nonne mihi domum tuam parvō pretiō vendere vīs? 14. Hī omnēs intelligunt Germānōs ā Sēquanīs mercēde arcessītōs esse. 15. Rē frūmentāriā quam celerrimē potuit comparātā, magnīs itineribus ad Ariovistum contendit. 16. Hīs rēbus cognitīs, Caesar Gallōrum animōs verbīs confirmāvit, pollicitusque est sibi (137) eam rem cūrae futūram (esse). Dixit magnam sē habēre spem (= spērāre) et beneficiō suō et auctōritāte adductum Ariovistum fīnem injūriīs factūrum (esse).

English into Latin.

1. Let us sell these houses at a very large price. 2. He will sell that book for fifty cents (ten sestertii). 3. Was he unwilling to fight for pay? 4. If they had been worthy of praise, we should have praised them. 5. A mountain of great height occupies (contineŏ) that place. 6. He will not go to the city, since he prefers to remain at home. 7. Ariovistus did not dare to come into Gaul, because Caesar was in the province with his army. 8. Men of unfriendly disposition (animus) cannot march through our territory.

LESSON LXXI.

CONCESSIVE CLAUSES; HISTORICAL INFINITIVE.

Clauses denoting Concession. Learn N. **183** & *a*, CAUTION, *b*.

Historical Infinitive. Learn N. **167**.

NOTICE that **tamen** (*yet*) is very often used as a *Correlative* (N. **195**, 8) to a Conjunction meaning *although*.

Questions.

What does the word *concession* mean? When must the Subjunctive be used with **etsi** and **tametsi**? What four uses may **qui** have with the Subjunctive? (N. **197**, 6.) Why is the *Historical* Infinitive so called? What is peculiar about its use? What are the chief uses of the Infinitive? (*Ans.* 1.) As a *Verbal Noun.* (2.) As a *Complement.* (3.) With a *Subject Accusative.* (4.) With a *Subject Nominative* (*Historical*). How may **quum** be spelled?

EXERCISE.

1. Quum Crassus imperātor creātus esset, tamen mīlitēs eum sequī nōlēbant. 2. Quum ad multam noctem pugnētur, nostrī nōn fugient. 3. Etsī mihi inimīcus esset (**175**, *a*, 2), eum nōn ōdissem. 4. Quae (**115**, *d*) tametsī Caesar intelligēbat, tamen proe-

lium sibi (136) committendum nōn existimāvit. 5. Quum ea ita sint, tamen, sī obsidēs ab iīs mihi dabuntur, et sī Aeduīs (131, a) dē injūriīs, quās ipsīs (= Aeduīs) sociīsque eōrum intulērunt, item sī Allobrogibus satisfacient, cum iīs pācem faciam. 6. Lēgātum, quī nihil morte (156) dignum fēcisset (183, b), interfēcērunt. 7. Quum mūrus dēfensōribus nūdātus sit, hostēs nōbīs sē dēdere nōlunt. 8. Servum graviter accūsat, quī (182, c) litterās nōn mīserit. 9. Septem cohortēs, quae nōbīs (137) subsidiō essent (180), mīsit. 10. Nēmō est (ējus modī), quī prō patriā (129, b) suā morī nōlit. 11. Caesar Aeduōs frūmentum flāgitāre. Diem ex diē Aeduī (eum) dūcere; frūmentum conferrī, comportārī, adesse dīcere. 12. Persuādent fīnitimīs, utī, cōdem ūsī consiliō (151, a), oppidīs vīcisque exustīs, ūnā (94, 2) sēcum proficiscantur.

English into Latin.

1. Although we are citizens, we are not free. 2. Although (etsī) the soldiers were ordered (jubeō) to advance, yet they did not obey. 3. Although we should have given-satisfaction-to (satisfied) the Remi, yet they would not make peace with us. 4. Let us accuse them severely, since they have said that they are not Romans. 5. We will burn our towns, about fifteen in number, lest the Gauls capture them.

LESSON LXXII.

TEMPORAL CLAUSES.

Clauses denoting Time. Learn N. 184 (entire).

Questions.

When does quum (cum), *when*, take the Subjunctive? Which of these are correct: quum fuī; quum eram; quum fuerō; quum amābam; quum monueram? What may dum mean? (N. 184, b; 183, d.) When do antequam and priusquam require the Subjunctive? What meanings may quum have? What mode is used with most of the particles of time? Express in two ways, *a thousand men* (43, e).

EXERCISE.

1. Quum esset Caesar in citeriōre Galliā in hībernīs, ita utī suprā diximus (**197**, 5 ; **111**, *a*), crēbrī ad eum nuntiī afferēbantur litterīsque Labiēnī certior fīēbat, omnēs Belgās (**199**, 3) contrā populum Rōmānum conjūrāre obsidēsque inter sē (**112**, *b*) dare: conjūrandī (**190**) causās multās esse.   2. Ubi neutrī transeundī (**190**) initium faciunt (**168**, *b*), Caesar suōs in castra reduxit.   3. Quī (**115**, *d*) quum sē suaque omnia in oppidum contulissent atque ab eō oppidō Caesar cum exercitū millibus passuum quinque abesset, omnēs mājōrēs nātū (**36**, *b ;* **153**) ex oppidō ēgressī sēsē in ējus fidem venīre dixērunt.   4. Eōdem tempore equitēs nostrī peditēsque, quī cum iīs fuerant, quōs prīmō hostium impetū pulsōs (esse) dixeram, quum sē in castra reciperent adversīs hostibus (**133**) occurrēbant ac rursus aliam in partem fugam petēbant ; et servī, quī ab summō jugō collis nostrōs victōrēs flūmen transīsse conspexerant, praedandī (**190**) causā profectī, quum respexissent et hostēs in nostrīs castrīs versārī vīdissent, fūgērunt.   5. Dum reliquae nāvēs convenīrent, exspectāvit.   6. Dum paucōs diēs ad Vesontiōnem reī frūmentāriae commeātūsque causā morātur (**184**, *b*, REMARK), iīdem principēs cīvitātum revertērunt petiēruntque utī sibi (**134**, REMARK) dē suā omniumque salūte cum eō agere licēret.   7. Dum haec faciant (**183**, *d*), urbem nōn expugnābimus.   8. Nē ējus suppliciō Divitiacī animum offenderet, verēbātur.   Itaque priusquam quidquam cōnārētur, Divitiacum ad sē vocārī jubet.   9. Quod (**115**, *d*) postquam barbarī fierī animadvertērunt, ad flūmen contendērunt.   10. Priusquam perīculum faceret, idōneum esse arbitrātus Cāium cum nāvī longā praemittit.   11. Quibus rēbus adductus nōn sibi (**136**) exspectandum (**199**, 2) existimāvit, dum in Santonōs Helvētiī pervenīrent.

English into Latin.

1. When the work had been finished (**perficiō**), he ordered two legions to follow him.   2. They waited until the troops should arrive.   3. When he comes (**168**, *a*), we will inform him concern-

ing these facts. 4. When this battle had been announced across the Rhine, the Remi sent legates to ask (180) aid. 5. As soon as (= after) Caesar arrived at the camp, he ordered a much higher rampart to be made. 6. When the camp had been fortified, the enemy began to return home. 7. When Caesar was setting-out into Italy, he sent Crassus with the twelfth legion and a part of the cavalry into-the-country-of (into) the Verăgri and Sedūni, who extend from the territory of the Allobroges and Lake Geneva (Lemannus) and the river Rhone to the Alps.

LESSON LXXIII.

GERUND AND GERUNDIVE.

Gerund. Learn N. 190.
Gerundive. Learn N. 189, *f*; 190, *a*.

REMARK. The Gerund has already been employed in these Lessons; so, also, has the Infinitive (as a verbal noun in the Nominative Case). The use of both is very easily understood, being like that of any *neuter* noun. The use of the Gerundive (for the Gerund) must be studied with special care (N. 190, *a*). *Study the Examples under the* NOTE. Notice that **ad**, with the Accusative of the Gerund or Gerundive, implies a *purpose*.

Questions and Practice.

What is used as the Nominative of the Gerund? What two common uses has the Gerundive? When should it be used instead of the Gerund? Give the rule for determining the form of the Noun and of the Gerundive. Give the Latin for: *the hope of seeing the soldiers; the opportunity* (**facultăs**) *for* (*of*) *leaving this place is not given.*

EXERCISE.

1. Nōs omnēs magistrum docendō sē docēre scīmus. 2. Hīs rēbus adductī et auctōritāte Orgetorigis permōtī, constituērunt ea, quae ad proficiscendum pertinērent (**181**, *c*), comparāre atque cum proximīs cīvitātibus pācem et amīcitiam confirmāre. 3. Proximō

diē Caesar ē castrīs utrisque cōpiās suās ēduxit, paulumque ā mājōribus castrīs prōgressus aciem instruxit hostibusque pugnandī potestātem fēcit. 4. Ita nostrī ācriter in hostēs signō (**157**) datō impetum fēcērunt, itaque (**195**, 5) hostēs celeriter prōcurrērunt, ut spatium pīla in hostēs conjiciendī nōn darētur. 5. Quum fīnem oppugnandī nox fēcisset, Iccius Rēmus (**106**), summā nōbilitāte (**152**) et grātiā inter suōs, quī oppidō praefuerat, ūnus ex hīs (**123**, *a*) quī lēgātī (**106**) dē pāce ad Caesarem vēnerant, nuntium ad eum mittit. 6. Causa mittendī fuit, quod iter per Alpēs, quō (**159**, REMARK 3) magnō cum perīculō mercātōrēs īre consuērant (**91**, 2, REMARK), patefierī volēbat. 7. Dixit perfacile (**109**, *b*) esse, quum virtūte omnibus (**133**) praestārent, tōtīus Galliae imperiō (**151**, *a*) potīrī. Id hōc (**149**) facilius eīs persuāsit, quod undique locī nātūrā Helvētiī continentur. 8. Frūmentum omne, praeterquam quod sēcum portātūrī erant, combūrunt, ut, domum reditiōnis spē (**157**) sublātā, parātiōrēs ad omnia perīcula subeunda essent. 9. Ubi nostrōs nōn esse virtūte inferiōrēs intellexit, locō (**157** (2)) prō castrīs ad aciem instruendam nātūrā (**149**) idōneō, duābus legiōnibus in castrīs relictīs, ut subsidiō (**137**, REMARK) dūcī possent, proeliī committendī signum dedit. 10. Ariovistus dīcit nōn sēsē Gallīs (**133**), sed Gallōs sibi bellum intulisse; omnēs Galliae cīvitātēs ad sē oppugnandum vēnisse. 11. Utrum suī mūniendī, an Galliae occupandae causā multitūdinem Germānōrum in Galliam transduxit? 12. Aliī aliam in partem (**195**, 9) perterritī ferēbantur.

English into Latin.

1. They gave the enemy no opportunity for (of) leaving the towns. 2. We have come for the purpose (**causa**) of storming your cities. 3. He thinks that time (**spatium**) ought not to be given to the enemy for (**ad**) adopting (**capiō**) plans. 4. While he delays in these places for the sake of securing (**parō**) ships, legates came to him from a large part of the Sequani, to say (**180**) that they wished to make peace with him. 5. We will not give the Remi an opportunity for (of) marching through our province. 6. Are the Helvetii desirous of carrying on wars with us?

LATIN LESSONS. 125

LESSON LXXIV.

SUPINE.

Supine. Learn N. **191** (entire).
How a Purpose may be expressed. Learn N. **180**.
Study N. **180** with great care, and apply it to the sentences of this Lesson.

EXERCISE.

1. Helvētiī agrōs Aeduōrum populābantur. Aeduī, quum sē suaque ab iīs dēfendere nōn possent, lēgātōs ad Caesarem mittunt rogātum auxilium. 2. Ob eam rem ex cīvitāte prōfūgit et Rōmam ad senātum vēnit auxilium postulātum, quod sōlus neque jūrejūrandō neque obsidibus tenēbātur. 3. Bellō Helvētiōrum confectō, tōtīus ferē Galliae lēgātī, principēs cīvitātum, ad Caesarem grātulātum convēnērunt. 4. Perfacile factū est haec cōnāta perficere, proptereā quod ipse suae cīvitātis imperium obtentūrus est. 5. Dixit sē pācem petītum vēnisse. 6. Sī hōc optimum factū fuisset (**175**, *b*, 2), eum interfēcissem. 7. Dumnorigī Aeduō, quī eō tempore principātum obtinēbat ac maximē plēbī (**131**, *b*) acceptus erat, ut idem cōnārētur (**172**, REMARK 2), persuādet, eīque fīliam suam in mātrimōnium dat. 8. Itaque rem suscipit, obsidēsque utī inter sēsē dent (**181**, *b*) perficit : Sēquanī,* nē itinere Helvētiōs prohibeant; Helvētiī,* ut sine maleficiō et injūriā transeant.

English into Latin.

Express these sentences in as many ways as possible, according to N. **180**.

1. He says that the troops of the Sequani have come to attack him. 2. We will send three legions to storm the winter-quarters of Ariovistus. 3. If he had come to see me, when I was at Rome,

---

* *Supply* obsidēs dent.

126 LATIN LESSONS.

I should have sent him to you. 4. Let us go to the city to see the king. 5. To cross the Rhine will be (a thing) very difficult to do. 6. Is this the best thing to do, or not? 7. If these things should be announced to our general, he would order (imperō) us (131, a) to (179, d) march two miles to attack the smaller camp. 8. Who were those men that sent you to congratulate me?

LESSON LXXV.

INDIRECT DISCOURSE: QUESTIONS.

An Indirect Quotation (N. **186**) may contain: —

(1) An *Indirect Statement* (Declaratory); (2) An *Indirect Question* (Interrogative); (3) An *Indirect Command* (Imperative). The Indirect Statement is described in N. **166**, and many examples of its use have been employed in the Exercises; as, **dux sēsē fortem esse dīcit.** ("Fortis sum" would be the *Direct Statement*.)

Indirect Statements. Review N. **166**.
Direct Questions. Review N. **101**.
Indirect Questions. Learn N. **177**, *b, c, d.* • An INDIRECT QUESTION may follow: —

(1) A Verb of *asking;* as, **rogābō quis sit,** *I will ask who he is.* (2) Any word that *hints* a question; as, **incertum est quid factūrus sit,** *it is uncertain* (= *I wonder*) *what he is going to do.* The Subjunctive mode (**īvisset**) would be required in the following: *I asked (wondered, found out, was uncertain, saw, understood, judged) whither he had gone.*

EXERCISE.

Notice the Sequence of Tenses (**172**).

1. Rogāvit utrum pugnātūrus esset, necne. Rogat num itūrus sim. 2. Utrum mē vīsum (**191**, *a*) vēnistī, annōn? 3. Quam in partem hostēs fūgērunt? 4. Vidēbō quam in partem Ariovistus iter fēcerit. 5. Quid factūrī sunt? 6. Nōbīs nōn constā-

bat (**93**, 1, *c*) quid dictūrus esset. 7. Utram (**195**, 7) in partem Arar fluit? 8. Arar (**3**) per fīnēs Aeduōrum et Sēquanōrum in Rhodanum influit incrēdibilī lēnitāte, ita ut oculīs, in utram partem fluat, jūdicārī nōn possit. 9. Hīs (**131**, *a*) imperāvit, ut, quae dīceret Ariovistus, cognōscerent et ad sē referrent. 10. Quod jussī sunt, faciunt; ac omnibus portīs (**159**, REMARK 3) ēruptiōne factā (**157**), cognōscendī quid fieret hostibus facultātem nōn relinquunt. 11. Prīmā lūce, duplicī aciē instructā, auxiliīs in mediam aciem conjectīs, quid hostēs consiliī (**122**, *a*) captūrī essent, exspectābat. 12. Dumnorigem ad sē vocat; quae in eō reprehendat, quae ipse intelligat, quae cīvitās querātur, ostendit; monet, ut in (*for*) reliquum tempus omnēs suspiciōnēs vītet. Dumnorigī custōdēs pōnit, ut, quae agat, quibuscum loquātur, scīre possit. 13. Quum incertus essem, ubi essēs, īre nōn audēbam. 14. Incertum est, utrum dux an mīles Cāius esse mālit. 15. Num Gallia est omnis dīvīsa in partēs quattuor? 16. Num Caesar Pompēiō (**154**) fortior esset, rogāvit. 17. Quum ab hīs quaereret, quae cīvitātēs quantaeque in armīs essent et quid (**142**, *c*) in bellō possent, sīc reperiēbat: plērōsque Belgās esse ortōs ab Germānīs.

English into Latin.

1. What-sort-of (**quālis**) a man is Marcus? I asked what-sort-of a house he had sold. 2. We will send-ahead the bravest soldiers to see in what direction the Remi have marched. 3. It was uncertain whether he had killed the slave, or not. 4. He asks whether we are at home. 5. Can Caesar ascertain whose forces have been conquered? 6. Tell me, my friend, whether this road (**via**) is very long, or not. 7. He says (**199**, 5) that they cannot judge how brave those men are.

LESSON LXXVI.

INDIRECT DISCOURSE (*continued*).

Imperative Sentences. Learn N. **187,** *c.*
General Laws of Modes and Tenses. Learn N. **187** & *a*, *l, c, d.*
Translate the Latin of the Example under N. **187,** *e* (both *Direct* and *Indirect*), as far as **voluisset.** Notice carefully ˜the changes in Mode and Tense. The *Indirect* form of the same extract is given in the Exercise below (sentence 4).

Questions.

What are the laws of modes and tenses in Indirect Discourse ? When will the verb of a Subordinate Clause be in the Subjunctive in *Direct* Discourse ? How is the *tense* of a verb in a Subordinate Clause decided ? What mode is used to express: a *Direct Statement ?* an *Indirect Command ?* an *Indirect Statement ?* a *Direct Question ?* a *Direct Command ?* an *Indirect Question ?*

EXERCISE.

Tell what form each verb would have, if it were in a Direct Quotation.

1. Dixit diem (= tempus) sē ad dēlīberandum sumptūrum (**199,** 2) ; sī quid vellent, reverterentur (**187,** *c*). 2. Hīs lēgātīs Caesar ita respondet : Quum ea ita sint (**183,** *a ;* **187**), tamen, sī obsidēs ab iīs sibi dentur, utī ea, quae polliceantur, (eōs) factūrōs intelligat, et sī Aeduīs dē injūriīs, quās ipsīs (= Aeduīs) sociīsque eōrum intulerint, item sī Allobrogibus satisfaciant, sēsē cum iīs pācem esse factūrum. Dīvicō respondet : Ita Helvētiōs ā mājōribus suīs īnstitūtōs esse, utī obsidēs accipere, nōn dare, consuērint (**79,** 4 ; **91,** 2, REMARK) ; ējus reī populum Rōmānum esse testem. Hōc respōnsō datō discessit. 3. Ad haec Ariovistus respondit : Jūs esse bellī, ut, quī vīcissent, iīs (**197,** 1), quōs vīcissent, quemadmodum vellent, imperārent : item populum Rōmānum victīs nōn ad alterius praescrīptum, sed ad suum arbitrium imperāre

consuesse. Sī ipse populō Rōmānō nōn praescrīberet, quemadmodum suō jūre ūterētur, nōn oportēre sēsē ā populō Rōmānō in suō jūre impedīrī. Aeduīs sē obsidēs redditūrum nōn esse, neque iīs neque eōrum sociīs injūriā bellum illātūrum, sī stīpendium penderent. Quum Caesar vellet, congrederētur (**187,** *c*); (eum) intellectūrum, quid (**142,** *c*) Germānī virtūte possent. 4. Is ita cum Caesare agit (**168,** *b*) : Sī pācem populus Rōmānus cum Helvētiīs faceret, in eam partem itūrōs (**199,** 2) atque ibi futūrōs Helvētiōs, ubi eōs Caesar constituisset atque esse voluisset.

LESSON LXXVII.

INDIRECT DISCOURSE : GENERAL PRACTICE.

Tell what form each verb would have, if it were in a Direct Quotation.

Eō conciliō dīmissō, iīdem principēs cīvitātum revertērunt petiēruntque, utī sibi (**134,** REMARK) dē suā omniumque salūte cum eō agere licēret. Eā rē impetrātā, sēsē omnēs flentēs Caesarī (**138**) ad pedēs prōjēcērunt. Locūtus est prō hīs Divitiacus Aeduus : Galliae tōtīus factiōnēs esse duās : hārum alterius prīn- 5 cipātum tenēre Aeduōs, alterius Arvernōs. Hī quum dē potentātū inter sē multōs annōs contenderent, factum esse, utī ab Arvernīs Sēquanīsque Germānī mercēde arcesserentur (**181,** *a*). Hōrum prīmō circiter millia quindecim Rhēnum trānsisse : posteāquam agrōs et cultum et cōpiās Gallōrum hominēs ferī ac barbarī ada- 10 massent (**79,** 4), trāductōs (**199,** 2) plūrēs; nunc esse in Galliā ad centum et vīgintī millium numerum. Cum hīs Aeduōs eōrumque clientēs armīs contendisse; magnam calamitātem pulsōs accēpisse, omnem nōbilitātem, omnem senātum, omnem equitātum āmīsisse. Quibus (**115,** *d*) proeliīs calamitātibusque fractōs, (eōs) quī et suā 15 virtūte et populī Rōmānī amīcitiā plūrimum ante in Galliā potuissent, coāctōs esse Sēquanīs obsidēs dare nōbilissimōs cīvitātis et

jūrejūrandō cīvitātem obstringere, sēsē neque obsidēs repetītūrōs (**199, 2**) neque auxilium ā populō Rōmānō implōrātūrōs. Ūnum sē esse ex omnī cīvitāte Acduōrum, quī addūcī nōn potuerit, ut jūrāret aut līberōs suōs obsidēs daret. Ob eam rem sē ex cīvitāte prōfūgisse
5 et Rōmam ad senātum vēnisse auxilium postulātum (**191**, *a*), quod sōlus neque jūrejūrandō neque obsidibus tenērētur. Sed pējus (**109**) victōribus Sēquanīs quam Aeduīs victīs accidisse, **Sequanis** propterea quod *Ariovistus, rex Germānōrum, in eōrum fīnibus consēdisset tertiamque partem agrī Sēquanī, quī esset optimus tōtīus Galliae,
10 occupāvisset et nunc dē alterā parte tertiā Sēquanōs dēcēdere jubēret, proptereā quod paucīs mensibus (**155**, *a*) ante Harūdum millia hominum vīgintī quattuor ad eum vēnissent, quibus locus ac sēdēs parārentur. Futūrum esse (**181**, *a*, REMARK) paucīs annīs, utī omnēs (Gallī) ex Galliae fīnibus pellerentur atque omnēs Germānī
15 Rhēnum transīrent.

LESSON LXXVIII.

INDIRECT DISCOURSE: GENERAL PRACTICE.

English into Latin.

1. I asked him whether he wished to go with me, since I had invited him, or to remain in the place which he had chosen. 2. They said that they thought that the Veneti were accustomed to use all the seas which were in-the-vicinity-of Gaul. 3. The king replied that he had crossed the Rhine (because he had been) invited by the Gauls, and that Caesar, alarmed by the messages which he had received, had enlisted two new legions, and had come to attack (**180**) him. 4. It was said that we had conspired among ourselves, (saying) that we would make war on the states (**133**). 5. They said that a beginning of war had been made by those, concerning whom the general had been informed, because they were unwilling to give hostages. 6. I shall ask whether he has promised to give

back (that he will give back) the hostages that we have sent. 7. Lucilius used-to-say that he wished those things which he wrote to be read neither by the very learned (doctus) nor by the very unlearned (indoctus). 8. We all know that the Helvetii informed Caesar that they intended to march through our province for this reason, because they had no other way. 9. He said that all these things must be done (agō) by Caesar, and that, if the Romans wished to conquer the forces which had been sent against them, they must fight bravely. (Express the last verb *impersonally*.) 10. The legates announced that all the Belgae were in arms, and that the Germans, who were dwelling on-this-side-of the Rhine, had joined themselves with them. 11. Caesar understood how great the danger was (**177,** *c*), and sent Galba to find out what states had conspired. 12. Having heard the consul's speech, the citizens all said that they would send their sons to the war, which was being carried on in Gaul, if he wished. 13. He said that he did not dare to cross the river, because it was uncertain in what direction the enemy intended to march (**177,** *c*).

MISCELLANEOUS SENTENCES FOR TRANSLATION INTO LATIN.

In these sentences many Latin words are used which are not given in the General Vocabularies. Such words follow the regular laws of Gender, Declension, Conjugation, etc. Sometimes a hint is given with regard to such words; as Plātō (-ōnis), (exclāmō, 1) *indicate that the Genitive of* Plātō *is* Plātōnis, *and that* exclāmō *is of the First Conjugation.*

1. Believe me (131, *a*), citizens, this man does not intend-to-go. 2. If you shall not be able to use (151, *a*) the sails (vēlum), use the oars (rēmus). 3. The Aedui having been conquered were compelled to give hostages to the Sequani. 4. If we must fight (*express in two ways*), let us fight as bravely as possible. 5. Having left ten cohorts near (ad) the sea, to serve as a guard (137) to the ships, he hastened toward the enemy. 6. If Caesar had been informed (175, *b*, 2) respecting the plans of the Gauls, he would have urged the Romans to send (179, *d*) an army into their country. 7. Dēmarātus, the father of king Tarquinius, fled from Corinth (Corinthus) to Tarquinii (-ōrum). 8. He says that our horsemen, having followed the enemy about three miles, captured very many of them. 9. The next (posterus) day he calls together the leaders of the forces, and tells (doceō) them that no city is more hostile (infestus) than the royal (rēgius) city (154). 10. Being praised by the king, the soldiers will fight more bravely. 11. If the Gauls had attacked (175, *b*, 2) the town that night, they would have taken it easily, since no one supposed (182, *b*) that they were-at-hand (adsum). 12. When Pompey had learned (reperiō) what (*plural*) had been done (gerō) at Corfīnium, he set out with two legions from Lūceria, and five days (155, *a*) after arrived at Brundisium. 13. They say that this city must be stormed; that the citizens may (197, 3) go out; that the enemy can be conquered. 14. Let the general send forward the greater part of his soldiers to attack (180) the camp. 15. The Gauls kept-sending ambassadors to me, the consul, who were-to-confer (colloquor) with me concerning peace. 16. He intends to march into Gaul that the auxiliaries may not be led out of those places. 17. He says that, if hostages should be given to him, he would make peace with them, and would not make war upon their territory (133). 18. Let us march into the enemy's lands (ager), that they may not winter in ours. 19. Do you not wish to remain at home? 20. Caius thinks that, if he should not send men as an aid (137) to our leader, the forces of Ariovistus would come to the camp, and would get-possession of all the weapons (151, *a*). 21. He said that, since he had been informed that the Germans had come (199, 3), he should set out as quickly as possible. 22. Although Titus had hoped (197, 7) that the courage of his (men)

LATIN LESSONS. 133

would be very great, yet he did not think that they would conquer so great forces. 23. My father has a house of great height (152), which was sold to him by a friend, Cassius by name, for a very small price (151, c). 24. This mountain is two miles (142, b) high, and is much higher than that hill which you see. 25. While (184, b, REMARK) these things were being done (agō) at Vēii (-ōrum), the citadel was in great danger. 26. The camp was pitched in a plain (campus), which was three miles (142, b) long and one-fifth of a mile (= how many paces?) wide. 27. At the same time, men were sent by Crassus to Caesar to inform (180) him that all those states had been made provinces of the Roman people. 28. Who were those men whom you sent to see (180) me? (*Express in five ways.*) 29. Such (so great) a report (opīniō) of this war will be spread-abroad (perferō), that legates will be sent to me by those nations (nātiō). 30. The king replies that he will not give-back the hostages, which he has received, but (and, ac) will make war on us (133). 31. We asked whether he had said that he would come to Rome. 32. The lieutenant announced that the Germans, whom Ariovistus was leading, had conquered the Romans (in) very many battles. 33. On the top of the hill the consul formed (instruō) a triple (triplex) line-of-battle (composed) of the legions which he had enlisted in hither Gaul. 34. The barbarians, frightened by the arrival of our army, said that they would surrender themselves and all their (property) to you. 35. He encouraged the soldiers of the tenth legion to advance (179 d; prōgredior) fearlessly (bravely). 36. Having finished (conficiō) the German (Germānicus) war (157), Caesar thought (statuō, 3) he ought to cross the Rhine; but, since he wished to cross without danger, he determined to make a bridge. 37. I have always been of such (is) a mind (152) as to think (that I thought) nothing could be better than bravery (154). 38. The men said that they had hesitated to cross the river, because it was both very wide and very deep. 39. Caesar, having received (157, REMARK 1) the arms and hostages, will set out *into the territory of the Ubii*. (*Express in two ways the words in italics.*) 40. When the senate had heard (184, a) that the barbarians excelled (praestō) our men (133) in bravery, it determined to send Caesar himself, hoping that, if he should go (187),the enemy would surrender the towns to him without a battle. 41. He came to free (180) the slaves. (*Express in five ways.*) 42. When the-contest-had-been-carried-on (pugnō) for more (amplus) than five days (154, b), Galba, having despaired-of (dēspērō) victory, began to go home by the same route as (115, f) he had come. 43. It was very difficult to conquer the tribes (gens, -tis) that had conspired together (= among themselves), because they all preferred to be killed fighting than to be captured. 44. If I were-to-be-accused (175, c, 2) by my fellow-citizens (cīvis), I should prefer to go into exile (exsilium) than to be looked-at (conspiciō) with the hostile (infestus) eyes of all. 45. He thinks that this fact (rēs) is very unlike that (132), does n't he? 46. The Romans' bravery was so great that they conquered the Boii and drove (agō) them many miles. 47. The leader said that the citizens ought to be called together, and that the city, which had been fortified by him, ought to be defended by them. 48. Do they intend (101, b) to be serviceable (ūtilis) to us or to the enemy? 49. The march of the third legion is said to have been hindered (impediō) by a thick (densus) forest and a broad river. 50. It happened that (181, a) in the consulship of Cicero and Antonius, many wretches (scelerātus) formed (faciō) a conspiracy (conjūrātiō) against the republic. 51. I have heard that Plātō (-ōnis) came to Tarentum in the consulship (157) of Camillus and Claudius, two very brave men. 52. He is said to have said that he thought it would be very easy to get possession of (151, a) the government (imperium) of all Gaul, since he surpassed (praestō) all (133) in wealth (dīvitiae, -ārum). 53. The Nervii, concerning whom we have written before, when they were coming with all their troops as aid (137) to the Aedui, this battle having been announced, returned home. 54. When I was at Athens (Athēnae), I used to see Marcus, whose house was very near mine (132). 55. If he is about-to-come to Rome without violence (vis), you may (197, 3) remain in the city, if you wish; but-if (sīn) he is going-to-storm the city, I fear that (179, e) we ourselves shall be killed. 56. Ought this man to be led to death by the consuls, whom he has protected at the risk (perīculum) of his life? 57. Your men were frightened, since one was running (currō) from one ship, another from another (195, 9). 58. When night had made (184, a) an end of the siege (of besieging), the leader, a man of great influence (152) among his (countrymen), came to seek (180) peace. 59. Let him, if he wishes, use arms (151, a) to (causā) defend (180) himself; let us not (178, 1) defend him. 60. He says that Namēius, who holds the chief place in (of) this embassy, has been sent to say that he intends-to-march through these places for this reason, because we are friendly to him. 61. The-inquiry-must-be-made (quaerō) whether he is unwilling to go, or not (177, d). 62. If death were feared (175, a, 2 & REMARK 4), Brūtus would not have fallen in battle, and the Decii would not have exposed (objiciō) themselves to the weapons of the enemy. 63. He said that he knew that Caesar had carried on very many wars both in Germany (Germānia) and in Gaul. 64. Being surrounded (circumveniō) by greater forces of the barbarians, they sustained all the attacks which the enemy made. 65. Let the cohorts, which the general's brother has sent, be led-back into camp. 66. The enemy's troops, which Labienus thinks the Romans have conquered, will storm our cities. 67. He says that the camp must be pitched six miles (155, a) from the Germans' camp. 68. Having sent (157, REMARK 1) the boy across the river, he said (199, 5) he should not go back without him. 69. When I go (168, a) to Rome, I shall see the king, concerning whom you have spoken. 70. It is not difficult to conquer, when the soldiers are very brave. 71. My mother says that she has sent all the letters (epistola) which she has written. 72. He replied that soldiers, who had been praised by their commander, were much (155, c) braver than those who had been blamed (culpō, 1). 73. The consul said that he had heard that all the larger cities had been fortified by the same leaders. 74. Lead out the two legions, Antonius, and follow the enemy. 75. The Germans, whom he was leading, said that they had not been conquered, and could not be conquered. 76. Slave, tell your king that Romans will surrender themselves to Romans, not to barbarians. 77. When the camp had been pitched at the foot of the mountain, we sent forward the same scouts (explōrător) to see (180) in what place the enemy were (177, c). 78. If I were you (175, a, 2), I should be happy. 79. If he were to ask (175, c, 2) me to go (179, d), I should go. 80. If he had been unwilling (175, b, 2) to come, they would have come alone. 81. He says that the boy (115, c) you saw is fond (studiōsus) of all the best pursuits (ars). 82. Caesar called together the leaders, of whom there was a great number in our camp. 83. You said that to conquer the Gauls was very difficult to do (191, b), because they were going-to-have a much braver leader. 84. Let us send as brave men as possible, since the Rhone must be crossed. 85. Another and greater danger is said to have frightened the wretched citizens. 86. Having overcome (157, REMARK 1) the second legion, and having captured our ships, seeing that they could not storm the camp, they had begun to return to the place from which they had set-out. 87. Word-was-brought-back (renuntiō) that the ascent (ascensus, 4) was very easy. 88. Publius Cousidius, who was regarded (habeō) (as) very skilled in military science (124), and had been in Lucius Sulla's army, is sent-ahead with the scouts (explōrător). 89. He said that you would find out who he was from the slave whom he had sent to you. 90. Nāsīca, when he had come to converse (colloquor) with the poet Ennius, and the maid (ancilla) had told him Ennius was not at home, thought that she had said (it) at her master's (dominus) order (jussū), and that he was within (intus). A few days (155, a) after, when Ennius had come to Nāsīca's (= to Nāsīca), Nāsīca cries out (exclāmō, 1) that he is not at home. 91. When Ennius had said that he knew (cognoscō) his voice, Nāsīca said (inquit, 91, 2, a; 193, 6, CAUTION), "You are a shameless (impudens) fellow (homō); I believed your maid, don't you believe my-ownself (ego ipse)?"

SHORT SENTENCES FOR GENERAL REVIEW.

92. I may do this. We must conquer the enemy (*write in two ways*). He came to see the city. Let us not say this. 93. Will Caesar be king, or not? He asks whether Caesar is going to set out, or not. Don't say that (178, b). 94. Who is that man? He thinks that he shall come. The soldiers that fight will be praised. He says this that he may be thought wise. 95. We are ordered to set out (*use both* jubeo *and* impero). The ships cannot be harmed. 96. When this battle was over (facio), he went to Rome (*write the* "when" *clause in two ways*). My son, go with me. Having followed them three miles, he returns to the city. 97. Having heard (of) this battle, they marched to Gaul as quickly as possible. Didn't you come home to see your brother? (*write in five ways*). Is this easy to do? No. The house is twenty feet wide. 98. If this should be done, he would be killed. The tower is of great height. The wall is very high. The tower is fifteen feet higher than the wall. 99. He sold the house for 5000 sestertii. He came to the city of Geneva. He marched from Gaul towards Rome. 100. We must inform him about the war. He feared that they would come. I fear that you will not be brave. He says that the town will not be taken.

CAESAR'S HISTORY OF THE GALLIC WAR.

BOOK I. — CHAPTERS 1-13.

References (to the NOTES) *and Explanations are given on pages 143-148.
Quantity is not indicated, except that of the Penult in new words.*

I. GALLIA est omnis divisa in partes tres, quarum unam incolunt Belgae, aliam Aquitani, tertiam, qui ipsorum lingua Celtae, nostra Galli appellantur. Hi omnes lingua, institutis, legibus inter se differunt. Gallos ab Aquitanis Garumna flumen, a Belgis
5 Matrŏna et Sequăna dividit. Horum omnium fortissimi sunt Belgae, propterea quod a cultu atque humanitate provinciae longissime absunt, minimeque ad eos mercatores saepe commeant, atque ea, quae ad effeminandos animos pertinent, important, proximique sunt Germanis, qui trans Rhenum incolunt, quibus-
10 cum continenter bellum gerunt; qua de causa Helvetii quoque reliquos Gallos virtute praecedunt, quod fere quotidianis proeliis cum Germanis contendunt, quum aut suis finibus eos prohibent, aut ipsi in eorum finibus bellum gerunt. Eorum una pars, quam Gallos obtinere dictum est, initium capit a flumine Rhodano; con-
15 tinetur Garumna flumine, Oceăno, finibus Belgarum; attingit etiam ab Sequanis et Helvetiis flumen Rhenum; vergit ad septentriones. Belgae ab extremis Galliae finibus oriuntur; pertinent ad inferiorem partem fluminis Rheni; spectant in septentriones et orientem solem. Aquitania a Garumna flumine ad
20 Pyrenaeos montes et eam partem Occăni, quae est ad Hispaniam, pertinet; spectat inter occasum solis et septentriones.

II. Apud Helvetios longe nobilissimus et ditissimus fuit Orgetŏrix. Is, Marco Messāla et Marco Pisōne consulibus, regni cupiditate inductus conjurationem nobilitatis fecit et civitati persuasit, ut de finibus suis cum omnibus copiis exirent; perfacile esse, quum virtute omnibus praestarent, totius Galliae imperio potiri. Id hoc facilius eis persuasit, quod undique loci natura Helvetii continentur: una ex parte flumine Rheno, latissimo atque 5 altissimo, qui agrum Helvetium a Germanis dividit; altera ex parte, monte Jura altissimo, qui est inter Sequanos et Helvetios; tertia, lacu Lemanno et flumine Rhodano, qui provinciam nostram ab Helvetiis dividit. His rebus fiebat, ut et minus late vagarentur et minus facile finitimis bellum inferre possent; qua de causa 10 homines bellandi cupidi magno dolore afficiebantur. Pro multitudine autem hominum et pro gloria belli atque fortitudinis, angustos se fines habere arbitrabantur, qui in longitudinem millia passuum ducenta et quadraginta, in latitudinem centum et octoginta patebant. 15

III. His rebus adducti et auctoritate Orgetorigis permoti, constituerunt ea, quae ad proficiscendum pertinerent, comparare; jumentorum et carrorum quam maximum numerum coëmere; sementes quam maximas facere, ut in itinere copia frumenti suppeteret; cum proximis civitatibus pacem et amicitiam confir- 20 mare. Ad eas res conficiendas biennium sibi satis esse duxerunt; in tertium annum profectionem lege confirmant. Ad eas res conficiendas Orgetŏrix deligitur. Is sibi legationem ad civitates suscepit. In eo itinere persuadet Castico Catamantaloedis filio, Sequano, cujus pater regnum in Sequanis multos annos obtinuerat 25 et a senatu populi Romani amicus appellatus erat, ut regnum in civitate sua occuparet, quod pater ante habuerat; itemque Dumnorigi Aeduo, fratri Divitiăci, qui eo tempore principatum in civitate obtinebat ac maxime plebi acceptus erat, ut idem conaretur, persuadet, eique filiam suam in matrimonium dat. Perfacile factu esse 30 illis probat conata perficere, propterea quod ipse suae civitatis imperium obtenturus esset; non esse dubium, quin totius Galliae plurimum Helvetii possent; se suis copiis suoque exercitu illis regna conciliaturum confirmat. Hac oratione adducti inter se fidem et jusjurandum dant, et, regno occupato, per tres potentis- 35 simos ac firmissimos populos totius Galliae sese potiri posse sperant.

IV. Ea res est Helvetiis per indicium enuntiata. Moribus suis Orgetorĭgem ex vinculis causam dicere coëgerunt. Damnatum
5 poenam sequi oportebat, ut igni cremaretur. Die constituta causae dictionis Orgetŏrix ad judicium omnem suam familiam, ad hominum millia decem, undique coëgit, et omnes clientes obaeratosque suos, quorum magnum numerum habebat, eodem conduxit; per eos, ne causam diceret, se eripuit. Quum civitas ob eam rem
10 incitata armis jus suum exsequi conaretur, multitudinemque hominum ex agris magistratus cogerent, Orgetŏrix mortuus est; neque abest suspicio, ut Helvetii arbitrantur, quin ipse sibi mortem consciverit.

V. Post ejus mortem nihilo minus Helvetii id, quod constitue-
15 rant, facere conantur, ut e finibus suis exeant. Ubi jam se ad eam rem paratos esse arbitrati sunt, oppida sua omnia numero ad duodecim, vicos ad quadringentos, reliqua privata aedificia incendunt; frumentum omne, praeterquam quod secum portaturi erant, comburunt, ut, domum reditionis spe sublata, paratiores ad omnia
20 pericula subeunda essent; trium mensium molita cibaria sibi quemque domo efferre jŭbent. Persuadent Raurăcis et Tulingis et Latovīcis, finitimis, uti, eodem usi consilio, oppidis suis vicisque exustis, una cum iis proficiscantur; Boiosque, qui trans Rhenum incoluerant et in agrum Norĭcum transierant Norēiamque oppugna-
25 rant, receptos ad se socios sibi adsciscunt.

VI. Erant omnino itinera duo, quibus itineribus domo exire possent: unum per Sequanos, angustum et difficile, inter montem Juram et flumen Rhodanum, vix qua singuli carri ducerentur; mons autem altissimus impendebat, ut facile perpauci prohibere
30 possent: alterum per provinciam nostram, multo facilius atque expeditius, propterea quod inter fines Helvetiorum et Allobrogum, qui nuper pacati erant, Rhodanus fluit, isque nonnullis locis vado transitur. Extremum oppidum Allobrogum est proximumque Helvetiorum finibus Geneva. Ex eo oppido pons ad Helvetios
35 pertinet. Allobrogibus sese vel persuasuros, quod nondum bono

animo in populum Romanum viderentur, existimabant; vel vi coacturos, ut per suos fines eos ire paterentur. Omnibus rebus ad profectionem comparatis, diem dicunt, qua die ad ripam Rhodani omnes conveniant. Is dies erat ante diem quintum Kalendas Apriles, Lucio Pisōne, Aulo Gabinio consulibus.

VII. Caesari quum id nuntiatum esset, eos per provinciam nostram iter facere conari, maturat ab urbe proficisci, et, quam maximis potest itineribus, in Galliam ulteriorem contendit et ad Genevam pervenit. Provinciae toti quam maximum potest militum numerum imperat (erat omnino in Gallia ulteriore legio una); pontem, qui erat ad Genevam, jubet rescindi. Ubi de ejus adventu Helvetii certiores facti sunt, legatos ad eum mittunt, nobilissimos civitatis, cujus legationis Nameius et Verudoctius principem locum obtinebant, qui dicerent, sibi esse in animo sine ullo maleficio iter per provinciam facere, propterea quod aliud iter haberent nullum; rogare, ut ejus voluntate id sibi facere liceat. Caesar, quod memoria tenebat Lucium Cassium consulem occisum, exercitumque ejus ab Helvetiis pulsum et sub jugum missum, concedendum non putabat; neque homines inimico animo, data facultate per provinciam itineris faciendi, temperaturos ab injuria et maleficio existimabat. Tamen, ut spatium intercedere posset, dum milites, quos imperaverat, convenirent, legatis respondit, diem se ad deliberandum sumpturum; si quid vellent, ad Idus Apriles reverterentur.

VIII. Interea ea legione, quam secum habebat, militibusque, qui ex provincia convenerant, a lacu Lemanno, qui in flumen Rhodanum influit, ad montem Juram, qui fines Sequanorum ab Helvetiis dividit, millia passuum decem novem murum, in altitudinem pedum sedecim, fossamque perducit. Eo opere perfecto praesidia dispōnit, castella commūnit, quo facilius, si se invīto transire conarentur, prohibere possit. Ubi ea dies, quam constituerat cum legatis, venit, et legati ad eum reverterunt, negat se more et exemplo populi Romani posse iter ulli per provinciam dare, et, si vim facere conentur, prohibiturum ostendit. Helvetii, ea spe dejecti, navibus junctis ratibusque compluribus factis, alii vadis

Rhodani, qua minima altitudo fluminis erat, nonnunquam interdiu, saepius noctu, si perrumpere possent, conati, operis munitione et militum concursu et telis repulsi, hoc conatu destiterunt.

IX. Relinquebatur una per Sequanos via, qua, Sequanis invitis, 5 propter angustias ire non poterant. His quum sua sponte persuadere non possent, legatos ad Dumnorīgem Aeduum mittunt, ut eo deprecatore a Sequanis impetrarent. Dumnŏrix gratia et largitione apud Sequanos plurimum poterat, et Helvetiis erat amicus, quod ex ea civitate Orgetorīgis filiam in matrimonium duxerat; 10 et cupiditate regni adductus novis rebus studebat, et quam plurimas civitates suo sibi beneficio habere obstrictas volebat. Itaque rem suscipit et a Sequanis impetrat, ut per fines suos Helvetios ire patiantur, obsidesque uti inter sese dent, perficit: Sequani, ne itinere Helvetios prohibeant; Helvetii, ut sine maleficio et injuria 15 transeant.

X. Caesari renuntiatur Helvetiis esse in animo per agrum Sequanorum et Aeduorum iter in Santŏnum fines facere, qui non longe a Tolosatium finibus absunt, quae civitas est in provincia. Id si fieret, intelligebat magno cum periculo provinciae futurum, 20 ut homines bellicosos, populi Romani inimicos, locis patentibus maximeque frumentariis finitimos haberet. Ob eas causas ei munitioni, quam fecerat, Titum Labienum legatum praefecit; ipse in Italiam magnis itineribus contendit duasque ibi legiones conscribit, et tres, quae circum Aquilēiam hiemabant, ex hibernis educit; et 25 qua proximum iter in ulteriorem Galliam per Alpes erat, cum his quinque legionibus ire contendit. Ibi Centrōnes et Graiocĕli et Caturīges, locis superioribus occupatis, itinere exercitum prohibere conantur. Compluribus his proeliis pulsis, ab Ocĕlo, quod est citerioris provinciae extremum, in fines Vocontiorum ulterioris 30 provinciae die septimo pervenit; inde in Allobrŏgum fines, ab Allobrogibus in Segusiāvos exercitum ducit. Hi sunt extra provinciam trans Rhodanum primi.

XI. Helvetii jam per angustias et fines Sequanorum suas copias transduxerant, et in Aeduorum fines pervenerant eorumque agros 35 populabantur. Aedui, quum se suaque ab iis defendere non possent, legatos ad Caesarem mittunt rogatum auxilium : Ita se omni tempore de populo Romano meritos esse, ut paene in conspectu exercitus nostri agri vastari, liberi eorum in servitutem abduci, oppida expugnari non debuerint. Eodem tempore Aedui Ambarri, necessarii et consanguinei Aeduorum, Caesarem certiorem faciunt, 5 sese depopulatis agris non facile ab oppidis vim hostium prohibere. Item Allobroges, qui trans Rhodanum vicos possessionesque habebant, fuga se ad Caesarem recipiunt et demonstrant, sibi praeter agri solum nihil esse reliqui. Quibus rebus adductus Caesar non exspectandum sibi statuit, dum, omnibus fortunis sociorum con- 10 sumptis, in Santŏnos Helvetii pervenirent.

XII. Flumen est Arar, quod per fines Aeduorum et Sequanorum in Rhodanum influit incredibili lenitate, ita ut oculis, in utram partem fluat, judicari non possit. Id Helvetii ratibus ac lintribus junctis transibant. Ubi per exploratores Caesar certior factus est, 15 tres jam copiarum partes Helvetios id flumen transduxisse, quartam vero partem citra flumen Arărim reliquam esse, de tertia vigilia cum legionibus tribus e castris profectus ad eam partem pervenit, quae nondum flumen transierat. Eos impeditos et inopinantes aggressus magnam eorum partem concidit; reliqui fugae sese 20 mandarunt atque in proximas silvas abdiderunt. Is pagus appellabatur Tigurīnus; nam omnis civitas Helvetia in quattuor pagos divisa est. Hic pagus unus, quum domo exisset patrum nostrorum memoria, Lucium Cassium consulem interfecerat et ejus exercitum sub jugum miserat. Ita, sive casu sive consilio deorum 25 immortalium, quae pars civitatis Helvetiae insignem calamitatem populo Romano intulerat, ea princeps poenas persolvit. Qua in re Caesar non solum publicas, sed etiam privatas injurias ultus est, quod ejus soceri Lucii Pisōnis avum, Lucium Pisōnem legatum, Tigurīni eodem proelio, quo Cassium, interfecerant. 30

XIII. Hoc proelio facto, reliquas copias Helvetiorum ut consequi posset, pontem in Arăre faciendum curat atque ita exercitum transducit. Helvetii repentino ejus adventu commoti, quum id, quod ipsi diebus viginti aegerrime confecerant, ut flumen transirent, illum uno die fecisse intelligerent, legatos ad eum mittunt; 5

cujus legationis Divĭco princeps fuit, qui bello Cassiāno dux Helvetiorum fuerat. Is ita cum Caesare agit: Si pacem populus Romanus cum Helvetiis faceret, in eam partem ituros atque ibi futuros Helvetios, ubi eos Caesar constituisset atque esse voluisset;
5 sin bello persequi perseveraret, reminisceretur et veteris incommodi populi Romani et pristinae virtutis Helvetiorum. Quod improviso unum pagum adortus esset, quum ii, qui flumen transissent, suis auxilium ferre non possent, ne ob eam rem aut suae magnopere virtuti tribueret aut ipsos despiceret; se ita a patribus majori-
10 busque suis didicisse, ut magis virtute quam dolo contenderent aut insidiis niterentur. Quare ne committeret, ut is locus, ubi constitissent, ex calamitate populi Romani et internecione exercitus nomen caperet aut memoriam proderet.

LATIN LESSONS. 143

CAESAR'S GALLIC WAR: Chapters 1-13.

REFERENCES AND EXPLANATIONS.

CHAPTER I.

Divisa, 189, b. — Quarum, 122. — Tertiam, qui = tertiam partem ii incolunt, qui. — Ipsorum, emphatic, *their own*. — Celtae, 107. — Lingua, institutis, legibus, 153. — Inter se, 112, b. — Dividit, *singular*, as the rivers form but *one* boundary (117, b, REMARK). — Horum, 122, a. — Atque, 96, a. — Minime saepe, *very seldom*. — Effeminandos, why not the Gerund? (190, a.) — Germanis, 132. — Quibuscum, 53, a. — Reliquos Gallos, 123, e. — Virtute, 153. — Suis finibus, 147. — Eorum, *of the enemy* (literally, *their*). To whom do suis, eos, ipsi, eorum refer? — Eorum una pars, *one part of their territory* (literally, *of them*, the people being used for their country); or we may supply finium, making eorum a *Possessive Genitive*. — Dictum est, the subject is quam Gallos obtinere, 188, b, 1. — Ab Sequanis, *on (from) the side of the Sequani*. — Ad Hispaniam, *near Spain*.

CHAPTER II.

Ditissimus, 36, a. — Marco Messala, etc., 157 (3). — Nobilitatis, civitati, collective force, *the nobles, the citizens*. — Civitati, 131, a. — Cum copiis, 150, a. — Exirent, 117, c ; 179, d. — Perfacile to potiri, Indirect Discourse; the verb of *saying* is implied in persuasit (186, a). The subject of esse is potiri, etc. (165, a). — Why is perfacile Neuter, and how does it differ from facile? (109, b ; 40, d.) — Give *two* reasons for the mode of praestarent (187, 182, b). — Omnibus, 133. — Imperio, 151, a. — Id, *that step*, or *course*. — Hoc, 149. — Loci natura, *by the nature of their situation*. — Una ex parte, *on one side*. — Latissimo, 40, b. — Nostram = Romanam. — Rebus, 149. — Fiebat, the subject is ut — possent (188, b, 2). — Vagarentur, possent, 181, a. — Finitimis, 133. — Homines, 106. — Bellandi, 190. — Pro, *in proportion to, considering*. — Qui (fines). — Millia, 142, b.

CHAPTER III.

Pertinerent, 181, c (ea = *such things*). — Comparare, coëmere, facere, confirmare, 165, b. — Quam, 40, c. — Suppeteret, 179. — Ad conficiendas, 190, a ; 137, a. — Satis, here equivalent to a *Predicate Adjective*. — Duxe-

144   LATIN LESSONS.

runt, *they reckoned.* — **In tertium annum,** *for* the third year. — **Sibi suscepit,** 133. — **Ad civitates,** *not* the Dative, because **legationem** implies *motion.* — **Persuadet, 168,** *b.* — **Castico, 131,** *a.* — **Filio, Sequano, 106.** — **Annos, 142,** *a.* — **Amicus, 107**; this title, *friend,* conferred by the Roman Senate, was highly prized by foreign rulers. — **Sua, 112,** *a.* — **Occuparet, conaretur, 172,** REMARK 2. — **Plebi, 131,** *b.* — **Acceptus** is here an Adjective. — **Perfacile,** etc., Indirect Discourse. **Perfacile** agrees with the subject of **esse** (**perficere conata**). — **Factu, 191,** *b.* — **Illis** probat, *he shows* (*to*) *them.* — **Obtenturus esset, 82,** *a;* **172,** REMARK 2; **187.** — **Esse,** the subject is **quin** — **possent** (**188,** *b,* 2), which is modified by **dubium** (**109,** *b*). — **Galliae, 122,** *b.* — **Plurimum, 94,** *d,* 1. — **Possent,** what mode in Direct Discourse? (**181,** *d.*) — **Copiis,** *wealth.* — **Conciliaturum, 199,** 2. — **Regno occupato, 157.** — **Galliae potiri, 151,** *a,* REMARK.

CHAPTER IV.

Per indicium, *by* (*through*) *informers* (literally, *information*). — **Moribus, 149.** — **Ex** — **dicere,** *to plead his cause* (= *make his defence*) *in* (*from*) *chains.* — **Damnatum,** agrees with **eum** (understood), the object of **sequi.** Translate, *if he should be condemned* (**189,** *d*). — **Oportebat,** the subject is (**eum**) **damnatum poenam sequi** (**188,** *b,* 1). — **Ut cremaretur,** in apposition with **poenam** (**181,** *e*). — **Die constituta,** *on the appointed day,* **160. Dies** is sometimes *feminine,* when it denotes a *fixed* time. — **Ad** (before **hominum**), Adverb of degree (*about*), modifying **decem.** — **Millia, 106.** — **Eodem,** Adverb. — **Diceret, 179.** — **Exsequi,** *assert.* — **Conaretur, cogerent, 184,** *a.* — **Magistratus,** Nominative. — **Ut arbitrantur, 197,** 5. — **Consciverit, 181,** *d.*

CHAPTER V.

Nihilo, 155. — **Ut** — **exeant,** in apposition with **id, 181,** *e.* — **Paratos,** Adjective. — **Numero, 153.** — **Ad** (before **duodecim**), Adverb. — **Domum, 159,** *b;* the *motion* is implied in **reditionis.** — **Spe, 157.** — **Ad subeunda, 190,** *a;* **137,** *a.* — **Essent, 172,** REMARK 2. — **Trium mensium,** etc., *three months'* supplies (**121**). — **Domo, 159,** *a.* — **Jubent,** why is the *Present Historical* used? — **Rauracis, 131,** *a.* — **Uti** = **ut.** — **Usi,** *having adopted.* — **Consilio, 151,** *a.* — **Oppidis, 157.** — **Una, 94,** 2. — **Cum iis,** we should expect to find **secum.** — **Oppugnarant, 79,** 4. — **Ad se** limits **receptos,** *received into their number.* — **Socios, 106.** — **Sibi, 133.**

CHAPTER VI.

Itineribus, 159, REMARK 3; the antecedent is sometimes repeated for emphasis. — **Domo, 159,** *a.* — **Possent, 181,** *c;* that is, *routes* (of such a kind) *that they could go out* by them. — **Unum, alterum,** appositives to **itinera.** —

LATIN LESSONS. 145

Qua, 94, 2. — Ducerentur, 181, *c (so narrow that,* etc.). — Singuli, 41, *a.* — Perpauci, 40, *d.* — Possent, 181. — Multo, 155. — Locis, 159, REMARK 2. — Vado, 151. — Finibus, 132. — Allobrogibus, 131, *a.* — Persuasuros, coacturos, 199, 2 ; this is Indirect Discourse, the introductory verb being existimabant (186, *u*). — Viderentur, 187. — Bono animo, *kindly disposed* (152). — Vi, how declined ? — Paterentur, Subjunctive for *two* reasons : 187, 179, *d.* — Eos = the Helvetii. — Suos refers to the Allobroges. — Conveniant, 179, *a.* — Ante diem, etc., study carefully 161, *b* & Rule 1. What were the three reckoning points in the month, and what was the date of each ? What part of speech is Apriles ? (161, *a.*) — Lucio, etc., 157 (3).

CHAPTER VII.

Nuntiatum esset, 184, *a.* — Eos conari, in apposition with id, 186, *a.* — Urbe, *the city* (Rome). — Ulteriorem = Transalpinam. — Ad Genevam, 159, REMARK 1. — Imperat, *levies.* — Nobilissimos, 109 ; 106. — Dicerent, 179, *a.* — Sibi esse . . . liceat, Indirect Discourse (Declaratory Sentence), 187, *a.* The principal verbs are esse and rogare ; the subordinate verbs are haberent and liceat. The subject of esse is facere iter ; the subject of rogare is se (understood). — Sibi (before esse), 135. — Voluntate, 149. — Sibi (before facere), 197, 2. — Liceat, Subjunctive for *two* reasons: 187 ; 179, *d.* What is the subject of liceat ? — Memoria tenebat = meminerat (151). — Occisum, pulsum, missum, concedendum, 199, 2. — Sub jugum, why not sub jugo ? (95, *c.*) What was the military jugum ? (see Vocabulary.) — Concedendum (esse), the subject is the *request* of the Helvetii. — Animo, 152. — Data facultate (157, REMARK 2), *if the opportunity should be given.* — Faciendi, 190, *a.* — Temperaturos, 199, 2. — Spatium = tempus. — Convenirent, 184, *b.* — Diem, *time.* — Vellent, 187, *c, d.* — Reverterentur, a *command* in Indirect Discourse. In the *Direct* form the Latin would be : Si quid voletis, revertimini. — Ad Idus, *on the* 13*th of April* (161, 3).

CHAPTER VIII.

Legione, militibus, 151. — Millia passuum, 123, *c ;* 142, *b.* — Decem novem, is this the usual position of a numeral ? (193, 1.) In what other ways can *nineteen* be expressed ? — Pedum, 121. — Disponit, 99, 2. — Quo, why not ut ? (179, *b.*) — Se invito, 157, REMARK 2. — Conarentur, 185 ; 172, REMARK 2. Notice that communit is followed by a *Primary* tense (possit) and also by a *Secondary* tense (conarentur). — Negat = dicit non (199, 5). — More, *in accordance with the practice* (149). — Iter, *the privilege of going.* — Ulli, 129. — Vim facere, *to employ force.* — Conentur, 187. — Prohibiturum, for se prohibiturum esse. — Spe (147), *disappointed (downcast) in this hope.* — Navibus junctis (151), *by making bridges of boats.* — Alii, *some,* meaning

10

that *most* of the Helvetii crossed by bridges of boats and rafts. — **Nonnunquam,**
195, 1. — **Possent (177,** REMARK 1), *having tried (to see) whether (if) they
could.* — **Operis munitione** (= **muro fossaque),** *by the strength of the works.*
— **Conatu, 147.**

CHAPTER IX.

Una via, *only the route.* — **Per Sequanos** = **per fines Sequanorum.** — **Qua,**
159, REMARK 3. — **Sequanis invitis,** 157, REMARK 2. — **His,** 131, *a.* — **Sua
sponte,** *of themselves;* that is, *without assistance.* — **Possent,** 182, *b.* — **Eo
deprecatore,** *through his intercession (he being an intercessor),* 157. — **Gratia,**
149. — **Plurimum, 94,** *d,* 1; **142,** *c.* — **Helvetiis,** 131, *b.* — **Novis rebus,** *for
a revolution (new things),* 131, *a.* — **Quam, 40,** *c.* — **Sibi** depends on **obstrictas.** — **Beneficio, 151.** — **Ut patiantur** is the object of **impetrat; uti dent,**
the object of **perficit, 181,** *b.* — **Inter se dent,** *exchange,* 53, *d.* — **Sequani,
Helvetii,** each the subject of **dent** (repeated). — **Ne prohibeant, ut transeant,
179.**

CHAPTER X.

Renuntiatur, *word is brought back,* **93, 2.** — **Helvetiis,** etc., see note on
sibi esse in animo, Chapter VII. What is the subject of **esse ?** — **Id si fieret,**
etc., Indirect Discourse, **187,** *a.* **Futurum** (esse) is the principal verb; its
subject is **ut... haberet, 188,** *b,* 2; **181,** *a.* — **Id** = **facere iter;** its position
is emphatic. — **Locis, 132.** — **Munitioni, 133.** — **Qua, 94,** 2. — **In Galliam,**
because **iter** implies *motion.* — **Locis occupatis, 157.** — **Itinere, 147.** — **Compluribus,** etc.; the order is: **his pulsis compluribus proeliis, 157.** — **Ab
Ocelo, 159,** REMARK 1. — **Citerioris (ulterioris) provinciae** = Hither (Farther)
Gaul. — **Extremum (oppidum),** *last, most westerly.* — **Die, 160.** — **Trans,** *west
of.* — **Primi,** emphatic position.

CHAPTER XI.

Angustias, see Chapter VI. (angustum et difficile). — **Possent, 182,** *b.* —
Sua, 109. — **Rogatum, 191,** *a.* — **Ita meritos esse de,** *(saying) that they had
deserved so well of.* — **Nostri,** with **exercitus.** — **Vastari** non debuerint, *ought
not to have been laid waste,* **173,** CAUTION. — **Eorum** = **sui.** — **Depopulatis,
80,** REMARK 3. — **Non facile** = **vix.** — **Demonstrant** = **eum certiorem faciunt.** — **Sibi praeter agri solum,** etc., *that they have nothing left (of a remainder) except the soil of their farms (of the field).* — **Sibi, 135.** — **Nihil,**
subject of **esse.** — **Reliqui, 122,** *a.* — **Quibus rebus, 115,** *d.* — **Exspectandum,
198, 199,** 2. — **Sibi, 136.** — **Fortunis, 157.** — **Pervenirent, 184,** *b.*

CHAPTER XII.

Flumen est Arar, *there is a river* (called) *the Arar* (Saône). — **Quod,** what is the antecedent? — **Lenitate, 150.** — **Utram, 195, 7.** — **Fluat, 177,** *c.* — **Possit, 181.** — **Per exploratores, 151,** CAUTION. — **Copiarum, 122,** *a.* — **Flumen, 141,** *c.* — **Ararim,** see Vocabulary. — **De tertia vigilia,** *in the third watch* (de shows that it was *after* the beginning of the watch). When did the third watch begin? (see Vocabulary.) — **Eorum, 122,** *a.* — **Concidit, 79, 6,** REMARK. — **Transierat, mandarunt, 79, 4.** — **In silvas,** *in the forests* (or *woods*). The Accusative indicates that they retreated *into,* and hid themselves *in.* — **Tigurinus, 107.** — **Divisa, 189,** *b.* — **Exisset, 79, 4; 184,** *a.* — **Memoria, 160.** — **Lucium Cassium,** what is the Vocative? — **Casu, 149.** — **Quae pars,** etc., = *ea pars civitatis Helvetiae, quae.* — **Populo, 133.** — **Princeps, 110,** *a.* — **Persolvit,** *paid* (in full, 99, 1). — **Qua in re, 115,** *d.* — **Publicas,** that is, *done to the state.* — **Privatas,** *personal* (done to his family). — **Quod ejus soceri,** etc., the order is: **quod Tigurini, eodem proelio (160), quo (interfecerant) Cassium, interfecerant Lucium Pisonem legatum (Cassii), avum ejus** (= Caesar's) **soceri Lucii Pisonis.**

CHAPTER XIII.

Hoc proelio facto = **post hoc proelium.** — **Copias, 123,** *e.* — **Ut posset,** purpose of **faciendum curat (172,** REMARK 2). — **In Arare,** *over the Arar.* — **Pontem faciendum, 189,** *h.* — **Intelligerent (184,** *a*), *when they saw.* — **Ut... transirent,** in apposition with **id (181,** *e*), namely, *the crossing of the river.* — **Bello Cassiano, 160; 110,** *c.* — **Dux Helvetiorum, 124.** — **Is ita cum Caesare agit** introduces a passage of Indirect Discourse **(186, 187),** extending through the remainder of the chapter. This is given under NOTE 187, *e,* together with the Latin of the *Direct* form, and the two should be carefully studied and compared. A general outline of each sentence is here given. **Si to Helvetiorum.** This sentence is *Declaratory,* as far as **voluisset;** the remainder is *Imperative.* The Principal Verbs in the Declaratory part are **ituros (esse), futuros (esse);** the Principal Verb in the Imperative part is **reminisceretur,** *let him remember* (*he should remember*) **(187,** *c*). — **Constituisset, Voluisset,** Future Perfect Indicative (*you shall have,* etc.) in Direct Discourse (see **187,** *e*). — **Bello, 151.** — **Persequi (eos),** *in pursuing them.* — **Perseveraret,** the subject is Caesar. — **Reminisceretur,** what form in Direct Discourse? — **Incommodi,** the defeat and death of Cassius **(125).** — **Quod** to **niterentur.** This sentence is *Imperative,* to **despiceret;** the remainder is *Declaratory.* The Principal Verbs in the Imperative part are **(ne) tribueret, despiceret,** *let him not* (= *that he should not*) *attribute* (the victory), etc., *or despise them;* the Principal Verb in the Declaratory part is **didicisse.** — **Quod, 182,** *d.* — **Improviso,** notice the derivation (literally = *in an un-fore-seen* manner). — **Possent,** what mode in

Direct Discourse ? (184, a.) — **Magnopere, 39.** — **Majoribus, 36,** b. — **Didicisse** = **institutos esse.** — **Insidiis niterentur,** to rely (that they should rely) on ambuscades (151). — **Contenderent, niterentur,** what mode in Direct Discourse ? (181, REMARK.) — **Quare** to **proderet.** This sentence is *Imperative*, the Principal Clause being **ne (Caesar) committeret:** let him not (= that he should not) cause the place where they should take (should have taken) their stand to receive (literally, cause that it should receive) a name, etc., or transmit the remembrance (of the defeat to future generations). — **Constitissent,** Future Perfect Indicative (we shall have taken our stand) in Direct Discourse. — **Caperet, proderet,** what mode in Direct Discourse ? (181, b.)

NOTES.

THE ESSENTIALS OF LATIN GRAMMAR.

ETYMOLOGY.

In Latin words, changes were often made which rendered them easier to pronounce. These are called *Euphonic* changes. Some of the most common changes are these : —

1. Consonant Changes.

(1.) **Qu** was regarded as a single consonant, equivalent to **C**. Hence we find **cūjus** as the genitive of **quī**; **secūtus** (from **sequor**) for **sequūtus**; **cum** for **quum**.

(2.) **S** between two vowels became **R**; as, **eram** and **erō** (from stem **es**); **flōris** (from **flōs**); **corporis** (from **corpus**).

(3.) **C** and **G** united with **S**, forming **X**; as **pacs** = **pax**; **regs** = **rex**; **regsī** = **rexī**. **H** did the same; as, **vehsī** = **vexī**; **trahsī** = **traxī**.

(4.) **D** and **T** were

  a. Suppressed before **S**; as, **pēs** for **peds**; **custōs** for **custods**; **virtūs** for **virtuts**; **pars** for **parts**.

  b. Changed to **S**; as, **possum** for **potsum**; **cessī** for **cedsī**. This change is called *Assimilation*. See (6), below.

(5.) **M** was changed to **N** before a *lingual;* as, **septen(m)decim**; **eun(m)dem** (so English iden-tity, from **īdem**).

(6.) Assimilation (from two Latin words, **ad**, *to*, and **similis**, *like*, is a change made in a consonant by which it becomes *like* the following consonant. The form of the word *assimilation* itself is the result of this change, d being changed to s.

It is very common in the case of Prepositions compounded with other words. A good example of it is seen in the verb **afferō**, a compound of **ad** and **ferō**. Its Present Indicative is **af-ferō**; Perfect Indicative, **at-tulī**; Supine, **al-lātum**.

2. Vowel Changes.

Vowel changes are frequent. Notes will be given on special changes when they shall occur. Some of those most common are given here : —

(1.) **E** changed to **I**; as, mīlitis (from **mīles**); principis (from **princeps**); verticis (from **vertex**); nōminis (from **nōmen**); retineō (from re + **teneō**).
(2.) **U** changed to **I**; as, capitis (from **caput**).
(3.) **O** changed to **I**; as, virginis (from **virgō**).
(4.) **O** changed to **U**; as, corpus (gen. corporis) for corpos.
(5.) **A** changed to **I**; as, conficiō (from con + **faciō**).
(6.) **A** changed to **E**; as, confectum (from con + **factum**).
(7.) **OE** changed to **Ū**; as, pūniō (from **poena**); mūniō (from **moenia**).
(8.) **AE** changed to **Ī**; as, occīdō (from ob + **caedō**).
(9.) **AU** changed to **Ū**; as, inclūdō (from in + **claudō**).

NOUNS.

Outline of Rules for Gender.

3. Gender decided by *meaning*.* These Rules apply to *all* Declensions ; *A small figure at the right of a word refers to* REMARKS *at the end of these tables.*

MASCULINE.[1]	FEMININE.[2]	NEUTER.
Names of *Males, Rivers, Winds,* and *Mountains.*	Names of *Females, Countries, Towns, Islands,* and *Trees.*	*Indeclinable Nouns; Infinitives, Phrases, Clauses,* and other parts of speech used as indeclinable nouns.

4. Gender decided by *ending* of Nominative Singular.

(1.) *First Declension.*

MASCULINE.	FEMININE.	NEUTER.
cf. 9, c.	a.	

(2.) *Second Declension.*

us,[3] er, ir.		um.

* Some names of *rivers, countries, towns,* etc., follow the rules of gender *by ending.*

NOTES. 151

(3.) *Third Declension.*

MASCULINE.	FEMININE.	NEUTER.
ō, or, ōs, er, ĕs (increasing in the Genitive to ĭdis or ĭtis).	ās, ēs (not increasing in the Genitive), is, ys, x, s (preceded by a consonant), dō, gō, iō (abstract and collective), ūs (Genitive, -ūdis or -ūtis).	a, e, ĭ, y, c, l, t, men (Genitive, -mĭnis), ar, ur, us (Genitive, -ŏris or -ĕris).

(4.) *Fourth Declension.*

us.[4]		ū.

(5.) *Fifth Declension.*

	ēs.[5]	

REMARKS. 1. Because vir (*man*), fluvius (*river*), ventus (*wind*), mons (*mountain*), are Masculine.

2. Because mulier (*woman*), terra (*land, country*), urbs (*city*), insula (*island*), arbor (*tree*), are Feminine.

3. Pelagus (*sea*), vīrus (*poison*), vulgus (*crowd*), are Neuter. Vulgus is rarely Masculine.

4. Manus (*hand*), domus (*house*), Īdūs (*the 15th, or 13th, of the month*), and several others, are Feminine.

5. Diēs (*day*) is Masculine or Feminine in the Singular, and Masculine in the Plural. Merīdiēs (*noon*) is Masculine.

General View of all Declensions.

5. STEM ENDINGS (or CHARACTERISTICS).

	I.	II.	III.	IV.	V.
STEM ENDING.	ă	ŏ	ĭ or a Consonant	ŭ	ē.

6. CASE ENDINGS.

Small figures at the right refer to "Different Forms" below.

Singular.

	I.	II.		III.		IV.		V.
	F.	M.	N.	M. F.	N.	M.	N.	F.
NOM.	ă	ŭs, ĕr, ĭr	ŭm	(various endings.)		ŭs	ū	ēs
GEN.	ae	ī	ī	ĭs	ĭs	ūs	ūs	ēī[5]
DAT.	ae	ō	ō	ī	ī	uī	ū	ēī[5]
ACC.	ăm	ŭm	ŭm	ĕm (ĭm)	like Nom.	ŭm	ū	ĕm
VOC.	ă	ĕ,[2] ĕr, ĭr	ŭm	like Nom.	"	ŭs	ū	ēs
ABL.	ā	ō	ō	ĕ (ĭ)	ĕ (ĭ)	ū	ū	ē

Plural.

	I.	II.		III.		IV.		V.
	F.	M.	N.	M. F.	N.	M.	N.	F.
Nom.	ae	ī	ă	ēs	ă (ia)	ūs	uă	ēs
Gen.	ārŭm	ōrŭm	ōrŭm	ŭm (iŭm)	ŭm (iŭm)	uŭm	uŭm	ērŭm
Dat.	īs[1]	īs	īs	ĭbŭs	ĭbŭs	ĭbŭs[4]	ĭbŭs	ēbŭs
Acc.	ās	ōs	ă	ēs[3]	ă (iă)	ūs	uă	ēs
Voc.	ae	ī	ă	ēs	ă (iă)	ūs	uă	ēs
Abl.	īs[1]	īs	īs	ĭbŭs	ĭbŭs	ĭbŭs[4]	ĭbŭs	ēbŭs

Different Forms.

1. Except deābus, fīliābus. 2. Except deus, fīlius, Cassius, etc. 3. Vowel stems have also īs. 4. Except words of two syllables, ending in cus (as lacus); also **portus** and a few others, which have ŭbus. 5. Except rēs, spēs, fidēs, which have ēī.

Formation of the Cases.

7. The following table will be helpful to the beginner, since it shows *how* the Cases were anciently formed from the Stems, in the Five Declensions, and what changes and contractions were afterwards made: —

	I.	II.	III.	IV.	V.
	Puellă-	Equŏ-	Reg-	Currŭ-	Diē-

Singular.

	I.	II.	III.	IV.	V.
Nominative.	*puella-* / puella	*equo-s* / equus	*reg-s* / rex	*curru-s* / currus	*die-s* / diēs
Genitive.	*puella-i* / puellae	*equo-i* / equī	*reg-is* / rēgis	*curru-is* / currūs	*die-i* / diēī
Dative.	*puella-i* / puellae	*equo-i* / equō	*reg-i* / rēgī	*curru-i* / curruī	*die-i* / diēī
Accusative.	*puella-m* / puellam	*equo-m* / equum	*reg-em* / rēgem	*curru-m* / currum	*die-m* / diem
Vocative.	*puella-* / puella	*equo-* / eque	*reg-s* / rex	*curru-s* / currus	*die-s* / diēs
Ablative.	*puella-d* / puellā	*equo-d* / equō	*reg-ed* / rēge	*curru-d* / currū	*die-d* / diē

NOTES.   153

	I. Puellă-	II. Equŏ-	III. Reg-	IV. Currŭ-	V. Diē-
	Plural.				
NOMINATIVE.	{ puella-i { puellae	equo-i equī	reg-es rēgēs	curru-es currūs	die-s diēs
GENITIVE.	{ puella-rum { puellārum	equo-rum equōrum	reg-um rēgum	curru-um curruum	die-rum diērum
DATIVE.	{ puella-is { puellīs	equo-is equīs	reg-ibus rēgibus	curru-bus curribus	die-bus diēbus
ACCUSATIVE.	{ puella-ms { puellās	equo-ms equōs	reg-ems rēgēs	curru-ms currūs	die-ms diēs
VOCATIVE.	{ puella-i { puellae	equo-i equī	reg-es rēgēs	curru-es currūs	die-s diēs
ABLATIVE.	{ puella-is { puellīs	equo-is equīs	reg-ibus rēgibus	curru-bus curribus	die-bus diēbus

Notice, in the above table, that the Ablative Singular originally ended in d. Afterwards, d was dropped and the *stem-vowel* was lengthened (in puellā, equō, currū). In rēge, the final vowel was *not* a stem-vowel, but a connecting vowel, and was not affected. Other changes, producing long vowels in final syllables, can be pointed out and explained by the teacher.

General Laws of Declension.

8. (1.) The Nominative and Vocative are always alike, in both numbers, except in nouns of the Second Declension ending in **us.**

(2.) The Accusative Singular of Masculines and Feminines always ends in **m**, and the Accusative Plural in **s**.

(3.) Neuter nouns have the Nominative, Accusative, and Vocative alike in both numbers, and these cases, in the Plural, always end in **a**.

(4.) In the Third, Fourth, and Fifth Declensions, the Nominative, Accusative, and Vocative Plural (*in all genders*) are alike.

(5.) The Dative and Ablative Plural are always alike.

(6.) The Genitive Plural always ends in **um**.

(7.) The vowels **i, o, u** are *long* when final.

(8.) The vowel **a** is short when final, except in the Ablative Singular.

(9.) Final **e** is *short* in the Third Declension, and *long* in the Fifth.

NOUNS: FIRST DECLENSION.

9. Latin nouns of the First Declension end in **a** in the Nominative Singular.

a. The Stem ends in **a** (called the *Stem-Vowel*, or *Characteristic*).

b. The Case Endings are given in 5.

c. The Gender of nouns of the First Declension is Feminine, except of a few that are Masculine from their meaning ; as, **nauta,** *a sailor ;* **agricola,** *a farmer ;* **poëta,** *a poet ;* **Belgae, Celtae** (names of tribes).

d. Observe that final **a** is long in the Ablative Singular.

e. **Filia,** *a daughter,* and **dea,** *a goddess,* have **filiābus** and **deābus** in the Dative and Ablative Plural, instead of **filiīs** and **deīs.** Were it not for some such peculiarity, these words could not be distinguished, in those cases, from **filius,** *a son,* and **deus,** *a god,* of the Second Declension.

NOUNS: SECOND DECLENSION.

10. Nouns of the Second Declension end in **us, er, ir** (Masculine), **um** (Neuter).

a. The Stem ends in **o.**

b. The Case Endings are given in **6.**

c. Nouns ending in **us** are exceptions to the law stated in NOTE **8** (1), as they have **e** in the Vocative Singular.

d. **Filius** and **genius** drop **e** in the Vocative ; so do proper names ending in **ius**; as, **filī** ; **Cassī** ; **Jūlī** (instead of **filie** ; **Cassie** ; **Jūlie**). This does not affect the accent ; as, **Mercŭ'rī** (for **Mercŭ'rie**).

e. The Genitive of nouns ending in **ius** or **ium** ends in **iī** or **ī** (that is, **iī** contracted). This does not affect the accent ; as, **ingĕ'nī** (for **ingĕ'niī**).

f. **Deus,** *a god,* is thus declined : Singular **deus, deī, deō, deum, deus, deō.** Plural N. and V. **deī, diī** (or, contracted, **dī**), G. **deōrum** (or, contracted, **deūm**), D. and ABL. **deīs, diīs** (or, contracted, **dīs**), Acc. **deōs.**

g. **Vulgus,** *the crowd,* is Neuter, and has the Accusative like the Nominative. It has no Plural.

NOUNS: THIRD DECLENSION.

11. Nouns of the Third Declension are divided into two classes : —

a. Nouns whose stem ends in a Consonant. They have **um** in the Genitive Plural ; as, **mīlitum.**

b. Nouns whose stem ends in the Vowel **i.** They have **ium** in the Genitive Plural ; as, **nāvium.**

12. The Nominative Singular of most nouns is formed by adding **s** to the stem.

a. If the stem ends in c or g, the Nominative will end in x (**1** (3)) ; as, lux (= lūc + s) ; rex (= rēg + s).

b. If the stem ends in t or d, those letters will be dropped before the final s of the Nominative (**1** (4) *a*) ; as, aetās (= aetāt + s) ; custōs (= custōd + s) ; lapis (= lapid + s).

13. In forming the Nominative, the vowel before the final consonant of the stem is often changed.

a. The most common change is from i to e ; as, mīles, jūdex, nōmen, nūbēs (from the stems mīlit-, jūdic-, nōmin-, nūbi-).

b. Other vowel changes are from i to u (as, caput, from stem capit-) ; i to o (as, virgō, multitūdō, from stems virgin-, multitūdin-) ; o to u (as, corpus, from stem corpor-) ; e to u (as, opus, from stem oper-).

REMARK. In the Genitives of corpus, opus, flōs, and others of like form, r takes the place of s, according to the law stated in **1** (2) ; as, corporis, operis, flōris, etc., instead of corposis, opesis, flōsis, etc.

14. Nominatives ending in o, (as, leō, multitūdō, virgō) have lost the final n of the stem. The stems of these nouns are leōn-, multitūdin-, virgin-. It will be seen from these examples that nouns ending in do and go also change the vowel (i) before n to o.

Consonant-Stems.

15. Nouns whose stem ends in a Consonant *increase in the Genitive;* that is, they have more syllables in that case than in the Nominative. Notice the REMARK below.

a. The final consonant of the stem may be a *Mute* or a *Liquid* (**4**, page 17) ; as, rēg-, duc-, capit-, custōd-, consul-, leōn-.

b. The Nominative Singular, except in the case of Neuters and nouns having Liquid stems, is formed by adding s to the stem. For Examples, see **12**, *a, b.*

REMARK. Pater, māter, frāter (Genitives, patris, mātris, frātris), *seem* not to increase in the Genitive. The reason is that the stems are really pater-, māter-, frāter-, and that they are contracted to patr-, mātr-, frātr- ; so that patris is for pateris, etc.

Vowel-Stems.

16. Nouns whose stem ends in the Vowel i *do not increase in the Genitive.* Notice the REMARK below.

156 NOTES.

a. The Nominative Singular, except of Neuters, is formed by adding **s** to the stem; as, nāvis (= nāvi + s).

b. As in nouns having Consonant-stems, i in the stem is frequently changed to **e** in the Nominative; as, mare, nūbēs (from stems mari-, nūbi-).

c. Nouns having vowel-stems end: —

(1.) In ēs and is (Feminine, with a few exceptions).

(2.) In e, al, ar (Neuter); *these have ī in the Ablative Singular.*

REMARK. Neuters (ending in al, ar), as animal, calcar (Genitives, animālis, calcāris), *seem* to increase in the Genitive. These forms, however, have lost a final e in the Nominative (as will be explained hereafter), and hence are to be regarded as nouns ending in āle, āre (26, *b*). Animāle, calcāre (Genitives, animālis, calcāris), *do not increase.*

Peculiarities of Vowel-Stems.

17. Nouns having i-stems differ from those having Consonant-stems in the following respects: —

a. The Genitive Plural ends in **ium**; Neuters have **ia** in the Nominative, Accusative, and Vocative, Plural. This seems irregular; but it is not at all so, as **um** and **a** are added to the *stem* (ending in i) just as to a stem ending in a consonant.

b. The Ablative Singular of all Neuters (ending in e, al, ar) ends in ī. The nouns ignis, nāvis, turris, and some others, have e or ī in the Ablative.

c. Some nouns have im in the Accusative Singular; others (as turris) have em or im. These can be best learned by practice.

d. The Accusative Plural (Masculine and Feminine) is often written īs; as, turrēs (or īs); nūbēs (or īs).

18. Monosyllables (*one-syllable* nouns), whose stem (in the Singular) ends in two consonants, are declined as *consonant-stems* in the Singular, but as *vowel-stems* in the Plural. That is, they increase in the Genitive, yet have ium in the Genitive Plural, and ēs or īs in the Accusative Plural; as, urbs, nox (Genitive Plural, urbium, noctium). The same principle applies to many nouns (*not* monosyllables) having stems (in the Singular) ending in two consonants; as, cohors, cliens (Genitive Plural, cohortium, clientium).

19. The Rules for Gender according to Nominative endings are given under N. 4.

a. The following nouns, in common use, are exceptions to these rules, being *Masculine*: dens, *a tooth*, fons, *a fountain*, mons, *a moun-*

NOTES. 157

tain, **pons**, *a bridge;* **ignis,** *fire,* **finis,** *a limit, end,* **collis,** *a hill.* According to the rules, these nouns should be *Feminine.*

b. There are many nouns not provided for by the rules : the gender of these must be learned by practice ; as, **jūs** (Genitive, **jūris**), *right, law* (Neuter); **iter** (Genitive, **itineris**), *journey, march* (Neuter).

NOUNS: FOURTH DECLENSION.

20. Nouns of the Fourth Declension end in **us** (Masculine),* **ū** (Neuter).

a. The Stem ends in **u.** The Case Endings are given under **6.**

b. The Nominative Singular of Masculines is formed by adding **s** to the stem ; as, **curru + s.**

c. From **7,** it will be seen that the Fourth Declension resembles the Third. The Genitive Singular of **currus,** for instance, is contracted from **curruis** to **currūs,** and hence the *long* u (**11,** *e,* p. 21). Other instances of contraction are shown in the Table under **7.**

d. Notice that, in the Dative and Ablative Plural, the **u** of the stem becomes **i;** also, that Neuter nouns have all cases in the Singular (except the Genitive) alike.

REMARK. Dissyllables (words of *two syllables*) ending in **cus** (as **lacus**), and a few others, have **ubus** in the Dative and Ablative Plural.

21. Most nouns of the Fourth Declension are formed from the Supine stem of verbs ; as, **exercitus, mōtus, adventus** (from **exerceō, moveō, adveniō**).

a. The Supines of verbs are therefore nouns of the Fourth Declension, but have only the Accusative and Ablative Singular.

b. **Domus** (*house* or *home*) belongs both to the Fourth and Second Declensions. Its inflection will be found under the References given in Lesson XXXV.

NOUNS: FIFTH DECLENSION.

22. Nouns of the Fifth Declension end in **ēs.** The Nominative = Stem **+ s.**

a. The Stem ends in **ē.** The Case Endings are given under **6.**

b. The Gender is Feminine ; except **diēs** (*day*), which is usually Masculine. **Merīdiēs** (*noon*) is also Masculine.

* **Manus, domus, Īdūs** (Plural), and a few others, are Feminine.

c. Only two nouns, diēs and rēs, have all the cases in the Plural. A few others have the Nominative and Accusative, Plural.

d. Contrary to the rule (11, b, p. 20), e is *long* before i in the Genitive and Dative Singular in all nouns except rēs, spēs, fidēs.

Compound Nouns.

23. There are, in Latin, several Compound Nouns. Of these, the two most common are: —

α. Respublica (= the noun rēs + the Feminine adjective publica), meaning *the public affair*, that is, *the state*. Both parts of the word are declined, — rēs as the noun (Fifth Declension) and publica as the feminine of bonus. Genitive = reīpublicae, or reī publicae.

b. Jusjūrandum (= the noun jūs + the Neuter participle jūrandum, from jūrō, *to swear*), meaning *an oath*. Jūs is the noun, Third Declension Neuter, and jūrandum is declined like bonum. Genitive = jūrisjūrandī.

c. Pater, māter, and some other nouns, are often joined with familiās (an old form of the Genitive, First Declension, = familiae). The first noun is declined regularly, but familiās does not change its form; as, patresfamiliās (*the heads of families*); mātresfamiliās (*matrons*).

ADJECTIVES.*

24. Latin Adjectives are declined like Nouns. As they must agree with a Noun or Pronoun in Gender, Number, and Case (108), they are declined in *three* Genders, *two* Numbers, and *six* Cases. They are divided into two classes: —

a. Adjectives whose Masculine and Neuter forms are like Masculine and Neuter nouns of the Second Declension, and whose Feminine form is like a Feminine noun of the First Declension; as, bonus (Masculine), bona (Feminine), bonum (Neuter). That is, they are declined exactly as servus, stella, bellum, would be, if declined *side by side*. These Adjectives are therefore called **Adjectives of the First and Second Declensions.**

b. Adjectives declined like Nouns of the Third Declension are called **Adjectives of the Third Declension.**

---

* Ūnus, alius, and others having the same peculiarities of declension, are described under Numeral Adjectives (43).

NOTES. 159

All Adjectives of the First and Second Declensions have a separate form for each gender; but Adjectives of the Third Declension differ in this respect, according to the rules stated in the next NOTE.

25. *Adjectives of the Third Declension* may have, in the Nominative Singular, (1) a separate ending for each gender; (2) one form for both Masculine and Feminine, and another for the Neuter; (3) the same form for *all* genders. For convenience, therefore, we say that an Adjective of the Third Declension has *three endings*, or *two endings*, or *one ending*. They can be distinguished by the following rules: —

a. Adjectives of *three endings* end in **er**; as, **ācer** (Masculine), **ācris** (Feminine), **ācre** (Neuter).

b. Adjectives of *two endings* end in **is**, or are in the Comparative Degree; as, **fortis** (*brave*); fortior (*braver*). These have, in the Nominative Singular, **fortis** (Masculine and Feminine), **forte** (Neuter); **fortior** (Masculine and Feminine), **fortius** (Neuter).

c. Adjectives of *one ending* include those *not* ending in **er** or **is**, and *not* in the Comparative Degree; as, **audax, ingens, vetus.**

26. a. Adjectives of the Third Declension ending in **er** are i-stems. The fact to be specially noticed is that they have **ī** *in the Ablative Singular*, and **ēs** or **īs** *in the Accusative Plural (Masculine and Feminine).*

b. Adjectives ending in **is** are i-stems. They have **ī** *in the Ablative Singular, and* **ēs** or **īs** *in the Accusative Plural (Masculine and Feminine).* Neuter nouns (Third Declension), ending in **al** and **ar**, are really Neuter forms of Adjectives ending in **is** (the **e** having disappeared); as, **animālis,** *living,* **animāle** (**animal**), *a living thing.*

c. Adjectives of *one ending* are i-stems. Notice, however, (1) that they *increase in the Genitive ;* (2) that they have **e** or **ī** in the Ablative Singular. In the Plural they are declined like **fortis**. (**Vetus**, *old*, and a few others have consonant-stems in both numbers.)

CAUTION. As these adjectives have *two endings* in the Accusative Singular (because the Accusative, Neuter, must be like the Nominative), it will be less confusing to decline them in two columns, thus : —

	M. F.	N.
Nominative	audax	audax.

d. *Comparatives* have *two endings* and Consonant (*Liquid*) stems; but notice that they have **e** or **ī** in the Ablative Singular. Also notice that the Accusative Plural (Masculine and Feminine) has **ēs** or **īs**.

CAUTION. Beginners are very apt to write the Nominative and Genitive Plural **ia, ium**. Notice that these forms have no **i**.

27. Plūs, *more*, is a Neuter Noun in the Singular, declined like jūs; hence, to express *more wisdom; more pain*, we must say plūs sapientiae; plūs dolōris (122, *b*).

In the Plural it is an Adjective, declined like the Plural of any other Comparative, except that it has ium in the Genitive.

28. As already stated, Adjectives of one ending, and also Comparatives, have e or ī in the Ablative Singular. The usual distinction is that the form ending in ī is used *adjectively*, and the form ending in e, *substantively*.

COMPARISON.

29. Adjectives expressing *quality* are compared, in Latin as in English, in three ways : (1) *regularly ;* (2) *irregularly ;* (3) by the use of the Adverbs *more* and *most.*

(1.) Regular Comparison.

30. The Comparative (Masculine) is formed by adding ior, and the Superlative by adding issimus (Masculine) to the stem of the Positive, *minus the stem vowel ;* as,

cārus, *dear ;*   cārior, *dearer ;*   cārissimus, *dearest.*
fortis, *brave ;*   fortior, *braver ;*   fortissimus, *bravest.*
audax, *bold ;*   audācior, *bolder ;*   audācissimus, *boldest.*

REMARK. The Comparative is always of the Third Declension, and the Superlative of the First and Second.

a. Participles, if used as Adjectives, are regularly compared ; as,

amans, amantior, amantissimus ; apertus, apertior, apertissimus.

(2.) Irregular Comparison.

31. Two classes of Adjectives do not form their Superlative according to the law of Regular Comparison : —

a. Adjectives ending in -er form the Superlative by adding rĭmus to the Positive ; as,

ācer, ācrior, ācerrimus ; miser, miserior, miserrimus.

b. Six Adjectives ending in -lis form the Superlative by adding lĭmus to the stem, minus the stem vowel i ; as, facilis, facilior, facillimus. The list is : —

facilis, *easy ;*   similis, *like ;*   gracilis, *slender.*
difficilis, *difficult ;*   dissimilis, *unlike ;*   humilis, *lowly.*

NOTES. 161

32. Compound Adjectives ending in -dĭcus, -fĭcus, -vŏlus (derived from the verbs dīcō, faciō, volō), form the Comparative and Superlative as though they were participial forms ending in ns ; as,

maledicus, *abusive (ill-speaking)*, maledicentior, maledicentissimus.
mūnificus, *liberal*, mūnificentior, mūnificentissimus.
benevolus, *benevolent (well-wishing)*, benevolentior, benevolentissimus.

33. The Adjectives bonus (*good*), malus (*bad*), magnus (*great*), parvus (*small*), multus (*much*), multī (plural of multus, meaning *many*), and a few others, are very irregular in their forms of comparison. Like the English *good, bad*, and other adjectives, the three degrees are formed from different stems. References to their forms of comparison are given in Lesson XXIX.

34. Five Adjectives have no Positive. They are, in the Comparative, citerior (*hither*), interior (*inner*), prior (*former*), propior (*nearer*), ulterior (*farther*). They are derived from Prepositions.

In English, also, we have Adjectives without a Positive, and derived from Prepositions ; as, (*in*), *inner, innermost* (or *inmost*).

35. These four have peculiar Superlatives : —
Exterus (*outside*), superus (*high*), inferus (*low*), posterus (*following*). These, also, are derived from Prepositions. References to their comparison are given in Lesson XXXIV.

36. The following are more or less peculiar in comparison : —

a. Dīves (*rich*), dīvitior or dītior, dīvitissimus or dītissimus.

b. Juvenis (*young*), minor nātū (*less by birth;* that is, *younger*), minimus nātū (*least by birth;* that is, *youngest*). Instead of minor nātū, minor alone is often used (nātū being understood), especially in the plural ; as, minōrēs, *descendants*. Senex (*old*), mājor nātū, maximus nātū. Or, mājōrēs alone is used for the Comparative (nātū being understood), in the sense of *elders* or *ancestors*.

(3.) **Comparison by** MORE *and* MOST.

37. Adjectives which have a vowel before the ending us usually form the Comparative and Superlative by the use of the Adverbs magis (*more*), and maximē (*most*) ; as, dubius (*doubtful*), magis dubius, maximē dubius.

Formation and Comparison of Adverbs.

38. Adverbs of *Manner* are formed from Adjectives. English Adverbs of Manner are formed by adding *ly* to Adjectives ; as, *dearly, bravely*.

In Latin Adverbs the ending of the Positive shows *from what Declension of Adjectives* the Adverb is derived.

 a. An Adverb is formed from the stem of an Adjective of the First and Second Declensions by changing the stem-vowel to ē; as, cārē, *dearly* (from stems cāro-, cāra-, *dear*). Other examples are: dignē (*worthily*); pulchrē (*beautifully*).

 b. An Adverb is formed from an Adjective of the Third Declension by adding ter to the stem; as, forti-ter (*bravely*), gravi-ter (*heavily*), audāci-ter* (*boldly*), ācri-ter (*eagerly*).

Adjectives ending in ns (Genitive, -ntis) drop ti from the stem before forming Adverbs; as, sapienter (*wisely*), for sapienti-ter; prūdenter (*prudently*).

 c. In Adverbs regularly compared, the Comparative is the same in form as the Neuter Accusative Singular of the Adjective (Comparative); as, cārius (*more dearly*), gravius (*more heavily*), ācrius (*more eagerly*), sapientius (*more wisely*), melius (*better*).

 d. The Superlative of the Adjective belongs to the First and Second Declensions. Therefore, according to the rule given above (*a*), the Superlative of the Adverb will end in ē; as, cārissimē, ācerrimē, facillimē, sapientissimē, pessimē.

Comparison of Adverbs: Peculiar Forms.

39. Bene, *well* (from bonus), melius, optimē.

Magnopere, *greatly;* magis, *more;* maximē, *most.* There is no simple Adverb derived from the Positive of magnus. Magnopere = magnō + opere, and is used as the Positive of the Adverb. Facile is regularly used instead of faciliter (see *a*, below).

 a. The Accusative and Ablative Singular of the Adjective (Neuter) are very often used as Adverbs; as, multum, multō (*much*). Facile is regularly used, as stated above.

 b. These Adverbs are compared in like manner, though not formed from Adjectives: —

   diū, *long* (*in time*), diūtius, diūtissimē.
   saepe, *often*, saepius, saepissimē.

Peculiar Meanings of Adjectives.

40. *a.* The Comparative may be variously translated; as, audācior, *bolder, rather bold, too bold.*

   * Audāciter is usually written audācter.

b. The Superlative may often be rendered by *very;* as, **vir optimus,** *a very excellent man.*

c. **Quam** (adverb of degree) with the Superlative has a peculiar force. Supplicium quam gravissimum means *as severe punishment as possible.* So quam plūrimī, *as many as possible.*

d. **Per** gives to a Positive almost the meaning of a Superlative; as, permagnus, *very great* (that is, *thoroughly great*).

NUMERAL ADJECTIVES.

41. Numeral Adjectives are ***Cardinal*** and ***Ordinal***, as in English (see **9,** *b,* page 2); as, ūnus, *one;* prīmus, *first.*

a. A third class of Numerals is composed of adjectives called ***Distributives.*** They answer the questions, *How many at a time? How many in a set?* Examples are singulī, *one by one;* bīnī, *two by two, in pairs.*

The lists of these Numerals are given in the Grammars and in the Appendix.

Declension of Numeral Adjectives.

42. *a.* Ordinal Adjectives are declined like **bonus.**

b. Distributive Adjectives are declined like the plural of **bonus.**

c. Cardinal Adjectives, from 4 to 100, inclusive, are *not declined.*

From 200 to 900, inclusive, they are declined like the plural of **bonus;** as, **ducentī, ae, a** (*two hundred*). The declension of the other Cardinal Adjectives is described in the next NOTE.

43. *a.* Ūnus is peculiar in its declension. In general it is like **bonus,** but it has ūnīus in the Genitive Singular, all genders (instead of ūnī, ūnae, ūnī), and ūnī in the Dative Singular, all genders (instead of ūnō, ūnae, ūnō).

In the Plural ūnī means *alone* or *only;* as, ūnī Ubiī, *the Ubii alone.*

b. Like ūnus are declined these adjectives, which are not Numerals, but are placed here because their irregularities are the same as those of ūnus: —

alius (neuter, aliud), *other.*
nullus, *no.*
sōlus, *alone.*
tōtus, *whole.*
ullus, *any.*
alter (genitive, alterīus), *the other* (of two).
neuter (genitive, neutrīus), *neither.*
uter (genitive, utrīus), *which* (of two).

c. Duo has peculiar forms of declension, which are given in the Grammars and the Appendix.

REMARK. Ambō (*both*) is declined like duo.

d. **Trēs** (Neuter, tria) is declined like the plural of **fortis**.
e. **Mille** may be a Noun or an Adjective.

As a Noun : (1) it is Neuter and is declined like **mare**, but it has, in the Singular, only the Nominative and Accusative (mille) ; (2) it is always followed by the Genitive (**123**, *c*); as, **mille hominum**; **duo millia** (or **milia**) **passuum** (*two miles*).

As an Adjective, it is *not declined*, and may be used in agreement with a noun in *any* case ; as, **mille virī**; **cum mille virīs**.

NUMERAL ADVERBS.

44. Numeral Adverbs answer the question, *How often ?* The list is given in the Grammars and the Appendix.

PRONOUNS.

45. Pronouns are of seven classes : —
1. Personal ; 2. Reflexive ; 3. Possessive ; 4. Demonstrative ; 5. Relative ; 6. Interrogative ; 7. Indefinite.

The Personal and Reflexive Pronouns are declined as Substantives ; their gender must be decided by the *sense*. All the other Pronouns are declined as Adjectives, having a separate form for each gender.

46. The *Personal Pronouns* are : First Person, **ego**, *I* (plural, **nōs**) ; Second Person, **tū**, *you* (plural, **vōs**). There is no Personal Pronoun of the Third Person in Latin ; but a Demonstrative (usually **is**) is used instead. As in English, this pronoun requires a separate form for each gender, and **is** supplies these forms. The declension of **is** is given under Demonstrative Pronouns.

REMARK. **Ego** and **is** (an), of course, have no Vocative.

47. *Reflexive Pronouns* (that is, pronouns that *turn*, or *refer, back*) are so called because they *refer back* to the subject of their sentence or clause. Hence they have no Nominative or Vocative. The Reflexive Pronouns of the First and Second Persons have case-forms precisely like the Genitive, Dative, Accusative, and Ablative of the Personal Pronouns. The list is : First Person, **meī**, *of myself* (**nostrī**, *of ourselves*); Second Person, **tuī**, *of yourself* (**vestrī**, *of yourselves*); Third Person, **suī**, *of himself, herself, itself* (**suī**, *of themselves*). The plural of **suī** is declined like the singular.

CAUTION. Notice that **suī** cannot be used as a Third Personal Pronoun, for two reasons : (1) it has no Nominative ; (2) it is *always used reflexively*. The following conjugation of **laudō** in the Present Indicative,

NOTES. 165

with a subject and object expressed, will help to make clear the use of the Personal and Reflexive Pronouns : —

Ego mē laudō, *I praise myself.*　　　　nōs nōs laudāmus.
tū tē laudās, *you praise yourself.*　　　vōs vōs laudātis.
is (ea) sē laudat, *he (she) praises himself (herself).*　iī (eae) sē laudant.

48. Possessive Pronouns are formed from the Personal and Reflexive Pronouns, and are declined as Adjectives of the First and Second Declensions. They are : —

meus (Vocative Singular, mī) *my,* or *mine;* tuus, *your,* or *yours;* suus, *his, her (hers), its;* noster, *our,* or *ours;* vester, *your,* or *yours;* suus, *their,* or *theirs.*

CAUTION. Suus (like suī) is used *reflexively.* When *his, her, its,* or *their,* is *not* reflexive, the Genitive of is should be used ; as, dominus servum suum vocāvit, et opus ējus laudāvit, *the master called his (the master's) slave, and praised his (the slave's) work.* Beginners often find the *meaning* of suus troublesome. It is an Adjective, and must agree with its noun in *gender, number,* and *case.* Being *reflexive,* its meaning must be decided, not from its *ending,* but from the meaning of the Subject. The following sentences will make this clear : —

Rex servum suum vocat, *the king calls* his *slave;* rēgīna servum suum vocat, *the queen calls* her *slave;* puerī mātrem suam amant, *the boys love* their *mother;* puellae patrem suum amant, *the girls love* their *father.*

49. Demonstrative Pronouns (that is, Pronouns that *point out*) agree with the Substantives which they limit in gender, number, and case. They are declined, for the most part, like Adjectives of the First and Second Declensions. They (particularly is) are often used as the Personal Pronoun of the Third Person (**46**). From their meaning, they all (except ipse) lack the Vocative. They are : —

hīc, *this* (near me);　　　　　　is, *that* (when used Adjectively).
ille, *that* (near him, or yonder);　ipse, *self.*
iste, *that* (near you);　　　　　īdem,* *the same,* = is + dem (an emphatic syllable).

REMARKS. 1. From their meaning, hīc, iste, ille, are often called *Demonstratives of the First, Second, and Third Persons.*

2. Is does not point out as definitely as hīc, ille, iste. It is very commonly used as an Antecedent to the Relative Pronoun ; as, is quī, *he who* (*one who, a man who*). Sometimes it has no greater force than the

---

* For change of **m** to **n** (as **eundem** for **eumdem**) see 1 (5).

Article *the;* as, **centum mīlitēs eō tempore habuit,** *he had one hundred soldiers at the time.*

3. **Ipse** is used to add emphasis to some Noun or Pronoun ; as, **vōs ipsī,** *you yourselves;* **vir ipse,** *the man himself* (or *the very man*).

50. The ***Relative Pronoun*** is **quī.** It has a separate form for each gender (**quī, quae, quod**), since it must agree in gender with its Antecedent. It is to be rendered *who, which, that,* according to the sense.

51. The ***Interrogative Pronoun*** resembles the Relative in declension. It has two forms, which are regularly used as follows : —

1. **quis, quae, quid,** used as a Substantive ; as, **quis mē laudat?** *who praises me?* **quid commīsit?** *what has he done?*

2. **quī, quae, quod,** used as an Adjective ; as, **quī homō mē laudat?** *what man praises me?* **quod facinus commīsit?** *what deed has he done?*

REMARK. Quis and quī are sometimes used for each other.

CAUTION. When the question refers to one of *two*, we must use **uter, utra, utrum** (*which of the two?*).

52. ***Indefinite Pronouns*** do not refer to *definite* objects. The simple Indefinite (= *any*) is **quis** (or **quī**). We very seldom find this form, however, except in *compounds*, which, with a very few exceptions, are declined exactly like the Relative and Interrogative Pronouns. The compounds (in common use) that have peculiar forms are **aliquis, sīquis, nēquis.** These, like the Interrogative Pronoun, have two forms, — **quis** (Substantive), and **quī** (Adjective). These compounds are declined, in general, like the Relative and Interrogative ; but notice that they regularly have final **a**, where the Relative and Interrogative have final **ae** (except in the Nominative Plural Feminine).

a. **Aliquis** (= **alius + quis**) means, literally, *some one or other.*
b. **Sīquis** and **nēquis** are written as compounds, or as separate words. This is because **sī** and **nē** are Conjunctions, and connect clauses as well as help in forming the compound pronouns.
c. The meanings of **aliquis, sīquis, nēquis,** are given here : —

SUBSTANTIVE.	ADJECTIVE.
aliquis, *any one, some one ;*	**aliquī,** *any, some.*
sīquis, *if any one ;*	**sīquī,** *if any.*
nēquis, *lest any one ;*	**nequī,** *lest any.*

d. Other Indefinite Pronouns (the first part declined like the Relative and Interrogative) are : **quīcumque,** *whoever* or *whosoever ;* **quīdam,** *a certain man* (or *a certain*); **quīvīs** (= **quī + vīs,** from **volō**), *any-you-please ;* **quisque,** *each, every.*

53. The following General Remarks on the Pronouns will be found useful: —

a. The Preposition cum (*with*) is joined as an Enclitic (**195**, 3) to the Ablative of the Personal, Reflexive, Relative, and Interrogative Pronouns; as, mēcum, nōbīscum, tēcum, vōbīscum, sēcum, quibuscum; but cum iīs (hīs, illīs).

b. Quisque (*each*) with a Superlative has a peculiar meaning; as, quisque sapientissimus, *all the wisest*. That is, if *each* is wisest, then *all* are. So also, quisque dītissimus, *all the richest*.

c. The Enclitic -que, added to the simple Indefinite, gives it a *universal* force; as, quis (*any*); quisque (*each, every*). This same force is given to an Adverb, by adding -que; as, ubi (*where*), ubique (*everywhere*); unde (*whence*), undique (*from every side, on every side*).

d. The Preposition inter, with a Reflexive Pronoun in the Plural, gives a peculiar force and meaning; as, inter nōs amāmus; inter vōs amātis; inter sē amant: *we (you, they) love each other*.

VERBS.

Special Note for Lesson II.

54. English Verbs are conjugated very much alike. In Latin, they are divided into four classes (called *Conjugations*), each Conjugation being somewhat unlike the others. They are called the First, Second, Third, and Fourth Conjugations. Just as we distinguish Declensions of Nouns by their Stems, so we distinguish one Latin Conjugation from the others by the Stem of its Present Tense, Indicative Mode, which we call the *Present Stem*. The following facts should be carefully studied : —

1. The ***Present Stem***, in the First Conjugation, like the stem of nouns of the First Declension, ends in a. The Present Stems of amō, vocō, and līberō, are amā, vocā, līberā.

2. English verbs have very few changes of *form* in conjugation. For instance, the Present Indicative of *love*, in its common use, has *loves* in the Third Person Singular, but *love* in all the other persons of both numbers. Hence, a Personal Pronoun, as *Subject*, is needed to show what the person of each form is. In Latin verbs, however, there is a special ending for each person, in both numbers ; and the Personal Pronoun can be omitted, because each ending shows what Personal Pronoun is to be supplied in translating. These endings are called ***Personal Endings***.

In the Present Indicative of all regular verbs these Personal Endings are : —

SINGULAR.
1. -ō (*I*).
2. -s (*you*).
3. -t (*he, she, it*).

PLURAL.
1. -mus (*we*).
2. -tis (*you*).
3. -nt (*they*).

3. Each form in the Present Tense is composed of the *Present Stem*, plus the proper *Personal Ending*. In the First Person Singular the stem-vowel a unites with the personal ending; as, vocō (for vocaō), amō (for amaō). The following examples show how these forms are built up, and the exact meaning of each element in them : —

ama + nt (*love they*), voca + mus (*call we*), da + t (*gives he*).

4. Vocō may be translated in three ways : *I call ; I am calling ; I do call* (section 17, *a, b,* page 4).

5. It is evident, from what has been stated (2, 3, 4), that a single verb-form contains a Subject and Predicate, and hence *may* be a complete sentence in itself ; as, amat, *he loves.*

Special Note for Lesson VI.

55. The verb Sum (*I am*) is Irregular and Intransitive. Like the English verb *to be,* it cannot make a statement, but requires some word (usually a Noun or Adjective) to *complete* its meaning ; that is, it acts as a *Copula,* and requires a *Complement.* This Complement, whether a Noun or Adjective, must be in the same case as the Subject. Study carefully section 37, *a,* page 10.

The Present Indicative of Sum is thus inflected : —

SINGULAR.
1. sum, *I am.*
2. es, *you are.*
3. est, *he is.*

PLURAL.
1. sumus, *we are.*
2. estis, *you are.*
3. sunt, *they are.*

Notice that the Personal Endings, in several óf the forms, are like those in the Present Tense of amō.

Transitive and Intransitive Verbs; Voice; Number; Person.

56. Latin Verbs, like those in English, may be Transitive or Intransitive. Transitive Verbs have two Voices, Active and Passive. Intransitive Verbs have no Passive Voice in ordinary use. As in English, Verbs have two Numbers and three Persons.

Modes.

57. Latin Verbs have four Modes, which are very similar to those in English having the same names. They are:—

a. The ***Indicative,*** which states a positive *fact*, or asks a *direct question;* as, **amat,** *he loves;* **quis vocat?** *who calls?*
b. The ***Subjunctive,*** which does *not* state *facts*, but expresses something as *uncertain, possible, impossible, desired,* &c.; as, **sī Rōmam videat, fēlix sit,** *if he should see Rome, he would be happy;* **servum laudēmus,** *let us praise the slave.*
c. The ***Imperative,*** which *commands;* as, **amīcōs amā,** *love your friends.*
d. The ***Infinitive,*** which, in Latin as in English, does not state or command, and has no person or number. It expresses the idea of the verb *indefinitely* (see section **15,** *e*, p. 4). As in English, it is very frequently used as a Verbal Noun; as, **scīre est regere,** *knowledge is power* (literally, *to know is to rule*): **cōnātur transīre,** *he tries to cross.*

Participles.

58. Latin Verbs have four Participles, or *Verbal Adjectives:*—

a. ***Active:*** *Present* and *Future Participles.*
b. ***Passive:*** *Perfect Participle* and *Gerundive* (or *Future Participle, Passive*).

REMARK. These Participles agree with their Substantives in gender, number, and case, and (with the exception of the Present Participle, which is of the Third Declension, one ending) are declined like **bonus.**

Gerund; Supine.

59. Latin Verbs have two *Verbal Nouns:*—

a. The ***Gerund,*** which is like the English Verbal Noun ending in *-ing.* It is declined like a noun of the Second Declension, but has no Nominative or Vocative. The Infinitive takes the place of the Nominative; as, **ars canendī,** *the art of singing;* **canere est jūcundum,** *singing (to sing) is pleasant.*
b. The ***Supine,*** which is a Verbal Noun of the Fourth Declension. It has only the Accusative and Ablative. Its uses are peculiar, and will be described hereafter **(191).**

Tenses.

This NOTE *should be studied in connection with sections* **16, 17,** *page* 4.

60. The Tenses named in this NOTE are those of the Indicative Mode. This Mode is the only one in which the Tenses properly distinguish *time.*

1. *Present;* as, amō, *I love.*
2. *Imperfect;* as, amābam, *I was loving.*
3. *Future;* as, amābō, *I shall love.*
4. *Perfect;* as, amāvī, *I have loved,* or *I loved.*
5. *Pluperfect;* as, amāveram, *I had loved.*
6. *Future Perfect;* as, amāverō, *I shall have loved.*

61. A comparison of these Tenses and their meanings with the Table on page 4 will show that, —

1. The *Present, Future,* and *Future Perfect* have the same meaning as the English tenses called by the same names.

2. The *Imperfect* is like the Past Imperfect (or *Progressive*); that is, it denotes an action as *going on* (or *customary*) in past time ; as, laudābat, *he was praising* (*he kept praising, he used to praise*). It must be carefully distinguished from the Perfect.

3. The *Perfect* has two meanings, as different from each other as though they represented two distinct tense-forms, instead of one. These are : —

   a. The meaning of the English *Present Perfect ;* as, laudāvī, *I have praised.* This is called the *Perfect Definite* (that is, I have *just finished* praising).

   b. The meaning of the English *Past* (Indefinite); as, laudāvī, *I praised.* This is called the *Perfect Indefinite* * (that is, I praised at *some indefinite time* in the past).

4. The *Pluperfect* is like the English *Past Perfect.*

SPECIAL NOTE.†

62. As the Perfect has two meanings, and is really equivalent to two tenses, it may be found less confusing to give a distinct *name* to each of these uses. We may, therefore, regard the Tenses as *seven* in number. The word *Aorist* means *Indefinite,* and therefore the tenses may be thus named : —

1. *Present ;* 2. *Imperfect ;* 3. *Future ;* 4. *Perfect* (English, *Present Per-*

---

* This is also called the *Perfect Historical.*

† This Note is for the use of those who prefer the *seven-tense* system, and may be omitted by others.

NOTES.   171

fect : *I have loved*); 5. *Aorist* (English, *Past* : *I loved*); 6. *Pluperfect*; 7. *Future Perfect*. The *Perfect* is the same as the *Perfect Definite*, and the *Aorist* is the same as the *Perfect Indefinite*.

Tenses of the different Modes.

63. *a.* The ***Indicative*** has all the tenses. As in English, it is the only Mode in which the tenses actually distinguish *time*.

b. The ***Subjunctive*** lacks the *Future* and the *Future Perfect*. How it supplies this lack will be explained hereafter. The real *time* denoted by the tenses of the Subjunctive must often be decided, as in English (**19**, page 6), by the *sense*.

c. The ***Imperative*** has two tenses : *Present* and *Future*. The Present, as in English, has only the Second Person. The Future has the Second and Third Persons ; *it is seldom used*.

d. The ***Infinitive*** has three tenses : *Present*, *Perfect*, and *Future*. The Future Infinitive, Active, is made up of the Future Active Participle and **esse** (Present Infinitive of **sum**). The Future Infinitive, Passive, is described later.

e. The tenses of the ***Participles*** have already been given (**58**).

Personal Endings.

64. In English, the verb-form *love* may be in the Present Indicative First or Second Person Singular, or in the First, Second, or Third Person Plural ; a Personal Pronoun, as subject, must be expressed, or other words given, before we can tell in what person the verb-form is. In a Latin tense, however, each of the six forms shows its person by its *ending*, and the Personal Pronouns may be, and usually are, omitted. These endings are therefore called *Personal Endings* (**54**, 2). Only the Indicative, Subjunctive, and Imperative have Personal Endings. The endings of the Perfect Indicative (Active) and the Imperative are peculiar, and are given separately. The following table shows the Personal Endings : —

a. *Personal Endings : Indicative and Subjunctive.*

	ACTIVE.		PASSIVE.	SUBJECT.
SINGULAR.	1. m (or ō) 2. s 3. t	SINGULAR.	1. r 2. ris (or re) 3. tur	*I.* *you.* *he, she, it.*
PLURAL.	1. mus 2. tis 3. nt	PLURAL.	1. mur 2. mĭnī 3. ntur	*we.* *you.* *they.*

b. *Perfect Indicative, Active.*

SINGULAR. {1. ī. 2. istī. 3. it. PLURAL. {1. imus. 2. istis. 3. ērunt (or ēre).

c. *Imperative.*

ACTIVE.
Present.
SING. 2. same as Pres. Stem.
PLUR. 2. te.

PASSIVE.
Present.
SING. 2. re (like the Pres. Inf. Act.).
PLUR. 2. mĭnī.

Future.
SING. 2. tō.
3. tō.
PLUR. 2. tōte.
3. ntō.

Future.
SING. 2. tor.
3. tor.
PLUR. 2. wanting.
3. ntor.

Conjugations.

65. Latin Verbs are divided into four Conjugations (**54**). They are distinguished by the vowel before re in the Present Infinitive Active. That part of the Present Infinitive which is left after taking away re is called the *Present Stem.* This Present Stem is here shown for the four Conjugations: —

CONJUGATION.	PRESENT INFINITIVE.	PRESENT STEM.
I.	amāre.	amā.
II.	monēre.	monē.
III.	regĕre.	regĕ.*
IV.	audīre.	audī.

Principal Parts.

66. The Principal Parts of a verb are so called because from them all the other forms of the verb are made up. They are *four* in number. The Roman figures indicate the Conjugations: —

	I.	II.	III.	IV.
Present Indicative.	amō.	moneō.	regō.	audiō.
Present Infinitive.	amāre.	monēre.	regĕre.	audīre.
Perfect Indicative.	amāvī.	monuī.	rexī.	audīvī.
Supine.	amātum.	monitum.	rectum.	audītum.

* The *Verb-Stem* of the Third Conjugation is usually *not* the same as the Present Stem. It is described in 79, 2, and *a.*

REMARK. As the Passive has no Supine, it has but three Principal Parts; as, *Present Indicative*, amor; *Present Infinitive*, **amārī**; *Perfect Indicative*, **amātus sum**.

Stems.

67. A Verb has three Stems: Present, Perfect, and Supine. The Present Stem has been described in **65**. To find the Perfect Stem, cut off ī from the Perfect Indicative. To find the Supine Stem, cut off um from the Supine. The Stems of the verbs given in **66** are:—

	PRESENT STEM.	PERFECT STEM.	SUPINE STEM.
I.	amā-	amāv-	amāt-
II.	monē-	monu-	monit-
III.	regĕ-	rex-	rect-
IV.	audī-	audīv-	audīt-

Formation of Tenses: Indicative Active.

68. *a.* The *Present* has no Tense Sign. It = Present Stem + Personal Endings. In the First and Third Conjugations, the stem-vowel is lost before o (as, amō = amaō). In the Third, there are vowel changes. In the Fourth, the Third Person Plural is audiunt (not audi-nt).

b. The *Imperfect* always has the Tense Sign **ba**. The vowel **e** (before **ba**) is always *long*.

c. The *Future* of the First and Second Conjugations always has the Tense Sign **bi**. The i disappears before o [as, amāb(i)ō, monēb(i)ō], and becomes u in the Third Person Plural.

The Future of the Third Conjugation consists of the Present Stem + Personal Endings. E becomes a in the First Person Singular. Verbs in io retain the i (like those of the Fourth Conjugation).

The Future of the Fourth Conjugation consists of the Present Stem + am, ēs, etc. It is inflected like that of the Third Conjugation.

d. The *Perfect* = Perfect Stem + Personal Endings of the Perfect, for all Conjugations.

e. The *Pluperfect* always has the Tense Sign **ĕra**.

f. The *Future Perfect* always has the Tense Sign **ĕri**. The i disappears before o [as, monuĕr(i)ō, amāvĕr(i)ō].

Formation of Tenses: Subjunctive Active.

69. *a.* The Present consists, in the First Person Singular of the
(1.) *First Conjugation*, of the Present Stem + m; a is changed to e.
(2.) *Second Conjugation*, of the Present Stem + am.

(3.) *Third Conjugation*, of the Present Stem + m; e changed to a.
(4.) *Fourth Conjugation*, of the Present Stem + am.
b. The Imperfect always has the Tense Sign re. It may be obtained by adding m to the Present Infinitive Active.
c. The Perfect always has the Tense Sign ĕri.
d. The Pluperfect always has the Tense Sign isse.

Formation of Tenses: Imperative Active.

70. The Present, Second Person Singular = Present Stem. As the forms of the Imperatives of the four Conjugations differ somewhat from each other, and are apt to confuse a beginner, this simple Rule will be found useful : *All the forms of the Imperative Active (except the Present, Second Singular) can be obtained from the Present Indicative (Second and Third Persons) by changing the Personal Endings to those of the Imperative.*

Formation of Tenses: Infinitive Active.

71. a. *Present* = Present Stem + re.
b. *Perfect* = Perfect Stem + isse.
c. *Future* = Future Participle + esse (Present Infinitive of sum).

Formation of Participles, Gerund, and Supine.

72. a. *Present Participle* = Present Stem + ns or ens; as, ama-ns, rege-ns, audi-ens.
b. *Future Participle* = Supine Stem + ūrus; as, amāt-ūrus.
c. *Gerund* = Present Stem + ndī or endī; as, ama-ndī, audi-endī.
d. *Supine* = Supine Stem + um; as, monit-um.

Formation of Tenses: Indicative Passive.

73. a. The *Present* is formed as in 68, a, but with Passive endings. Notice, however, that in the Third Conjugation, the Second Person Singular has ĕ and not i; as, regĕris (Active, regis).
b. The *Imperfect* has the regular Tense Sign and Passive endings.
c. The *Future* of the First and Second Conjugations has the Regular Tense Sign ; but notice that the Second Person Singular has bĕ (not bī); as, amābĕris, monēbĕris. The Future of the Third and Fourth Conjugations has the same general form as the Future Active, with Passive endings ; as, regēris, audiēris.
d. The Perfect Stem is not used in the Passive Voice. The *Perfect, Pluperfect,* and *Future Perfect,* Passive, are compound, consisting of the *Perfect Passive Participle* with sum, eram, erō.

NOTES. 175

Formation of Tenses: Subjunctive Passive.

74. *a.* The *Present* and *Imperfect* are formed as the same tenses are in the Active, but with Passive endings.

b. The *Perfect* and *Pluperfect* are compound, and consist of the *Perfect Passive Participle* with **sim** and **essem**.

Formation of Tenses: Imperative Passive.

75. Notice : —

a. That the Second Person Singular, Present, is the same in form as the *Present Infinitive Active.*

b. That there is no Second Person Plural in the Future.

c. That the other forms can be obtained from the Present Indicative Passive according to **70.**

Formation of Tenses: Infinitive Passive.

76. *a.* In the First, Second, and Fourth Conjugations the *Present* is formed by changing final **e** of the Present Infinitive Active to **ī**. In the Third it is formed from the *Present Stem* by changing **ĕ** to **ī**; as, **amāri**, but **regī**.

b. The *Perfect* = *Perfect Passive Participle* + **esse**.

c. The *Future* = *Supine* (Accusative) + **īrī**. The word **īrī** is the Present Infinitive Passive of **eō** (*I go*), and **amātum īrī** has the idea of *going to be loved*. This tense of the Infinitive is a peculiar form and one seldom used. What takes its place will be explained hereafter.

Formation of Passive Participles.

77. *a.* The *Perfect* = Supine Stem + **us**; as, **amāt-us**.

b. The *Gerundive* (or *Future Participle*) = Present Stem + **ndus** or **endus**; as, **ama-ndus, audi-endus**.

Synopsis.

78. A Synopsis is a general outline of a Verb. The following Synopsis of **amō**, *I love*, shows from what Stem each form is made. In the Synopsis of any other Conjugation the same *Modes, Tenses*, etc., would be formed from the same Stems. The only differences would be those peculiar to each Conjugation, and described in **68–77.**

ACTIVE.

STEM.	Present, amā-	Perfect, amāv-	Supine, amāt-
INDICATIVE.	Present, amō Imperfect, amābam Future, amābō	Perfect, amāvī Pluperfect, amāveram Future Perfect, amāverō	
SUBJUNCTIVE.	Present, amem Imperfect, amārem	Perfect, amāverim Pluperfect, amāvissem	
IMPERATIVE.	Present, amā Future, amātō		
INFINITIVE.	Present, amāre	Perfect, amāvisse	Future, amātūrus esse
PARTICIPLES.	Present, amans		Future, amātūrus
GERUND.	Genitive, amandī Dative, etc. amandō, etc.		
SUPINE.			Accusative, amātum Ablative, amātū

PASSIVE.

STEM.	Present, amā-		Supine, amāt-
INDICATIVE.	Present, amor Imperfect, amābar Future, amābor		Perfect, amātus sum Pluperfect, amātus eram Future Perfect, amātus erō
SUBJUNCTIVE.	Present, amer Imperfect, amārer		Perfect, amātus sim Pluperfect, amātus essem
IMPERATIVE.	Present, amāre Future, amātor		
INFINITIVE.	Present, amārī		Perfect, amātus esse Future, amātum īrī
PARTICIPLES.	Ger'dive, amandus		Perfect, amātus
GERUND.			

NOTES. 177

Some Peculiarities of the Four Conjugations.

79. Most verbs of the First and Fourth Conjugations have Principal Parts that are quite similar. The Perfect Stem is formed by adding v, and the Supine Stem by adding t, to the Present Stem; but the Second and Third Conjugations, and some verbs of the First and Fourth, have peculiarities which should be carefully noticed.

1. Only a few verbs of the Second Conjugation form their Perfect and Supine Stem by adding v and t to the Present Stem. Dēleō, *I destroy;* fleō, *I weep;* and the compounds of pleō, *I fill* (as, compleō), are those in common use; as, compleō, complēre, complēvī, complētum.

Most verbs of the Second Conjugation form the Perfect by changing v to u (3, p. 17), and the e of the stem disappears; as, monuī (for moneuī = monēvī). They form the Supine by changing *long* e of the stem to *short* i; as, monĭtum (for monētum).

2. The Third Conjugation (like the Third Declension) has the greatest variety of forms of all the Conjugations. These differences occur in the Perfect and Supine, and can be best learned by practice. In other Conjugations the Present Stem (sometimes slightly changed) is usually found in all the Principal Parts; but, in the Third Conjugation, the final ĕ of the Present Stem rarely appears, in any form, in the Perfect and Supine Stems. **Rege-**, therefore, is called the Present Stem of **regō**, but **reg-** is the *Verb-Stem.*

   a. The Third Conjugation is like the Third Declension in another respect: in many verbs s is added to the Verb-Stem to form the Perfect Stem (as, reg + s = Perfect Stem rex), just as s is added to the Stem to form the Nominative Singular; as, reg + s = rex, *a king.* Likewise mīsī (Perfect of mittō) = mitt-sī.

3. ***Verbs of the Third in* iō.** Some verbs of the Third Conjugation end in iō, and have some forms, in the Present-Stem Tenses, like those of the Fourth Conjugation. They are called *Verbs in* iō. Capiō, *I take,* is one of this class. Notice this simple Rule for remembering its irregularities: *Verbs in* iō *have the forms of the Fourth Conjugation wherever the Fourth has* i *followed by a vowel.* Hence we have capiō (audiō); capiēbam (audiēbam); capiens (audiens); but capere (audīre).

4. **V** is often dropped in the Perfect, Pluperfect, and Future Perfect; as, audieram (= audīveram); iit (= īvit). Sometimes a contraction takes place; as, amasse (= amāvisse); consuesse (= consuēvisse).

5. **Dīcō, dūcō, faciō, ferō** (but see 88, REMARK), drop final e in the Imperative Present, Second Singular, making dīc, dūc, fac, fer.

6. The Perfect Stem of some verbs doubles the first two (sometimes three) letters of the Present Stem, often with vowel changes. This is

called *Reduplication* (that is, *redoubling*); as, currō (Perfect, cucurrī); dō (Perfect, dedī); stō (stetī); pellō (pepulī); cadō (cecidī); caedō (cecīdī); discō (didicī); poscō (poposcī).

REMARK. In compounds, *the reduplication is dropped;* as, repellō, repulī; incĭdō (= in + cădō), incĭdī; incĭdō (= in + caedō), incīdī. But compounds of dō and stō *always*, and those of currō and some others *often*, retain it; as, addō (addidī); instō (institī); dēcurrō (dēcucurrī).

7. Many verbs of the Third Conjugation do *not* add s to form the Perfect Stem. The following verbs, in common use, should be noticed:—

a. Legō (Perfect, lēgī), *I choose, read.*

Three compounds of legō, however, have x in the Perfect: dīligō (*not* dēligō), intelligō, negligō.

b. Vertō (Perfect, vertī), *I turn.*

c. Verbs having nd before final o; as, scandō (scandī); incendō (incendī); contendō (contendī).

8. Section 4, *d* (p. 18), will be found useful, as explaining many of the consonant changes taking place in the Third Conjugation; as, reg-ō, rectum; scrīb-ō, scriptum.

Deponent Verbs.

80. Deponent Verbs have a *Passive form* but an *Active meaning*. The name (*Deponent*) means *putting off*, or *aside*, because they lay aside (dēpōnunt) the Passive sense. They occur in all four Conjugations, and are inflected like the Passive of other verbs of these Conjugations. Of course, the Present Imperative, Second Singular, has the same form as the Present Infinitive Active *would have.*

CAUTION. Notice that, in Deponent Verbs, —

a. The *Future Infinitive* is taken from the ***Active Voice;*** as, hortātūrus esse (*not* hortātum īrī).

b. The forms of *both voices* are found after the Infinitive Mode; that is, a Deponent Verb has *all four Participles, the Gerund,* and *the Supine.*

REMARKS. 1. Deponents are the only Latin verbs that have a Perfect Participle *with an Active meaning.* 2. The Gerundive is regularly *Passive* in meaning; as, mīlitēs cohortandī sunt, *the soldiers must be exhorted.* 3. The Perfect Participle is sometimes *Passive* in meaning.

Semi-Deponent Verbs.

81. Four verbs have no Perfect Stem, and are half Active and half Passive in form. They form the Present-Stem tenses, etc., regularly,

NOTES. 179

according to their Conjugations. All other forms they borrow from the Passive; hence they are called Semi-Deponent (*half-deponent*). Their meaning is Active. The list is: audeō, audēre, ausus sum, *I dare;* gaudeō, gaudēre, gāvīsus sum, *I rejoice;* soleō, solēre, solitus sum, *I am accustomed;* fīdō, fīdere, fīsus sum, *I trust.*

Periphrastic Conjugations.

82. The word *Periphrastic* is derived from two Greek words, and means *roundabout speaking.* The English word *circumlocution* (circum, *around,* and loquor, *I speak*) means the same thing. The *Future Infinitives*, Active and Passive, are examples of *roundabout speaking.* Amātūrus esse means, literally, *to be about to love;* amātum īrī has the general idea of the English *going to be loved.* Other forms might be mentioned, which, like the English *I am going to go,* state something in a roundabout way. In Latin there are two Conjugations (compound in their forms), which, from the frequency of their use, are called *the* Periphrastic Conjugations. They are thus formed: —

a. The First, or **Active, Periphrastic Conjugation** consists of the *Indicative, Subjunctive,* and the *Present and Perfect Infinitive* of sum, with the *Future Active Participle.* It expresses *intention,* or that something is *going to happen;* as, amātūrus sum, *I am about to love, intend to love, am going to love.*

REMARK. The Subjunctive has no Future Tense. The Present is sometimes used with a Future meaning; but when Future time is to be *accurately* stated, and *distinguished* from Present time, the form sim with the Future Active Participle must be used. Amātūrus sim may, therefore, be called the *Future Subjunctive* of amō; as, dubium est utrum fīlium amātūrus sit, necne, *it is doubtful whether he will love his son, or not* (utrum amet = *whether he loves*).

b. The Second, or **Passive, Periphrastic Conjugation** has the same Mode and Tense forms as the First; but the *Gerundive* is used. It expresses *necessity, duty,* etc.; as, amandus sum, *I ought to be loved, must be loved;* amandus fuī, *I was (worthy) to be loved, ought to have been loved.*

Irregular Verbs.

83. Each Conjugation forms its Principal Parts according to its own laws. Many verbs in these Conjugations, however, do not strictly obey these laws. For example, petō and quaerō belong to the Third Conjugation; yet they have petīvī, quaesīvī, in the Perfect (more like the Fourth than the Third Conjugation). We do not, however, call such verbs

Irregular, because their stems and inflection are, *in general*, like those of their own conjugation. We call those verbs *Irregular*, which have two or three stems entirely unlike each other (like English *am, was, been; go, went, gone*), or which have some forms of inflection not to be found in the four Conjugations. In studying an Irregular Verb, always notice how much of it is *regular*, as well as what are the *irregular* forms. The most common *Irregular Verbs* are sum, ferō, eō, fīō (and their compounds), volō, nōlō, mālō.

84. Sum, *I am*, has these stems : Present, es ; Perfect, fu ; Supine, fut (found only in the Future Participle). Its chief peculiarities are : —

a. In the Present Indicative, sum, sumus, sunt, have lost the e (as though 'sum, etc.). The same is true in the Present Subjunctive; as, sim (for esim).

b. The stem es becomes er in the Imperfect and Future Indicative, according to 1 (2).

c. The *Supine, Gerund,* and *Present Participle* are wanting. The Present Participle (used as an adjective) is found in three compounds : potens, absens, praesens. Therefore we may say that, *if* sum *had a Present Participle, it would be* ens.

d. Instead of futūrus esse we often find fore, and instead of essem, forem is sometimes used.

85. Two Compounds of sum have peculiar forms : —

1. Possum, *I am able, I can*, is made up of the adjective potis, *able,* and sum, *I am.* Only the first syllable of potis (pot) is employed, so that the verb is really potsum (1 (4) *b*). The same change occurs wherever pot would stand before s ; as, possunt, possim (for potsunt, potsim). Potesse is shortened to posse (hence the Imperfect Subjunctive is possem), and f is dropped from fuī, etc. (potuī, potuisse, etc., for potfuī, potfuisse).

It has a Present Participle (used only as an adjective); but no *Imperative, Future Participle, Gerund,* or *Supine.*

2. Prōsum, *I am helpful, I assist*, takes d before e ; as, prōdesse, prōdest, prōderam, etc. The form prōd is used to separate the vowels, just as re, *back,* and eō, *I go,* form the compound redeō, *I go back* (like the English *an,* not *a,* before words beginning with a vowel).

86. Ferō, *I bear,* has three stems, very unlike each other : Present, fere (sometimes fer); Perfect, tul ; Supine, lāt. The tenses formed from the Present Stem are exactly like those of the Third Conjugation with these exceptions : —

a. The vowel e (or i) is lost : (1) in certain forms of the Present Indicative, Active and Passive ; (2) in the Imperfect Subjunctive,

NOTES. 181

Active and Passive ; (3) in the Imperative (certain forms), Active and Passive ; (4) in the Infinitive, Active and Passive. The Present Infinitive Passive (ferrī) is the most irregular of all the forms. If like the Third Conjugation, it would be ferī (like regī); but it has rr, as though it had been shortened from ferĕrī.

87. Eō, *I go*, has the stems ī, īv, it ; hence it resembles a verb of the Fourth Conjugation. It has these irregularities : —

a. The vowel i, unlike the Fourth Conjugation, is *short* in the Supine stem ; as, ītūrus.

b. The Present stem is changed to e before a, o, u ; as, eō, eunt, eam.

c. The Future Indicative is ībō, a mixture of the First (or Second) and Fourth Conjugations.

d. The Present Participle has euntis, etc., in the Genitive and other cases, instead of ientis (as, audientis). The Gerund is eundī (not iendī, as in audiendī).

REMARK. Although eō is Intransitive, yet some of its compounds (with Prepositions) are Transitive, and are followed by the Accusative ; as, adeō, *I approach;* transeō, *I cross;* subeō, *I undergo*.

88. Fīō, *I am made, I become*, is used as the Passive of faciō, and also, as its second meaning indicates, as an Intransitive verb, in the sense of *become, happen* (that is, *to be brought about*). Some of its tenses evidently *are* the Passive of faciō. Its peculiarities are : —

a. The Present Infinitive is fierī.

b. The Imperfect Subjunctive is formed as though the Present Infinitive were fiere.

c. Tenses formed from the Present stem have Active *endings*, but (frequently) Passive *meanings*.

REMARK. Compounds of faciō with *prepositions* are regular in both Voices, with vowel changes (2) ; as, conficior, conficī, confectus sum. Other compounds do not change the vowel a to i, and have fīō in the Passive ; as, patefaciō, *I open* (Passive, patefīō, patefierī, patefactus sum). Therefore this simple rule may be followed : Faciō *always has* fīō *in the Passive;* but ficiō *is regular.* Examples : *Imperatives,* fac,. perfice, patefī, conficere ; *Infinitives,* facere, patefierī, conficere, perficī.

89. Volō, *I am willing, wish*, resembles, in some respects, the Third Conjugation (as in the Future Indicative). It has these peculiarities : —

a. The Present Infinitive *would be* volere, if of the Third Conjugation. The o is changed to e (= velere); then, as in ferere, the second e is dropped (= velre); then the r is assimilated (*made like*) to the l (= velle). This same e is also seen in the Present and Imperfect Subjunctive (velim, vellem).

b. The Present Indicative would have volis, volit, volimus, volitis. Volis is shortened to vīs; volit to vult (= volt); volitis to vultis (= voltis). Volimus becomes volumus (like sumus).

c. Velim (Present Subjunctive) = volam.

d. Lack of forms, as shown in the Grammars and Appendix.

90. Volō has two compounds: nōlō, *I am unwilling*, and mālō, *I would rather, I prefer*. Nōlō = nōn volō; mālō = magis volō (as though it were mavolō). Their similarity to volō will be seen in their conjugation.

REMARK. Notice that nōlō is the only one of the "volō class" that has an Imperative. Notice, also, that this Imperative is a mixture of the Fourth and Third Conjugations.

Defective Verbs.

91. Defective Verbs are such as lack many tenses, or parts of tenses. The most important Defective verbs are these three, which have no tenses formed from the Present stem: —

1. Coepī, *I began*. The verb incipiō, *I begin* (in + capiō), supplies the place of the Present; as, incipiunt crēdere, *they begin to believe*. When coepī is followed by a Passive Infinitive, it is expressed in a Passive form; as, urbem aedificāre coepērunt, *they began to build the city;* but urbs aedificārī coepta est.

2. Meminī, *I remember*, and ōdī, *I hate*. These verbs have, in the Perfect, Pluperfect, and Future Perfect, the meaning of the Present, Imperfect, and Future. From the fact that they employ the tenses of *completed* action to express the meaning of the tenses of *incomplete* action, they are often called *Preteritive* (praeter + īre, *to pass by*); that is, they have only the tenses of *completed* action. Meminī has these Imperative forms: mementō, mementōte (Future).

REMARK. The Perfect of noscō, *I begin* (or *learn*) *to know*, and also that of consuescō, *I become accustomed*, have the same peculiarity, and mean, *I know* (that is, *I have finished beginning, and now know*); *I am accustomed* (that is, *have become accustomed*). See **98, d**.

a. Inquam, *say I, quoth I*, has only one complete tense, the Present Indicative. It is used in *direct quotations only*, and never stands first; as, "Venīte," inquit, "in castra."

b. These have Imperative forms only: salvē! avē! *hail!*

Impersonal Verbs.

92. *Study section* **26**, *page* 8. In Latin, as in English, an *Impersonal Verb* is one having no *personal* subject, and is used only in the Third

Person Singular; but these verbs are more numerous in Latin than in English, forming a class of words very important and very frequently used. With such verbs we often, in English, use *it* as a subject; as, *it rains*. We hardly know what part of speech to call *it*. In Latin no such word was expressed; as, pluit, *it rains*.

CAUTION. It must be clearly understood, at the very first, that *every Latin verb has a subject;* and that, if the subject is not *expressed*, it is to be *understood*. The subject of an Impersonal Verb is its general *idea* (that is, its *stem*). Pluit means *rain is falling;* tonat, *thunder crashes, roars*, etc. There are a few Impersonal Verbs in Latin that we cannot translate into English, giving the full value to the *stem* as subject, since the same thought is *differently expressed* in the two languages. For instance, me oportet really means *necessity compels me;* but the English would be *I must*, and therefore we must so render it. Almost all Impersonal Verbs, however, *can* and *should* be rendered with the *stem* (or *thought*) as subject; as, pugnātur, *fighting* (or, *the fight*) *is carried on* (not *they fight*, or *it is fought*).

93. Impersonal Verbs, in Latin, are of two kinds: (1) Those whose *regular* use is Impersonal; (2) Those *often* used Impersonally.

1. *Verbs regularly Impersonal.* These are: —
a. Verbs denoting *states of the weather*, etc. (as in English); as, pluit, *it rains;* ningit, *it snows;* grandinat, *it hails;* tonat, *it thunders;* lūcescit, *it grows light;* vesperascit, *it's getting dark,* or *drawing towards evening.* The *real* subjects of these verbs (their *stems*) might be thus expressed: *rain, snow,* or *hail, is falling; thunder sounds, crashes,* etc.; *light* (lux) *begins to appear,* or *break; evening* (vesper) *draws near.*

b. Verbs denoting *mental state.* These must be rendered according to the *English use* of such words; as, mē pudet, *I am ashamed* (literally, *a feeling of shame possesses me*). The most common of these verbs are given here, with the Accusative Case, which is regularly used with them as *object,* though, in translating, the English requires the Accusative to be rendered as though it were the *subject:* mē miseret, *I pity;* vōs poenitet, *you are sorry for, you repent;* tē pudet, *you are ashamed.*

c. Verbs having a *Phrase* or *Clause* as subject (as in English). Many of these are also used with *personal* subjects. Some of them are: libet, *it pleases;* licet, *it is permitted* (English, *license*); oportet, *it is necessary;* accidit, *it happens;* accēdit, *there is another (added) reason* (usually translated, *it is added*); vidētur, *it seems best;* restat, *it remains;* praestat, *it is better.*

2. Very many verbs may be *used Impersonally*. Some of them have been given above (*c*) ; as, **accidit, accēdit, vidētur.** A very large class of them is composed of Passive forms of Intransitive verbs. *Intransitive verbs can be used in the Passive only Impersonally.* A variety of such forms is given under **198**. A few of those most commonly used are given here (notice that *the stem of the verb is the subject*): **pugnātur, pugnātum est, pugnandum est,** *fighting is, was, must be carried on ;* **nōbīs mātūrandum est,** *haste must be made on our part* (or, *we must hurry*); **nocētur,** *harm is done, injury is inflicted ;* **manētur,** *a stay* (or *stop*) *is made ;* **ītur,** *a march is made, is in progress ;* **imperātum est,** *the order was given.*

ADVERBS.

94. *Learn section* **28**, page 9.

Adverbs have the same use in Latin as in English, and are divided into the same classes. Latin Adverbs may be, —

a. Derived from Adjectives or Participles (see **38**); as, **cārē, ācriter, doctē.** The Comparative of an Adverb is regularly the same in form as the Neuter Accusative of the Adjective (Comparative). See, also, *d*, below.

b. Derived from Nouns ; as, **diū, noctū, partim.**

c. Simple ; as, **saepe.**

d. Besides the forms mentioned in *a, b, c,* there are forms of adjectives and pronouns *used as adverbs.* They can usually be explained as *cases.*

1. The Accusative and Ablative, Neuter, are often used as adverbs. The Accusative usually denotes *Degree* or *Extent* (**142**, *c*), and the Ablative, *Degree of Difference* (**155**); as, **plūrimum potest,** *he is very* (or *most*) *powerful* (literally, *he is powerful to a very great degree*); **hostium impetūs paulum tardātī sunt,** *the attacks of the enemy were checked a little* (literally, *to a slight extent*); **nuntiī multō crēbriōrēs erant,** *the messages were* (*by*) *a great deal more frequent.*

2. The Feminine Ablative Singular is often used as an adverb (the noun being omitted); as, **quā, ūnā, ultrā, inf(e)rā (parte** or **viā),** *whither* (*by which way*), *together* (*by one way*), *beyond* (*on the farther side*), *below* (*on the under side*).

PREPOSITIONS.

95. Prepositions, in Latin as in English, are *connectives* (see **29**, page 9). When not used as connectives, they are adverbs [*] (as in English) ;

---

[*] This is the original use.

NOTES. 185

as, paulō post (or ante) vēnit, *he came a little while after* (or *before*). They are followed by the Accusative or Ablative. The Accusative is used with about *thirty* prepositions; the Ablative with about *one third* as many. Those (in common use) which are *always* used with the Ablative are *seven* in number. They are given below in rhyme, that they may be more easily remembered:—

ā (or ab), dē;
cum, ex (or ē);
sine, prō, prae.

a. Two of these have double forms: ā and ē are used *only* before words beginning with a *consonant;* ab and ex before those beginning with a vowel *or* consonant (somewhat like *a* and *an* in English); as, ā (or ab) flūmine, ē silvā; but ab urbe, ab hōc oppidō (see 4, *b*, page 17), ex agrō.

b. Notice that ā (ab) means *away from;* ē (ex), *out of;* as, ā flūmine, *from the river*, that is, *from the river-bank;* but ē flūmine, *out of the river*.

c. In and sub with the Accusative answer the question *Whither?* with the Ablative, the question *Where?* as, in oppidum vēnit, *he came into the town;* sub jugum missī sunt, *they were sent under the yoke;* but in hortō ambulat, *he is walking in the garden;* sub monte castra pōnit, *he pitches his camp at the foot of the mountain*.

CONJUNCTIONS.

96. Conjunctions, in Latin as in English (see 30, page 9), are:—

(1.) *Co-ordinate;* as, et, *and;* sed, *but*.

(2.) *Subordinate;* as, sī, *if;* quod, *because;* ut, *that, so that;* nē, *lest, that not;* quum, *when, since, although*.

a. There are three words meaning *and:* —

1. Et, *and*, connects *independent* words, phrases, and clauses.

2. Que, *and*, always an Enclitic (195, 3), connects words, etc. that naturally form a *pair* of objects or thoughts, or convey one general idea; as the names of two men in partnership, a general *and* his army, the senate *and* the people. Que is joined to the *second* of the two words connected. If it connects clauses, it is joined to the first word of the second clause.

3. Atque (sometimes written āc) = ad + que, and hence means *and in addition, and too, and also*. It indicates that the second word, etc., is more important than the first; as, mīlitēs atque imperātor, *the soldiers and the commander, too*. It is often used after words denoting *comparison,* etc., meaning *as* or *than;* as, aliter āc, *otherwise than*.

b. Regularly, with several words, et was either used *before all but the first*, or was omitted entirely; as, equī et arma et obsidēs, or equī, arma, obsidēs.

INTERJECTIONS.

97. Interjections are used as in English (see 31, page 9).

DERIVED AND COMPOUND WORDS.

Endings.

98. Many derived words have endings that give them special meanings. A few of those most common are given in this NOTE.

a. *Nouns* composed of the Supine stem of Verbs + or denote the *male agent;* as, amātor, monitor, rector, audītor, inventor, victor. Some nouns, derived from other *nouns*, have the same ending tor, and denote the *agent;* as, viātor, *a traveller* (from via). A change of tor to trix gives a noun denoting the *female agent;* as, victrix, inventrix.

b. *Nouns* and *Adjectives* ending in ulus (a, um) denote *smallness*, and are called *Diminutives;* as, rīvus, *a stream*, rīvulus, *a rivulet*, or *streamlet;* parvus, *small*, parvulus, *very small;* adolescens, *a youth*, adolescentulus, *a mere youth*.

c. *Adjectives* ending in ōsus denote *fulness;* as, studiōsus, *zealous, studious (full of study)*; bellicōsus, *warlike (filled with the desire of war)*.

d. *Verbs* ending in scō denote the *beginning of an act;* as, noscō, *I begin to know*, or *learn;* cognoscō, *I find out;* lūcescit, *day begins to break*. They are called *Inceptives* (from incipiō, *I begin*), and are of the Third Conjugation. See 91, 2, REMARK. The noun adolescens, *a youth*, is really the Present Participle of adolescō, *I grow up*, and means one who is *getting his full growth*.

e. *Derivative Verbs* ending in tō or itō denote *repeated* or *vigorous action;* as, jactō (from jaciō), *I hurl, keep throwing;* clāmitō (from clāmō), *I keep shouting;* ventitō (from veniō), *I keep coming;* also, verbs formed from Supine stems; as, versor (from vertō), *I keep turning, busy myself, am engaged in*. These verbs are called *Frequentatives*, and are of the First Conjugation.

Compound Words: Prefixes.

99. 1. Many Latin *Prepositions*, when used as the first part of Compound Verbs, have the force of adverbs, and give a special meaning to the compounds. Some of these meanings are evident, and need no explanation. The following have some special force: —

NOTES. 187

ā, ab, *away, off;* as, abiit, *he has gone away;* quinque mīlia (or mīlibus) passuum abest, *he is five miles off.*

com, con (adverbial forms of cum), *together, thoroughly, earnestly;* as, conveniunt, *they assemble;* conferunt, *they collect;* conjungere, *to join together;* conficiō, *I complete;* cohortor, *I exhort earnestly;* collaudat, *he praises highly.*

dē, *down, away;* as, dēmissō capite, *with downcast head (look);* dējectus, *downcast (discouraged);* dēdūcō, *I withdraw, lead away.*

in, *on, against;* as, Gallīs bellum inferō, *I make war on the Gauls.*

ob, *towards, to meet;* as, occurrō, *I run to meet.*

per, *through, thoroughly (through and through);* as, epistolam perlēgī, *I've read the letter through;* perterritus, *thoroughly frightened.*

2. The following prefixes (never written alone) give a special meaning and force to Verbs : —

dis (or dī), *apart, here and there, away;* as, discēdō, *I go away;* mīlitēs dispōnit, *he places soldiers here and there;* ventus ignem distulit, *the wind spread the fire in every direction.*

in (English, *in* or *un*) gives a *negative* force; as, innocentia, *blamelessness, uprightness* (literally, *a not doing harm*); imperītus, *unskilled;* integer (in + tangō, *I touch*), *whole, unwearied.*

re (red), *back, behind;* as, redūcō, *I lead back;* mē recipiō (re + capiō), *I retreat, betake myself;* equitēs relīquit, *he left the cavalry behind.*

sē; *apart, away;* as, sēcēdō, *I go away;* sējungō, *I disjoin, separate.*

NOTES ON SYNTAX.

THE SENTENCE.

100. Sentences, in Latin as in English, are : —
Declaratory ; as, **vir fortis est,** *the man is brave.*
Interrogative ; as, **quis aeger est ?** *who is sick ?*
Imperative ; as, **fortēs este,** *be brave* ; **veniant,** *let them come.*
Exclamatory ; as, **quam sapiens fuit !** *how wise he was!*

Interrogative Sentences.

101. Questions, in English or Latin, may be *single* or *double*. *Is the man brave ? Did n't he call ?* are *single* questions.

Is the man brave, or cowardly ? Did he praise, or blame ? Did you call, or not ? are *double* questions.

In Latin, every question requires an *interrogative word*. This word may be an Interrogative Pronoun or Adverb ; as, **quis es ?** *who are you ?* **unde (cūr) vēnistī ?** *whence (why) have you come ?* Most of these words have a meaning and use as in English. A few, however, need special mention : —

 a. In *Single Questions,* expecting the answer *yes* or *no*, we must use a word indicating *what answer is expected.*

 If an *answer* merely is expected (either *yes* or *no*), use **-ne.** This word is always an Enclitic (**195**, 3), and is joined to the first word in the sentence ; as, **puerīne vēnērunt ?** *have the boys come ?*

 If *yes* is expected, use **nonne** ; as, **nonne vir bonus est ?** *is he not a good man ?* or, *he is a good man, is n't he ?* Notice that **-ne** is an Enclitic in **nonne.**

 If *no* is expected, use **num** ; as, **num mīles fortis mortem timet ?** *does a brave soldier fear death ?*

 b. In *Double Questions* an interrogative word is used with *each part* of the question. The words most commonly used are **utrum** (or **-ne,** enclitic) in the first part, and **an** in the second. **Utrum** is really the Neuter of the Adjective **uter** (**51**, CAUTION), and means, *which* (*thing*) *of these two is the fact ?* It is not to be translated into English. **An** means *or.* If the second part is merely *or not,* use **annōn**; as, **utrum pugnāvit an fūgit?** *did he fight, or flee?* **utrum patriam amat, annōn?** *does he love his country, or not?*

REMARK. *Yes* and *no*, in answer to questions, have no equivalent (in single words) in common use. Such an answer should usually be expressed by repeating the verb (with a negative adverb, if *no* is the answer); as, **vēnitne?** *has he come?* **vēnit,** *yes (he has come)*; **suntne amīcī tuī?** *are they your friends?* **nōn sunt,** *no (they are not).*

Subject and Predicate.

102. Every sentence must contain a Subject and a Predicate.

a. The Subject of a Finite Verb must be in the Nominative Case. It answers the question *Who?* or *What?* and must be a noun or some word or collection of words used as a noun (see **36**, page 10); as, **benefacere reī publicae pulchrum est,** *to contribute to the welfare of* (literally, *to do good to*) *the state is honorable* (Subject, **benefacere reī publicae**).

The Subject, if a Personal Pronoun, is very frequently omitted, as the Personal Ending of the verb shows what it is; therefore, *a sentence may consist of but one word;* as, **vocātis,** *you are calling.*

b. The Predicate may consist of a verb alone, or with modifiers; as, **agricola vocat,** *the farmer calls;* **mīles pugnat,** *the soldier fights;* **agricola puellam vocat,** *the farmer calls the girl;* **mīles fortiter pugnat,** *the soldier fights bravely.*

REMARK. The Direct Object of a Transitive Verb is in the Accusative Case; as, **puellam** in the sentence above.

Copula and Complement.

103. *Review* **37,** *a,* page 10. The verb **sum,** *I am,* is the *Copula* in Latin. A noun or adjective, in the same case as the subject, is the *Complement.* The Copula and the Complement form the Predicate; as, **puer bonus est,** *the boy is good;* **Brūtus meus amīcus fuit.**

a. Review **37,** *b, c,* page 10. In Latin, as in English, there are other *Copulative Verbs* besides **sum**; as, **fīō,** *I am made, become;* **videor,** *I seem, appear;* and the Passive of verbs signifying *to choose, to call, to think,* etc.; as, **imperātor creor (appellor, habeor),** *I am elected (called, considered) general.*

Modifiers.

104. *Review* **38,** page 11. As in English, a Subject or a Predicate may be modified by a

Word; as, **milites fortes urbem expugnaverunt,** *brave soldiers stormed the city.*
Phrase; as, **exercitus sub jugum missus est,** *the army was sent under the yoke.*
Clause; as, **oppidum, quod hostes ceperunt, magnum fuit,** *the town, which the enemy took, was large.*

Sentences Classified.

105. *Review* **40,** page 11. Sentences, in Latin as in English, are:—

Simple; as, **magister puero librum dat,** *the teacher gives a book to the boy.*

Compound; as, **veni, vidi, vici,** *I came, I saw, I conquered.*

Complex; as, **puerum laudat, ut a puero laudetur,** *he praises the boy that he may be praised by the boy.*

Apposition.

106. A noun used to describe or explain another Noun, or Pronoun, and meaning *the same* person or thing, is put (by Apposition) in the same case **(46,** page 13); as, **Labienus legatus ad urbem Romam venit,** *Labienus, the lieutenant, came to the city* (of) *Rome.* Notice that *Rome* is *not* in the Genitive, as it denotes the same thing as *city.*

    a. If the Appositive describes two or more nouns, it must be in the Plural; as, **per Marcum Silanum et Titum Sextium legatos delectum habuit,** *he held a levy (of troops) through (using as agents) Marcus Silanus and Titus Sextius,* his lieutenants.

Predicate Nominative.

107. A Noun used to complete the Predicate, with **esse,** or any other Copulative Verb **(103),** agrees with the Subject in case, and is called the *Predicate Nominative* **(46,** *a,* page 13); as, **Cicero vir fortissimus fuit,** *Cicero was a very brave man.*

    REMARK. This same principle applies to a *Predicate Adjective* **(108,** 1).

ADJECTIVES.

108. An Adjective or Participle (that is, a *Verbal Adjective*) agrees with its Noun, or Pronoun, in gender, number, and case; as, **copiae bonae,** *good troops;* **viri fortissimi,** *very brave men.*

    REMARK. This, of course, applies to all Pronouns having three gender-forms (Possessive, Demonstrative, etc.).

1. An Adjective may be *Attributive* or *Predicate*.

An Attributive Adjective modifies its noun *directly;* that is, it is not connected with it by **esse**, or some other verb; as, **vir fortis bonus cīvis est**, *a brave man is a good citizen.*

A Predicate Adjective is one which helps to form the Predicate, and is connected with its noun by **esse**, or some other Copulative Verb.

2. An Attributive Adjective, modifying more than one noun, usually agrees with the nearest and is to be understood with the rest : or it is sometimes repeated; as, **omnēs agrī et maria**; or, **agrī omnēs omniaque maria**, *all lands and seas.*

3. A Predicate Adjective agrees with the Subject in gender, number, and case; as, **puer studiōsus est**, *the boy is studious.*

4. A Predicate Adjective, agreeing with two or more nouns, must be in the Plural; as, **nauta et mīles fortēs erunt**, *the sailor and the soldier will be brave.*

5. If the subjects are of different genders, a Predicate Adjective will be

  a. Masculine Plural, if the subjects denote *living beings;* as, **pater et māter mortuī sunt**, *my father and mother are dead.*

  b. Neuter Plural, if the subjects denote things *without life;* as, **amor et amīcitia simillima sunt**, *love and friendship are (things) very much alike.*

Adjectives used as Nouns.

109. Adjectives may be used as Nouns: the Masculine, Feminine, and Neuter denoting *men, women,* and *things.* This is more common in the Plural than in the Singular; as, **Rōmānī**, *the Romans;* **omnia**, *all things* (or *property*); **nostrī**, *our men* (or *soldiers*); **fīnitimī**, *the neighbors;* **novissimī**, *the rearmost (soldiers);* **hīberna** (castra), *winter-quarters;* **bona**, *goods.*

  a. Sometimes Adjectives are so used in the Singular; as, **patria** (terra), *native land, fatherland;* **fera** (bestia), *a wild beast.*

  b. The Neuter Singular of an Adjective very often agrees with an Infinitive or Clause used as a Substantive (see **36**, REMARK, page 10); as, **dulce et decōrum est prō patriā morī**, *to die for one's country is (a) delightful and honorable (thing or service).*

  c. Sometimes the Neuter Plural is used as a Noun, when the *general sense* must decide its translation; as, **bona**, *goods;* **praeterita**, *past events* (English, *bygones*); **haec respondit**, *he made this reply.*

Special Uses of Adjectives.

110. a. An Adjective is sometimes used where, in English, we should use an Adverb, an Infinitive, or a Relative Clause. The Adjective usually

"describes the condition of the actor, rather than the manner of the action;" as, **prīmus vēnit,** *he came first (was the first to come, was the first who came);* **invītus (laetus, libens) vēnī,** *I came unwillingly (joyfully, gladly).*

b. Often, in Latin, an Adjective is used, *agreeing with a Noun,* where the English idiom would require a Noun followed by a Genitive; as, **summus mons,** *the top of the mountain;* **mediō in colle,** *on the middle of the hill (half-way up the hill);* **extrēmā hieme,** *in the last part of winter;* **prīmā aestāte** (or **initā aestāte**), *in the early part* (or *beginning*) *of summer;* **reliquī Belgae,** *the rest of the Belgae.*

c. Adjectives, agreeing with Nouns, are often employed in Latin, where the English idiom requires a *possessive* form, or a *phrase;* as, **domus aliēna,** *another person's house;* **bellum servīle,** *the war with the slaves;* **bellum Veneticum,** *the war with the Veneti.*

d. When two Adjectives agree with one Noun, they are regularly connected by a Conjunction; as, **virī multī et bonī,** *many good men* (literally, *men many and good*).

REMARK. This rule does not apply to Numerals or Adjective Pronouns; as, **decem** (or **illī**) **virī bonī.**

PRONOUNS.

Personal.

111. Personal Pronouns (as Subjects) are omitted, unless required for emphasis; as, **vēnī, vīdī, vīcī,** *I came, I saw, I conquered;* **ego tē laudāvī, tū mē culpāvistī,** *I have praised you, (but) you have blamed me.*

a. The speaker or writer often uses the First Person *Plural,* when he does not wish to make *himself* prominent in what he is saying (that is, he avoids *ego*tism). Authors and editors often do the same in English; this use of the Subject is often called "the editor's *we*;" as, **Labiēnus, quem suprā dīximus,** *Labienus, whom we* (= *I*) *have mentioned above.*

Reflexive.

112. The Reflexive Pronouns refer to the Subject of the sentence. The use of the Reflexives of the First and Second Persons (**meī, tuī**) can be easily understood, but special care must be taken in the use of the Reflexive of the Third Person (**suī**), and of the Possessive Pronoun (**suus**), which is the Adjective form of **suī (47, 48).**

a. In a Subordinate Clause, **suī** and **suus** may refer either to the subject of their own clause, or to that of the principal clause; as, **Sabīnus postulāvit ut hostēs sē suaque omnia dēderent,** *Sabinus demanded that the enemy should surrender themselves and all their property;* **Ariovistus imperat ut obsidēs ad castra sua redūcantur et sibi reddantur,** *Ariovistus gives orders that the hostages shall be brought back to his camp and restored to him.*

b. **Inter sē** means *to each other, from each other, each other, mutually;* as, **obsidēs inter sē dēdērunt,** *they gave hostages to each other* (that is, *exchanged hostages*); **inter sē cohortātī sunt,** *they encouraged each other* (*gave mutual encouragement*).

Possessive.

113. The Possessive Pronouns are usually omitted, when they are not emphatic, and can be easily understood from the general meaning of the sentence; as, **māter valet,** *my (your) mother is well.* They follow the same law of *agreement* as Adjectives.

On the proper use of **suus** and **ējus** (**eōrum, eārum**), see **48,** CAUTION.

a. The Possessives are often used as Nouns (**109**); as, **nostrī,** *our men;* **suōs hortātus est,** *he encouraged his men.*

Demonstrative.

114. The Demonstrative Pronouns may be used: —

1. As *Adjectives;* as, **ille mīles, hīc puer, vir ipse, ea nox,** *that soldier there, this boy here, the man himself* (or *the very man*), *that night.*

2. As *Personal Pronouns.* In this use is is very common, so that it is often called the *Third Personal Pronoun* (**46**); as, **is vēnit,** *he came;* **ea flēbat,** *she was weeping;* **Caesar id animadverterat,** *Caesar had noticed it* (*that thing* or *fact*). So also, **ipse dixit,** *he (himself) has said so;* **illī sē recēpērunt,** *they retreated.*

a. **Ipse,** *self,* gives emphasis to the word with which it agrees, and may be translated in several ways; as, **vir ipse,** *the very man* (or *the man himself*); **ipsī sē interfēcērunt,** *they killed themselves with their own hands.*

b. **Ille** sometimes means "the former" (that is, *the more distant*), and **hīc,** *the latter* (that is, *the nearer*), of two persons or things described; as, **ille huic subvenit,** *the former comes to aid the latter* (somewhat like **alter — alter**).

c. **Hīc** is often used like the English *as follows;* as, **haec est ratiō oppugnātiōnis,** *the style of attack is as follows;* **haec respondit,** *he thus replied* (*replied these things,* or *words*).

Relative.

115. In Latin, as in English, a Relative Pronoun takes the Gender, Number, and Person, of its Antecedent; *its Case depends on the form of its own clause;* as, **urbs, quam vidēs, Rōma est,** *the city, which you see, is Rome;* **ego, quī tē laudāvī, rex sum ; mīlitēs, ā quibus urbs capta est, fortēs sunt.**

    a. The Antecedent is often omitted ; as, **(eōs) quī iter cognoscerent mīsit,** *he sent men to investigate the route;* **quod jussī sunt, (id) faciunt,** *they do what they have been ordered (to do).*

    b. **Quod, id quod,** or **quae rēs,** may be used to refer to a clause, or *idea,* as Antecedent ; as, **nostrī redintegrātīs vīribus, quod in spē victōriae saepe accidit, pugnāre coepērunt,** *our men began to fight with renewed strength, which* (that is, *the renewal of strength*) *often happens in the hope of victory (when soldiers hope for victory).*

    c. The Relative is often omitted in English ; it is *never* omitted in Latin. Its importance as a *connective* is shown by its use ; as, **vir, quem vidēs, Caesar est,** *the man (whom) you see is Caesar.*

    d. A Relative at the beginning of a sentence must often be translated as a Demonstrative ; as, **quibus rēbus cognitīs, profectus est,** *having ascertained these facts, he started.*

    e. In Latin, as in English, a Relative Adverb may take the place of a Relative Pronoun with a Preposition ; as, **ad eum locum vēnit, ubi fuerant** (or, **unde profūgerant**), *he came to the place, where they had been* (or, *whence they had fled*). In this example, **ubi** = **in quō** ; **unde** = **ā quō.**

    f. In English, *as* is often a Relative Pronoun, especially after *such* and *same.* In Latin, therefore, **quī** (after **īdem**) should be translated *as.* **Quālis** and **quantus** (Relative Adjectives) should be translated *as* after **tālis,** *such,* and **tantus,** *such, so great* (**195,** 8).

Interrogative and Indefinite.

116. The general meaning and use of Interrogative and Indefinite Pronouns can be best learned from **51** and **52,** and from the Vocabulary.

VERBS.

117. A Finite Verb agrees with its Subject in Number and Person ; as, **puellae vocant,** *the girls call;* **hostēs superantur,** *the enemy are overcome;* **beātī estis,** *you are happy.*

REMARK. As already stated (111), the Subject is generally omitted, if it is a Personal Pronoun.

a. When a verb has two or more Singular subjects connected by a co-ordinate conjunction, it will be : —

1. Plural (as in English), if it agrees with them taken *together;* as, **virtūs et vitium inter sē contrāria sunt,** *virtue and vice are contrary to each other.*

2. Singular (as in English), if it agrees with them *separately;* as, **neque puer neque puella audit,** *neither the boy nor the girl hears* ; **vel homō vel fīlius ējus hōc fēcit,** *either the man or his son has done this.*

b. With *two or more subjects* the verb often agrees with the nearest, and is understood with the others ; as, **castra et imperātor magnō in perīculō versābātur,** *the camp and commander were in great danger.*

REMARK. Two Singular subjects may denote *one* thing, and then the verb is *singular;* as in the English, *bread and milk is healthful.*

c. A *Collective Noun* (as in English) may take a Singular verb, when the body *as a whole* is spoken of ; but when the *separate objects* are thought of, the verb must be Plural ; as, **cīvitās jūs suum armīs exsequī cōnāta est,** *the state attempted to assert its right by force of arms;* but **cīvitātī persuāsit ut exīrent,** *he persuaded the state to go out* (that the *citizens* should go out).

d. In Latin, as in English, when a verb has several subjects, *of different persons,* it will be in the *First Person* rather than in the *Second* or *Third,* and in the *Second* rather than in the *Third;* as, **ego et tū et Cassius valēmus,** *Cassius, you, and I* (= *we*) *are well;* **tū et fīlius tuus valētis.**

THE CASES.

NOMINATIVE.

118. The Nominative is the case of the Subject, as in English. It may also be an Appositive or a Predicate Noun, as already described (**106, 107**).

GENITIVE.

119. The Genitive is most frequently used to modify another Noun, denoting a *different* person or thing. It is unlike the Appositive, since the latter denotes the *same* person or thing as the word it describes. It may be translated by the Possessive, or by *of* with a Noun; as, **templa deōrum**, *the temples of the gods;* **pater puerī**, *the boy's father.*

CAUTION. In such expressions as *the city of Rome*, *of* must not be rendered by the Genitive, because *Rome* denotes the *same* thing as *city*. The Latin should be **urbs Rōma** (Appositive).

Genitive denoting Possession.

120. The Genitive denotes the *Possessor*, answering the question *Whose?* as, **fīlius servī**, *the slave's son;* **castra Caesaris**, *Caesar's camp*.

Genitive of Quality.

121. The Genitive (with an Adjective) denotes *Quality*, answering the question *Of what kind?* or (as in the English *ten-foot pole, five days' march*), *Of what length, height, depth?* etc.; as, **vir magnae sapientiae**, *a man of great wisdom;* **rēs ējus modī** (or **ējusmodī**), *affairs of that sort;* **iter quinque diērum**, *a five days' journey* (or *march*); **fossa trium pedum**, *a ditch of three feet* (*a three-foot ditch*).

    a. The Genitive of Quality is used to denote *Indefinite Value*. This is expressed by the Genitive Singular of an Adjective (Neuter, agreeing with **pretiī**, understood). Among the forms so used are **magnī, parvī, tantī, quantī**; as, **magnī tuae epistolae sunt**, *your letters are of great value.*

Partitive Genitive.

122. The Genitive denotes the *whole* of which a *part* is taken. This is called the *Partitive Genitive*. It is used:—

    a. With Nouns, Pronouns, and Adjectives; as, **pars equitum**, *a part of the horsemen;* **quis vestrum?** *which of you?* **uter consulum?** *which of the (two) consuls?* **nihil reliquī est**, *there is nothing left (of a remainder).*

    b. With Neuter Adjectives and Adverbs of Degree (both used as Nouns); as, **plūs dolōris**, *more grief;* **tantum spatiī** (or **locī**), *so much space;* **satis ēloquentiae** (or **pecūniae**), *enough eloquence* (or *money*).

123. Notice these facts concerning the *Partitive Genitive:*—

    a. Cardinal numbers regularly (and other words sometimes) take the Ablative with **ē (ex)** or **dē**, and *not* the Partitive Genitive; as, **quinque ex mīlitibus; ūnus dē nōbīs.**

NOTES. 197

b. **Nostrum** and **vestrum** are used as Partitive Genitives; **nostrī** and **vestrī** as Objective Genitives (**124**); as, **quis nostrum? uter vestrum?** But we must say **nostrī oblītus**, *forgetful of us.*

c. **Mille** (the *noun*) is followed by the Partitive Genitive; as, **quinque millia passuum**, *five miles;* **sex millia hominum.**

d. CAUTION. *All of us; all of you; all of the soldiers;* etc., must not be expressed by the Partitive Genitive, since *all* does not denote a *part*, but the *whole*. The Latin should be, **nōs omnēs**, *we all;* **vōs omnēs; mīlitēs omnēs.**

e. CAUTION. *The top of the mountain; the middle of the night; the rest of the Gauls;* etc., must not be expressed by a noun and a Partitive Genitive (**110**, *b*), but thus: **summus mons; media nox; reliquī Gallī.**

Subjective and Objective Genitive.

124. Many Nouns and Adjectives have the general meaning of Transitive Verbs; for instance, **amor** in the expression **amor patriae**, *love of country*. If this were to be expressed in the form of a sentence, it would be **nōs** (**tū, ego, is**, etc.) **patriam amāmus** (**amās, amō, amat**, etc.), *we (you, I, he) love (loves) our (your, my, his) country*. That is, **patriae**, as well as **patriam**, is the *Object* of the *love*. So also, **cupidī bellī sumus** = **bellum cupimus**. Hence such a Genitive is called the *Objective Genitive*. If a Genitive of *Possession* were used, it would represent the *actor*, or *Subject*, and hence such a Genitive is called the *Subjective Genitive*. **Amor Deī** (*love of God*) may mean **Deus nōs amat**, or **nōs Deum amāmus**; the former would represent the *Subjective Genitive*, and the latter the *Objective Genitive*. The following examples will illustrate both: **mīlitis amor bellī**, *the soldier's* (Subjective) *love of war* (Objective) = **mīles bellum amat.** — **rērum novārum cupidī sunt**, *they are desirous of a revolution* (Objective) = **iī rēs novās cupiunt.** — **rērum nōn imperītus** (or **ignārus**) **fuit**, *he was not unskilled in* (or *ignorant of*) *affairs* (Objective). — **Helvētiōrum injūriae populī Rōmānī magnae erant**, *the injuries inflicted by* (literally, *of*) *the Helvetii* (Subjective) *upon* (literally, *of*) *the Roman people* (Objective) *were great*.

Genitive with Verbs of Remembering and Forgetting.

125. Verbs meaning *to remember, to forget* (that is, *to be mindful of, to be forgetful of*), are regularly followed by the Genitive; as, **nunquam illīus noctis oblīviscar**, *I shall never forget that night;* **mortis ējus meminī**, *I remember his death.*

Genitive after Sum.

126. *a.* As in English, the noun which the Genitive limits is not always expressed. Nouns meaning *duty, part, nature, mark, property,* are often omitted, as in these examples: mīlitis Rōmānī est aut vincere aut morī, *it is a Roman soldier's (duty) either to conquer or die;* imperātōris est jubēre, *it is a commander's duty (right) to order;* omnia sunt victōris, *all things are (the property) of the victor* (that is, *belong to the victor*).

REMARK. If, however, a Personal Pronoun is used in the English sentence, the Latin requires the Neuter of the corresponding Possessive Pronoun; as, tuum est vidēre nē malī mihi noceant, *it is your (duty) to take care (see to it) lest bad men harm me.* In this sentence tuum agrees with vidēre (109, *b*).

b. The Genitive is often used after sum, equivalent to the English *composed of;* as, dē hīs duōbus generibus alterum est Druidum, alterum equitum, *of these two classes, one is composed of the Druids, the other of the knights.*

Genitive with Impersonal Verbs.

127. *a.* The Impersonal Verbs miseret, *it causes pity;* poenitet, *it causes repentance;* pudet, *it causes shame;* taedet, *it causes weariness;* piget, *it causes vexation,* take an Accusative (of the person) as Direct Object, and a Genitive expressing *the cause of the feeling* (93, *b*); as, eōs poenitet hōrum consiliōrum, *they repent of these plans* (literally, *it causes them repentance for these plans*).

b. The Impersonal Verbs rēfert and interest (*it is to the advantage of, it concerns*) take the Genitive of the person *to whose advantage anything is.* The subject of these verbs is usually an Infinitive, or an Accusative with the Infinitive; as, interest omnium rectē facere, *it is to the interest of all to act rightly;* interest reī publicae manūs hostium distinērī, *it is to the state's advantage that the bands of the enemy be kept apart.*

Other Uses of the Genitive.

128. The Genitive is used before causā, grātiā (*for the sake of*); instar (indeclinable noun, meaning *likeness*); prīdiē (*the day before*); postrīdiē (*the day after*); as, amīcitiae causā Caesarem secūtus est, *he followed Caesar for friendship's sake;* haec saepēs instar mūrī est, *this hedge is like (the likeness of) a wall;* prīdiē (postrīdiē) ējus diēī, *the day before (the day after) that day.*

NOTES. 199

REMARK. Pridiē and postridiē are contracted forms of priōrī diē and posterō diē; so that pri(ōrī)diē ējus diēī really means *on that day's predecessor*, and posterōdiē (in its shortened form) ējus diēī = *on that day's successor.*

DATIVE.

129. The Dative denotes the *Indirect Object*, and answers the question *To* or *For whom* (or *what*)? as, agricolae pecūniam nautīs dant, *the farmers give money to the sailors;* nōn scholae sed vītae discimus, *we learn, not for the school, but for life;* puer mihi nōmen dixit, *the boy told (to) me his name;* multa parentibus dēbēmus, *we owe much (many things) to our parents.*

CAUTION. *a.* In the sentences, *he comes to the city; we follow him to the gate*, there is no Dative, because *city* and *gate* do not denote the *indirect object* of an action. When the verb expresses *motion*, the Preposition ad with the Accusative must be used; as, ad urbem venit. But see 159.

b. When *for* means *in defence of, in behalf of*, prō with the Ablative must be used; as, dulce est prō patriā morī, *it is sweet to die for (one's) country.*

Dative with Intransitive Verbs.

130. Intransitive Verbs can, of course, take only an Indirect Object; as, rēs legiōnī fēlīciter ēvēnit, *the affair turned out successfully (happily) for the legion.*

Dative of Advantage or Disadvantage.

131. The Dative is very often used to denote *Advantage* or *Disadvantage;* that is, to denote that something is *helpful* or *injurious* (to any one), *pleasant* or *disagreeable* (to him), *fit* or *unfit* (for his use), etc. The Dative is thus used with very many Verbs and Adjectives; as, domus dominīs aedificātur, nōn mūribus, *a house is built for its owners, not for the mice;* Aeduī Rōmānīs amīcī erant, *the Aedui were friendly to the Romans;* Caesarī Ariovistus inimīcus fuit, *Ariovistus was hostile to Caesar.*

a. The following Verbs (and others of similar meaning) would be Transitive in English; in Latin they are regularly Intransitive, and take a Dative of Advantage or Disadvantage: —

1. Verbs meaning *to benefit* or *injure, please* or *displease, command* or *obey, serve* or *resist.*

2. Verbs meaning *to believe* or *distrust, persuade, pardon, envy, threaten, be angry.*

CAUTION. These verbs, if used in the Passive, must be *Impersonal* (134).

b. Some of the Adjectives taking a Dative of Advantage or Disadvantage are these : —
Friendly, amīcus ; *unfriendly,* inimīcus ; *useful,* ūtilis ; *useless,* inūtilis ; *fit,* aptus ; *unfit,* incommodus ; *acceptable,* grātus ; *dear,* cārus ; *displeasing,* ingrātus ; *faithful,* fidēlis ; *angry,* īrātus.

CAUTION. Juvō, *I help,* takes the Accusative. Imperō, *I command,* takes the Dative ; but jubeō, *I order,* takes the Accusative.

c. The Dative of Advantage or Disadvantage is often used where we should expect to find the Ablative of Separation (147). It is thus used with Verbs compounded with ab, dē, ex, and sometimes with other words. It usually represents a *person;* as, mihi hunc timōrem ēripe, *relieve me of this fear (take this fear from me);* scūtō mīlitī dētractō, *having snatched a shield from a soldier.*

Dative with Adjectives: Like, Equal, Near.

132. The Dative is used (as in English) to limit Adjectives meaning *like* (and *unlike*), *equal* (and *unequal*), *near;* as, puer similis patrī est, *the boy is like (to) his father;* hostēs nostrīs (mīlitibus) nōn parēs sunt, *the enemy are not equal to (a match for) our soldiers;* proximī Germānīs sunt, *they are nearest to the Germans;* fīnitimī Galliae fuērunt, *they were neighboring to Gaul (bordered on Gaul).*

a. As prope (*near*) is a Preposition, the Adjective and Adverb derived from it very often take the Accusative, as though they were Prepositions ; that is, they retain the force of the Preposition prope ; as, Crassus proximus mare Oceanum hiemāverat, *Crassus had passed the winter very near the Atlantic.*

Dative with Compounds.

133. Compound Verbs containing the Prepositions ad, ante, con, in, inter, ob, post, prae, prō, sub, super, and sometimes circum, usually take the Dative of Indirect Object ; as, virtūte omnibus praestābant, *they excelled all in valor;* aliquid eī accidit, *something has happened to him;* Rōmānī Germānīs bellum inferunt, *the Romans make war on the Germans;* moenibus multitūdō circumjecta est, *the multitude was thrown about the walls* (that is, *surrounded them*).

CAUTION. Of course, if the *simple* verb is *Transitive* (as, mittō) the compound verb will *remain* Transitive, and take the Accusative of the Direct Object ; as, proelium committō, *I join battle;* equitēs praemittō, *I send the horsemen ahead.*

Dative with Impersonal Verbs.

134. In English, Intransitive Verbs have no Passive; in Latin, they may have a Passive, but it must be *Impersonal*. All verbs that take only the Dative, therefore, can be used in the Passive *only* Impersonally. This includes those verbs mentioned in **93, 2**, as well as such verbs as **veniō, eō, pugnō, contendō, currō**; as, **puerō nocētur,** *harm is done to the boy (the boy is harmed)*; **mīlitibus imperātur,** *a command is given to the soldiers (the soldiers are commanded)*; **lēgibus pārendum est,** *obedience must be rendered to the laws (the laws must be obeyed)*; **nōn parcitur hostibus,** *no quarter is given to the enemy (the enemy are not spared)*.

REMARK. The Impersonal Verbs **libet** (*it pleases*) and **licet** (*it is permitted*) take the Dative; as, **licet mihi īre,** *I may go* (literally, *it is permitted me to go*).

Dative of Possessor.

135. Instead of **habeō** with the Accusative, the Dative is very often used with the verb **sum,** to denote the *Possessor;* as, **nōbīs sunt librī,** *we have books;* **virō quinque equī sunt,** *the man has five horses.*

a. The Dative is also used with the compounds of **sum** (except **possum,** which takes the Infinitive, and **absum,** which takes the Ablative, usually with **ā** or **ab**); as, **Caesarī exercitus nōn dēfuit,** *an army was not wanting (lacking) to Caesar.*

Many of these are provided for by **133.**

Dative of Agent.

136. The Dative is regularly used with the Gerundive to denote the *Agent.* This is sometimes called the Dative of *Apparent* Agent, since the *real* Agent is expressed by the Ablative with **ā** or **ab** (**151,** CAUTION). The Dative, in this use, denotes that something must be done *on a person's part, as far as he is concerned, for his advantage,* etc.; yet it may usually be more simply rendered as though it were Ablative; as, **omnia Caesarī agenda erant,** *all things had to be done by Caesar (on Caesar's part);* **mīlitibus castra relinquenda sunt,** *the camp must be abandoned by the soldiers.*

Two Datives.

137. Some verbs take *two* Datives; one denotes the *Purpose,* and the other is the Dative of *Advantage* or *Disadvantage;* as, **mīlitēs subsidiō Sabīnō mittit,** *he sends soldiers as aid (relief) to Sabinus;* **haec rēs magnō impedīmentō nostrīs erat,** *this circumstance proved a great hindrance to our men.*

REMARK. The Dative of *Purpose* is sometimes used without the Dative of Advantage or Disadvantage.

a. A Phrase (containing ad) is very often used to express a Purpose; as, mīlitēs ad pugnandum alacrēs erant, *the soldiers were eager for fighting;* ad urbem videndam vēnit, *he came to see the city* (180).

Dative instead of the Genitive.

138. The Dative is often used where we should expect a Genitive. It will always be found, however, that the Dative expresses *more* than simple Possession; as, *advantage, disadvantage,* etc.; as, Gallī Titō ad pedēs sē prōjiciunt, *the Gauls throw themselves at Titus's feet* (literally, *throw themselves before* (prō) *Titus, at his feet*); Pulfiōnī scūtum transfīgitur, *Pulfio's shield is pierced through.*

ACCUSATIVE.

139. The Accusative denotes the *Direct Object* of a Transitive Verb; as, magister puerum laudat, *the teacher praises the boy;* oppidānī portās clausērunt, *the townspeople closed the gates.*

a. Verbs of *motion,* which are Intransitive (as simple verbs), often become Transitive when compounded with ad, circum, in, trans; as, urbem adiit, *he approached the city;* consilia ineunt, *they form (enter upon) plans;* nostrōs circumvēnērunt, *they entrapped* (English, "*got around*") *our men;* flūmen transītis, *you are crossing the river.*

Cognate Accusative.

140. In English, an Objective Case may be used after an Intransitive Verb (as well as after a Transitive Verb) to *repeat the idea* contained in the Verb; as, *he went his way; we ran a race; I have dreamed a dream.* It is called in English the *Cognate Objective* (*Cognate,* from con + nascor, means *kindred, related*); in Latin, it is called the *Cognate Accusative;* as, mīrum somnium somniāvī, *I have dreamed a wonderful dream;* jusjūrandum jūrāvī, *I have sworn an oath;* viam trīduī prōcessit, *he advanced a three days' journey.*

Two Accusatives.

141. Some Verbs take *two Accusatives:* —

a. Verbs of *making, calling, thinking* (as well as verbs of similar meaning), take two Accusatives (of the *same* Person or Thing), just as in English they take two Objectives; as, Ancum Martium rēgem

NOTES. 203

populus creāvit, *the people elected Ancus Martius king;* Rŏmulus urbem Rōmam vocāvit, *Romulus called the city Rome;* tē virum sapientem putō, *I think you a wise man.* When these verbs become Passive, one Accusative becomes the *Subject*, the other becomes the *Predicate Nominative* (as in English); as, urbs Rōma vocāta est.

b. Verbs of *asking* and *teaching* (as well as verbs of similar meaning) take two Accusatives (one denoting the Person and the other the Thing), as in English ; as, sententiam mē rogāvit, *he asked me my opinion;* Caesar frūmentum Aeduōs flāgitābat, *Caesar kept demanding corn of the Aedui;* pācem tē poscimus, *we demand peace of you.* In the Passive, the Accusative of the Person becomes the *Subject;* the Accusative of the Thing remains (as in English); as, sententiam rogātus sum, *I was asked my opinion.*

REMARK 1. Cēlō, *I conceal*, takes two Accusatives, like verbs of *asking* ; as, mē haec cēlābās, *you were concealing these things from me* (that is, you were concealing these *things*, and were keeping *me* "in the dark"); amīcum sermōnem cēlāvit.

REMARK 2. Petō, *I seek;* postulō, *I demand;* quaerō, *I ask*, do not take two Accusatives (like rogō). They take the Accusative of the *thing*, but the *Ablative* of the *person* (as the *source* of information) with a Preposition. Petō and postulō take ā or ab ; quaerō takes ā (ab), dē, or ē (ex); as, pācem ā Rōmānīs petunt ; auxilium ā mē postulāvit ; dē iīs causam quaesīvit (*he asked them the reason*).

c. Some Transitive verbs, compounded with trans, take two Accusatives, one being the object of the simple verb, and the other depending on the Preposition ; as, equitēs Rhodanum transduxit (= equitēs trans Rhodanum duxit); so also, cōpiās flūmen transmīsit (= cōpiās trans flūmen mīsit).

REMARK. In the Passive, the Accusative depending on the Preposition may remain ; as, mājor multitūdō Germānōrum Rhēnum trans- dūcitur.

Accusative used Adverbially.

142. The Accusative is very often used *adverbially*, especially to denote *degree* or *extent*. In very many instances it is like the English Objective similarly used (see 54, page 15). Some of these uses are : —

a. The Accusative denotes *length of time*, answering the question, *How long?* as, quinque diēs morābitur, *he will delay five days;* trīduum ibi manēbat, *he remained there for the space of three days;* septem annōs in Galliā vixit.

b. The Accusative denotes *extent of space*, answering the questions *How far? How high? How long?* etc. ; as, **octo millia passuum prōcessit** (**prōgressus est**), *he advanced eight miles ;* **mūrus centum pedēs longus est**, *the wall is 100 feet long ;* **domus quadrāgintā pedēs alta fuit**, *the house was 40 feet high.*

c. The Accusative has an adverbial force (of *degree, extent, cause*, etc.) in many expressions. Some of these, as **multum, plūrimum**, etc., have been mentioned under **94,** *d,* 1. Examples are : —
Suēvī nōn multum frūmentō, sed maximam partem lacte atque pecore vīvunt, *the Suevi do not live much on corn, but for the most part on milk and* (*the flesh of*) *cattle ;* **plūrimum potest,** *he is very powerful* (*he is able to a very great extent*); **quid venītis,** *why do you come?* (English, *what for?*); **fāma tantum valuit,** *the report had so great influence* (*availed to such a degree*).

REMARK. The Accusative of *Place to which* is described in **159,** *b.*

Accusative as Subject.

143. The Accusative is used as the Subject of the Infinitive Mode. In English the Objective is often used in the same way (see **56,** page 16). This use of the Accusative is more fully described in **166.**

Accusative with Prepositions.

144. The Accusative and Ablative are used with Prepositions. The list of those (most common) that take the Ablative is given under **95**; *those not contained in this list require the Accusative.* But see **95,** *c.*

VOCATIVE.

145. The Vocative is the case of Direct Address; as, **studiōsī este, puerī,** *boys, be studious.* It is like the English Independent Case, as, in the example, **puerī** has no dependence on any other word in the sentence.

ABLATIVE.

146. The Ablative usually expresses *Adverbial* ideas ; that is, it answers the questions *From what? By what? Why? How? Where? When? With what?* etc. In English, the same ideas are expressed by phrases containing the Prepositions *from, by, in, with,* and sometimes others ; as, **virum culpā līberat,** *he frees the man from blame ;* **pallidus īrā fuit,** *he was pale with anger* (tells *why*); **clārā vōce dixit,** *he spoke in a loud tone* (tells *how*); **posterō diē hostēs superāvit,** *he overcame the enemy the following day* (tells *when*).

Ablative of Separation.

147. The Ablative (= *from*) is very frequently used to denote *Separation;* as, mē timōre līberās, *you free me from fear;* fīnitimī agrīs expulsī sunt, *the neighbors were driven from their lands;* cōnātū dēstitērunt, *they desisted from their attempt.*

    a. **Opus** (indeclinable, used in Nominative and Accusative) and **ūsus**, meaning *need*, take the Ablative, like verbs expressing *separation* or *privation;* as, opus est magistrātibus et pecūniā, *there is need of magistrates and money.*

Ablative of Origin, or Source.

148. The Ablative (= *from*) denotes *Origin* or *Source*, especially with such a Participle as nātus, *born (from)*; ortus, *sprung (from)*; as, Lūcius Catilīna nōbilī genere nātus fuit, *Lucius Catiline came from noble stock.*

Ablative of Cause.

149. The Ablative denotes *Cause*, answering the question *Why? In accordance with what?* as, pallidus īrā fuit, *he was pale with anger;* senectūte mortuus est, *he died of old age;* victōriā suā glōriantur, *they boast of their victory;* stīpendium jūre bellī capit, *he takes the tribute by* (*in accordance with*) *the law of war.*

    a. The Ablative causā is often used *after* a Genitive to express *cause;* as, reī publicae causā, *for the republic's sake;* reī frūmentāriae (or commeātūs) causā, *for the sake of supplies of corn* (or *supplies*).

Ablative of Manner.

150. The Ablative denotes *Manner*, answering the question *How?* as, clārā vōce dixit, *he spoke in a loud tone;* magnō flētū auxilium ā Caesare petunt, *with a flood of tears* (*great weeping*) *they seek aid of Caesar;* magnā vī contendērunt, *they strove with might and main.*

    a. CAUTION. If *with* means *in company with, in conflict with,* cum must be used. The Ablative is then called the *Ablative of Accompaniment;* as, cum decimā legiōne vēnit, *he came with the tenth legion;* cum hostibus pugnant; cum Germānīs bellum gerunt.

    REMARK. In military reports, or in describing military movements, cum is often omitted.

Ablative of Means or Instrument.

151. The Ablative denotes *Means* or *Instrument*, answering the questions *By what? With what?* as, **hostium fīnēs ferrō et igne vastant,** *they lay waste the enemy's territory with sword and flames;* **Deus mundum omnibus rēbus bonīs explēvit,** *God has filled the world with all blessings (good things);* **legiōne fossam perdūcit,** *he digs (conducts) a ditch with (the help of) the legion.*

CAUTION. If the Noun or Pronoun denotes the *person by whom* something is done, it requires the preposition **ā (ab)**. It is then called, not the *Means*, but the **Agent;** as, **pater ā fīliīs amātur,** *the father is loved by his sons;* **nāvēs mīlitibus ā Caesare complētae sunt,** *the ships were filled with soldiers* (Means) *by Caesar* (Agent).

The *indirect agent* is expressed by **per** with the Accusative; as, **Caesar per explōrātōrēs certior factus est,** *Caesar was informed through scouts* (**ab explōrātōribus** = *by the scouts in person*). See also **136**.

a. The Ablative of Means is used with the Deponent Verbs **ūtor, fruor, fungor, potior, vescor,** and also **vīvō** (with the meaning, *live upon*); as, **aurō et argentō ūtuntur,** *they use (employ) gold and silver;* **eādem conditiōne dēditiōnis ūsus est,** *he enjoyed the same condition (or terms) of surrender;* **lacte vescuntur,** *they live on (feed on) milk;* **pecore vīvunt,** *they live on (the flesh of)cattle;* **castrīs potītī sunt,** *they got possession of the camp.*

REMARK. Potior sometimes takes the Genitive, in the sense of *become master of;* as, **tōtīus Galliae potior,** *I become master of all Gaul.*

b. The Adjectives **frētus, contentus, praeditus** (= **prae + datus**), take the Ablative of Means ; as, **frētī virtūte suā,** *relying on their bravery;* **paucīs rēbus contentus fuit,** *he was content with a few things;* **virtūte praeditus et cōpiīs frētus, Marcellus hostēs vīcit,** *endowed (gifted) with bravery, and relying on his troops, Marcellus conquered the enemy.*

c. The Ablative denotes the *Price* paid for anything. It is the *means by which* it is obtained or exchanged ; as, **vīgintī talentīs ūnam ōrātiōnem vendidit,** *he sold one oration for 20 talents;* **haec victōria Caesarī multō sanguine stetit,** *this victory cost Caesar much blood* (literally, *stood to his account*); **librum duodecim sestertiīs ēmit,** *he bought the book for 12 sesterces* (about 60 cents).

Ablative of Quality.

152. The Ablative of *Quality* is used to describe a person or thing, answering the questions *Of what kind? What sort of? Of what appear-*

ance! etc. See Genitive of Quality (121). EXAMPLES: **Germānī virī corporum ingentī magnitūdine fuērunt,** *the Germans were men of huge size of body;* **moenia urbis magnā altitūdine sunt,** *the walls of the city are of great height;* **horridō aspectū sunt,** *they are of dreadful appearance (have a dreadful look, are "dreadful-looking").*

a. Although the Genitive *may* be used to denote *Quality*, yet the Ablative is more common. The Genitive *must* be used to denote actual measurement (in *days, feet,* etc.); as in the Examples under **121.**

Ablative of Respect.

153. The Ablative often answers the question *In what respect?* and is then called the *Ablative of Respect* (or *Specification*). It is used with Nouns, Adjectives, and Verbs; as, **rex nōmine fuit,** *he was a king in name;* **Gallōs reliquōs virtūte praecēdunt,** *they surpass the rest of the Gauls in bravery;* **puer patrī omnibus rēbus similis est,** *the boy is like his father in all respects;* **mājōrēs nātū sumus,** *we are older (greater in respect to birth).*

REMARK. The Ablative of the Supine is an Ablative of Respect (**191,** *b*).

Ablative with Comparatives.

154. The Ablative may be used after Comparatives, instead of quam (with the Nominative or Accusative); as, **Tullus Hostīlius Rōmulō** (= quam Rōmulus) **ferōcior fuit,** *Tullus Hostilius was more warlike than Romulus;* **scīmus sōlem mājōrem esse terrā** (= quam terram), *we know that the sun is greater than the earth;* **castra amplius millibus passuum octo in lātitūdinem patēbant,** *the camp extended more than eight miles in width.*

a. A few Ablatives (like **opīniōne, spē**) are used with a Comparative, and have the force of entire clauses; as, **celerius opīniōne omnium vēnit,** *he came quicker than any one supposed he would* (literally, *quicker than the opinion,* or *expectation, of all*).

b. Quam is often omitted after **plūs, minus, amplius, longius,** without affecting the case of the following noun; as, **amplius** (Accusative) **tria millia** (Accusative) **passuum castra patēbant,** *the camp extended more than three miles;* that is, *three miles* (Accusative) *and more* (Accusative).

Ablative expressing Measure of Difference.

155. The Ablative denotes the *Measure* (or *Degree*) of *Difference* between two objects compared, telling *by how much* one thing is greater or less than another. Notice a similar use of the Objective in English (**54,** 7, page 15). EXAMPLES: ille vir tōtō capite altior est, *that man is a whole head taller;* Hibernia dīmidiō minor est quam Britannia, *Ireland is a half smaller than England;* tempus multō brevius est, *the time is much shorter.*

 a. The Ablative expressing Measure of Difference is found with all words and phrases which contain a Comparative *idea;* as, hīc locus aequō spatiō ab castrīs Ariovistī et Caesaris aberat, *this spot was the same distance* (*off*) *from the camp of Ariovistus and* (*that of*) *Caesar;* paulō post (ante) vēnit, *he came a little after* (or *before*) ; flūmen trīgintā millibus passuum infrā (suprā) eum locum fuit, *the river was* 30 *miles below* (or *above*) *that place.*

 b. The Ablative of Measure of Difference is very often expressed in the form of *correlatives* (**195,** 8), as, quō — eō (or hōc); quantō — tantō, which are to be translated *the — the;* as, quō mājor vīs aquae sē incitāverit, hōc (eō) artius continēbuntur, *the* (*by how much*) *greater the force of the current shall have been, the* (*by so much*) *more tightly will they be held together.*

 c. The Ablative with Comparatives (**154**) and the Ablative of Measure of Difference are very often found in the same sentence; as, servus multō fortior dominō suō est, *the slave is much braver than his master;* turris quinque pedibus mūrō altior est, *the tower is five feet higher than the wall.*

Ablative with Dignus and Indignus.

156. The Adjectives **dignus**, *worthy*, and **indignus**, *unworthy*, take the Ablative ; as, ignāvus vītā indignus est, *a coward does n't deserve to live* (*is unworthy of life*) ; mīlitēs laude dignī erant, *the soldiers were worthy of praise.*

Ablative Absolute.

157. The Ablative is often used *independently* of the rest of the sentence, and is then called the *Ablative Absolute* (*absolute* means *freed from dependence*). In English, the Independent Case is employed in the same way with Participles, and has three uses : —

 (1.) Substantive + Participle ; as, *the camp having been fortified, he came to Rome.*

 (2.) Substantive + *being* + Adjective ; as, *the soldiers being brave, the enemy were overcome.*

 (3.) Substantive + *being* + Substantive ; as, *Caesar being the judge, you will be condemned.*

The verb *to be* is a Copula; hence *brave* is a Predicate Adjective, and *judge*, a Predicate Noun. The verb **sum** has no Present Participle, however, and therefore, in expressing these examples in Latin, *being* must be omitted in the *second* and *third*. Of course, *brave* must agree with *soldiers*, and *judge* must be in Apposition with *Caesar*. Therefore, the Latin for these examples will be : —

(1.) Substantive + Participle, castrīs mūnītīs, Rōmam vēnit.

(2.) Substantive + (*being*) + Adjective, mīlitibus fortibus, hostēs victī sunt.

(3.) Substantive + (*being*) + Substantive, **Caesare jūdice**, condemnāberis.

Judging from **potens** (Present Participle of **possum**), we may say that the Present Participle of **sum** *would be* **ens**; so that **mīlitibus (entibus) fortibus**, and **Caesare (ente) jūdice**, will show how much alike the English and Latin are in the use of the *absolute* case and the Predicate Noun or Adjective.

REMARK 1. Verbs in Latin (except the Deponents) have no Perfect Active Participle. The Ablative Absolute is *required*, to supply this lack as nearly as possible; as, *having seen the city; having heard the speech*, must be translated thus: **urbe vīsā** (*the city having been seen*); **ōrātiōne audītā** (*the speech having been heard*). In these sentences, however, there will be no Ablative Absolute, as the Participles are *Active* in meaning: *having followed the enemy, our men killed a large number of them; having delayed five days, he set out.* They must be written thus: **hostēs secūtī** (Nominative), **nostrī magnum numerum eōrum occīdērunt**; **quinque diēs morātus** (Nominative), **profectus est**.

REMARK 2. The Ablative Absolute phrase, like the English Independent phrase, is usually equivalent to a *shortened clause*, and should generally be translated as a Subordinate Clause ; as, **mīlitibus fortibus**, *because the soldiers were brave;* **ōrātiōne habitā**, *when the speech had been delivered;* **sē invītō**, *although he was* (or *if he should be*) *unwilling* (or *without his permission*).

REMARK 3. It is much more common than the English Independent Case, and often cannot be translated *literally* so as to make good sense. The student must use that translation which is best and *smoothest;* for example : —

Caesare jūdice, *if Caesar is judge, because Caesar is judge;* **Cicerōne et Antōniō consulibus**, *when Cicero and Antony were consuls, in the consulship of Cicero and Antony;* **hostibus victīs**; (1) *when* (*although, since, because*) *the enemy have been conquered;* (2) *having conquered the enemy;* (3) *the enemy having been conquered;* (4) *after having conquered the enemy.*

PLACE.

158. The Ablative *with a Preposition* denotes place *where* (or *in which*) and *whence* (or *from which*); as, in **Galliā**, *in Gaul;* ab **oppidō**, *from the town;* ex **silvā**, *out of the forest.*

Place *to which* is expressed by the Accusative *with a Preposition;* as, ad **urbem**, *to the city;* ad **castra**, *to the camp.* Remember, this is the *rule;* the next NOTE gives the *exceptions.*

159. To express Place *where* (*in* or *at which*), *whence* (*from which*), *whither* (*to which*), Prepositions are *omitted* with the following : —
(1) *Names* of Cities and Towns ; (2) **domus** (*home*), **rūs** (*country*); (3) *small* Islands. These nouns obey the following Rules : —

a. Place *from which* is expressed by the Ablative ; as, **Catilīna Rōmā fūgit**, *Catiline has fled from Rome;* **rūre revocātus est**, *he was recalled from the country.*

b. Place *to which* is expressed by the Accusative ; as, **domum īvit**, *he went home;* **Corinthō Rōmam profectus est**, *he set out from Corinth for Rome.*

c. Place *in* (or *at*) *which* is expressed by a case called the *Locative* (**locus**, *place*), which is mentioned in **20**, REMARK, page 24, as the *seventh* Latin case. It is found in the First, Second, and Third Declensions, has a Singular and a Plural form, and has endings like the Genitive Singular or Ablative (Singular and Plural). This table shows the endings of the Locative Case : —

DECLENSION.	I.	II.	III.
Singular.	ae.	ī.	e (rarely ī).
Plural.	īs.	īs.	ibus.

Some names of Cities and Towns have no Singular form ; as, **Athēnae** (ārum), *Athens;* **Vēiī** (ōrum), *Veii;* **Sardēs** (ium), *Sardis.* The above table and its correct use can be remembered by this

RULE : To express Place *where*, names of Cities and Towns, also **domus**,* **rūs**, and small Islands, must have the form of the
Genitive, if of the First or Second Declension AND Singular Number.
Ablative, if of the Third Declension OR Plural Number.

EXAMPLES : **Capuae; Karthāgine; Vēiīs; Athēnīs; Sardibus; Rōmae; Lugdūnī** (Nominative Singular, **Lugdūnum**) ; **domī**: *at (or in) Capua, Carthage, Veii, Athens, Sardis, Rome, Lyons; at home.*

* **Domus**, meaning *home*, is of the Second Declension (**21**, *b*).

NOTES. 211

REMARK 1. To express *towards, in-the-vicinity-of, near, from-the-vicinity* (or *neighborhood*) *-of*, Prepositions must be used ; because without them we could not tell whether **Rōmam īvit** meant *he went to Rome,* or *towards Rome.* These examples will show what Prepositions should be used for such meanings : ad **Rōmam profectus est,** *he started towards (in-the-direction-of) Rome ;* ad **Genēvam pervēnit,** *he arrived in-the-vicinity-of Geneva ;* ad (circum, apud) **Capuam hiemāvit,** *he passed the winter near Capua ;* **ā Capuā vēnit,** *he came from-the-neighborhood-of Capua.*

REMARK 2. There are some common, *every-day* words (locō, parte, etc.), which often express Place *where* without a Preposition. These can be best learned by experience.

REMARK 3. The Ablative expressing the *way by which* (or *through which*) is an Ablative of *Means;* as, **viā breviōre īvit,** *he went by a shorter way;* **hostēs locīs impedītīs sequitur,** *he follows the enemy through places difficult of passage.*

TIME.

160. The Ablative answers the questions *When ? Within what time ?* (like the English Objective with a Preposition, expressed or understood). The Accusative (**142**, *a*) answers the question *How long ?* (like the English Objective); as, **sōlis occāsū,** *at sunset;* **bellō servīlī,** *in the war with the slaves* (*servile war*); **tōtam noctem iērunt,** *they marched all night;* **quinque hōrās pugnābant,** *they fought five hours;* **Kalendīs Martiīs,** *on the first of March* (*on the March Kalends*).

DATES.

161. The Romans did not number the days of the month as we do. There were three fixed points in each month, and any particular day was reckoned as so many days *before* the nearest of these points. These three points were called : —

1. **Kalendae** (ārum), *the Kalends:* the first day of the month.
2. **Nōnae** (ārum), *the Nones* (so called from **nōnus,** *ninth;* being *nine* days before the *Ides*): the 7th of March, May, July, and October, and the 5th of the other months.
3. **Īdūs** (uum), Feminine, *the Ides:* the 15th of March, May, July, and October, and the 13th of the other months. It was the pay-day for interest, tuitions, etc.

   a. The names of the Months are Adjectives ; as, **Kalendae Aprīlēs** (often written **Kal. Apr.**), *the 1st of April ;* **Īdibus Novembribus** (**Id. Nov.**), *on the 13th of November.*

b. To express *March* 28*th*, the Romans said *the 5th day before the April Kalends*, because they included the day *from which* and the day *to which* they counted. We should suppose that this would be expressed thus : quintō diē ante Kalendās Aprīlēs; but they said ante diem quintum Kalendās Aprīlēs, *as though* ante diem *were a Preposition followed by the Accusative.*

RULE 1. To find how many days before the Kalends an English day of the month falls, add *two* to the number of days in that month, and subtract the number of the given date ; as, March 28th = 31 + 2 (33) — 28 = 5 ; that is, March 28th = the 5th day before the April Kalends. By adding *two*, they counted in the first day of the next month, because it was an extra day, *beyond the month;* this, with the day *from which* they reckoned, made the two extra days.

RULE 2. To find how many days before the Nones or Ides an English day of the month falls, add *one*, and subtract the number of the given date ; as, ante diem quartum Nōnās Jūniās = (5 + 1) − 4 = June 2; ante diem quartum Īdūs Septembrēs = (13 + 1) − 4 = Sept. 10.

MODES OF THE VERB.

Indicative.

162. The Indicative Mode is used

a. To state something as a *fact;* as, puerum laudat, *he praises the boy;* vēnī, vīdī, vīcī, *I came, I saw, I conquered.*

b. To ask a *direct* question ; as, quis putat Cassium ignāvum esse? *who supposes that Cassius is a coward?* pugnātne servus? *does the slave fight?*

The forms of questions are given in **101.**

Imperative.

163. The Imperative Mode expresses a *direct* command (that is, one to the Second Person); as, convocā, magister, puerōs, *teacher, call the boys together;* studiōsī este, *be industrious;* cavē, *beware.*

CAUTION. To express a *prohibition* (negative command) a peculiar idiom is required. This is given in **178**, CAUTION 2.

Subjunctive.*

164. The Subjunctive Mode has a variety of uses ; the simplest are : —

* Only a few of the simplest uses are given in this section; the Mode is more fully described hereafter. This Note gives such uses of the Subjunctive as can be readily appreciated by contrast with the Indicative and the Imperative.

NOTES. 213

a. To state something as *doubtful* or *possible;* as, **sī Caesar pugnet, Germānōs superet,** *if Caesar should fight, he would overcome the Germans.*
(The Indicative states a *fact.*)

b. To ask an *indirect* question; as, **rogat quid dīcam,** *he asks what I am saying.* It is also used to ask a question implying *doubt* or *uncertainty;* as, **quis putet Cassium ignāvum esse?** *who would suppose that Cassius is a coward?*
(The Indicative asks a *direct* question, and one which does *not* imply a doubt.)

c. To express an *indirect* command; that is, commanding an act in which the First or Third Person is to be the *actor,* but the command is not addressed *to* the First or Third Person (see REMARK, below). It may express all such ideas as *exhortation, warning,* etc.; as, **magister puerōs convocet,** *let the teacher call the boys together;* **omnēs studiōsī sīmus,** *let us all be studious;* **caveat,** *let him beware.*
(The Imperative expresses a *direct* command.)

REMARK. If, in an Imperative sentence, the First or Third Person is required, the Subjunctive must be used. This table will show the forms of *command, exhortation,* etc., for **amō** and **sum,** in all Persons, Present Tense :—

Singular.

1. **amem,** *let me love.*
2. **amā,** *love (thou).*
3. **amet,** *let him (her, it) love.*

1. **sim,** *let me be.*
2. **es,** *be (thou).*
3. **sit,** *let him (her, it) be.*

Plural.

1. **amēmus,** *let us love.*
2. **amāte,** *love (ye).*
3. **ament,** *let them love.*

1. **sīmus,** *let us be.*
2. **este,** *be (ye).*
3. **sint,** *let them be.*

d. To express *purpose,* answering the questions, *Why? For what?* as, **Caesar mīlitēs mīsit ut urbem expugnārent,** *Caesar sent soldiers to take (that they might take) the city.* Notice that **expugnārent** does not state a *fact,* but something *intended,* or *possible.*

INFINITIVE.

165. The Infinitive is usually employed as an indeclinable Verbal Noun (as in English).

a. The Infinitive is often used as Subject of a Verb (*impersonal*). Of course, a Predicate Adjective will be *Neuter* (**109,** *b*). EXAMPLES: **esse melius quam vidērī est,** *to be is better than to seem;* **dulce prō patriā morī est,** *to die for (one's) native land is sweet.*

b. The Infinitive is used after many verbs, sometimes as Object, and sometimes to fill out their meaning. In the latter use it is called the *Complementary Infinitive* (that is, it *completes* the thought); as, **Caesar bellum cum Germānīs gerere constituit,** *Caesar determined to carry on war with the Germans;* **urbem expugnāre nōn possunt,** *they cannot take the city by storm;* **iter facere coepit,** *he began to march.*

Infinitive with Subject Accusative.

166. Verbs and expressions of *telling, thinking, perceiving, knowing* (and others of similar meaning), are followed by the *Infinitive, with the Accusative as Subject.* This use of the Infinitive may be more easily understood, if stated thus : —

I. Verbs of *saying* are followed by the Accusative with the Infinitive, when they introduce, not a *Direct Statement* (that is, the *exact* words of the speaker), but an *Indirect Statement* (that is, the general *idea* of what he said, but not his exact words). Such an Indirect Statement, in English, is introduced by the Conjunction *that;* but the word *that* is omitted in Latin. EXAMPLES : (Direct Quotation) "*The sailors fight*," " **Nautae pugnant;**" (Indirect Statement) *He says that the sailors fight,* **Dīcit nautās pugnāre.**

II. A beginner, however, often finds it hard to understand why a verb of *thinking* should follow the same rule as a verb of *telling.* The reason is that, when a person *thinks,* he "says to himself," as in this sentence : *I said to myself* (= *thought, determined, hoped*) *that I should be elected.*

A similar construction is seen in English (**56,** page 16) after verbs of *seeing* and *hearing;* as, *I heard him* (*to*) *call; he saw the boy* (*to*) *jump.*

In Latin, the *Accusative with the Infinitive* is a very common construction, after verbs of *saying,* etc. ; as, **dīcit** (**negat, respondet, putat, spērat, audit, crēdit**) **Rōmānōs superātūrōs esse Gallōs,** *he says* (*denies, replies, thinks, hopes, hears, believes*) *that the Romans will overcome the Gauls.*

CAUTION. Verbs of *asking* do not *state* anything, and therefore cannot take the Accusative and Infinitive. They should be followed by a Subjunctive of *Purpose* or *Indirect Question* (see **179,** *d;* **177,** *b*).

NOTES. 215

Historical Infinitive.

167. Latin writers often use the Present Infinitive, instead of the Imperfect and Perfect Indicative (without *have*). It is then called the *Historical Infinitive*. In this use its Subject is in the *Nominative Case*. Perhaps some verb (like **coepī**), upon which the Infinitive depends, has been omitted. It is used in lively descriptions ; as, **flāgitāre, dūcere,** and **dīcere,** in these sentences : **Caesar Aeduōs frūmentum flāgitāre. Diem ex diē Aeduī dūcere; frūmentum conferrī, comportārī, adesse dīcere,** *Caesar kept demanding corn of the Aedui. The Aedui kept putting* (*him*) *off, day after day ; they said* (*at one time*) *that the corn was being collected,* (*at another*) *that it was on the way,* (*and again*) *that it was at hand.*

TENSES.

168. *Indicative.* The Indicative has all the Tenses, which are described in **61.**

a. Both the Future and Future Perfect are sometimes required, when the English verb contains the *idea* of a Future, but does not have a Future *form* (**17,** NOTE, page 5) ; as, **sī Rōmam vēnerit** (or **veniet**), **fēlix erō,** *if he comes* (that is, *shall have come, shall come*) *to Rome, I shall be happy.*

b. The Present Tense is often used for a *past* tense, to represent a past event vividly, as though *now* taking place. It is then called the **Present Historical** (like the *Historical Infinitive,* **167**), because it really describes past events ; as, **dum haec geruntur, dux nuntiōs mittit,** *while these things are going on, the leader sends messengers.* Webster, when pleading a case before a jury, thus used the Present Historical : " The deed is done. He (the criminal) retreats, retraces his steps to the window, passes out through it as he came in, and escapes. The secret is his, and it is safe."

REMARK. The Present Historical is almost always used with **dum,** *while,* though the other verbs in the sentence may be in tenses denoting *past* time ; as, **dum haec parantur, Saguntum jam oppugnābātur,** *while these preparations are being made, Saguntum was already under siege* (*being besieged*).

169. *Imperative Tenses.* The Imperative Mode has only one tense (the Present) in common use. The Future is used in laws and commandments (like the English, "Thou shalt not steal"). The Present Imperative tells the time of *giving* the command, the time of *obeying* may be *future* (as in English). The Present has only one Person, the Second ; how the lack of the First and Third Persons is supplied is explained in **164**, *c*, REMARK.

170. Subjunctive Tenses. The Subjunctive Mode has no Future or Future Perfect. This lack is sometimes supplied (for the Future) by the use of the Active Periphrastic Conjugation (as shown in **82**, REMARK), and sometimes by using the Present Subjunctive as a Future and the Perfect as a Future Perfect (as described in **175**). The Imperfect Subjunctive also has a peculiar use (described in **175**, REMARK 1). In a word, the *time* denoted by the Subjunctive tenses must often be decided by the *sense*, and not by the *name* of the tense (see **19**, page 6).

Primary and Secondary Tenses.

171. Tenses expressing Present or Future time are called *Primary* (or *Principal*); those expressing Past time are called *Secondary* (or *Historical*). *Historical* means *describing past events* (as in the terms, *Historical Present* and *Historical Infinitive*). The tenses are thus divided : —
Primary : Present, Future, Perfect (Definite), Future Perfect.
Secondary : Imperfect, Perfect (Indefinite, or *Aorist*), Pluperfect.

Sequence of Tenses.

172. The tense of a verb in the Subjunctive, in a Dependent Clause, is determined by the tense of the verb on which it depends. That is, Present or Future time must be followed by Present or Future time, and Past time must be followed by Past time. This law is called the *Sequence of Tenses* (from **sequor**, *I follow*), and can be thus stated : *Primary tenses follow Primary tenses, and Secondary tenses follow Secondary.* This is illustrated by the following : —

PRIMARY.
{ veniō ut tē videam, *I come that I may see you.*
  veniam " "   " *I shall* " " " "
  vēnī   " "   " *I have*   " " " "
  vēnerō " "   " *I shall have* " " " " }

SECONDARY.
{ veniēbam ut tē vidērem, *I was coming that I might see you.*
  vēnī   " "   " *I came*   " " "
  vēneram " "   " *I had come* " " " }

Also, **rogō quid agās**, *I ask what you are doing* (Present Subjunctive).
rogābō quid actūrus sīs, *I will ask what you are going to do*, or *will do* (Future Subjunctive).

REMARK 1. The Imperfect Subjunctive (*not* the Perfect) is regularly used after Secondary tenses ; as, **vidērem** in the examples above.

REMARK 2. The Historical Present (**168**, *b*), being really a *past* tense, is regularly followed by a past tense ; as, **Helvētiī lēgātōs ad Caesarem mittunt, quī pācem peterent,** *the Helvetii send envoys to Caesar to ask for peace.*

173. *Infinitive Tenses*. The tenses of the Infinitive are named *Present, Perfect,* and *Future;* but the Present may have the meaning of a Present or Imperfect, and the Perfect may have that of the Perfect or Pluperfect. *The time of an Infinitive tense is determined by the time of the verb on which it depends.* If the Infinitive denotes, —

(1.) The *same* time as the principal verb, use the *Present.*
(2.) Time *before* that of the principal verb, use the *Perfect.*
(3.) Time *after* that of the principal verb, use the *Future.*

Compare these rules carefully with the following examples : **dīcit mīlitem pugnāre,** *he says that the soldier fights;* **dixit magistrum puerōs laudāre,** *he said that the teacher was praising the boys;* **putat Rōmānōs fortissimōs fuisse,** *he thinks that the Romans have been very brave;* **nuntiāvit Gallōs nostrōs superāvisse (superātūrōs esse),** *he announced that the Gauls had overcome (would overcome) our men.*

CAUTION. With verbs denoting *necessity, permission, ability* (as, **oportet, licet, possum**) the Present Infinitive must be translated by the *Perfect,* when those verbs are in the Perfect ; as, **oportuit mē īre** (not **īvisse**), *I ought to have gone* (*it was necessary for me to go*); **mihi venīre licuit,** *I might have come* (*it was permitted me to come*); **urbem vidēre potuistī,** *you could have seen the city* (*you were able to see*).

CONDITIONAL SENTENCES.

174. A Conditional Sentence consists of a Principal Clause, making a *statement,* and a Subordinate Clause, connected by **sī** (*if*), or a compound of **sī** (as, **nisi,** *unless;* **etsī,** *although;* **sīn,** *but if*). The clause containing **sī** is called the *Condition;* the clause containing the statement (that is, the Principal Clause) is called the *Conclusion.* The Condition is also called the *Protasis;* the Conclusion, the *Apodosis.*

Conditional Sentences are divided, —

(1.) According to the *time* denoted by them.
(2.) According to the *kind of statement* made, or the *thought* expressed.
 a. Time. Conditional Sentences may express Past, Present, or Future time.
 b. Kind of Statement. As the Mode of a verb expresses the " mood " of the speaker, he will use the Indicative to make a *simple statement* (that is, a statement without any hint of *doubt*); but he will use the Subjunctive to state something which he regards as *uncertain* (that is, *possible*) or *contrary to the truth* (that is, *impossible*).

NOTES.

Table of Conditional Sentences.

175. This Table shows what *time* and what *thought* a Conditional Sentence may express. Remember that the Subjunctive has no Future or Future Perfect. The Present is also used as a Future (as in *c*), and the Perfect as a Future Perfect (as in REMARK 3).

TIME.	THOUGHT EXPRESSED.	MODE AND TENSE.	EXAMPLE.
a. Present.	1. Fact,	Indic. Pres. (both clauses),	si valet, laetor, *if he is well, I rejoice.*
	2. Contrary to Fact,	Subj. Imperf.* (both clauses),	si valēret, laetārer, *if he were well, I would rejoice (now).*
b. Past.	1. Fact,	Indic. Imperf. (both clauses),	si valēbat, laetābar, *if he was well, I was rejoicing.*
		Indic. Perf.† (both clauses),	si valuit, laetātus sum, *if he was well, I rejoiced.*
	2. Contrary to Fact,	Subj. Pluperf. (both clauses),	si valuisset, laetātus essem, *if he had been well, I would have rejoiced.*
c. Future.	1. Fact,	Indic. Fut.‡ (both clauses),	si valēbit, laetābor, *if he shall be well, I will rejoice.*
	2. Doubt,	Subj. Pres.‡ (both clauses),	si valeat, laeter, *if he should be well, I would rejoice.*

* REMARK 1. This form of Conditional Sentence is apt to puzzle a beginner more than any other, because the Imperfect Subjunctive denotes *present* time. Review carefully 19, *b*, page 6, and notice how exactly alike the English and Latin are in this respect. We say, "If it *were* so now" (as it is *not*).

† REMARK 2. Of course, the Perfect Indicative may have a double idea of time (61, 3); and the example may also be translated, *if he has been well, I have rejoiced.*

‡ REMARK 3. If the action of the Condition is completed *before* the time of the Conclusion, we must use the Future Perfect Indicative, instead of the Future, and (to express a *doubt*) we must use the Perfect Subjunctive (= the Future Perfect), instead of the Present; as, sī mīlitēs hortātus erit, fortiter pugnābunt, *if he shall have encouraged the soldiers, they will fight bravely;* sī mīlitēs hortātus sit, fortiter pugnent, *if he should have encouraged the soldiers, they would fight bravely.*

REMARK 4. Besides the forms of Conditional Sentences given in the above Table, others will be found whose form will depend entirely upon the *sense*; for example, those which will either combine *past* and *present* time, or in which the Conclusion may have the form of a *command*; as, sī fortis fuisset, victor esset, *if he had been brave, he would (now) be victor;* sī vult, veniat, *if he wishes, let him come.*

Subjunctive of Wish.

176. The Subjunctive is used to express a *wish*. Of course, the Indicative cannot denote such an idea, as the thing wished for must be *possible* or *impossible*. "There is an *if* about every wish;" and, in Latin, a sentence expressing a *wish* is really a clause of a Conditional Sentence, following the laws stated in **175**, *a* (2), *b* (2), *c* (2).

With the Subjunctive of Wish the particles **utinam**, **Ō sī** (*would that*) are often used.

a. A wish for something *impossible at the present time* requires the Imperfect Subjunctive; as, (utinam) cōpiās mājōrēs habērēmus! *would that we (now) had greater forces!*

b. A wish for something *impossible in past time* requires the Pluperfect Subjunctive; as, (utinam, Ō sī) mīlitēs fortiōrēs fuissent! *would that the soldiers had been braver!*

c. A wish for something *possible in the future* requires the Present Subjunctive; as, (utinam) pater veniat! *would that my father would come!*

CAUTION. A *negative wish* requires **nē**, and *not* **nōn**; as, **nē vīvam, sī sciō**, *I wish I may not live, if I know.*

Subjunctive in Questions.

177. *a.* The Subjunctive is used to ask a question implying a *doubt* (see examples under **164**, *b*).

b. The Subjunctive is used to ask an *Indirect Question;* as, **rogāvit quis sē vccāret**, *he asked who was calling him* (Direct Question, "**Quis mē vocat?**")

c. The question is often *hinted*, but not really *asked;* as, **cognōvit quid fēcerit**, *he has found out (by inquiry) what he has done;* **dīc mihi quid faciās**, *tell me (for I wish to know) what you are doing;* **quae agat, quibuscum loquātur, scit**, *he knows (by inquiry) what he does (and) with whom he converses.*

d. Indirect Questions are either *single* or *double;* like Direct Questions, they require interrogative words. (Review **101**.) Notice, however, these two points in which they differ from Direct Questions:
(1.) In a *Single* Indirect Question, **num** (*whether*) is regularly used, but it does *not* necessarily expect the answer *No;* (2.) In *Double* Indirect Questions, **utrum — an** (or **-ne — an**) are used, as in Direct Questions; but *or not* is expressed by **necne** (**annōn** being used in Direct Questions); as, **rogāvit utrum amīcus an inimīcus essem**, *he asked whether I were a friend or foe;* **dubium est utrum ventūrus sit, necne**, *it is doubtful whether he will come, or not.*

REMARKS. 1. Sometimes **sī** is used in the sense of *whether* (as in English). This use is common with **exspectō**, in a *single* question; as, **sī venīrent exspectāvī**, *I waited* (*to see*) *whether they would come.* 2. **Ut** (*how*) is sometimes used in questions; as, **docēbat ut omnī tempore tōtīus Galliae principātum Aeduī tenuissent.**

Subjunctive of Command, Exhortation, etc.

178. Any form of Command not *direct* (that is, implying that the First or Third Person is the actor, and expressing *exhortation, warning,* etc.) requires the Subjunctive.

CAUTIONS. 1. To express a *negative* form of *exhortation,* etc., **nē**, and *not* **nōn**, must be used; as, **nē pugnēmus**, *let us not fight.*

2. To express a *prohibition* (that is, a negative command to the Second Person), the Imperative must *not* be used. There are several forms that may be used; these two, however, are most common:—

a. For the Singular, **nē** with the *Perfect* Subjunctive; as, **nē hōc flūmen transierīs**, *don't cross this river* (literally, *do not have crossed,* etc.). The use of the Perfect arises from the fact that the Romans often wished to describe an act as *finished.*

b. For the Singular *or* Plural, use **nōlī** (Imperative of **nōlō**) with the Complementary Infinitive; as, **nōlīte ignāvī esse**, *do not be cowardly* (literally, *be unwilling to be*).

Subjunctive of Purpose.

179. The Subjunctive is used to express a *purpose,* answering the questions *Why? For what?* A Purpose may be *positive* or *negative;* the conjunction **ut** (also written **utī**), *that, in order that,* is commonly used with the *positive,* and **nē**, *that not, lest,* with the *negative;* as, **vēnit ut urbem vidēret**, *he came that he might see* (*to see*) *the city;* **pugnāmus nē servī sīmus**, *we fight that we may not be slaves.*

CAUTIONS. 1. *The Infinitive must not be used to denote a Purpose* (see first example). 2. **Ut nōn** *must not be used for a negative Purpose, but for a negative Result* **(181).**

a. The Relative **quī** is very often used to introduce a clause of Purpose, being equal to **ut is** is (**ego, tū**, etc.); as, **cōpiās mīsit quae** (= **ut eae**) **urbem expugnārent**.

b. The Ablative **quō** (= **ut eō**) is regularly used, instead of **ut**, when there is a *Comparative* in the clause. It is thus both a Conjunction (**ut**) and an Ablative of Measure of Difference **(155)**; as, **lēgem brevem esse oportet, quō facilius intellegātur**, *a law should be short, that it may* THE *more easily be understood.*

c. **Quōminus** (also written **quō minus**, *by which the less*) takes the Subjunctive, with the meanings *that not, from*, etc., after verbs signifying to *hinder, prevent, object*, being equivalent to **nē**, *lest;* as, **quid Caesarem impedit quōminus urbem oppugnet?** (*hinders from assaulting*); **recūsāvit quōminus sub imperiō populī Rōmānī esset** (*refused to be*).

d. Verbs of *asking, commanding* (except **jubeō**), *urging, permitting* (except **patior**), and others of like meaning, take a Subjunctive of Purpose, *and not the Accusative with the Infinitive, as they do not make a statement;* as, **legiōnēs hortātus est ut pugnārent**, *he urged the legions to fight.*

e. Verbs of *fearing* take the Subjunctive : with **nē**, when the event is not desired; with **ut**, when it *is* desired. Translate **nē** by *that* or *lest*, **ut** by *that not*, and the Present Subjunctive like the Future Indicative. Study these examples carefully, and notice that "*not*" comes from the *thought*, rather than from **ut**: **vereor nē leō veniat**, *I fear that (lest) the lion will come* (literally, *I have my fears about his not coming*); **vereor ut vincat**, *I fear that he will not conquer* (literally, *I have my fears about his conquering*).

f. **Ut** is often omitted, especially after verbs of *asking, commanding*, and others of similar meaning; as, **huic mandat, Rēmōs adeat**, *he instructs him to visit the Remi.*

180. There are, in common use, *five ways* of expressing a Purpose; but *the Infinitive is not one of them. He came to see the city* may be written : —

1. vēnit ut urbem vidēret.
2. vēnit quī urbem vidēret.
3. vēnit ad urbem videndam (**190**, a).
4. vēnit urbis videndae causā (**190**, a).
5. vēnit urbem vīsum (**191**, a).

Subjunctive of Result.

181. The Subjunctive is used to denote a *result*. A *positive* Result regularly has, for its conjunction, **ut**, *so that;* a *negative* Result has **ut nōn**, *so that not.*

REMARK. The Subjunctive of Result is common after **sīc** (**ita, tam**), *so;* **tālis**, *such;* **tantus**, *so great;* **is**, *such;* **ējusmodī**, *of such a kind.*

a. A Subjunctive of Result is used with Impersonal Verbs like **accidit** (fit), *it happens;* **sequitur**, *it follows;* and other verbs and expressions of like meaning. Of course, *the thing that happens*, etc., is the real Subject of such a verb; as, **accidit, ut lūna plēna esset**, *it happened to be full moon* (*that the moon was full*); **sequitur, ut haec falsa sint**, *it follows that these things are false.*

REMARK. The Future Infinitive Passive (as **amātum īrī**) is seldom found. In its place is used **futūrum esse** (or **fore**) followed by a Subjunctive of Result ; as, **dixit fore (futūrum esse) ut omnēs interficerentur** (*not* **omnēs interfectum īrī**), *he said that (it would happen that) all would be killed*.

   b. A Result clause may also be the Object of a verb ; as, **fēcērunt ut profectiō consimilis fugae vidērētur**, *they made their departure seem very like a flight;* **nē committat ut locus hōc nōmen capiat**, *let him not cause the place to take this name*.

   c. The Relative **quī** is often equivalent to **ut is, ego**, etc., introducing a Result. This use of the Subjunctive expresses a Result of some *quality* of the Antecedent, and hence is called the *Characteristic Result*. Sometimes the thought of Result is not at once evident, and we must supply some such word as **tālis, tantus, ējusmodī**, to modify the Antecedent and give to it the idea of *quality*, which the Romans associated with it ; as, **nōn is** (= **tālis**) **sum quī** (= **ut ego**) **perīculō terrear**, *I am not such (a coward) as to be (that I am) terrified by danger;* **tempestās (tanta) coörta est, quae** (= **ut ea**) **nāvēs rējiceret**, *a storm arose (so great) which (that it) drove the vessels back*.

   d. **Quīn**, a peculiar compound of the Relative Pronoun and **nōn** (or **nē**), is used with the Subjunctive after words implying *doubt*, and is translated by *that, but that*. The **quī** is an old Ablative, equivalent to **quō**; so that **quīn** = **ut eō nōn**. **Quīn** is sometimes used instead of **quōminus** (**179**, *c*) after verbs of *hindering*, etc. Examples are : **nōn est dubium** (or **nōn dubitō**) **quīn fortis sit**, *there is no doubt* (or *I do not doubt*) *that he is brave;* **nunquam mē poteris dēterrēre, quīn haec loquar**, *you can never deter me from saying these things*.

CAUTIONS. 1. If the thought is, *I doubt whether*, or *it is doubtful whether*, the Subjunctive of *Indirect Question* must be used ; as, **fortisne an ignāvus sit, dubium est**. 2. **Dubitō**, meaning *I hesitate*, takes the Infinitive ; as, **nostrī flūmen transīre nōn dubitāvērunt**.

   e. A clause of Result is often used as an *appositive ;* as, **id, quod constituerant, facere cōnantur, ut ē fīnibus suīs exeant** (**ut — exeant** is in apposition with **id**).

How to express Cause or Reason.

182. *a*. **Quod** (*because*), **quoniam** (*since*), **quia** (*because*), regularly require the Indicative.

NOTES. 223

b. **Quum** (or **cum**), meaning *since*, and introducing a reason, requires the Subjunctive; as, **quum fortis sit, vincet,** *since he is brave, he will conquer.*

c. The Relative **quī** is often equal to **quum** is (**ego**, etc.) meaning *since he* (*I*, etc.), and takes the Subjunctive of Cause; as, **condemnātus est, quī amīcum interfēcerit,** *he has been condemned, since he has killed his friend.*

d. **Quod** is often used to introduce a Substantive Clause (**188,** b) which may be Subject or Object; as, **quod Rēgulus rediit mīrābile vidētur,** *the fact that Regulus returned seems strange.* It is generally best translated by *the fact that,* or *as to the fact that.*

e. For **quod** (*because*) with the Subjunctive, see **187,** f.

How to express Concession.

183. *Concession* means *granting;* for instance, *although he is innocent* means *granting that,* etc.

a. **Quum** (or **cum**), meaning *although,* requires the Subjunctive of Concession; as, **quum paucī sint, fortissimī sunt,** *although they are few, they are very brave.*

CAUTION. **Etsī, tametsī,** meaning *although,* being compounds of **sī,** take the Indicative or the Subjunctive according to the laws of Conditional Sentences (**175**). **Quamquam** (*although*) takes the Indicative.

b. The Relative **quī** is often equal to **quum** is (**ego**, etc.) meaning *although he* (*I,* etc.), and takes the Subjunctive of Concession; as, **culpātur, quī innocens sit,** *he is blamed, although he is innocent.*

c. **Quamvīs** (= **quam** + **vīs,** Second Person Singular of **volō**) means, literally, *as much as you please,* but is translated *although.* It requires the Subjunctive; as, **quamvīs fortēs sint,** *although they are brave* (*let them be as brave as you please*).

d. **Dum, modo, dummodo,** meaning *provided,* require the Subjunctive of Concession; as, **dum eat,** *provided he go.*

Clauses of Time.

184. a. **Quum** (or **cum**), *when,* regularly takes the Subjunctive in the *Imperfect* and *Pluperfect* tenses, but the Indicative in the others; as, **quum in citeriōre Galliā esset; quum quaesīvisset.** The Imperfect and Pluperfect, *Indicative,* sometimes occur, emphasizing a *fact.*

CAUTION. **Ubi,** *when,* **postquam** (or **posteāquam**), *after,* and others of like meaning, take the Indicative.

b. **Dum**, meaning *until*, and implying *purpose*, takes the Subjunctive; when it means *while*, or *until* (not denoting *purpose*), it takes the Indicative; as, **dum reliquae nāvēs convenīrent, exspectāvit**, *he waited until the rest of the ships should assemble;* but **dum paucōs diēs morātur**, *while he tarries a few days.*

REMARK. **Dum**, meaning *while*, regularly takes the Present Historical (**168**, *b*, REMARK), as **morātur**, in the above example.

c. **Antequam** and **priusquam**, meaning *before*, take the Subjunctive, when there is an idea of *doubt* or *purpose;* but when they simply connect two *facts*, one occurring before the other, they take the Indicative; as, **priusquam quidquam cōnārētur, Divitiacum ad sē vocārī jubet**, *before he should attempt anything*, etc.; **ad eum locum contendit, antequam hostēs oppidum expugnārent**, *he hastened to that place, before the enemy should capture the town* (= *lest*, **nē**); but **neque prius fugere dēstitērunt quam ad flūmen pervēnērunt**.

REMARK. **Antequam** and **priusquam**, as in the last example, are often written as separate words.

Subjunctive "by Attraction."

185. The Subjunctive is often used in a dependent clause, not for any reason of its own, but *because the verb on which it depends is in the Subjunctive.* Such a clause must be so closely connected with the other Subjunctive clause as to become a *necessary*, or *explanatory*, part of it, and its verb is said to be in the Subjunctive *by Attraction;* as, **velit** in this sentence: **nēmō tam potens est ut omnia quae velit efficere possit**, *no one is so powerful as to be able to accomplish all that he wishes.* That is, **velit** is a part of the Result.

INDIRECT DISCOURSE (Ōrātiō Oblīqua).

186. A Direct Quotation gives the exact words of the speaker; an Indirect Quotation gives the general *idea* of what he said, but not his exact words. We call the former *Direct Discourse* (**Ōrātiō Recta**); the latter, *Indirect Discourse* (**Ōrātiō Oblīqua**). In changing from the Direct to the Indirect, the First Person regularly becomes the Third.

a. Review the whole of **166**; also **177**, *b, c, d.* The constructions of Indirect Discourse are found, not only after *Verbs* of *saying, asking, thinking, perceiving, knowing*, but also in connection with any Verb, Noun, or Adjective, containing the same *idea;* as, **cognōvit virum fortem esse** (Object), *he ascertained that the*

NOTES.

man was brave ; cognitum est virum fortem esse (Subject), *it was ascertained,* etc.; certior factus est exercitum vēnisse, *he was informed that the army had come;* spēs (fāma) erat Caesarem ventūrum esse, *there was a hope (report) that Caesar would come;* dīc mihi quid faciās, *tell me what you are doing.*

Laws of Modes and Tenses in Indirect Discourse.

187. In changing from the Direct to the Indirect Discourse, *the Verbs of all Subordinate Clauses become (or remain) Subjunctive.* The Mode of the Principal Verb depends on the *kind of sentence.* The modes ordinarily found in both Principal and Subordinate Clauses, and in Declaratory, Interrogative, and Imperative Sentences, are shown in this Table : —

SENTENCE.	CLAUSE.	DIRECT DISCOURSE.	INDIRECT DISCOURSE.
a. *Declaratory.*	Principal.	Indicative.	Accusative with Infinitive.
	Subordinate.	Indicative.*	Subjunctive.
b. *Interrogative.*	Principal.	Indicative.	Subjunctive.
	Subordinate.	Indicative.*	Subjunctive.
c. *Imperative.*	Principal.	Imperative.	Subjunctive.
	Subordinate.	Indicative.*	Subjunctive.

* REMARKS. 1. Of course, if the Subjunctive (expressing *Purpose, Result, Cause,* etc.) were used in the Direct Discourse, instead of the Indicative, it would be *retained* in the Indirect Discourse.

2. If a Subordinate Clause is *not a part of the quotation,* but is merely explanatory, its verb may be in the Indicative ; as, dixit oppidum, quod vidēs, Ariovistī fuisse, *he said that the town,* which you see, *had been (the property) of Ariovistus.*

d. *Tenses in Indirect Discourse.* The Tense of the Subjunctive in Indirect Discourse is decided by the laws for the *Sequence of Tenses* **(172)**. Remember that the tense of the *introductory verb* (dīcō, respondeō, putō, etc.) must be carefully noticed in applying these laws.

e. This passage (Caesar's *Gallic War,* I. 13) will furnish applications of these principles : —

DIRECT DISCOURSE.	INDIRECT DISCOURSE.
Divico said to Caesar : — "Si pacem populus Romanus cum Helvetiis *faciet*, in eam partem *ibunt* atque ibi *erunt Helvetii*, ubi eos *constitueris* atque esse *volueris:* sin bello persequi *perseverabis, reminiscere** et veteris incommodi populi Romani, et pristinae virtutis Helvetiorum. Quod improviso unum pagum adortus *es*, cum ii qui flumen *transierant* suis auxilium ferre non *possent*, ne ob eam rem aut *tuae* magnopere virtuti *tribueris* [**178**, 2 (*a*)], aut *nos despexeris:* nos ita a patribus majoribusque *nostris didicimus*, ut magis virtute quam dolo *contendamus*, aut insidiis *nitamur*. Quare *noli committere* [**178**, 2 (*b*)], ut is locus ubi *constiterimus* ex calamitate populi Romani et internecione exercitus nomen *capiat*, aut memoriam *prodat.*"	Divico said to Caesar (that) : — Si pacem populus Romanus cum Helvetiis *faceret*, in eam partem *ituros* atque ibi *futuros Helvetios*, ubi eos Caesar *constituisset* atque esse *voluisset:* sin bello persequi *perseveraret, reminisceretur* et veteris incommodi populi Romani, et pristinae virtutis Helvetiorum. Quod improviso unum pagum adortus *esset*, cum ii qui flumen *transissent* suis auxilium ferre non *possent*, ne ob eam rem aut *suae* magnopere virtuti *tribueret*, aut *ipsos despiceret:* se ita a patribus majoribusque *suis didicisse*, ut magis virtute quam dolo *contenderent*, aut insidiis *niterentur*. Quare ne *committeret*, ut is locus ubi *constitissent* ex calamitate populi Romani et internecione exercitus nomen *caperet*, aut memoriam *proderet.*

f. The sentence, *The leader praised the soldier because he had fought bravely*, may have two meanings : (1) that the *speaker* gives the reason ; (2) that the speaker quotes the *leader's* reason. The Latin for the first is **quod pugnāverat**; for the second, **quod pugnāvisset**, because it is quoting the leader's reason (Subordinate Clause) *indirectly*. The sentence, *The boy did not come, because he was sick,* may be written : **puer, quod aeger erat, nōn vēnit**; or **puer, quod aeger esset, nōn vēnit**. The first is the reason given by *any one;* the second is the *boy's* reason (= *as he said*).

SUBSTANTIVE CLAUSES.

188. "A Substantive Clause is one which, like a Noun, is the Subject or Object of a verb, or in Apposition with the Subject or Object." (Review **42**, *a*, page 12.)

   a. Of course, the verb of which a Substantive Clause is Subject must be Impersonal, or used Impersonally ; as, **accidit ut lūna plēna esset; utrum vincat an vincātur, incertum est.**

* Imperative.

b. Substantive Clauses are, —
1. Infinitive with Subject Accusative: **mē īre oportet.**
2. Subjunctive Clauses of
  - (a.) *Purpose* (after *ask, fear, command,* etc.; **179,** *d, e*).
  - (b.) *Result* (after *happen, effect, doubt,* etc.; **181,** *a, b, d*).
3. Indicative with **Quod** (*the fact that*); **182,** *d*.
4. Indirect Questions; as in the second example under *a* (above).

PARTICIPLES.

189. A Participle is a *Verbal Adjective;* that is, it agrees with some Noun or Pronoun in *gender, number,* and *case*. Participles are declined, the Present Active being in the Third Declension (*one termination*), like **recens,** and the others in the First and Second, like **bonus.**

  a. The *names* of the Tenses of Participles (except of the Future) give no accurate idea of the *time* expressed. The time of the Present and Perfect Participles (like that of the Present and Perfect Infinitive, **173**) depends on the time of some other verb. The Present Participle denotes an action as *going on,* and the Perfect Participle as *completed, at the time of that verb;* as, **pugnans (vulnerātus) cadit (cecidit),** *he falls (fell) fighting (wounded)*.

  b. A Participle may be used as a Predicate Adjective; as, **Gallia in trēs partēs est dīvīsa,** *Gaul is divided (in a divided condition) into three parts.*

  c. The Active Voice (except in Deponent Verbs) has no Perfect Participle. Its place is supplied by the Ablative Absolute (in which the Perfect Passive Participle is used), or by the Pluperfect Subjunctive with **quum** (*when, after,* etc.); as, *having seen the city,* **urbe vīsā,** or **quum urbem vīdisset.**

  d. A Participle is often best translated by a *clause;* as, **eum prōcurrentem vulnerāvit,** *he wounded him as he ran forward;* **eōs transductōs necāvit,** *he carried them over and put them to death.*

  e. The Future Active Participle is most frequently used with **sum** to form the Active Periphrastic Conjugation (**82,** *a*). The form **esse** is frequently omitted (**199,** 2).

  f. The Gerundive (or Future Passive Participle) has two regular uses:

  (1.) With **sum,** to form the Passive Periphrastic Conjugation (**82,** *b*), when it always denotes *necessity;* as, **urbs dēlenda est,** *the city must be destroyed;* **mātūrandum est,** *haste must be made.*

  (2.) Instead of the Gerund, as explained in **190,** *a*.

g. The Gerundive is also used as a Predicate Participle; as, nōn vidētur ferendus, *he does not seem bearable.*

h. The Gerundive is used with cūrō (*I care for, provide for*) and some other verbs to denote a Passive *Purpose;* as, nāvēs aedificandās cūrāvit, *he arranged for the building of ships.*

GERUND.

190. The Gerund is a Verbal Noun of the Second Declension, lacking the Nominative and Vocative, and used only in the Singular. The Infinitive supplies the place of its Nominative; as, scīre est regere, *knowledge is power* (*knowing is ruling*); bellandī cupidī sunt, *they are desirous of waging war;* facultās regrediendī nōn datur, *an opportunity for (of) retreating is not afforded.*

a. A Transitive Gerund (that is, one from a Transitive Verb) *sometimes* takes an Object in the Accusative, but regularly it does not. This Rule should be followed: *When the Gerund would take a Direct Object, the Gerundive should be used instead. The Noun or Pronoun that would be the Object takes the case that the Gerund would have, and the Gerundive agrees with it, as an Adjective.* For instance, *the hope of seeing the cities* should not be written spēs urbēs videndī, but spēs urbium videndārum : also, ad pācem petendam (*not* petendum); facultās ējus locī relinquendī (Gerundive), *an opportunity for (of) leaving that place.*

SUPINE.

191. The Supine is a Verbal Noun of the Fourth Declension, having only the Accusative and Ablative Singular.

a. The Accusative (often called the *Former Supine*) is used after verbs of *motion*, and denotes *purpose* **(180)**. If it is from a Transitive Verb, it may take a Direct Object; as, vēnērunt pācem petītum, *they came to seek peace.*

REMARK. The Future Infinitive Passive (as, laudātum īrī) is a peculiar instance of the use of the Supine in um. The form īrī is the Passive Infinitive of eō (*I go*); so that dīcit nocitum īrī means *he says that harm is going to be done.*

b. The Ablative of the Supine is an *Ablative of Respect*, or *Specification* **(153)**, and is most frequently used with Adjectives ; as, probat perficere cōnāta perfacile factū esse, *he shows that to accomplish their undertakings is (a thing) very easy to do* (literally, *with respect to the doing*).

NOTES.   229

ORDER OF WORDS IN A LATIN SENTENCE.

192. No absolute laws can be given for the order of words in a Latin sentence, as it is constantly changed to make one or more words *emphatic*. There is, however, a *regular* arrangement, which is usually observed in ordinary prose. This ***Regular Order*** is: 1. The Subject; 2. Modifiers of the Subject; 3. Modifiers of the Verb; 4. The Verb.

193. A few rules for the position of certain words are here given:—

1. An ***Adjective,*** expressing *Quality*, (if not emphatic) follows the word which it describes; but a ***Numeral*** precedes.

2. A ***Genitive*** (if not emphatic) follows the word on which it depends; as, liber puerī, *the boy's book*. Puerī liber means *the boy's book* (and *not* the girl's).

3. ***Direct and Indirect Object.*** The Direct Object stands nearer the Verb than the Indirect; as, puerō librum dat.

4. ***Pronouns.*** A Demonstrative Pronoun precedes its Noun. A Relative Pronoun stands first in its clause, because it is a *connective*. An Interrogative Pronoun stands first, because, as an interrogative word, it serves to introduce the sentence or clause (like nonne, num).

5. An ***Adverbial*** element (Adverb, Ablative, Phrase) regularly stands immediately before the word which it modifies.

CAUTION. Nē — quidem, *not even*, must have the emphatic word between them; as, nē Caesar quidem, *not Caesar even*.

6. Est, sunt, etc. (*there is, there are*), often stand first.

CAUTION. Inquit, *quoth he*, must follow one or more words of the quotation.

7. A Preposition very frequently stands between its noun and the adjective modifying the noun; as, magnō in perīculō; omnibus cum cōpiīs.

8. In the order of Personal Pronouns, the Latin is the reverse of the English; as, ego·et tū, *you and I;* ego et Caesar, *Caesar and I.*

ANALYSIS OF SENTENCES.

194. Sections **34** to **44**, pages 9–13, should be carefully studied. The same general principles apply to the analysis of both English and Latin sentences. They are here stated in brief form: (1.) Tell whether it is Simple, Compound, or Complex.

    *a. **Simple Sentence.*** (2.) Tell whether it is Declaratory, Interrogative, Imperative, or Exclamatory. (3.) Tell its Subject and Predicate. (4.) Name the modifiers of the Subject (if there are any). (5.) Name the modifiers of the Verb (if there are any), and tell what each expresses, — *manner, cause,* etc.

230   NOTES.

b. *Compound Sentence.* Analyze each Clause as a Simple Sentence, and name the Connective, if one is expressed.

c. *Complex Sentence.* Analyze the Principal Clause as a Simple Sentence. Name the Subordinate Clauses ; tell what each modifies, and *why;* analyze each as a Simple Sentence, naming its Connective.

GENERAL FACTS AND USEFUL HINTS.

195. 1. Two negatives equal an affirmative ; as, **nullī,** *none;* **nonnullī,** *some;* **nunquam,** *never;* **nonnunquam,** *sometimes.*

2. **Nē quidem,** *not even,* always have the emphatic word between them; as, **nē equitēs quidem,** *not the horsemen even.*

3. An *Enclitic* is a word which is *always* attached to another. The word means *leaning on,* as though Enclitics were too weak to stand alone. The most common Enclitics are **-que** (*and*), **-ne** (asking a question), and **cum** (*with*) when used with Personal, Reflexive, Relative, and Interrogative Pronouns. As an illustration of the *weakness* of **-que,** compare the English *bread 'n' milk, horse 'n' carriage* (as those expressions are sometimes hastily pronounced).

4. When an Enclitic is added to a word, the *accent* is placed on the syllable before the Enclitic; as, **itine'ribus,** but **itineribus'que; Ci'cerō,** but **Cicerō'ne** (as, **Cicerōne valet?** *is Cicero well ?*).

5. **Itaque** may be a Conjunction meaning *therefore* (**i'taque**), or **ita + que,** meaning *and so* (**ita'que**). In the former sense it stands at the beginning of a sentence ; in the latter, the **que** connects the clauses of a sentence.

6. Two Adjectives (not Numerals) modifying a noun are regularly connected by **et** or **que**; as, **urbēs multae et magnae,** *many great cities.*

7. **Quis** = *who?* (of several). **Uter** = *which one?* (of two). **Alius** = *another* (of several). **Alter** = *the other* (of two). **Aliēnus** = *another's;* as, **servus aliēnus,** *another's slave.*

8. Words used *in pairs* are called *Correlatives* (because they relate to each other).

Usually, the first has a *Demonstrative* idea, the second, a *Relative* force. The most common Correlatives are : —

alius — alius, *one — another.*
aliī — aliī, *some — others.*
alter — alter, *the one — the other.*
alterī — alterī, *the one party — the other party.*
aut — aut, *either — or.*

eō — quō, *thither — whither.*
et — et, *both — and.*
ibi — ubi, *there — where.*
inde — unde, *thence — whence.*
is — quī, *he — who.*

NOTES. 231

neque (nec) — neque (nec), *neither — nor*.
nōn sōlum — sed etiam, *not only — but also*.
quum — tum, *not only — but also*.
quum — tamen, *although — yet*.
tālis — quālis, *such — as*.
tametsī — tamen, *although — yet*.
tantus — quantus, *as great — as*.
tot — quot, *as many — as*.
tum — quum, *at that time — when*.
vel — vel, *either — or*.

9. Alius has a peculiar use. To express these sentences: *some did one thing, and some another; one was running from one ship, another from another*, it would *seem* right (in view of 8, above) to say, aliī aliud fēcērunt, aliī aliud; alius aliā ex nāvī currēbat, alius ex aliā. This, however, would be merely repeating the same words, and therefore the Latins simply said, aliī aliud fēcērunt; alius aliā ex nāvī currēbat. Also, alius aliī auxilium tulērunt, *they bore aid to one another (one to another)*.

196. "When shall I use Quīn, and when Quōminus?" A good authority says: "The use of quōminus springs from the courtesy of the Latin language. It is more *polite* to say, 'I will hinder you so that you shall *the less* do what you wish,' than to say, 'so that you shall *not* (quīn) do it.' So after recūsō the refusal is less point blank with quōminus than with quīn."

197. 1. Imperō takes the Dative; jubeō, the Accusative.
2. Licet takes the Dative of Advantage; oportet, the Accusative.
3. *May* (meaning *permission*), *can, must, might* (meaning *permission*), *could, should* (meaning *duty*), are *not* signs of the Subjunctive, but require separate verbs. *May* and *might* require the proper tense of licet; *can* and *could* require possum; *must, ought, should*, require oportet or the Gerundive.
4. Nē may be an Adverb; as, nē eāmus, *let us not go*. Nē may be a Conjunction; as, vereor nē veniat, *I fear that he will come* (*lest he may come*). Ně is an Interrogative word, always *Enclitic;* as, audīvitne? *did he hear?*
5. Ut (meaning *as*) takes the Indicative, forming with it a parenthetical clause; as, ut āiunt, *as they say*.
6. The Relative Quī may be equivalent to

Ut is, ego, etc., expressing *Purpose* (**179**, *a*).
Ut is, ego, etc., expressing *Result* (**181**, *c*).
Quum is, ego, etc., expressing *Cause* (**182**, *c*).
Quum is, ego, etc., expressing *Concession* (**183**, *b*).

7. Quum (cum) meaning
When, takes the Subjunctive in the *Imperfect* and *Pluperfect* tenses; but the Indicative in the other tenses.

Since, takes the Subjunctive in *all* tenses.
Although, takes the Subjunctive in *all* tenses.

8. **Jubeō**, *I order;* **vetō**, *I forbid;* **cōgō**, *I compel;* **patior**, *I allow*, are regularly followed by the Accusative and Infinitive, and not by **ut** and the Subjunctive.

198. These forms, as well as others from the same Verbs, are often used Impersonally : —

pugnātur, *fighting is carried on;* **nocētur**, *harm is done;* **nōn exspectandum est**, *no delay must be made;* **quaeritur**, *the question is asked;* **cogitandum est**, *thought must be taken;* **imperātum est**, *the order was given;* **mātūrandum est**, *haste must be made;* **ad arma concurritur**, *a general* (con) *rush to arms is made;* **pārendum est**, *obedience must be rendered;* **prōspiciendum est**, *provision must be made* (**reī frūmentāriae**, *for the corn supply*); **praecavendum est**, *care (precaution) must be taken;* **hīs rēbus occurrendum (esse) existimāvit**, *he thought that a remedy must be found for these things;* **parcitur hostibus**, *quarter is given to the enemy;* **lēgibus ūtendum est**, *use must be made of the laws*.

199. 1. **Dubitō** takes
The *Infinitive*, when it means *hesitate*.
Dubitō and **dubius** take
The *Subjunctive* with **quīn**, when meaning *doubt* (or *doubtful*) *that*.
The *Subjunctive of Indirect Question;* as, **dubitat utrum hōc facile an difficile sit**.

2. **Esse** is very often omitted, especially with the *Future Participles*. This should never cause any difficulty, as the Infinitive will always be *required* by a word of *saying, thinking*, etc. ; as, **Caesar sē castra mōtūrum (esse) dixit; exspectandum (esse) nōn existimāvit**, *he did not think that any delay should be made*.

3. Remember that not only *verbs*, but *words* and *phrases*, of *saying, thinking*, etc., require the Accusative and Infinitive; as, **fāma erat, eum interfectum esse; habeō spem maximam hostēs pācem factūrōs (esse); Caesarem certiōrem faciō mē vēnisse**.

4. Case of the Person after Verbs of *asking:* —
Rogō takes the *Accusative;* **petō, postulō**, the *Ablative* with **ā** (**ab**); **quaerō**, the *Ablative* with **ā** (**ab**), **dē**, or **ē** (**ex**).

5. To express *I say — not*, use **negō** rather than **dīcō nōn**; as, **negat sē venīre posse**, *he says that he can't come*.

HINTS ON TRANSLATION.

200. The beginner will notice, of course, that the order of words in a Latin sentence is often very different from the order of words in the same

sentence when expressed in English. For example, in this sentence, **Apud Helvetios longe nobilissimus et ditissimus fuit Orgetorix,** *Among the Helvetii by far the noblest and richest (man) was Orgetorix,* the subject stands last; yet the sentence makes perfectly good sense when read exactly in the order of the Latin words.

In every Latin sentence the same method of translation should be observed, *as nearly as possible.* It will often be necessary, after the general meaning of a sentence has been found, to change the order of certain words to secure a better English order; but the pupil who has mastered the *idea,* in just the order of words that the Latin presents, will find no difficulty in giving the sentence a more natural English order.

To the Teacher. A good example for practice is the sentence on page 139, lines 25-29. If the teacher will read with the class several such sentences each day, even before the class has mastered the meaning and forms of all the words contained in those sentences, the pupils will very soon be able to "hold the sentence in suspense" until the whole has been read and the entire thought developed.

APPENDIX.

FORMS OF DECLENSION, CONJUGATION, ETC.

The References are to the NOTES, *in which Principles and Exceptions are more fully stated.*

NOUNS.

1. FIRST DECLENSION (N. 9): STEM-VOWEL, A.

	Singular.	Plural.
NOMINATIVE.	silva, *a (the) forest.*	silvae, *forests.*
GENITIVE.	silvae, *of a forest.*	silvārum, *of forests.*
DATIVE.	silvae, *to (for) a forest.*	silvīs, *to (for) forests.*
ACCUSATIVE.	silvam, *a forest.*	silvās, *forests.*
VOCATIVE.	silva, *O forest!*	silvae, *O forests!*
ABLATIVE.	silvā, *with (by, etc.) a forest.*	silvīs, *with (by, etc.) forests.*

a. For the Declension of Dea and Filia, see N. 9, *e.*

2. SECOND DECLENSION (N. 10): STEM-VOWEL, O.

Singular.	*slave* (M.)	*boy* (M.)	*field* (M.)	*man* (M.)	*gift* (N.)
NOM.	servus	puer	ager	vir	dōnum
GEN.	servī	puerī	agrī	virī	dōnī
DAT.	servō	puerō	agrō	virō	dōnō
ACC.	servum	puerum	agrum	virum	dōnum
VOC.	serve	puer	ager	vir	dōnum
ABL.	servō	puerō	agrō	virō	dōnō
Plural.					
NOM.	servī	puerī	agrī	virī	dōna
GEN.	servōrum	puerōrum	agrōrum	virōrum	dōnōrum
DAT.	servīs	puerīs	agrīs	virīs	dōnīs
ACC.	servōs	puerōs	agrōs	virōs	dōna
VOC.	servī	puerī	agrī	virī	dōna
ABL.	servīs	puerīs	agrīs	virīs	dōnīs

a. For the Declension of Filius and Proper Names in ius (as, Cassius), see N. 10, *d.*

b. For the Declension of Deus, see N. 10, *f.*

236   APPENDIX.

3. THIRD DECLENSION: I. (N. 15, a, b) STEM ENDING IN A CONSONANT (*Mute*).

Singular.	king (M.)	judge (M.)	soldier (M.)	manhood (F.)	head (N.)
NOM.	rex	jūdex	mīles	virtūs	caput
GEN.	rēgis	jūdicis	mīlitis	virtūtis	capitis
DAT.	rēgī	jūdicī	mīlitī	virtūtī	capitī
ACC.	rēgem	jūdicem	mīlitem	virtūtem	caput
VOC.	rex	jūdex	mīles	virtūs	caput
ABL.	rēge	jūdice	mīlite	virtūte	capite
Plural.					
N., ACC., V.	rēgēs	jūdicēs	mīlitēs	virtūtēs	capita
GEN.	rēgum	jūdicum	mīlitum	virtūtum	capitum
DAT., ABL.	rēgibus	jūdicibus	mīlitibus	virtūtibus	capitibus

4. THIRD DECLENSION: II. (N. 15, a, b) STEM ENDING IN A CONSONANT (*Liquid*).

Singular.	consul (M.)	sister (F.)	maiden (F.)	name (N.)	body (N.)
NOM.	consul	soror	virgō	nōmen	corpus
GEN.	consulis	sorōris	virginis	nōminis	corporis
DAT.	consulī	sorōrī	virginī	nōminī	corporī
ACC.	consulem	sorōrem	virginem	nōmen	corpus
VOC.	consul	soror	virgō	nōmen	corpus
ABL.	consule	sorōre	virgine	nōmine	corpore
Plural.					
N., ACC., V.	consulēs	sorōrēs	virginēs	nōmina	corpora
GEN.	consulum	sorōrum	virginum	nōminum	corporum
DAT., ABL.	consulibus	sorōribus	virginibus	nōminibus	corporibus

REMARK. Pater, Māter, Frāter (GENITIVES, Patris, Mātris, Frātris) *do not increase in the Genitive* (N. 15, REMARK).

5. THIRD DECLENSION: III. (N. 16, 17) STEM ENDING IN A VOWEL (I).

Singular.	tower (F.)	cloud (F.)	sea (N.)	animal (N.)	spur (N.)
NOM.	turris	nūbēs	mare	animal	calcar
GEN.	turris	nūbis	maris	animālis	calcāris
DAT.	turrī	nūbī	marī	animālī	calcārī
ACC.	turrem (im)	nūbem	mare	animal	calcar
VOC.	turris	nūbēs	mare	animal	calcar
ABL.	turre (ī)	nūbe	marī	animālī	calcārī
Plural.					
NOM.	turrēs	nūbēs	maria	animālia	calcāria
GEN.	turrium	nūbium	marium	animālium	calcārium
DAT.	turribus	nūbibus	maribus	animālibus	calcāribus
ACC.	turrēs (īs)	nūbēs(īs)	maria	animālia	calcāria
VOC.	turrēs	nūbēs	maria	animālia	calcāria
ABL.	turribus	nūbibus	maribus	animālibus	calcāribus

APPENDIX. 237

6. Third Declension: IV. (N. 18) Stem ending in a Consonant (Singular) and a Vowel (Plural).

	Singular. city (F.)	mountain (M.)	night (F.)	cohort (F.)	client (C.)
Stem.	(urb-)	(mont-)	(noct-)	(cohort-)	(client-)
Nom.	urbs	mons	nox	cohors	cliens
Gen.	urbis	montis	noctis	cohortis	clientis
Dat.	urbī	montī	noctī	cohortī	clientī
Acc.	urbem	montem	noctem	cohortem	clientem
Voc.	urbs	mons	nox	cohors	cliens
Abl.	urbe	monte	nocte	cohorte	cliente
Plural.					
Stem.	(urbi-)	(monti-)	(nocti-)	(cohorti-)	(clienti-)
Nom.	urbēs	montēs	noctēs	cohortēs	clientēs
Gen.	urbium	montium	noctium	cohortium	clientium
Dat.	urbibus	montibus	noctibus	cohortibus	clientibus
Acc.	urbēs (Is)	montēs (Is)	noctēs (Is)	cohortēs (Is)	clientēs (Is)
Voc.	urbēs	montēs	noctēs	cohortēs	clientēs
Abl.	urbibus	montibus	noctibus	cohortibus	clientibus

7. Third Declension: Irregular Forms.

	Singular. old man (M.)	force (F.)	ox, cow (C.)	Jupiter (M.)
Nom.	senex	vīs	bōs	Jŭpiter
Gen.	senis	vīs	bovis	Jovis
Dat.	senī	...	bovī	Jovī
Acc.	senem	vim	bovem	Jovem
Voc.	senex	vīs	bōs	Jŭpiter
Abl.	sene	vī	bove	Jove
Plural.				
N., Acc., V.	senēs	vīrēs	bovēs	
Gen.	senum	vīrium	boum	
Dat., Abl.	senibus	vīribus	bōbus (būbus)	

8. Fourth Declension (N. 20): Stem-Vowel, U.

	Singular. chariot (M.)	Plural.	Singular. horn (N.)	Plural.
Nom.	currus	currūs	cornū	cornua
Gen.	currūs	curruum	cornūs	cornuum
Dat.	curruī	curribus	cornū	cornibus
Acc.	currum	currūs	cornū	cornua
Voc.	currus	currūs	cornū	cornua
Abl.	currū	curribus	cornū	cornibus

a. **Domus,** *house, home* (N. 21, *b*), belongs to the Second and Fourth Declensions.

	Singular.	Plural.
Nom.	domus	domūs
Gen.	domūs (domī*)	domuum (domōrum)
Dat.	domuī (domō)	domibus
Acc.	domum	domōs (domūs)
Voc.	domus	domūs
Abl.	domō (domū)	domibus

9. Fifth Declension (N. 22): Stem-Vowel, E.

	Sing. *day* (m.)	Plur.	Sing. *thing* (f.)	Plur.	*faith* (f.)
Nom.	diēs	diēs	rēs	rēs	fidēs
Gen.	diēī	diērum	rĕī (N. 22, *d*)	rērum	fidĕī
Dat.	diēī	diēbus	rĕī	rēbus	fidĕī
Acc.	diem	diēs	rem	rēs	fidem
Voc.	diēs	diēs	rēs	rēs	fidēs
Abl.	diē	diēbus	rē	rēbus	fidē

ADJECTIVES.

10. First and Second Declensions (N. 24, *a*): US.

Magnus, *great.*

Singular.	Masculine.	Feminine.	Neuter.
Nom.	magnus	magna	magnum
Gen.	magnī	magnae	magnī
Dat.	magnō	magnae	magnō
Acc.	magnum	magnam	magnum
Voc.	magne	magna	magnum
Abl.	magnō	magnā	magnō
Plural.			
Nom.	magnī	magnae	magna
Gen.	magnōrum	magnārum	magnōrum
Dat.	magnīs	magnīs	magnīs
Acc.	magnōs	magnās	magna
Voc.	magnī	magnae	magna
Abl.	magnīs	magnīs	magnīs

a. First and Second Declensions: ER.

Līber, *free.*

	Singular.				Plural.	
	M.	F.	N.	M.	F.	N.
N.	līber	lībera	līberum	līberī	līberae	lībera
G.	līberī	līberae	līberī	līberōrum	līberārum	līberōrum
D.	līberō	līberae	līberō	līberīs	līberīs	līberīs
Ac.	līberum	līberam	līberum	līberōs	līberās	lībera
V.	līber	lībera	līberum	līberī	līberae	lībera
Ab.	līberō	līberā	līberō	līberīs	līberīs	līberīs

* Really the Locative Case (N. 159, *c*).

APPENDIX. 239

Niger, *black.*

	Singular.			Plural.	
M.	F.	N.	M.	F.	N.
Nom. niger	nigra	nigrum	nigrī	nigrae	nigra
Gen. nigrī	nigrae	nigrī	nigrōrum	nigrārum	nigrōrum
Dat. nigrō	nigrae	nigrō	nigrīs	nigrīs	nigrīs
Acc. nigrum	nigram	nigrum	nigrōs	nigrās	nigra
Voc. niger	nigra	nigrum	nigrī	nigrae	nigra
Abl. nigrō	nigrā	nigrō	nigrīs	nigrīs	nigrīs

11. First and Second Declensions: Genitive in ĪUS, Dative in Ī. *For the entire list of these Adjectives (with English meanings), see N. 43, b. The declension of the Singular of* **ūnus, alius, uter,** *and* **alter** *is here given. The Plural endings are like those of* **bonus.**

M.	F.	N.	M.	F.	N.
Nom. ūnus	ūna	ūnum	uter	utra	utrum
Gen. ūnīus	ūnīus	ūnīus	utrīus	utrīus	utrīus
Dat. ūnī	ūnī	ūnī	utrī	utrī	utrī
Acc. ūnum	ūnam	ūnum	utrum	utram	utrum
Abl. ūnō	ūnā	ūnō	utrō	utrā	utrō

M.	F.	N.	M.	F.	N.
Nom. alius	alia	aliud	alter	altera	alterum
Gen. alīus	alīus	alīus	alterius	alterius	alterius
Dat. aliī	aliī	aliī	alterī	alterī	alterī
Acc. alium	aliam	aliud	alterum	alteram	alterum
Abl. aliō	aliā	aliō	alterō	alterā	alterō

12. Third Declension: Three Endings: ER (N. 25, a; 26, a).

Ācer, *sharp.*

	Singular.			Plural.	
M.	F.	N.	M.	F.	N.
Nom. ācer	ācris	ācre	ācrēs	ācrēs	ācria
Gen. ācris	ācris	ācris	ācrium	ācrium	ācrium
Dat. ācrī	ācrī	ācrī	ācribus	ācribus	ācribus
Acc. ācrem	ācrem	ācre	ācrēs (īs)	ācrēs (īs)	ācria
Voc. ācer	ācris	ācre	ācrēs	ācrēs	ācria
Abl. ācrī	ācrī	ācrī	ācribus	ācribus	ācribus

13. Third Declension: Two Endings:* **IS (N. 25, b; 26, b).**

Fortis, *brave.*

Singular.		Plural.	
M. and F.	N.	M. and F.	N.
Nom. fortis	forte	fortēs	fortia
Gen. fortis	fortis	fortium	fortium
Dat. fortī	fortī	fortibus	fortibus
Acc. fortem	forte	fortēs (īs)	fortia
Voc. fortis	forte	fortēs	fortia
Abl. fortī	fortī	fortibus	fortibus

* The Declension of Comparatives is given in **15.**

14. Third Declension: One Ending (N. 25, c; 26, c).

	Singular.		Plural.	
	M. and F.	N.	M. and F.	N.
Nom.	audax (*bold*)	audax	audācēs	audācia
Gen.	audācis	audācis	audācium	audācium
Dat.	audācī	audācī	audācibus	audācibus
Acc.	audācem	audax	audācēs (īs)	audācia
Voc.	audax	audax	audācēs	audācia
Abl.	audāce (ī)	audāce (ī)	audācibus	audācibus

Recens, *recent.*

Nom.	recens	recens	recentēs	recentia
Gen.	recentis	recentis	recentium	recentium
Dat.	recentī	recentī	recentibus	recentibus
Acc.	recentem	recens	recentēs (īs)	recentia
Voc.	recens	recens	recentēs	recentia
Abl.	recente (ī)	recente (ī)	recentibus	recentibus

a. In the following Adjectives (one ending) only the Nominative and Genitive, Singular and Plural, are given to show the general form of declension:—

	Sing.	M. and F.	N.	M. and F.	N.	M. and F.	N.
	Nom.	pār (*equal*)	pār	dīves (*rich*)	dīves	vetus (*old*)	vetus
	Gen.	paris	paris	dīvitis	dīvitis	veteris	veteris
		(Abl. parī)					

Plural.

Nom.	parēs	paria	dīvitēs	(dītia)	veterēs	vetera
Gen.	parium	parium	dīvitum	dīvitum	veterum	veterum

	Singular.	M. and F.	N.	M. and F.	N.
	Nom.	praeceps (*headlong*)	praeceps	iens (*going*)	iens
	Gen.	praecipitis	praecipitis	euntis	euntis

Plural.

Nom.	praecipitēs		praecipitia		euntēs	euntia
Gen.	praecipitium		praecipitium		euntium	euntium

15. Comparatives have Two Endings, and are thus declined:—

	Singular.		Plural.	
	M. and F.	N.	M. and F.	N.
Nom.	fortior	fortius	fortiōrēs	fortiōra
Gen.	fortiōris	fortiōris	fortiōrum	fortiōrum
Dat.	fortiōrī	fortiōrī	fortiōribus	fortiōribus
Acc.	fortiōrem	fortius	fortiōrēs (īs)	fortiōra
Voc.	fortior	fortius	fortiōrēs	fortiōra
Abl.	fortiōre (ī)	fortiōre (ī)	fortiōribus	fortiōribus

APPENDIX. 241

a. Plūs (N. 27) is a Neuter Noun in the Singular, and an Adjective in the Plural.

	Singular.		Plural.	
	NEUTER.	M. and F.		N.
NOM.	plūs	plūrēs		plūra
GEN.	plūris	plūrium		plūrium
DAT.	wanting	plūribus		plūribus
ACC.	plūs	plūrēs (īs)		plūra
ABL.	plūre	plūribus		plūribus

COMPARISON OF ADJECTIVES.

16. Regular Comparison. (See N. 30.)
The following classes of Adjectives are somewhat Irregular in Comparison:
a. Adjectives ending in er. (See N. 31, *a*.)
b. Six Adjectives in lis. (See N. 31, *b*.)
c. Adjectives ending in dicus, ficus, and volus. (See N. 32.)

17. Irregular and Defective Comparison. (See N. 33.)
a. bonus, melior, optimus, *good, better, best.*
malus, pējor, pessimus, *bad, worse, worst.*
magnus, mājor, maximus, *great, greater, greatest.*
parvus, minor, minimus, *little, less, least.*
multus, ———, plūrimus, *much, most* (Masculine).
multa, ———, plūrima, *much, most* (Feminine).
multum, plūs (APP. 15, *a*.), plūrimum, *much, more, most* (NEUTER).
multī, plūrēs, plūrimī, *many, more, most.*

b. These Adjectives have no Positive (see N. 34); they are derived from Prepositions: —

PREP.	POS.	COMP.	SUP.
(cis, citrā),	......	citerior,	citimus, *hither, hithermost.*
(in, intrā),	......	interior,	intimus, *inner, innermost (inmost).*
(prae, prō),	......	prior,	prīmus, *former, first.*
(prope),	......	propior,	proximus, *nearer, nearest (next).*
(ultrā),	......	ulterior,	ultimus, *farther, farthest.*

c. These are also derived from Prepositions (N. 35); the Positive is generally used as a Noun: —

POS.	COMP.	SUP.
exterus,	exterior,	extrēmus (or extimus) *outer, outermost.*
inferus,	inferior,	infimus (or īmus), *lower, lowest.*
posterus,	posterior,	postrēmus (or postumus), *hinder (later), last*
superus,	superior,	suprēmus (or summus), *higher, highest.*

d. For the Comparison of dīves, juvenis, senex, see N. 36, *a, b.*
e. For Comparison by magis and maximē, see N. 37.
18. For the Formation and Comparison of ADVERBS, see N. 38, 39.

242   APPENDIX.

19. The **Numeral Adjectives** (N. 41) and **Adverbs** (N. 44) are:—

	CARDINAL, answering the question, *how many?*	ORDINAL, answering the question, *which in order?*	DISTRIBUTIVE, answering the question, *how many each?*	ADVERBS, answering the question, *how often?*
1	ūnus, a, um	prīmus, a, um	singulī, *one by*	semel, *once*.
2	duo, ae, o	secundus or alter	bīnī [*one*.	bis
3	trēs, tria	tertius	ternī or trīnī	ter
4	quattuor	quartus	quaternī	quater
5	quīnque	quīntus	quīnī	quīnquiēs
6	sex	sextus	sēnī	sexiēs
7	septem	septimus	septēnī	septiēs
8	octo	octāvus	octōnī	octiēs
9	novem	nōnus	novēnī	noviēs
10	decem	decimus	dēnī	deciēs
11	undecim	undecimus	undēnī	undeciēs
12	duodecim	duodecimus	duodēnī	duodeciēs
13	tredecim	tertius decimus	ternī dēnī	tredeciēs
14	quattuordecim	quartus decimus	quaternī dēnī	quattuordeciēs
15	quīndecim	quīntus decimus	quīnī dēnī	quīndeciēs
16	sēdecim	sextus decimus	sēnī dēnī	sēdeciēs
17	septendecim	septimus decimus	septēnī dēnī	septiēs deciēs
18	duodēvīgintī (octodecim)	duodēvīcēsimus	duodēvīcēnī	duodēvīciēs
19	undēvīgintī (novendecim)	undēvīcēsimus	undēvīcēnī	undēvīciēs
20	vīgintī	vīcēsimus	vīcēnī	vīciēs
21	ūnus et vīgintī (vīgintī ūnus)	vīcēsimus prīmus	vīcēnī singulī	semel et vīciēs
30	trīgintā	trīcēsimus	trīcēnī	trīciēs
40	quadrāgintā	quadrāgēsimus	quadrāgēnī	quadrāgiēs
50	quīnquāgintā	quīnquāgēsimus	quīnquāgēnī	quīnquāgiēs
60	sexāgintā	sexāgēsimus	sexāgēnī	sexāgiēs
70	septuāgintā	septuāgēsimus	septuāgēnī	septuāgiēs
80	octōgintā	octōgēsimus	octōgēnī	octōgiēs
90	nōnāgintā	nōnāgēsimus	nōnāgēnī	nōnāgiēs
100	centum	centēsimus	centēnī	centiēs
101	centum et ūnus	centēsimus prīmus	centēnī singulī	centiēs semel
200	ducentī, ae, a	ducentēsimus	ducēnī	ducentiēs
300	trecentī	trecentēsimus	trecēnī	trecentiēs
400	quadringentī	quadringentēsimus	quadringēnī	quadringentiēs
500	quīngentī	quīngentēsimus	quīngēnī	quīngentiēs
600	sexcentī	sexcentēsimus	sescēnī	sexcentiēs
700	septingentī	septingentēsimus	septingēnī	septingentiēs
800	octingentī	octingentēsimus	octingēnī	octingentiēs
900	nongentī	nongentēsimus	nongēnī	nongentiēs
1000	mille	millēsimus	singula millia	milliēs
2000	duo millia	bis millēsimus	bīna millia	bis milliēs

APPENDIX. 243

20. Numeral Adjectives. The following require special notice:—
a. Ūnus is declined in 11, a, of the APPENDIX.
b. Duo and trēs * are thus declined:—

	M.	F.	N.	M. and F.	N.
N., V.	duo	duae	duo	trēs	tria
GEN.	duōrum	duārum	duōrum	trium	trium
DAT.	duōbus	duābus	duōbus	tribus	tribus
ACC.	duōs (duo)	duās	duo	trēs (trīs)	tria
ABL.	duōbus	duābus	duōbus	tribus	tribus

c. **Mille** (N. 43, e) is indeclinable, as an Adjective; as a Noun (*Neuter*) it has, in the Singular, NOM. mille; ACC. mille. In the Plural it is declined like the Plural of mare, thus: NOM. millia; GEN. millium, etc.

PRONOUNS.

21. The **Personal Pronouns** † (N. 46) are thus declined:—

	FIRST PERSON.		SECOND PERSON.	
N.	ego, *I*.	nōs, *we*.	tū, *thou*.	vōs, *ye* or *you*.
G.	meī, *of me*.	nostrum (trī), *of us*.	tuī	vestrum (vestrī)
D.	mihi, *to (for) me*.	nōbīs, *to (for) us*.	tibi	vōbīs
AC.	mē, *me*.	nōs, *us*.	tē	vōs
V.	*wanting*.	*wanting*.	tū	vōs
AB.	mē, *by (from, with) me*.	nōbīs, *by* (etc.) *us*.	tē	vōbīs

22. The **Reflexive Pronouns of the First and Second Persons** are described in N. 47.

The **Reflexive Pronoun of the Third Person** is declined alike in both numbers:—

GEN. suī, *of himself, herself, itself, themselves*.
DAT. sibi, *to* (or *for*) *himself, herself*, etc.
ACC. sē or sēsē, *himself, herself*, etc.
ABL. sē or sēsē, *by (from, with) himself, herself*, etc.

23. The **Possessive Pronouns** are declined like **magnus** and **niger** (see N. 48). Meus has mī in the Vocative Singular Masculine.

24. The **Demonstrative Pronouns** (N. 49) are thus declined:—

	Singular.			Plural.		
	M.	F.	N.	M.	F.	N.
NOM.	hīc	haec	hōc, *this*.	hī	hae	haec, *these*.
GEN.	hūjus	hūjus	hūjus	hōrum	hārum	hōrum
DAT.	huīc	huīc	huīc	hīs	hīs	hīs
ACC.	hunc	hanc	hōc	hōs	hās	haec
ABL.	hōc	hāc	hōc	hīs	hīs	hīs
NOM.	is	ea	id, *that*.	iī (eī)	eae	ea, *those*.
GEN.	ējus	ējus	ējus	eōrum	eārum	eōrum
DAT.	eī	eī	eī	iīs (eīs)	iīs (eīs)	iīs (eīs)
ACC.	eum	eam	id	eōs	eās	ea
ABL.	eō	eā	eō	iīs (eīs)	iīs (eīs)	iīs (eīs)

* Declined like the Plural of fortis.
† How is the lack of a *Third Personal Pronoun* supplied? (N. 46.)

	Singular.			Singular.		
	M.	F.	N.	M.	F.	N.
Nom.	ille*	illa	illud, *that.*	ipse*	ipsa	ipsum, *self.*
Gen.	illīus	illīus	illīus	ipsīus	ipsīus	ipsīus
Dat.	illī	illī	illī	ipsī	ipsī	ipsī
Acc.	illum	illam	illud	ipsum	ipsam	ipsum
Abl.	illō	illā	illō	ipsō	ipsā	ipsō

Iste, ista, istud, *that (near you),* is declined like ille.

Īdem, *the same.*

	Singular.			Plural.		
	M.	F.	N.	M.	F.	N.
Nom.	īdem	eadem	idem	iīdem (eī-)	eaedem	eadem
Gen.	ējusdem	ējusdem	ējusdem	eōrundem	eārundem	eōrundem
Dat.	eīdem	eīdem	eīdem	iīsdem or eīsdem		
Acc.	eundem	eandem	idem	eōsdem	eāsdem	eadem
Abl.	eōdem	eādem	eōdem	iīsdem or eīsdem		

25. The **Relative Pronoun Quī** (N. 50), is thus declined:—

Who, Which, That.

	Singular.			Plural.		
	M.	F.	N.	M.	F.	N.
Nom.	quī	quae	quod	quī	quae	quae
Gen.	cūjus	cūjus	cūjus	quōrum	quārum	quōrum
Dat.	cuī	cuī	cuī	quibus	quibus	quibus
Acc.	quem	quam	quod	quōs	quās	quae
Abl.	quō	quā	quō	quibus	quibus	quibus

26. The **Interrogative Pronoun Quis** (Quī, N. 51) is declined in the Plural like the Relative. The Singular is:—

Who? Which? What?

Nom.	quis (quī)	quae	quid (quod)
Gen.	cūjus	cūjus	cūjus
Dat.	cuī	cuī	cuī
Acc.	quem	quam	quid (quod)
Abl.	quō	quā	quō

27. The **Indefinite Pronouns** are described in N. 52. The simple forms (Quis, Quī) are rare. Most of the Compounds are declined like the Relative and Interrogative. **Aliquis, sī quis, nē quis,** are thus declined:—

Some one, Any.

	Singular.			Plural.		
Nom.	aliquis†	aliqua	aliquid†	aliquī	aliquae	aliqua
Gen.	alicūjus	alicūjus	alicūjus	aliquōrum	aliquārum	aliquōrum
Dat.	alicuī	alicuī	alicuī	aliquibus	aliquibus	aliquibus
Acc.	aliquem	aliquam	aliquid	aliquōs	aliquās	aliqua
Abl.	aliquō	aliquā	aliquō	aliquibus	aliquibus	aliquibus

* The Plural of ille and ipse is like that of **magnus** or **bonus**.

† Or **aliquī** (Masculine), **aliquod** (Neuter), when used as an adjective.

APPENDIX. 245

VERBS: FIRST CONJUGATION.

28. ACTIVE VOICE. — Amō, *I love.*

Principal Parts.

Pres. Indic.	*Pres. Infin.*	*Perf. Indic.*	*Supine.*
amō,	amāre,	amāvī,	amātum.

Stems: Present, amā; Perfect, amāv; Supine, amāt.

INDICATIVE MODE.

Present Tense.

SINGULAR.	PLURAL.
amō, *I love.*	amāmus, *we love.*
amās, *you love.*	amātis, *you love.*
amat, *he (she) loves.*	amant, *they love.*

Imperfect.

amābam, *I was loving.*	amābāmus, *we were loving.*
amābās, *you were loving.*	amābātis, *you were loving.*
amābat, *he was loving.*	amābant, *they were loving.*

Future.

amābō, *I shall love.*	amābimus, *we shall love.*
amābis, *you will love.*	amābitis, *you will love.*
amābit, *he will love.*	amābunt, *they will love.*

Perfect.

amāvī, *I have loved, I loved.*	amāvimus, *we have loved, we loved.*
amāvistī, *you have loved, you loved.*	amāvistis, *you have loved, you loved.*
amāvit, *he has loved, he loved.*	amāvērunt (ēre), *they have loved, they loved.*

Pluperfect.

amāveram, *I had loved.*	amāverāmus, *we had loved.*
amāverās, *you had loved.*	amāverātis, *you had loved.*
amāverat, *he had loved.*	amāverant, *they had loved.*

Future Perfect.

amāverō, *I shall have loved.*	amāverimus, *we shall have loved.*
amāveris, *you will have loved.*	amāveritis, *you will have loved.*
amāverit, *he will have loved.*	amāverint, *they will have loved.*

APPENDIX.

SUBJUNCTIVE.*

Present.

SINGULAR.	PLURAL.
amem	amēmus
amēs	amētis
amet	ament

Imperfect.

amārem	amārēmus
amārēs	amārētis
amāret	amārent

Perfect.

amāverim	amāverimus
amāveris	amāveritis
amāverit	amāverint

Pluperfect.

amāvissem	amāvissēmus
amāvissēs	amāvissētis
amāvisset	amāvissent

IMPERATIVE.

Present.

2. amā, *love (thou).* 2. amāte, *love (ye).*

Future.

2. amātō, *thou shalt love.* 2. amātōte, *ye shall love.*
3. amātō, *he shall love.* 3. amantō, *they shall love.*

INFINITIVE.

Present. amāre, *to love.*
Perfect. amāvisse, *to have loved.*
Future. amātūrus esse, *to be about to love.*

PARTICIPLES.

Present. amans, *loving.*
Future. amātūrus, *about to love*

GERUND.

GEN. amandī, *of loving.*
DAT. amandō, *to (for) loving.*
ACC. amandum, *loving.*
ABL. amandō, *by loving.*

SUPINE.

ACC. amātum, *to love.*
ABL. amātū, *to love.*

* The Subjunctive has a great variety of meanings; they can be best learned by a study of the different uses of the mode, as they are presented in the Lessons.

VERBS: FIRST CONJUGATION.

29. Passive Voice. — **Amor,** *I am loved.*

Principal Parts.

Pres. Ind.	*Pres. Inf.*	*Perf. Ind.*
amor,	amārī,	amātus sum.

Stems: *Present,* amā; *Supine,* amāt.

INDICATIVE MODE.

Present Tense.

SINGULAR.	PLURAL.
amor, *I am loved.*	amāmur, *we are loved.*
amāris (re), *you are loved.*	amāminī, *you are loved.*
amātur, *he (she, it) is loved.*	amantur, *they are loved.*

Imperfect.
I was loved.

amābar	amābāmur
amābāris (re)	amābāminī
amābātur	amābantur

Future.
I shall be loved.

amābor	amābimur
amāberis (re)	amābiminī
amābitur	amābuntur

Perfect.
I have been loved, was loved.

amātus sum	amātī sumus
amātus es	amātī estis
amātus est	amātī sunt

Pluperfect.
I had been loved.

amātus eram	amātī erāmus
amātus erās	amātī erātis
amātus erat	amātī erant

Future Perfect.
I shall have been loved.

amātus erō	amātī erimus
amātus eris	amātī eritis
amātus erit	amātī erunt

SUBJUNCTIVE.

Present.

SINGULAR.	PLURAL.
amer	amēmur
amēris (re)	amēminī
amētur	amentur

Imperfect.

amārer	amārēmur
amārēris (re)	amārēminī
amārētur	amārentur

Perfect.

amātus sim	amātī sīmus
amātus sīs	amātī sītis
amātus sit	amātī sint

Pluperfect.

amātus essem	amātī essēmus
amātus essēs	amātī essētis
amātus esset	amātī essent

IMPERATIVE.

Present.

2. amāre, *be (thou) loved.* | amāminī, *be (ye) loved.*

Future.

2. amātor, *thou shalt be loved.* | 2. *wanting.*
3. amātor, *he shall be loved.* | 3. amantor, *they shall be loved.*

INFINITIVE.

Present. amārī, *to be loved.*
Perfect. amātus esse, *to have been loved.*
Future. amātum īrī, *to be about to be loved.*

PARTICIPLES.

Perfect. amātus, *having been loved.*
Gerundive. amandus, *to-be-loved, deserving to be loved.*

VERBS: SECOND CONJUGATION.

Moneō, *I warn, advise.*

Prin. Parts:	Pres. Ind.	Pres. Inf.	Perf. Ind.	Supine.
30. ACTIVE:	moneō,	monēre,	monuī,	monitum.
31. PASSIVE:	moneor,	monērī,	monitus sum.	

Stems: *Present,* monē; *Perfect,* monu; *Supine,* monit.

NOTICE *that only a few tenses of* moneō *are here given in full; the others have the same tense-signs and endings as in* amō.

(30) ACTIVE. (31) PASSIVE.

INDICATIVE.	SUBJUNCTIVE.	INDICATIVE.	SUBJUNCTIVE.
	Present.		
SINGULAR.		SINGULAR.	
moneō	moneam	moneor	monear
monēs	moneās	monēris (re)	moneāris (re)
monet	moneat	monētur	moneātur
PLURAL.		PLURAL.	
monēmus	moneāmus	monēmur	moneāmur
monētis	moneātis	monēminī	moneāminī
monent	moneant	monentur	moneantur
	Imperfect (*like* amō).		
monēbam, etc.	monērem, etc.	monēbar, etc.	monērer, etc.
	Future (*like* amō).		
monēbō, etc.		monēbor, etc.	
	Perfect (*like* amō).		
monuī, etc.	monuerim, etc.	monitus sum, etc.	monitus sim, etc.
	Pluperfect (*like* amō).		
monueram, etc.	monuissem, etc.	monitus eram, etc.	monitus essem, etc.
	Future Perfect (*like* amō).		
monuerō, etc.		monitus erō, etc.	

IMPERATIVE.

	SING.	PLUR.		SING.	PLUR.
Pres.	2. monē	monēte	Pres. 2.	monēre	monēminī
Fut.	2. monētō	monētōte	Fut. 2.	monētor	*wanting.*
	3. monētō	monentō	3.	monētor	monentor

INFINITIVE.

Pres. monēre Perf. monuisse | Pres. monērī Perf. monitus esse
Fut. monitūrus esse | Fut. monitum īrī

PARTICIPLES.

Pres. monens Fut. monitūrus | Perf. monitus G've. monendus

GERUND. monendī, ō, um, ō } VERBAL NOUNS.
SUPINE. monitum, monitū }

VERBS: THIRD CONJUGATION.

Regō, *I direct, rule.*

Prin. Parts:	Pres. Ind.	Pres. Inf.	Perf. Ind.	Supine.
32. ACTIVE:	regō,	regere,	rexī,	rectum.
33. PASSIVE:	regor,	regī,	rectus sum.	

Stems: *Present,* rege (N. 79, 2); *Perfect,* rex; *Supine,* rect.

(32) ACTIVE.

INDICATIVE.	SUBJUNCTIVE.

Present.

SINGULAR.

regō	regam
regis	regās
regit	regat

PLURAL.

regimus	regāmus
regitis	regātis
regunt	regant

(33) PASSIVE.

INDICATIVE.	SUBJUNCTIVE.

SINGULAR.

regor	regar
regeris (re)	regāris (re)
regitur	regātur

PLURAL.

regimur	regāmur
regiminī	regāminī
reguntur	regantur

Imperfect (*like* moneō).

| regēbam | regerem | regēbar | regerer |

Future.

SINGULAR.

regam	regar
regēs	regēris (re)
reget	regētur

PLURAL.

regēmus	regēmur
regētis	regēminī
regent	regentur

Perfect (*like* moneō).

| rexī | rexerim | rectus sum | rectus sim |

Pluperfect (*like* moneō).

| rexeram | rexissem | rectus eram | rectus essem |

Future Perfect (*like* moneō).

| rexerō | | rectus erō | |

IMPERATIVE.

	SING.	PLUR.		SING.	PLUR.
Pres.	2. rege	regite	Pres.	2. regere	regiminī
Fut.	2. regitō	regitōte	Fut.	2. regitor	*wanting*
	3. regitō	reguntō		3. regitor	reguntor

ACTIVE.	PASSIVE.

INFINITIVE. { **Pres.** regere **Perf.** rexisse   **Pres.** regī **Perf.** rectus esse
{ **Fut.** rectūrus esse   **Fut.** rectum īrī

PARTICIPLES. **Pres.** regens **Fut.** rectūrus **Perf.** rectus G've. regendus

VERBAL NOUNS. GERUND. regendī, etc.   SUPINE. rectum, rectū.

VERBS: THIRD CONJUGATION.

34. VERBS IN IO.
This class of Verbs is described in NOTE 79, 3.

Prin. Parts:	*Pres. Ind.*	*Pres. Inf.*	*Perf. Ind.*	*Supine.*
ACTIVE:	capiō, *I take.*	capere	cēpī	captum
PASSIVE:	capior	capī	captus sum	

Stems: *Present*, cape; *Perfect*, cēp; *Supine*, capt.

ACTIVE.
INDICATIVE.	SUBJUNCTIVE.

PASSIVE.
INDICATIVE.	SUBJUNCTIVE.

Present.

SINGULAR.
capiō	capiam	capior	capiar
capis	capiās	caperis (re)	capiāris (re)
capit	capiat	capitur	capiātur

PLURAL.
capimus	capiāmus	capimur	capiāmur
capitis	capiātis	capiminī	capiāminī
capiunt	capiant	capiuntur	capiantur

Imperfect.
capiēbam	caperem	capiēbar	caperer

Future.
capiam		capiar	
capiēs		capiēris (re)	
capiet, etc.		capiētur, etc.	

Perfect.
cēpī	cēperim	captus sum	captus sim

Pluperfect.
cēperam	cēpissem	captus eram	captus essem

Future Perfect.
cēperō		captus erō	

IMPERATIVE.
Pres. 2. cape	capite	Pres. 2. capere	capiminī
Fut. 2. capitō	capitōte	Fut. 2. capitor	*wanting*
3. capitō	capiuntō	3. capitor	capiuntor

INFINITIVE.
Pres. capere	Perf. cēpisse	Pres. capī	Perf. captus esse
Fut. captūrus esse		Fut. captum īrī	

PARTICIPLES.
Pres. capiens   Fut. captūrus | Perf. captus   G've. capiendus

GERUND. capiendī, ō, um, ō } VERBAL NOUNS.
SUPINE. captum, captū .

VERBS: FOURTH CONJUGATION.

Audiō, *I hear*.

Prin. Parts:	Pres. Ind.	Pres. Inf.	Perf. Ind.	Supine.
35. ACTIVE:	audiō	audīre	audīvī	audītum
36. PASSIVE:	audior	audīrī	audītus sum	

Stems: *Present*, audī; *Perfect*, audīv; *Supine*, audīt.

(35) ACTIVE.

(36) PASSIVE.

INDICATIVE. SUBJUNCTIVE. INDICATIVE. SUBJUNCTIVE

Present.

SINGULAR.

audiō	audiam	audior	audiar
audīs	audiās	audīris (re)	audiāris (re)
audit	audiat	audītur	audiātur

PLURAL.

audīmus	audiāmus	audīmur	audiāmur
audītis	audiātis	audīminī	audiāminī
audiunt	audiant	audiuntur	audiantur

Imperfect.

audiēbam	audīrem	audiēbar	audīrer

Future.

SINGULAR.

audiam	audiar
audiēs	audiēris (re)
audiet	audiētur

PLURAL.

audiēmus	audiēmur
audiētis	audiēminī
audient	audientur

Perfect.

audīvī	audīverim	audītus sum	audītus sim

Pluperfect.

audīveram	audīvissem	audītus eram	audītus essem

Future Perfect.

audīverō		audītus erō	

IMPERATIVE.

Pres. 2. audī	audīte	Pres. 2. audīre	audīminī
Fut. 2. audītō	audītōte	Fut. 2. audītor	*wanting.*
3. audītō	audiuntō	3. audītor	audiuntor

INFINITIVE.

Pres. audīre   Perf. audīvisse | Pres. audīrī   Perf. audītus esse
Fut. audītūrus esse | Fut. audītum īrī

PARTICIPLES.

Pres. audiēns   Fut. audītūrus | Perf. audītus   G've. audiendus

GERUND. audiendī, ō, um, ō } VERBAL NOUNS.
SUPINE. audītum, ū

APPENDIX. 253

DEPONENT VERBS: ALL CONJUGATIONS.

37. (See Note 80.)
The Principal Parts and meanings of these verbs are given in the Vocabulary.

INDICATIVE.

	I.	II.	III.	IV.
Pres.	hortor	vereor	sequor	potior
	hortāris (re)	verēris (re)	sequeris (re)	potīris (re)
	hortātur	verētur	sequitur	potītur
	hortāmur	verēmur	sequimur	potīmur
	hortāminī	verēminī	sequiminī	potīminī
	hortantur	verentur	sequuntur	potiuntur
Imp.	hortābar	verēbar	sequēbar	potiēbar
Fut.	hortābor	verēbor	sequar	potiar
Perf.	hortātus sum	veritus sum	secūtus sum	potītus sum
Plup.	hortātus eram	veritus eram	secūtus eram	potītus eram
F. P.	hortātus erō	veritus erō	secūtus erō	potītus erō

SUBJUNCTIVE.

Pres.	horter	verear	sequar	potiar
Imp.	hortārer	verērer	sequerer	potīrer
Perf.	hortātus sim	veritus sim	secūtus sim	potītus sim
Plup.	hortātus essem	veritus essem	secūtus essem	potītus essem

IMPERATIVE.

hortāre, ātor   verēre, ētor   sequere, itor   potīre, ītor

INFINITIVE.

Pres.	hortārī	verērī	sequī	potīrī
Perf.	hortātus esse	veritus esse	secūtus esse	potītus esse
Fut.	hortātūrus esse	veritūrus esse	secūtūrus esse	potītūrus esse

PARTICIPLES.

Pres.	hortans	verens	sequens	potiens
Fut.	hortātūrus	veritūrus	secūtūrus	potītūrus
Perf.	hortātus	veritus	secūtus	potītus
G've.	hortandus	verendus	sequendus	potiendus

VERBAL NOUNS.

Ger.	hortandī, etc.	verendī, etc.	sequendī, etc.	potiendī, etc.
Sup.	hortātum, ū	veritum, ū	secūtum, ū	potītum, ū

38. Semi-Deponent Verbs. (See Note 81.)

audeō, audēre, ausus sum, *dare;* gaudeō, gaudēre, gavīsus sum, *rejoice;* fīdō, fīdere, fīsus sum, *trust;* soleō, solēre, solitus sum, *be wont.*

PERIPHRASTIC CONJUGATIONS.

39. *a.* **First (or Active).**—Amātūrus sum, *I am about to love* (see N. 82).

Amātūrus, Monitūrus, Rectūrus, Audītūrus,—

	Present.	Imperf.	Future.	Perfect.	Pluperf.	Fut. Perf.
INDIC.	sum	eram	erō	fuī	fueram	fuerō
SUBJ.	sim	essem	.....	fuerim	fuissem	.....
INFIN.	esse	.....	.....	fuisse	.....	.....

b. **Second (or Passive).**—Amandus sum, *I must be loved.*

Amandus, Monendus, Regendus, Audiendus,—

	Present.	Imperf.	Future.	Perfect.	Pluperf.	Fut. Perf.
INDIC.	sum	eram	erō	fuī	fueram	fuerō
SUBJ.	sim	essem	.....	fuerim	fuissem	.....
INFIN.	esse	.....	.....	fuisse	.....	.....

IRREGULAR VERBS.

40. Sum, *I am.* (See NOTE 84.)

	Pres. Ind.	Pres. Inf.	Perf. Ind.	Supine.
Prin. Parts:	sum,	esse,	fuī,	wanting.

Stems: *Pres.* es ; *Perf.* fu ; *Sup.* fut (found in the Future Participle).

INDICATIVE.

Present.

SINGULAR. | PLURAL.
sum, *I am.* | sumus, *we are.*
es, *thou art (you are).* | estis, *you are.*
est, *he (she, it) is.* | sunt, *they are.*

Imperfect.

eram, *I was.* | erāmus, *we were.*
erās, *you were.* | erātis, *you were.*
erat, *he (she, it) was.* | erant, *they were.*

Future.

erō, *I shall be.* | erimus, *we shall be.*
eris, *you will be.* | eritis, *you will be.*
erit, *he will be.* | erunt, *they will be.*

Perfect.

fuī, *I have been (was).* | fuimus, *we have been (were).*
fuistī, *you have been (were).* | fuistis, *you have been (were).*
fuit, *he has been (was).* | fuērunt (ēre), *they have been (were).*

Pluperfect.

fueram, *I had been.* | fuerāmus, *we had been.*
fuerās, *you had been.* | fuerātis, *you had been.*
fuerat, *he had been.* | fuerant, *they had been.*

Future Perfect.

fuerō, *I shall have been.* | fuerimus, *we shall have been.*
fueris, *you will have been.* | fueritis, *you will have been.*
fuerit, *he will have been.* | fuerint, *they will have been.*

SUBJUNCTIVE OF Sum.

	Present.	Imperfect.	Perfect.	Pluperfect.
SINGULAR.	sim	essem[1]	fuerim	fuissem
	sīs	essēs	fueris	fuissēs
	sit	esset	fuerit	fuisset
PLURAL.	sīmus	essēmus	fuerimus	fuissēmus
	sītis	essētis	fueritis	fuissētis
	sint	essent	fuerint	fuissent

IMPERATIVE.

Present. 2. es, *be thou.* este, *be ye.*
Future. 2. estō, *thou shalt be.* estōte, *ye shall be.*
3. estō, *he shall be.* suntō, *they shall be.*

INFINITIVE.

Present. esse, *to be.*
Perfect. fuisse, *to have been.*
Future. futūrus esse,[2] *to be about to be.*

PARTICIPLES.

Present. *wanting*
Future. futūrus

[1] For essem, forem is often used. [2] For futūrus esse, fore is often used.

Compounds of Sum.

41. Possum (*I am able, can*) = potis (*able*) + sum. Possum = potsum; t becomes s before s (N. 1 (4) *b*), as, pos-sum, and is retained before e, as, pot-es. The verb is described in N. 85, 1.

Prin. Parts: possum, posse (for pot-esse), potuī (for pot-fuī).

INDICATIVE.	SUBJUNCTIVE.	INDICATIVE.	SUBJUNCTIVE.
Present.		**Perfect.**	
possum, *I am able, can.*	possim	potuī, *I could.*	potuerim
potes, *you can.*	possīs	**Pluperfect.**	
potest, *he can.*	possit	potueram	potuissem
possumus, *we can.*	possīmus	**Future Perfect.**	
potestis, *you can.*	possītis	potuerō	
possunt, *they can.*	possint	IMPERATIVE.	
Imperfect.		*wanting*	
poteram, *I could.*	possem	INFINITIVE.	
Future.		Pres. posse Perf. potuisse	
poterō, *I shall be able.*		PARTICIPLES.	
		Pres. potens (used as an adjective), *powerful.*	

a. In Prōsum, *I profit, help,* prō becomes prōd before e, as in the Present Indicative: (*Singular*) prō-sum, prōd-es, prōd-est; (*Plural*) prō-sumus, prōd-estis, prō-sunt. Other instances are prōd-eram, prōd-erō.

APPENDIX.

IRREGULAR VERBS.

42. Ferō, *I bear.* (See NOTE 86.)

Prin. Parts: ACTIVE: ferō, ferre, tulī, lātum.
PASSIVE: feror, ferrī, lātus sum.

ACTIVE.

	INDICATIVE.	SUBJUNCTIVE.
Pres.	ferō	feram
	fers	ferās
	fert	ferat
	ferimus	ferāmus
	fertis	ferātis
	ferunt	ferant
Imperf.	ferēbam	ferrem
Fut.	feram	
Perf.	tulī	tulerim
Plup.	tuleram	tulissem
F. Perf.	tulerō	
IMP. Pres.	fer	ferte
Fut.	fertō	fertōte
	fertō	feruntō
INF. Pres. ferre	Perf. tulisse
Fut. lātūrus esse
PART. Pres. ferens Fut. lātūrus
GER. ferendī, etc. SUP. lātum, ū

PASSIVE.

INDICATIVE.	SUBJUNCTIVE.
feror	ferar
ferris (re)	ferāris (re)
fertur	ferātur
ferimur	ferāmur
feriminī	ferāminī
feruntur	ferantur
ferēbar	ferrer
ferar	
lātus sum	lātus sim
lātus eram	lātus essem
lātus erō	
ferre	feriminī
fertor	*wanting*
fertor	feruntor
Pres. ferrī	Perf. lātus esse
Fut. lātum īrī	
Perf. lātus	G've. ferendus

43. IRREGULAR VERBS: **EŌ,** *I go.* (See NOTE 87.)

Prin. Parts: eō, īre, īvī, itum.

INDICATIVE.	SUBJUNCTIVE.
Pres. SING. eō, īs, it	eam, eās, eat
PLUR. īmus, ītis, eunt	eāmus, eātis, eant
Imperf. ībam, ībās, ībat	īrem, īrēs, īret
ībāmus, ībātis, ībant	īrēmus, īrētis, īrent
Future. ībō, ībis, ībit	
ībimus, ībitis, ībunt	
Perf. īvī	īverim
Pluperf. īveram	īvissem
Fut. Perf. īverō	

IMPERAT. Pres. ī, īte; Fut. ītō, ītō, ītōte, euntō.
INFIN. Pres. īre   Perf. īvisse   Fut. itūrus esse
PART. Pres. iens (GENITIVE, euntis)   Fut. itūrus
GERUND.   eundī, etc.   SUPINE. itum, itū

APPENDIX. 257

44. IRREGULAR VERBS: Fīō (*I am made, become*) is the Passive of **Faciō**
(See NOTE 88.)

INDICATIVE.	SUBJUNCTIVE.
Pres. SING. fīō, fīs, fit	fīam, fīās, fīat
PLUR. fīmus, fītis, fīunt	fīāmus, fīātis, fīant
Imp. fīēbam, fīēbās, etc.	fierem, fierēs, etc.
Fut. fīam, fīēs, etc.	
Perf. factus sum	factus sim
Plup. factus eram	factus essem
Fut. Perf. factus erō	

IMPERAT. Pres. fī, fīte; Fut. fītō, fītō, fītōte, fīuntō
INFIN. Pres. fierī   Perf. factus esse   Fut. factum īrī
PART. Perf. factus   G've. faciendus

45. IRREGULAR VERBS: Volō and its compounds (see NOTES 89, 90):—
volō, velle, voluī, *to wish*.
nōlō (= nōn volō), nolle, nōluī, *to be unwilling*.
mālō (= magis volō), malle, māluī, *to wish rather, prefer*.

Present.

INDIC.	SUBJ.	INDIC.	SUBJ.	INDIC.	SUBJ.
volō	velim	nōlō	nōlim	mālō	mālim
vīs	velīs	nonvīs	nōlīs	māvīs	mālīs
vult	velit	nonvult	nōlit	māvult	mālit
volumus	velīmus	nōlumus	nōlīmus	mālumus	mālīmus
vultis	velītis	nonvultis	nōlītis	māvultis	mālītis
volunt	velint	nōlunt	nōlint	mālunt	mālint

Imperfect.

| volēbam | vellem | nōlēbam | nollem | mālēbam | mallem |

Future.

| volam | | nōlam | | mālam | |

Perfect.

| voluī | voluerim | nōluī | nōluerim | māluī | māluerim |

Pluperfect.

| volueram | voluissem | nōlueram | nōluissem | mālueram | māluissem |

Future Perfect.

| voluerō | | nōluerō | | māluerō | |

IMPERATIVE.

Pres. nōlī, nōlīte, *do not*.
Fut. nōlītō, nōlītōte, *thou shalt not, ye shall not.*
nōlītō, nōluntō, *he shall not, they shall not.*

INFINITIVE.

velle   voluisse   nolle   nōluisse   malle   māluisse

PARTICIPLES.

volens, *willing*.   nōlens, *unwilling*.

DEFECTIVE VERBS.

46. (See NOTE 91.) The following have (in common use) only the tenses formed from the Perfect Stem: coepī,* *I began* (*have begun*); meminī,† *I remember*; ōdī,† *I hate*.

Synopsis. $\begin{Bmatrix} \text{coep-} \\ \text{memin-} \\ \text{ōd-} \end{Bmatrix}$ ī, eram, erō, erim, issem, isse

REMARK 1. Passive forms of coepī (as coeptus sum) are used with the *Passive Infinitive* (N. 91, 1).

REMARK 2. Inquam and other Defective verbs are described in N. 91, *a, b*.

IMPERSONAL VERBS.

47. (See NOTE 92.) Impersonal verbs are used in the Third Person Singular of the Indicative and Subjunctive Modes (all tenses), and also in the Infinitive. A synopsis of three classes of Impersonal verbs is here given, as well as their Principal Parts: —

1. **Regularly Impersonal** (licet, Second Conjugation).
2. **Used Impersonally in the Active** (constat, accidit, First and Third Conjugations).
3. **Used Impersonally in the Passive** (pugnātur, nocētur [see N. 134]).

Prin. Parts: constat, constāre, constitit, *it is evident*.
licet, licēre, licuit, *it is permitted*.
accidit, accidere, accidit, *it happens*.
pugnātur, pugnārī, pugnātum est, *fighting is carried on*.
nocētur, nocērī, nocitum est, *harm is done*.

constat	licet	accidit	pugnātur	nocētur
constābat	licēbat	accidēbat	pugnābātur	nocēbātur
constābit	licēbit	accidet	pugnābitur	nocēbitur
constitit	licuit	accidit	pugnātum est	nocitum est
constiterat	licuerat	acciderat	pugnātum erat	nocitum erat
constiterit	licuerit	acciderit	pugnātum erit	nocitum erit
constet	liceat	accidat	pugnētur	noceātur
constāret	licēret	accideret	pugnārētur	nocērētur
constiterit	licuerit	acciderit	pugnātum sit	nocitum sit
constitisset	licuisset	accidisset	pugnātum esset	nocitum esset
constāre	licēre	accidere	pugnārī	nocērī
constitisse	licuisse	accidisse	pugnātum esse	nocitum esse
constātūrum esse	licitūrum esse		pugnātum īrī	nocitum īrī

* The Present-stem tenses of coepī are borrowed from incipiō, *I begin*.

† Nōvī, *I know* (from noscō), and consuēvī, *I am wont* (from consuescō), as well as meminī and ōdī, are used in the Perfect, Pluperfect, and Future Perfect, with the meaning of the Present, Imperfect, and Future; that is, they are **preteritive verbs** (N. 91, 2 and REMARK).

SPECIAL VOCABULARIES AND EXAMPLES.

These Vocabularies have been prepared for the first 29 Lessons. The same Latin words are also given in the General Vocabulary. Beyond the 29th Lesson, Special Examples are given for such Lessons as require them.

Abbreviations.

adv., *adverb.*
conj., *conjunction.*
f., *feminine gender.*
m., *masculine gender.*
n., *neuter gender.*
prep., *preposition.*

LESSON I.

agricola, ae, m. *farmer.*
causa, ae, f. *cause, reason.*
glōria, ae, f. *glory.*
lingua, ae, f. *tongue, language.*
memoria, ae, f. *memory.*
mensa, ae, f. *table.*
nauta, ae, m. *sailor.*

pecūnia, ae, f. *money.*
Rōma, ae, f. *Rome.*
rosa, ae, f. *rose.*
silva, ae, f. *forest.*
stella, ae, f. *star.*
via, ae, f. *way, road.*
victōria, ae, f. *victory.*

LESSON II.

amō, *I love.*
laudō, *I praise.*

puella, ae, f. *girl.*
pugnō, *I fight.*
vocō, *I call.*

LESSON III.

ager, agrī, m. *field.*
amīcus, ī, m. *friend.*
dō, *I give.*
equus, ī, m. *horse.*
liber, librī, m. *book.*
līberō, *I free, release.*

magister, trī, m. *master, teacher.*
puer, ī, m. *boy.*
Rōmānus, ī, m. *a Roman.*
servus, ī, m. *slave.*
vir, virī, m. *man.*

LESSON IV.

Nouns.
bellum, ī, n. *war.*
dōnum, ī, n. *gift.*
praemium, ī, n. *reward.*
templum, ī, n. *temple.*

Adjectives.
aeger, aegra, aegrum, *sick.*
bonus, bona, bonum, *good.*
līber, lībera, līberum, *free.*
magnus, magna, magnum, *great, large.*
miser, misera, miserum, *wretched.*
niger, nigra, nigrum, *black.*
parvus, parva, parvum, *small.*

LESSON V.

cōpia, ae, f. (in the Singular) *abundance, plenty;* (in the Plural) *forces, troops, supplies.*
et, conj. *and.*
Gallī, ōrum, m. *the Gauls.*
Genēva, ae, f. *Geneva.*
Germānī, ōrum, m. *the Germans.*
gladius, I, m. *sword.*

lēgātus, I, m. *legate, lieutenant.*
occupō, *I occupy, seize.*
oppidum, I, n. *town* (fortified).
portō, *I carry.*
Sabīnus, I, m. *Sabinus.*
superō, *I overcome.*
Titus, I, m. *Titus.*
vastō, *I lay waste.*

LESSON VI.

acūtus, a, um, *sharp.*
albus, a, um, *white.*
altus, a, um, *high, lofty, deep.*
attentus, a, um, *attentive.*
beātus, a, um, *happy, fortunate.*
clārus, a, um, *bright, clear.*
exemplum, I, n. *example.*
insula, ae, f. *island.*
lātus, a, um, *wide, broad.*

longus, a, um, *long.*
multus, a, um, *much, many.*
numerus, I. m. *number.*
perīculum, I, n. *peril, danger.*
porta, ae, f. *gate, door.*
regnum, I, n. *kingdom.*
sum, *I am.*
timidus, a, um, *timid.*

LESSON VIII.

dea, ae, f. *goddess.*   fīlia, ae, f. *daughter.*   mūrus, I, m. *wall.*

Principal Parts of Verbs.

PRES. INDIC.	PRES. INFIN.	PERF. INDIC.	SUPINE.
amō,	amāre,	amāvī,	amātum, *love.*
dō,	dare,	dedī,	datum, *give.*
laudō,	laudāre,	laudāvī,	laudātum, *praise.*
līberō,	līberāre,	līberāvī,	līberātum, *free.*
monstrō,	monstrāre,	monstrāvī,	monstrātum, *show.*
narrō,	narrāre,	narrāvī,	narrātum, *tell.*
portō,	portāre,	portāvī,	portātum, *carry.*
pugnō,	pugnāre,	pugnāvī,	pugnātum, *fight.*
servō,	servāre,	servāvī,	servātum, *save, protect*
vastō,	vastāre,	vastāvī,	vastātum, *lay waste.*

LESSON IX.

The new Verbs used in this Lesson are given in the Vocabulary for Lesson VIII

fābula, ae, f. *story.*
frūmentum, I, n. *corn.*

injūria, ae, f. *injury, wrong.*
nōn, adv. *not.*

LESSON XI.

auxilium, I, n. (in Sing.) *aid;* (in Plur.) *auxiliaries.*
Cāius, I, m. *Caius.*
Cassius, I, m. *Cassius.*
concilium, I, n. *council.*
fīlius, I, m. *son.*
Jūlius, I, m. *Julius.*

Marcus, I, m. *Marcus.*
meus, a, um, *my, mine.*
nuntiō, āre, etc. *announce.*
patria, ae, f. *fatherland, native land.*
Pompēius, I, m. *Pompey.*
proelium, I, n. *battle.*

LESSON XIII.

aedificō, āre, etc., *build.*
alius, a, ud, *other.*
alter, era, erum, *the other* (of two).
nātūra, ae, f. *nature.*
neuter, tra, trum, *neither.*
nullus, a, um, *no, none.*
poëta, ae, m. *poet.*

sōlus, a, um, *only, alone.*
tōtus, a, um, *entire, whole.*
ullus, a, um, *any.*
ūnus, a, um, *one.*
uter, tra, trum, *which* (of two).
vacō, āre, etc., *be empty, unoccupied.*
vīta, ae, f. *life.*

LESSON XIV.

caput, capitis, n. *head.* [CAPIT-AL]
consul, consulis, m. CONSUL.
corpus, corporis, n. *body.* [CORPOR-AL]
malus, a, um, *bad, evil.*
mīles, mīlitis, m. *soldier.* [MILITARY.]

nōmen, nōminis, n. *name.* [NOMIN-ATE]
rex, rēgis, m. *king.* [REG-AL]
soror, sorōris, f. *sister.*
virgō, virginis, f. *maiden.* [VIRGIN]

LESSON XVI.

altitūdō, inis, f. *height.*
cīvitās, ātis, f. *state.*
custōs, ōdis, m. *keeper, guard.*
dux, ducis, m. and f. *leader, chief.*
flōs, flōris, m. *flower.*
frāter, tris, m. *brother.*
honor, ōris, m. *honor.*
lātitūdō, inis, f. *width.*
legiō, ōnis, f. *legion.*

leō, ōnis, m. *lion.*
longitūdō, inis, f. *length.*
lux, lūcis, f. *light.*
māter, tris, f. *mother.*
mōs, mōris, m. *custom.*
opus, eris, n. *work, task.*
pater, tris, m. *father.*
princeps, ipis, m. *chief, prince.*
tempus, oris, n. *time.*
virtūs, ūtis, f. *manhood, courage.*

LESSON XVII.

animal, ālis, n. *animal.*
arx, arcis, f. *citadel.*
calcar, āris, n. *spur.*
collis, is, m. *hill.*
dux, ducis, m. and f. *leader, chief.*
fīnis, is, m. (in Sing.) *end, limit;* (in Plur.) *territory.*
Gallia, ae, f. *Gaul.*
hostis, is, m. and f. *enemy* (regularly in the Plural, to denote *the enemy as a body*).
ignis, is, m. *fire.*
mare, is, n. *sea.*
mons, montis, m. *mountain.*
nāvis, is, f. *ship.*
nox, noctis, f. *night.*
nūbēs, is, f. *cloud.*
pars, partis, f. *part.*
pulcher, chra, chrum, *beautiful.*
turris, is, f. *tower.*
urbs, urbis, f. *city.*
vectīgal, ālis, n. *tax.*

LESSON XIX.

arma, ōrum, n. *arms.*
Caesar, aris, m. *Caesar.*
castra, ōrum, n. *camp.*
expugnō, āre, etc., *storm, take by storm.*
ignāvus, a, um, *cowardly.*
injustus, a, um, *unjust.*
jūdex, icis, m. *judge.*
justus, a, um, *just.*

Examples.

Urbem expugnāre potes, *you can (are able to) storm the city.*
Hostēs superāre potuistī, *you could have (were able to) overcome the enemy.*

LESSON XX.

dīcit (3d. Conj.), *he says.*
iter, itineris, n. *way, journey, march.*
negō, āre, etc., *deny, say not.*
putō, āre, etc., *think, suppose.*
spērō, āre, etc., *hope.*

Examples.

"Urbs magna est," (he says) "*The city is great.*"
Dīcit urbem magnam esse, *he says (that) the city is great.*
Spērat urbēs magnās futūrās esse, *he hopes (that) the cities will be great.*
Putat iter longum fuisse, *he thinks (that) the journey was (has been) long.*

LESSON XXI.

Examples.

FACT.
{ Sī pugnat, hostēs superat, *if he fights, he overcomes the enemy.*
Sī pugnābat, hostēs superābat, *if he was fighting, he was overcoming,* etc.
Sī pugnābit, hostēs superābit, *if he fights (shall fight), he will overcome,* etc.
Sī pugnāvit, hostēs superāvit, *if he fought (has fought), he overcame (has overcome),* etc.
Sī pugnāverit, hostēs superābit, *if he fights (shall have fought), he will overcome,* etc. }

FUTURE POSSIBLE. Sī pugnet, superet, *if he should fight, he would overcome.*

FUTURE POSSIBLE. Sī pugnāverit, superet, *if he should have fought, he would overcome.*

PRES. IMPOSSIBLE. Sī pugnāret, superāret, *if he were fighting* (now), *he would be overcoming.*

PAST IMPOSSIBLE. Sī pugnāvisset, superāvisset, *if he had fought, he would have overcome.*

LESSON XXII.

ā, or ab, prep. (in this Lesson) *by*.
decimus, a, um, *tenth*.
lapis, idis, m. *stone*.
signum, ī, n. *sign, signal*.

tēlum, ī, n. *weapon*.
tuba, ae, f. *trumpet*.
vulnerō, āre, etc., *wound*.

Examples.

Titus gladiō vulnerātur, *Titus is wounded with a sword* (MEANS).
Urbēs ab Ariovistō expugnantur, *the cities are stormed by Ariovistus* (AGENT).
Oppidum ā (or ab) mīlitibus servātum est, *the town was saved by the soldiers* (AGENT).

LESSON XXIII.

dēfensor, ōris, m. *defender*.
nūdō, āre, etc., *strip*.
-que, enclitic conj. (N. 195, 3) *and*.

servitūs, ūtis, f. *slavery*.
suspiciō, ōnis, f. *suspicion*.
timor, ōris, m. *fear*.

Examples.

Urbem timōre līberō, *I free the city from fear.*
Mūrus dēfensōribus nūdātus est, *the wall has been stripped of defenders.*

LESSON XXIV.

Examples.

Compare the Examples for Lesson XXI.

Sī ignāvī fuissēmus, urbs expugnāta esset, *if we had been cowardly, the city would have been taken by storm.*
Sī pugnārēs, laudārēris, *if you were fighting* (now), *you would be praised.*
Sī laudēris, pugnēs, *if you should be praised* (hereafter), *you would fight.*
Sī laudātus sīs, pugnēs, *if you should have been praised* (hereafter), etc.

LESSON XXVI.

aestās, ātis, f. *summer.*
alacer, cris, cre, *eager, active.*
brevis, e, *brief, short.*
celer, eris, ere, *swift, quick.*
difficilis, e, *difficult.*
facilis, e, *easy.*
fortis, e, *brave.*
gravis, e, *heavy.*
homō, inis, m. and f. *man* (i. e. human being).

immortālis, e, *immortal.*
levis, e, *light.*
mortālis, e, *mortal.*
omnis, e, *all, every.*
onus, eris, n. *load, burden.*
socius, ī, m. *ally, companion.*
tristis, e, *sad.*
ūtilis, e, *useful.*

LESSON XXVII.

audax, ācis, *bold.*
dīves, itis, *rich.*
fēlix, īcis, *happy.*
flōrens, entis, *flourishing.*
infēlix, īcis, *unhappy.*
ingens, tis, *huge, mighty.*
nōbilis, e, *noble.*

pār, paris, *equal.*
potens, tis, *powerful.*
recens, tis, *recent.*
Rōmānus, a, um, *Roman.*
sapiens, tis, *wise.*
vetus, eris, *old.*

LESSON XXVIII.

amans, tis, *loving, affectionate.*
amīcus, a, um, *friendly.*
Aeduī, ōrum, m. *the Aedui.*
Ariovistus, ī, m. *Ariovistus.*
cārus, a, um, *dear.*

eques, itis, m. *horseman;* (Plural) *cavalry.*
lex, lēgis, f. *law.*
pedes, itis, m. *foot-soldier;* (Plural) *infantry.*

LESSON XXIX.

ācriter, *sharply, fiercely.*
attentē, *attentively.*
audacter, *boldly.*
celeriter, *swiftly, quickly.*
dīligenter, *diligently, carefully.*
dissimilis, e, *dissimilar, unlike.*
facile, *easily.*

fortiter, *bravely.*
inimīcus, a, um, *unfriendly;* (as a noun) *foe, personal enemy.*
quam, adv. *than.*
sapienter, *wisely.*
similis, e, *similar, like.*

Example.

Virtūs mīlitum mājor quam ducis fuit, *the soldiers' bravery was greater than the leader's.*

NO SPECIAL VOCABULARIES WILL BE GIVEN FOR THE REMAINING LESSONS; FOR SOME OF THEM, HOWEVER, SPECIAL EXAMPLES ARE PROVIDED.

LESSON XXXIV.

Cīvēs malī cīvitātī inimīcī sunt, *bad citizens are hostile to the state.*
Locus castrīs magis idōneus est, *the place is more suitable for a camp.*
Puer sorōrī similis est, *the boy is like (his) sister.*
Gallīs Belgae proximī sunt, *the Belgae are nearest to the Gauls.*
Summus mons ab hostibus tenētur, *the top of the mountain is held by the enemy.*
Servīs parēs sunt, *they are a match for (equal to) the slaves.*

LESSON XXXV.

ā dextrō (sinistrō) cornū, *on (from) the right (or left) wing.*
castra movet, *he breaks up (moves) camp.*
Caesar domī est, *Caesar is at home.*

LESSON XL.

PRIMARY.
{ Laudō Cāium, ut ā Cāiō lauder, *I praise Caius, that I may be praised by Caius.*
Laudābō Cāium, ut ā Cāiō lauder, *I shall praise Caius, that I may be praised by Caius.*
Laudāvī Cāium, ut ā Cāiō lauder, *I have praised Caius, that I may be praised by Caius.*
Laudāverō Cāium, ut ā Cāiō lauder, *I shall have praised Caius, that I may be praised by Caius.*

SECONDARY.

> Laudābam Cāium, ut ā Cāiō laudārer, *I was praising Caius, that I might be praised by Caius.*
> Laudāvī Cāium, ut ā Cāiō laudārer, *I praised Caius, that I might be praised by Caius.*
> Laudāveram Cāium, ut ā Cāiō laudārer, *I had praised Caius, that I might be praised by Caius.*

LESSON XLI.

Multī rēgem laudant, *many (men) praise the king.*
Omnia omnibus nōn sunt ūtilia, *all things are not useful for all (men).*
Multa audit, *he hears many (things).*
Jūdicēs justī esse videntur, *the judges seem to be just.*

LESSON XLIV.

Consul ab urbe discēdens servum interficī jussit, *the consul, (as he was) departing from the city, ordered the slave to be killed.*
Litterās ā puerō scriptās mīsit, *he sent the letter (which had been) written by the boy.*
Dux hostēs ad flūmen secūtus legiōnem reduxit, *the leader, having followed the enemy to the river, led back the legion.*
Lapidēs conjectōs rējiciunt, *they throw back the stones (which had been) hurled.*
Per Galliam iter fēcit, *he marched through Gaul.*
Titum dē victōriā certiōrem fēcī, *I informed (made more certain) Titus about the victory.*

LESSON XLVII.

Impetus paulum tardātus est, *the attack was checked a little.*
Plūrimum poterat, *he was very powerful* (i. e. *to a very great extent*).
Maximam partem frūmentō vīvunt, *for the most part they live on corn.*
Plūs auctōritātis habet, *he has more (of) authority.*
Dē tertiā vigiliā, *in the third watch.*
Castra tantum spatiī patēbant, *the camp extended over so much (of) space.*
Prīmā lūce, *at day-break.* Multō diē, *late in the day.* Prīmā nocte, *in the early part of the night.*
Exercitus (from exerceō), *a drilled army;* agmen (from agō), *an army on the march;* aciēs, *a line-of-battle.*

LESSON XLVIII.

Rogat Caesarem, ut veniat, *he asks Caesar to come (that he may come).*
Mīlitēs hortātus sum, ne fugerent, *I exhorted the soldiers not to flee (that they should not flee).*
Nītēmur ut vincāmus, *we shall strive to conquer.*
Alterī fortēs erant, alterī fūgērunt, *the one party were brave, the other fled.*

LESSON LX.

Pugnātūrī sumus, *we are going to fight.*
Hōc mihi faciendum est, *this (thing) must be done by me; I must do this.*
Quis nōbīs mittendus fuit? *who ought to have been sent by us? whom ought we to have sent?*
Dūcendī erunt, *they will have to be led.*

LESSON LXIV.

The subject of each Impersonal form is printed in italics.

Mihi nōn exspecta-ndum est, *I must not wait (delay must not be made by me).*
Pugnā-tum est, *fighting was carried on.*
Ute-ndum est armīs, *use must be made of the arms.*
Licuit Cāiō Rōmam venīre, *Caius might have come to Rome (it was permitted to Caius to come to Rome).*
Oportuit *mē injūriās ferre, I ought to have borne the injuries (it was necessary for me to bear the injuries).* This sentence may also be written: Injūriae mihi ferendae fuērunt.
Optimum vīsum est *cōpiās mittere, it seemed best to send troops.*
Urbem expugnāre potuit, *he could have stormed the city.*

LESSON LXV.

Fit ut nāvēs capiantur, *it happens that the ships are taken.*
Dixit fore ut sub jugum mitterēmur, *he said that we should be sent under the yoke* (literally, *that it would come to pass that*, etc.).
Nōn est dubium quīn justus sit, *there is no doubt (it is not doubtful) that he is just (about his being just).*
Caesar nōn is (= tālis) fuit, quī (= ut is) fugeret, *Caesar was not the man to flee* (literally, *not such a man that he would flee*).

GENERAL VOCABULARY.

Latin - English.

ABBREVIATIONS.

abl., *ablative.*
adj., *adjective.*
acc., *accusative.*
adv., *adverb.*
coll., *collective.*
comp., *comparative.*
conj., *conjunction.*
def., *defective.*
deg., *degree.*
dem., *demonstrative.*
dep., *deponent.*
diff., *difference.*
dim., *diminutive.*
distrib., *distributive.*
f., *feminine.*

fut., *future.*
gen., *genitive.*
impers., *impersonal.*
indecl., *indeclinable.*
indef., *indefinite.*
inf., *infinitive.*
interrog., *interrogative.*
irr., *irregular.*
m., *masculine.*
n., *neuter.*
nom., *nominative.*
num., *numeral.*
part., *participle.*
pass., *passive.*
perf., *perfect.*

pers., *personal.*
plur., *plural.*
pos., *positive.*
poss., *possessive.*
prep., *preposition.*
pres., *present.*
pron., *pronoun.*
quest., *question.*
refl., *reflexive.*
rel., *relative.*
semi-dep., *semi-deponent.*
sing., *singular.*
sup., *superlative.*
voc., *vocative.*

Numeral Adjectives (except ūnus, duo, trēs, mille) are *not given in this Vocabulary, but may be found in the lists, page* 242.

A.

ā, ab, prep. with abl. [Ā is used only before a consonant; ab, before a vowel or consonant], *from, by, on the side of;* ā dextrō cornū, *on the right wing.* Sometimes used as an adverb (= *off*); as, ab mīllibus passuum quīnque, *five miles off.*
abdō, dere, didī, ditum (ab + dō), *remove, hide.* Sēsē in silvās, *to go into the forests and hide.*
abdūcō, ere, xī, ctum (ab + dūcō), *lead away, withdraw.*
abeō, īre, īvī (iī), itum (ab + eō), *go away, depart.*
absum, esse, fuī (ab + sum), *be absent (away), be distant, be wanting.*

āc, conj. See atque.
acceptus, a, um, part. as adj. (accipiō), *acceptable, welcome, beloved.*
accidō, ere, accidī (ad + cadō), *fall upon, happen;* accidit (impers.), *it happens.*
accipiō, ere, cēpī, ceptum (ad + capiō), *receive, accept.*
accūsō, āre, āvī, ātum (ad + causa), *accuse, blame.*
ācer, ācris, ācre, *sharp, keen, eager, vigorous.*
aciēs, ēī, f., old gen., aciē (root ac in ācer), *sharp edge, keenness, line of battle.*
ācriter, ācrius, ācerrimē (ācer), *vigorously, keenly, fiercely.*

acūtus, a, um, *sharp, pointed.*
ad, prep. with acc., *to, towards, near, in (into) the vicinity of, according to, for.*
ad, adv. (with numerals), *about.*
adamō, āre, āvī, ātum (ad + amō), *love exceedingly, covet.*
addūcō, ere, xī, ctum (ad + dūcō), *lead to, induce, influence.*
adeō, īre, īvī (iī), itum (ad + eō), *go to, approach, visit.*
adhibeō, ēre, uī, itum (ad + habeō), *summon, invite.*
adorior, īrī, ortus sum, dep. (ad + orior, *rise up against*), *attack.*
adscīscō, ere, scīvī, scītum (ad + sciō), *receive, admit.*
adsum, esse, adfuī or affuī (ad + sum), *be near, be present, aid.*
adventus, ūs, m. (ad + veniō), *coming, arrival.*
adversus, a, um (ad + vertō, *turn*), *contrary, opposite, face to face.*
aedificium, ī, n. (aedificō), *building.*
aedificō, āre, āvī, ātum, *build, construct.*
Aeduus, a, um, *of the Aedui, Aeduan.*
Aeduus, ī, m. *an Aeduan;* (plur.) *the Aedui,* a Gallic tribe.
aeger, gra, grum, *sick, feeble.*
aegrē, aegrius, aegerrimē (aeger), *with difficulty, scarcely, hardly.*
aequus, a, um, *equal, just, right.*
aestās, ātis, f., *summer.*
afferō, ferre, attulī, allātum (ad + ferō), *bring (to).*
afficiō, ere, fēcī, fectum (ad + faciō), *affect, influence;* dolōre afficī, *to be greatly vexed,* or *distressed.*
ager, agrī, m., *field, territory.*
aggredior, edī, essus sum, dep. (ad + gradior), *go against, attack.*
agmen, inis, n. (agō), *army* (on the march); prīmum agmen, *the van;* novissimum agmen, *the rear.*
agō, ere, ēgī, actum, *lead, drive, act, do, treat* (= *discourse*).

agricola, ae, m. (ager + colō), *farmer.*
agricultūra, ae, f. (ager + colō), *agriculture.*
alacer, cris, cre, *eager, active.*
albus, a, um, *white.*
aliēnus, a, um (alius), *another's, foreign, unfavorable.*
aliquis (quī), qua, quid (quod), indef. pron., *some, any, some one, any one* (or *thing*).
alius, a, ud (gen. alīus), *other, another;* alius .... alius, *one* .... *another;* aliī aliam in partem, *some in one direction and some in another.*
Allobrogēs, um, m. (sing. Allobrox), *the Allobroges,* a people in the southeastern part of Gaul.
Alpēs, ium, f., *the Alps.*
alter, era, erum (gen. alterius), *the other* (of two), *the second;* alter .... alter, *the one* .... *the other.*
altitūdō, inis, f. (altus), *height, depth.*
altus, a, um, *high, tall, lofty, deep.*
amans, tis (amō), part. as adj., *loving, affectionate.*
Ambarrī, ōrum, m., *the Aedui Ambarri,* clients of the Aedui, north of the Allobroges.
amīcitia, ae, f. (amīcus), *friendship.*
amīcus, a, um (amō), *friendly.*
amīcus, ī, m. (amō), *friend.*
āmittō, ere, mīsī, missum (ā + mittō), *send away, let go, lose.*
amō, āre, āvī, ātum, *love, be fond of.*
amor, ōris, m. (amō), *love, affection.*
amplius, adv. (comp. of amplē), *more, further.*
amplus, a, um, *of large extent, spacious.*
an, interrog. adv., *or.*
angustiae, ārum, f. (angustus), *narrow pass, defile.*
angustus, a, um, *narrow.*
animadvertō, ere, tī, sum (animus + ad + vertō, *turn*), *notice, punish* (Eng. "attend to").

GENERAL VOCABULARY. 271

animal, ālis, n., *living creature, animal.*
animus, ī, m., *mind, disposition;* esse in animō, *intend.*
annōn, interrog. adv., *or not;* used only in direct questions.
annus, ī, m., *year.*
ante, prep. with acc., *before.*
ante, adv., *before, ago;* paulō ante, *a little while ago.*
anteā, adv. (ante + is), *before, formerly.*
antequam, or ante .... quam, conj. (literally, *before than,* or *that*), *before.*
Antōnius, ī, m., *Antonius,* a Roman name.
appellō, āre, āvī, ātum, *call, name.*
Aprīlis, e, *of April;* Kalendae Aprīlēs, *the April Kalends, the first of April.*
apud, prep. with acc., *near, with, among, in the presence of.*
Aquilēia, ae, f., *Aquileia,* a town at the head of the Adriatic.
Aquītānī, ōrum, m., *people of Aquitania, the Aquitanians.*
Aquītānia, ae, f., *Aquitania,* the southwestern division of Gaul.
Arar, aris, m. (acc. Ararim), *the Arar,* now the Saône, tributary of the Rhone.
arbitrium, ī, n., *judgment, will.*
arbitror, ārī, ātus sum, dep., *judge, think.*
arcessō, ere, īvī, ītum, *summon, invite.*
Ariovistus, ī, m., *Ariovistus,* a king of the Germans.
arma, ōrum, n., *arms, weapons.*
ars, artis, f., *skill, art, science, pursuit.*
Arvernī, ōrum, m., *the Arverni,* a Gallic people.
arx, arcis, f., *citadel, stronghold.*
Athēnae, ārum, f., *Athens,* a city of Greece.
atque (or āc), conj. (ad + que), *and too, and also;* with words of comparison, *as, than.*

attentē, adv. (attentus), *attentively, diligently.*
attentus, a, um, *attentive.*
attingō, ere, tigī, tactum (ad + tangō), *touch, border on, reach.*
auctōritās, ātis, f., *authority, influence, power.*
audacter (or audāciter), adv. (audax), *boldly, courageously.*
audax, ācis (audeō), *bold, audacious, daring.*
audeō, ēre, ausus sum, semi-dep. (N. 81), *dare, venture.*
audiens, part. as adj. (audiō), *obedient.*
audiō, īre, īvī, ītum, *hear, hear of.*
auferō, ferre, abstulī, ablātum (ab + ferō), *bear away, remove.*
Aulus, ī, m., *Aulus,* a Roman personal name.
aut, conj., *or;* aut .... aut, *either .... or.*
autem, conj., *but, moreover, however.*
auxilium, ī, n., *aid, assistance;* (plur.) auxiliaries, *auxiliary troops.*
avus, ī, m., *grandfather.*

B.

barbarus, a, um, *foreign, strange;*
barbarī, ōrum, m., *barbarians.*
beātus, a, um, *happy, fortunate.*
Belgae, ārum, m., *the Belgae,* a people of Northern Gaul.
bellicōsus, a, um (bellum), *warlike, eager for war.*
bellō, āre, āvī, ātum (bellum), *carry on war, fight.*
bellum, ī, n., *war.*
bene, adv. (bonus), *well, successfully.*
beneficium, ī, n. (bene + faciō), *favor, kindness.*
Bibracte, is, n., *Bibracte,* the chief city of the Aedui.
biduum, ī, n. (bis + diēs), *space of two days.*
biennium, ī, n. (bis + annus), *space of two years.*

Boiī, ōrum, m. *the Boii*, a wandering people of Germany and Gaul.
bonus, a, um, *good, friendly, well-disposed;* bona, ōrum, n., *goods, property.*
brevis, e, *short, brief.*
Britannia, ae, f., *the island of Britain.*

C.

cadō, ere, cecidī, cāsum, *fall, perish.*
caedō, ere, cecīdī, caesum, *cut, kill.*
Caesar, aris, m., *Caius Julius Caesar*, a famous Roman general, conqueror of Gaul.
Cāius, ī, m., *Caius*, a Roman personal name.
calamitās, ātis, f., *calamity, disaster, loss.*
calcar, āris, n. (calx, *heel*), *spur.*
Calendae, see Kalendae.
capiō, ere, cēpī, captum, *take, seize, select, adopt, reach.*
caput, itis, n., *head, capital* (chief city).
carrus, ī, m., *cart, wagon.*
Carthāgō, see Karthāgō.
cārus, a, um, *dear, beloved, precious.*
Cassiānus, a, um (Cassius), *pertaining to Cassius, Cassian;* bellō Cassiānō, *in the war with Cassius.*
Cassius, ī, m., *Cassius*, a Roman name; *Lucius Cassius*, the consul slain by the Helvetii.
castellum, ī, n. (dimin. of castrum), *fort, redoubt.*
Casticus, ī, m., *Casticus*, a chief of the Sequani.
castra, ōrum, n. (sing. castrum, *fort*), *camp, encampment.*
cāsus, ūs, m. (cadō), *that which befalls, chance, misfortune, accident.*
Catamantaloedēs, is, m., *Catamantaloedes*, father of Casticus.
Caturigēs, um, m., *the Caturiges*, a Gallic tribe.

causa, ae, f., *cause, reason, excuse;* causam dīcere, *to plead a case;* causā (with a gen. preceding), *for the sake (of).*
celer, eris, ere, *swift, quick.*
celeriter, adv. (celer), *swiftly, quickly.*
cēlō, āre, āvī, ātum, *hide, conceal.* N. 141, Remark 1.
Celtae, ārum, m., *the Celts, Gauls,* a people of central Gaul.
Centrōnēs, um, m., *the Centrones,* a Gallic tribe.
centuriō, ōnis, m. (centum), *centurion,* captain of 100.
certus, a, um, *sure, certain;* certiōrem facere, *to inform.*
cibārius, a, um (cibus, *food*), *pertaining to food;* cibāria, ōrum, n., *provisions, supplies.*
Cicerō, ōnis, m., *Marcus Tullius Cicero*, a famous Roman orator.
circiter, adv. of degree, *about, nearly.*
circum, prep. with acc., *about, around, near, in the neighborhood of.*
circumdūcō, ere, xī, ctum, (circum + dūcō), *lead around, draw around.*
circumveniō, īre, vēnī, ventum (circum + veniō), *come around, surround, deceive, cheat.*
cis, prep. with acc., *on this side of.*
Cisalpīnus, a, um (cis + Alpēs), *on this side of the Alps* (south of the Alps), *Cisalpine.*
citerior, us (cis; N. 34), *on this side, hither.*
citrā, prep. with acc. (cis), *on this side of.*
cīvis, is, m. and f., *citizen, fellow-citizen.*
cīvitās, ātis, f. (cīvis), *state, citizenship.*
clārus, a, um, *bright, clear, loud.*
claudō, ere, sī, sum, *shut, close;* claudere agmen, *close the line of march, bring up the rear.*
cliens, tis, m. and f., *dependant, subject, client.*

Cnēius, I, m., *Cnēius*, a Roman personal name.
coëmō, ere, ēmī, emptum (con + emō), *buy, buy up.*
coepī, isse, def. vb. (N. 91, 1), *began, have begun;* part. coeptus.
cognoscō, ere, nōvī, nitum (con + noscō), *become acquainted with, ascertain, find out, know.* N. 91, 2, Rem.
cōgō, ere, coēgī, coactum (con + agō), *bring together, collect, force, compel.*
cohors, tis, f., *cohort,* the tenth part of a legion.
cohortor, ārī, ātus sum, dep. vb. (con + hortor), *encourage, exhort.*
collātus, part. of conferō.
collis, is, m., *hill.*
colloquor, I, cūtus sum, dep. vb. (con + loquor), *speak with, converse, confer.*
colō, ere, uī, cultum, *till, cultivate, honor.*
combūrō, ere, bussī, bustum, (con + ūrō, *burn*), *burn up.*
commeātus, ūs, m. (commeō), *means of transport, supplies, provisions.*
commeō, āre, āvī, ātum (con + meō, *go*), *go back and forth, visit.*
committō, ere, mīsī, missum (con + mittō), *join, connect;* proelium committere, *to join battle, begin an engagement.* Also, *cause, give occasion.*
commoveō, ēre, mōvī, mōtum (con + moveō), *move greatly, excite, alarm.*
commūniō, īre, īvī, ītum (con + mūniō), *fortify on all sides, intrench, secure.*
comparō, āre, āvī, ātum (con + parō), *make ready, get, procure, bring together.*
compleō, ēre, ēvī, ētum (con + pleō, *fill*), *fill up, finish, complete;* montem, *cover.*
complūrēs, ia (con + plūrēs), *several (together), very many.*

comportō, āre, āvī, ātum (con + portō), *bring together, collect.*
con, inseparable prefix, *together* (or adds emphasis).
cōnātum, I, n., also cōnātus, ūs, m. (cōnor), *attempt, undertaking.*
concēdō, ere, cessī, cessum, *yield, grant, concede.*
concidō, ere, cidī (con + cadō), *fall, perish.*
concīdō, ere, cīdī, cīsum (con + caedō), *cut to pieces, cut down, kill.*
conciliō, āre, āvī, ātum (concilium), *unite, win, procure, secure.*
concilium, I, n., *council, assembly.*
concursus, ūs, m. (con + currō), *running together, onset, attack.*
condemnō, āre, āvī, ātum (con + damnō), *sentence, condemn.*
condūcō, ere, xī, ctum (con + dūcō), *lead together, collect, hire.*
conferō, ferre, tulī, collātum (con + ferō), *bring together, collect;* sē conferre, *to betake themselves.*
confertus, a, um, *close, crowded.*
conficiō, ere, fēcī, fectum (con + faciō), *finish, accomplish, exhaust.*
confīrmō, āre, āvī, ātum (firmus), *make firm, establish, assure, encourage.*
congredior, I, gressus sum, dep. vb. (con + gradior, *go*), *meet* (with), *contend, "come on."*
conjiciō, ere, jēcī, jectum (con + jaciō), *throw together, hurl, put.*
conjungō, ere, xī, ctum (con + jungō), *join together, unite.*
conjūrātiō, ōnis, f. (conjūrō), *conspiracy.*
conjūrō, āre, āvī, ātum (con + jūrō), *swear together, conspire.*
cōnor, ārī, ātus sum, dep. vb., *endeavor, try, attempt.*
consanguineus, a, um (con + sanguis, *blood*), *related by blood;* as a noun, *kindred, relatives.*
consciscō, ere, scīvī, scītum (con + sciō), *approve;* sibi mortem, *to commit suicide.*

conscrībō, ere, psī, ptum (con + scrībō), *write in a list, enrol, enlist, levy.*
consequor, I, cūtus sum (con + sequor), dep. vb., *follow after, overtake, obtain.*
consīdō, ere, sēdī, sessum (con + sīdō, *settle*), *settle, encamp.*
consilium, I, n., *counsel, advice, plan, design, purpose, wisdom, council of war.*
consimilis, e (con + similis), *quite like, very similar.*
consistō, ere, stitī, stitum (con + sistō), *take a stand, halt, depend on, consist in.*
conspectus, ūs, m. (conspiciō), *full view, sight, presence.*
conspiciō, ere, spexī, spectum (con + speciō, *look*), *behold, look at, perceive, see.*
constituō, ere, uī, ūtum (con + statuō) *place together, establish, determine, erect.*
constitūtus, a, um, part. as adj., *established, appointed.*
constō, āre, stitī, stātum (con + stō), *stand firm, agree; constat,* impers., *it is evident, settled, "stands to reason."*
consuescō, ere, suēvī, suētum (con + suescō, *be wont*), *become accustomed, be wont;* consuēvī, *I am accustomed.* N. 91, 2, Rem.
consul, ulis, m., *consul,* one of two chief magistrates at Rome, elected annually.
consūmō, ere, sumpsī, sumptum (con + sūmō), *spend, destroy, consume.*
contendō, ere, dī, tum (con + tendō, *stretch, strain*), *strive, hasten, contend, fight.*
contentus, a, um (contineō), *content, satisfied.*
continenter, adv. (contineō), *uninterruptedly, without cessation.*
contineō, ēre, uī, tentum (con + teneō), *hold together, hem in, bound.*

contrā, prep. with acc., *against, opposite.*
conveniō, īre, vēnī, ventum (con + veniō), *come together, assemble, meet;* convenit, impers., *it is fitting, agreed.*
convocō, āre, āvī, ātum (con + vocō), *call together, summon.*
cōpia, ae, f., *plenty, abundance;* cōpiae, ārum, f., *forces, troops, supplies, wealth.*
Corinthus, I, f., *Corinth,* a city in Greece.
cornū, ūs, n., *horn, wing* (of an army); ā sinistrō cornū, *on the left wing.*
corōna, ae, f., *crown, wreath.*
corpus, oris, n., *body, person.*
Crassus, I, m., *Crassus,* a Roman name.
crēber, bra, brum, *frequent, numerous.*
crēdō, ere, didī, ditum, *trust, believe.*
cremō, āre, āvī, ātum, *burn.*
creō, āre, āvī, ātum, *create, make, elect, appoint.*
culpō, āre, āvī, ātum, *blame.*
cultus, ūs, m. (colō), *culture, luxury, civilization.*
cum, prep. with abl., *with, in company with.*
cum = quum.
cupiditās, ātis, f. (cupidus), *eagerness, desire, ambition.*
cupidus, a, um, *eager, desirous, fond.*
cupiō, ere, īvī, ītum, *desire, long for, wish.*
cūr, interrog. adv., *why? for what purpose?*
cūra, ae, f., *care, regard, attention.*
cūrō, āre, āvī, ātum (cūra), *care for, manage, attend to;* with gerundive, *cause to be done; as,* pontem faciendum cūrāre, *cause a bridge to be built.*
currō, ere, cucurrī, cursum, *run.*
currus, ūs, m. (currō), *chariot, wagon.*

GENERAL VOCABULARY. 275

cursus, ūs, m. (currō), *running, speed, course.*
custōs, ōdis, m. and f., *keeper, guard.*

D.

damnō, āre, āvī, ātum, *condemn, sentence.*
dē, prep. with abl., *from, down from, of, concerning, about (of), during, in;* dē secundā vigiliā, *in the second watch.* In compounds, *down, away.*
dea, ae, f., *goddess.*
dēbeō, ēre, uī, itum (dē + habeō), *owe, ought, must.*
dēcēdō, ere, cessī, cessum (dē + cēdō, *go away*), *retire, withdraw, depart, die.*
dēdō, ere, didī, ditum (dē + dō), *give up, surrender, deliver up.*
dēdūcō, ere, xī, ctum (dē + dūcō), *lead down, withdraw, conduct.*
dēfendō, ere, dī, sum (dē + fendō, only in compounds), *ward off, defend, protect.*
dēfensor, ōris, m. (dēfendō), *defender.*
dējectus, a, um (dējiciō), part. as adj., *downcast, disappointed.*
dēleō, ēre, ēvī, ētum, *destroy, overthrow.*
dēlīberō, āre, āvī, ātum, *weigh, consider, deliberate.*
dēligō, ere, lēgī, lectum (dē + legō, *select*), *choose out, select.*
dēmonstrō, āre, āvī, ātum (dē + monstrō), *point out, show, declare.*
dēpopulor, ārī, ātus sum, dep. vb. (dē + populor), *plunder, lay waste, devastate.*
dēprecātor, ōris, m. (dē + precor, *pray*), *intercessor, mediator.*
dēsistō, ere, stitī, stitum (dē + sistō, *stand*), *cease, desist.*
dēspiciō, ere, spexī, spectum (dē + speciō, *look*), *look down on, despise.*
deus, ī, m., *god, deity.*

dexter, tra, trum, *on the right hand, right;* dextra (manus, understood), *right hand.*
dīcō, ere, xī, ctum, *say, mention, tell, appoint;* causam dīcere, *to plead a case.*
dictiō, ōnis, f. (dīcō), *speaking, pleading.*
dictum, ī, n. (dīcō), *word, command;* dictō audiens, *obedient.*
didicī, perf. of discō.
diēs, ēī, m. (sometimes f.), *day, time;* multō diē, *late in the day;* diem ex diē, *day after day.*
differō, ferre, distulī, dīlātum (dis + ferō), *differ.*
difficilis, e (dis + facilis), *difficult, difficult to pass.*
difficultās, ātis, f. (difficilis), *trouble, difficulty.*
dignus, a, um, *worthy, deserving.*
dīligens, tis, *diligent, attentive, careful.*
dīligenter, adv. (dīligens), *with care, punctually.*
dīmittō, ere, mīsī, missum (dis + mittō), *send different ways, dismiss, send out.*
dis (or dī), inseparable prefix, *apart, in various directions, hither and thither.*
discēdō, ere, cessī, cessum (dis + cēdō), *depart, go away.*
discō, ere, didicī, *learn.*
dispōnō, ere, posuī, positum (dis + pōnō), *place here and there, distribute, station.*
dissimilis, e, *unlike, dissimilar.*
dītior, see dīves. N. 36, *a.*
diū, -tius, -tissimē, *for a long time, long.*
dīves, dītior, dītissimus, *rich.*
Divicō, ōnis, m., *Divico,* a Helvetian noble.
dīvidō, ere, vīsī, vīsum, *divide, separate.*
dīvīsus (dīvidō), part. as adj., *divided.*
Divitiacus, ī, m., *Divitiacus,* brother of Dumnorix, an Aeduan, friend of Caesar.

dō, dare, dedī, datum, *give, grant, permit, allow.*
doceō, ēre, uī, ctum, *teach, inform, show, instruct.*
dolor, ōris, m., *pain, grief.*
dolus, ī, m., *cunning, deceit, fraud.*
domus, ūs (ī), f., *house, home;* domī, *at home.*
dōnum, ī, n. (dō), *gift, present.*
dubitātiō, ōnis, f. (dubitō), *doubt, hesitation.*
dubitō, āre, āvī, ātum, *doubt, hesitate* (with inf.).
dubius, a, um, *doubtful, uncertain.*
dūcō, ere, xī, ctum, *lead, guide, bring, reckon, think, put off;* in mātrimōnium, *marry.*
dum, conj., *while, until, provided.*
Dumnorix, igis, m., *Dumnorix,* brother of Divitiacus, an Aeduan.
duo, ae, o, num. adj., *two.*
duplex, icis (duo + plicō, *fold*), *twofold, double.*
dux, ducis, m. and f. (dūcō), *leader, guide, chief.*

E.

ē (or ex), *out of, from.*
ēdūcō, ere, xī, ctum (ē + dūcō), *lead forth, draw out.*
effēminō, āre, āvī, ātum (ex + fēmina, *woman*), *make womanish, weaken, enervate.*
efferō, ferre, extulī, ēlātum (ex + ferō), *carry* or *bear forth, carry out, lift up, elate.*
ego, meī, pers. pron., *I.*
ēgredior, ī, gressus sum, dep. vb. (ē + gradior, *go*), *go forth* or *out, depart.*
ējiciō, ere, jēcī, jectum (ē + jaciō), *cast out, drive forth, expel;* sē ējicere, *rush forth.*
ējusmodī (or ējus modī), gen. of is + modus (N. 121), *of that sort* or *kind, such.*
ēmittō, ere, mīsī, missum (ē + mittō), *send forth* or *out, let go, cast.*

ēnuntiō, āre, āvī, ātum (ē + nuntiō), *report, announce, declare.*
eō, īre, īvī, itum, irr., *go, march.*
eō, adv. (abl. of is), *thither;* as abl. of degree of diff., quō magis... eō minus, *the more ... the less.*
eōdem, adv. (abl. of īdem), *to the same place.*
eques, itis, m. (equus), *horseman;* (plur.) equitēs, um, *cavalry, knights.*
equitātus, ūs, m. (equus), *cavalry* (in a *body*).
equus, ī, m., *horse.*
ēripiō, ere, uī, reptum (ē + rapiō), *snatch away, take away, rescue.*
ēruptiō, ōnis, f. (ē + rumpō, *break*), *bursting forth, sortie, sally.*
et, conj., *and, also, even;* et ... et, *both ... and.*
etiam, conj. (et + jam), *and also, even, indeed, yet, besides;* sed etiam, *but also.*
etsī, conj. (et + sī), *even if, although.*
exemplum, ī, n., *example.*
exeō, īre, īvī, itum (ex + eō), *go forth* or *out, march out.*
exercitus, ūs, m. (exerceō, *train*), *trained army, army, infantry.*
existimō, āre, āvī, ātum (ex + aestimō, *regard*), *judge, think, consider.*
expedītus, a, um (ex + pēs, *foot*), literally, *freed* (from a snare), *unencumbered, light-armed, without baggage, free from obstacles, handy, passable.*
explōrātor, ōris, m. (explōrō, *search out*), *spy, scout.*
expugnō, āre, āvī, ātum (ex + pugnō), *take by storm, storm, capture.*
exsequor, ī, cūtus sum, dep. vb. (ex + sequor), *follow out, finish, assert, maintain.*
exspectō, āre, āvī, ātum (ex + spectō), *look for, wait for, await, delay, wait to see.*
exterus, a, um (ex), more common in the comp. and sup., **exterior,**

GENERAL VOCABULARY. 277

extrēmus (or extimus), *outer, foreign.*
extrā, prep. with acc., also adv., *on the outside of, beyond, besides.*
extrēmus, a, um (exterus), *outermost, farthest, most remote, extreme, last.*
exūrō, ere, ussī, ustum (ex + ūrō, *burn*), *burn up, consume.*

F.

fābula, ae, f. (for, *speak*), *story.*
facilis, e (faciō), *easy* (to do), *easy, practicable.*
facile, adv. (facilis), *easily, readily.*
faciō, ere, fēcī, factum ; (pass.) fīō, fierī, factus sum, *make, do, perform, construct;* cōpiam facere, *furnish a supply;* certiōrem facere, *to inform.*
factiō, ōnis, f. (faciō), *faction, party.*
facultās, ātis, f. (faciō), *ability, opportunity, abundance, supply;* (plur.) *resources.*
familia, ae, f., *household, retinue of slaves or dependents, family.*
fēlix, Icis, *happy.*
ferē, adv., *almost, nearly, for the most part, generally.*
ferō, ferre, tulī, lātum, irr., *bear, carry, bring, endure, produce.*
ferus, a, um, *wild, barbarous, cruel.*
fidēlis, e (fidēs), *trusty, faithful.*
fidēs, eī, f. (fīdō), *trust, confidence, faith, pledge, promise, security, protection.*
fīdō, ere, fīsus sum, semi-dep., *trust.*
fīlia, ae, f., *daughter.*
fīlius, I, m., *son.*
fīniō, Ire, īvī, ītum (fīnis), *limit, bound.*
fīnis, is, m., *end, limit, boundary;* (plur.) *territory, country.*
fīnitimus, a, um (fīnis), *bordering upon, adjoining;* as a noun (plur.), *neighbors.*

fīō, fierī, factus sum, irr., pass. of faciō, *be made, become; fit,* impers., *it happens;* certior fīō, *I am informed.*
firmus, a, um, *firm, strong, powerful, valiant.*
flāgitō, ārĕ, āvī, ātum, *demand* (earnestly or repeatedly), *dun.*
fleō, ēre, ēvī, ētum, *weep, cry, lament.*
flētus, ūs, m., *weeping, tears.*
flōrens, tis (flōs), *flourishing, prosperous.*
flōs, ōris, m., *flower.*
flūmen, inis, n. (fluō), *river.*
fluō, ere, xī, xum, *flow.*
fore = futūrus esse ; forem = essem.
fortis, e (ferō), *strong, brave, valiant.*
fortiter, adv. (fortis), *bravely, courageously.*
fortitūdō, inis, f. (fortis), *bravery, fortitude.*
fortūna, ae, f. (fors, *chance*), *fortune, chance.*
fossa, ae, f. (fodiō, *dig*), *ditch.*
frangō, ere, frēgī, fractum, *break, crush, subdue.*
frāter, tris, m., *brother, ally.*
frētus, a, um, *relying upon, depending on.* N. 151, *b.*
frūmentārius, a, um (frūmentum), *belonging to corn, abounding in corn ;* rēs frūmentāria, *corn-supply, supplies.*
frūmentum, I, n., *corn, grain.*
fuga, ae, f., *flight, rout.*
fugiō, ere, fūgī, fugitum, *flee, escape, shun.*
fundō, ere, fūdī, fūsum, *pour out, scatter, rout.*

G.

Gabīnius, I, m., *Gabinius,* a Roman name.
Gallia, ae. f., *Gaul,* including Belgium, France, and the greater part of Switzerland.

Gallicus, a, um, *Gallic.*
Gallus, ī, m., *a Gaul;* as a noun, Gallī, *the Gauls.*
Garumna, ae, m., *the Garonne, a river of Gaul.*
gaudeō, ēre, gāvīsus sum, semi-dep., *rejoice, be glad.*
Genēva (or Genāva), ae, f., *Geneva, a city of the Allobroges.*
genus, eris, n., *birth, race, kind.*
Germānia, ae, f., *Germany.*
Germānus, a, um, *German;* as a noun, Germānī, *the Germans.*
gerō, ere, gessī, gestum, *bear, carry on* (war), *perform.*
gladius, ī, m., *sword.*
glōria, ae, f., *glory, fame.*
glōrior, ārī, ātus sum (glōria), dep., *boast, glory.*
Grāiocelī, ōrum, m., *the Graioceli, a people of Hither Gaul.*
grātia, ae, f. (grātus), *favor, esteem, popularity, influence, friendship;* grātiā (abl.), *for the sake (of).*
grātulor, ārī, ātus sum, dep. (grātus), *congratulate, wish joy.*
grātus, a, um, *grateful, agreeable, acceptable.*
gravis, e, *heavy, severe.*
graviter, adv. (gravis), *heavily, severely.*

H.

habeō, ēre, uī, itum, *have, hold, regard, consider, deliver* (a speech).
Harūdēs, um, m., *the Harudes, a German tribe.*
Helvētius, a, um, *Helvetian;* as a noun, Helvētiī, ōrum, *the Helvetians,* people of Helvetia (Switzerland).
hīberna, ōrum, n. (hiems), *winter-quarters* (really an adj., castra being understood).
hīc, haec, hōc, dem. pron., *this, he, she, it, the latter, as follows.*
hiemō, āre, āvī, ātum (hiems), *pass the winter, winter.*
hiems, emis, f., *winter.*

Hispānia, ae, f., *Spain.*
homō, inis, m. and f., *a human being* (man or woman), *man, person.* (See vir.)
honor, ōris, m., *honor, esteem, office.*
hōra, ae, f., *hour.*
hortor, ārī, ātus sum, dep. *exhort, encourage, urge.*
hostis, is, m. and f., *enemy* (public); inimīcus, *personal enemy.*
hūmānitās, ātis, f., *humanity, kindness, refinement, politeness.*

I.

ibi, adv. (is), *there, in that place.*
Iccius, ī, m., *Iccius,* a chief of the Remi.
īdem, eadem, idem, dem. pron. (is + dem, emphatic), *the same.*
idōneus, a, um, *fit, suitable.*
Īdūs, uum, f. plur., *the Ides,* the 15th of March, May, July, October; 13th of the other months.
ignārus, a, um, *ignorant, inexperienced.*
ignāvus, a, um, *idle, cowardly.*
ignis, is, m., *fire.*
ignoscō, ere, nōvī, nōtum (in, not + noscō), *overlook, pardon, forgive.*
illātus, part. of inferō.
ille, illa, illud, dem. pron., *that* (yonder), *he, she, it, the former, the well-known* or *famous.*
immortālis, e (in, *not* + mortālis), *immortal, eternal.*
impedīmentum, ī, n. (impediō), *hindrance;* (plur.) *heavy-baggage.*
impediō, īre, īvī, ītum (in + pēs), *entangle, hinder, impede.*
impedītus, a, um (impediō), part. as adj., *hindered, impeded, obstructed.*
impendeō, ēre (in + pendeō, *hang*), *overhang, impend, threaten.*
imperātor, ōris, m. (imperō), *commander-in-chief, general, chief.*
imperītus, a, um (in, *not* + perītus, *skilled*), *unskilled, ignorant, unacquainted with.*

GENERAL VOCABULARY. 279

imperium, I, n. (imperō), command, authority, order, power, government, empire.
imperō, āre, āvī, ātum, command, order, rule over, levy (troops).
impetrō, āre, āvī, ātum, accomplish, effect, obtain by request.
impetus, ūs, m., attack, onset, violence.
implōrō, āre, āvī, ātum, entreat, implore, beg for.
impōnō, ere, posuī, positum (in + pōnō), place on, impose on.
importō, āre, āvī, ātum (in + portō), bring in, import.
imprōvīsō, adv. (in, not + prōvideō, foresee), on a sudden, unexpectedly.
īmus, see inferus.
in, prep. with acc. and abl. (1) With acc. (answering question *Whither?*), into, against, towards.; in reliquum tempus, *for the future;* in Santonōs, *into the country of the Santoni.* (2) With abl. (answering question *Where?*), in, on, among, over.
incendō, ere, dī, sum, set fire to, burn, inflame, excite.
incertus, a, um (in, not + certus), uncertain, doubtful.
incipiō, ere, cēpī, ceptum (in + capiō), take up, begin, commence; supplies the present-stem tenses of coepī.
incitō, āre, āvī, ātum, hasten, rouse, incite, spur on.
incolō, ere, coluī (in + colō), dwell, inhabit.
incommodum, I, n. (in, not + commodum, advantage), misfortune, disaster.
incrēdibilis, e (in, not + crēdō), incredible.
inde, adv. (is), from that place, thence.
indicium, I, n. (index, informer), information; per indicium = per indicēs.
indīcō, ere, xī, ctum (in + dīcō), declare, proclaim.

indignus, a, um (in, not + dignus), unworthy, wrong.
indūcō, ere, xī, ctum (in + dūcō), bring on or in, move, induce, influence.
ineō, īre, īvī, itum (in + eō), go into, enter, begin; consilium ineō, *I form a plan.*
infēlix, īcis (in, not + fēlix), unhappy.
inferō, ferre, intulī, illātum (in + ferō), bring in (upon, or against); signa inferre, advance (to the attack); bellum inferre, to make war on; spē illātā, hope being inspired.
inferus, a, um, below; Comp. inferior, lower, inferior; Sup. infimus (īmus), lowest, lowest part of.
influō, ere, xī, xum (in + fluō), flow into, flow, empty into.
infrā, prep. with acc.; also an adv., below.
ingens, tis, huge, vast, mighty.
inimīcus, a, um (in, not + amīcus), unfriendly, hostile; as a noun, an enemy (personal).
initium, I, n. (ineō), beginning.
injūria, ae, f. (in, not + jūs), injury, wrong; injūriā (abl.), unjustly.
injustus, a, um (in, not + justus), unjust, wrong.
inopīnans, tis (in, not + opīnor, think), not expecting, unawares.
inquam, def. (N. 91, a), say.
insidiae, ārum, f. (in + sedeō, sit), ambush, plot, treachery, stratagem.
insigne, is, n. (insignis), mark, badge; (plur.) insignia, badges of office.
insignis, e (in + signum), marked, distinguished, noted, remarkable.
instituō, ere, uī, ūtum (in + statuō, establish), establish, arrange, draw up (in battle array), bring up, train, educate.
institūtum, I, n. (instituō), custom, practice.
instruō, ere, xī, ctum (in + struō, build), construct, arrange, draw up (in battle array).

insula, ae, f., *island.*
integer, gra, grum (in, *not* + tangō), *sound, fresh.*
intelligō, ere, lexī, lectum (inter
   + legō), *perceive, understand,
   know.*
intentus, a, um, *intent, attentive.*
inter, prep. with acc., *between,
   among, during;* inter sē amant,
   they love each other.
intercēdō, ere, cessī, cessum
   (inter + cēdō, *go*), *go between,
   intervene.*
interdiū, adv. (inter + diēs), *by
   day, in the day-time.*
intereā, adv. (inter + is), *in the
   meantime, meanwhile.*
interficiō, ere, fēcī, fectum (inter
   + faciō), *kill, slay.*
intermittō, ere, mīsī, missum
   (inter + mittō), *cease, interrupt,
   discontinue, let pass.*
interneciō, ōnis, f. (inter + necō,
   kill), *massacre.*
intrā, prep. with acc.; also adv.,
   within.
inveniō, īre, vēnī, ventum (in +
   veniō), *come upon, find, discover,
   invent.*
invītō, āre, āvī, ātum, *invite, summon.*
invītus, a, um, *unwilling;* mē invītō, *without my consent.*
ipse, a, um, dem. pron., *self, very,
   he, she, it.*
īrātus, a, um (īra, *anger*), *angry,
   enraged.*
is, ea, id, dem. pron., *that, this, he,
   she, it.*
iste, a, ud, dem. pron., *that* (near
   you), *that* (of yours).
ita, adv. (is), *in that manner, so, to
   such a degree;* ita ut (utī), *just as.*
Italia, ae, f., *Italy.*
itaque, conj. (ita + que), *and so,
   therefore, accordingly.* N. 195, 5.
item, adv. (is), *likewise, also.*
iter, itineris, n. (eō), *way, road,
   journey, march, pass;* iter magnum, *forced march.*

J.

jaciō, ere, jēcī, jactum, *throw,
   hurl.*
jam, adv., *now, already.*
jubeō, ēre, jussī, jussum, *order,
   bid, command.*
jūdex, icis, m. (jūs + dīcō), *judge.*
jūdicium, ī, n. (jūdex), *court, trial,
   judgment, decision.*
jūdicō, āre, āvī, ātum (jūdex),
   judge, decide.
jugum, ī, n. (jungō), *yoke; a yoke
   formed by two upright spears sup-
   porting a third (horizontal), under
   which a defeated army was made to
   pass in token of subjection; ridge
   of a mountain or hill.*
Jūlius, ī, m., *Julius,* a Roman name;
   also, as an adj., *pertaining to* (*of*)
   July.
jūmentum, ī, n. (jungō), *beast of
   burden* (ox, horse).
jungō, ere, nxī, nctum, *join, connect.*
Jūra, ae, m., *Jura,* a mountain-
   chain extending from the Rhine to
   the Rhone.
jūrō, āre, āvī, ātum (jūs), *take an
   oath, swear, promise under oath.*
jūs, jūris, n., *law, right.*
jusjūrandum, jūrisjūrandī,
   (jūs + jūrō), *oath.*
justus, a, um (jūs), *just, right.*

K.

Kalendae (or Calendae), ārum,
   f., *the Calends,* first day of each
   month.
Karthāgō (or Carthāgō), inis, f.,
   Carthage, a city of North Africa.

L.

Labiēnus, ī, m., *Labienus,* Caesar's
   ablest lieutenant.
labor, ōris, m., *toil, labor, hard-
   ship.*

GENERAL VOCABULARY. 281

lacus, ūs, m., *lake.*
laetor, ārī, ātus sum, dep. (laetus, *glad*), *rejoice, exult.*
lapis, idis, m., *stone.*
largītiō, ōnis, f. (largior, *bestow gifts*), *liberality, generosity, bribery.*
lātitūdō, inis, f. (lātus), *breadth, width.*
Latovīcī (or Latobrīgī), ōrum, m., *the Latovīci*, a Gallic people.
lātus, part. of ferō.
lātus, a, um, *wide, broad, spacious.*
laudō, āre, āvī, ātum (laus), *praise, commend.*
laus, laudis, f., *praise, glory.*
laxō, āre, āvī, ātum, *loosen, open, expand;* manipulōs laxāre, *to open the ranks.*
lēgātiō, ōnis, f., *embassy, legation.*
lēgātus, ī, m., *ambassador, legate, lieutenant.*
legiō, ōnis, f., *legion,* consisting of ten cohorts of foot-soldiers and 300 cavalry ; the total number varied from 4,200 to 6,000.
legō, ere, lēgī, lectum, *choose, select, read.*
Lemannus, ī, m., *Lake Geneva.*
lēnitās, ātis, f. (lēnis, *gentle*), *gentleness, smoothness.*
leō, ōnis, m., *lion.*
levis, e, *light.*
lex, lēgis, f., *law.*
līber, era, erum, *free.*
liber, brī, m., *book.*
līberē, adv. (līber), *freely, unreservedly.*
līberī, ōrum, m., *children.*
līberō, āre, āvī, ātum (līber), *make free, release, liberate.*
lībertās, ātis, f. (līber), *liberty, freedom.*
licet, ēre, uit, impers., *it is allowed* or *permitted;* mihi licet īre, *I may go.*
Lingonēs, um, m., *the Lingones*, a Gallic people.
lingua, ae, f., *tongue, language.*
linter, tris, f., *boat, skiff.*

littera (or lītera), f., (sing.) *letter* (of the alphabet); (plur.) *letter* (that is, an *epistle*), *document.*
locus, ī, m., (plur.) loca, ōrum, n., *place, situation, condition.*
locūtus, part. of loquor.
Londīnium, ī, n., *London.*
longē, adv. (longus), *by far, far.*
longitūdō, inis, f. (longus), *length.*
longus, a, um, *long, distant.*
loquor, ī, locūtus sum, dep., *speak, talk, tell, say.*
Lūcīlius, ī, m., *Lucilius*, a Roman name.
Lūcius, ī, m., *Lucius*, a Roman name.
lūna, ae, f., *moon.*
lux, lūcis, f., *light;* prīmā lūce, *at daybreak.*

M.

magis, adv. (magnus), *more, rather.*
magister, trī, m. (mag-, root of magnus), *master, teacher.*
magistrātus, ūs, m. (magister), *office of magistrate, magistracy, magistrate.*
magnitūdō, inis, f. (magnus), *greatness, size.*
magnopere, adv. (magnō + opere), *very much, greatly, exceedingly.*
magnus, a, um (comp. mājor; sup. maximus), *great, large;* iter magnum, *forced march.*
mājor (with or without nātū), *older* (N. 36, b), plur. as noun, *ancestors, elders.*
maleficium, ī, n. (male + faciō), *wrong-doing, crime, mischief.*
mālō, malle, māluī, irr. (magis + volō), *choose rather, prefer.*
malus, a, um (comp. pējor; sup. pessimus), *bad, evil.*
mandō, āre, āvī, ātum (manus + dō), *put into one's hands, commit, consign, command;* fugae sē, *to betake one's self to flight.*
maneō, ēre, mansī, mansum, *stay, remain, abide.*

manipulus, i, m., *maniple*, a company of soldiers, three of which formed a cohort.
manus, ūs, f., *hand, band* (of troops).
Marcus, i, m., *Marcus*, a Roman name.
mare, is, n., *sea.*
māter, tris, f., *mother.*
mātrimōnium, i, n. (māter), *marriage*; in mātr. dūcere, *to marry.*
Mātrona, ae, m., *the Matrona* (now the Marne), a river in Gaul.
mātūrō, āre, āvī, ātum, *hasten, make haste.*
maximē, adv. (maximus), *very greatly, especially, exceedingly.*
maximus, sup. of magnus.
medius, a, um, *middle, midway, in the middle of*; mediō in colle, *half-way up the hill.*
melior, comp. of bonus.
meminī, isse, def., *remember, bear in mind.* N. 91, 2.
memor, oris, *mindful.*
memoria, ae, f. (memor), *memory, recollection.*
mens, mentis, f., *mind, reason, judgment.*
mensa, ae, f., *table.*
mensis, is, m., *month.*
mercātor, ōris, m., *merchant, trader.*
mercēs, ēdis, f., *pay, wages, bribe.*
mereor, ērī, itus sum, dep., *deserve, be worthy of, earn.*
merīdiēs, ēī, m. (medius + diēs), *midday, noon, south.*
Messāla, ae, m., *Messala,* a Roman name.
metus, ūs, m., *fear, dread.*
meus, a, um, poss. pron. (ego, meī), *my, mine.*
mīles, itis, m., *soldier* (infantry).
mille, adj. indecl., *thousand.*
mille (nom. and acc. sing.), n., *thousand*; (plur.) mīllia (or mīlia), um, n., *thousands*; tria mīllia passuum, *three miles.*
minimē, adv. (minimus), *least, by no means*; minimē saepe, *very seldom.*

minimus, sup. of parvus, *least.*
minor, comp. of parvus, *smaller, less.*
minus, adv., comp. of parum, *less*; sī minus, *if not.*
mīror, ārī, ātus sum, dep. (mīrus), *wonder at, admire.*
mīrus, a, um, *wonderful, strange.*
miser, era, erum, *wretched, unfortunate.*
mittō, ere, mīsī, missum, *send, let go, cast.*
modo, adv. (modus), *only.*
modus, i, m., *measure, manner, mode, way*; ējus modī, *of that sort.*
moenia, ium, n. (mūniō), *walls* (of a town), *fortifications.*
molitus, part. as adj. (molō, *grind,* Eng. *mill*), *ground.*
moneō, ēre, uī, itum, *remind, warn, advise.*
mons, montis, m., *mountain.*
monstrō, āre, āvī, ātum, *show, point out.*
morior, morī, mortuus sum, dep., *die*; fut. part., moritūrus.
moror, ārī, ātus sum, dep., *delay, tarry, hinder.*
mors, mortis, f. (morior), *death.*
mortālis, e (mors), *mortal*; as a noun, *a mortal, a human being.*
mortuus, part. as adj. (morior), *dead.*
mōs, mōris, m., (sing.) *manner, custom, practice*; (plur.) *character.*
moveō, ēre, mōvī, mōtum, *move, excite*; castra movēre, *break up camp.*
mulier, eris, f., *woman.*
multitūdō, inis, f. (multus), *multitude, crowd.*
multō, adv. (abl. of multus, as deg. of diff.), *much, by far.*
multum, adv. (acc. neut. of multus), *much, very, exceedingly.*
multus, a, um (comp. neut. plūs; sup. plūrimus) *much*; (plur.) *many, numerous*; multō diē, *late in the day.*
mūniō, īre, īvī, ītum, *fortify, defend, protect.*

GENERAL VOCABULARY. 283

mūnītiō, ōnis, f. (mūniō), *fortification, rampart.*
mūrus, ī, m., *wall, rampart.*

N.

nam, conj., *for.*
Nameius, ī, m., *Nameius,* a Helvetian chief.
narrō, āre, āvī, ātum, *tell, relate.*
nascor, nascī, nātus sum, dep., *be born, arise, be produced.*
nātū, m., only in the abl. (nascor), *by birth, in age;* mājor nātū (N. 36, b), *older;* as noun, *elders, ancestors.*
nātūra, ae, f. (nascor), *birth, nature.*
nauta, ae, m. (nāvis), *sailor, seaman.*
nāvis, is, f., *ship;* nāvis longa, *ship of war.*
nē, conj., *that not, lest, so that not.*
nē, adv. (especially with subjunctive of command, etc.), *not;* nē ... quidem, *not even* (emphatic word between).
ne, interrog. enclitic particle. See N. 195, 3.
nec = neque.
necessārius, a, um, *necessary, related;* as a noun, m., *relative, kinsman.*
necne, adv., *or not;* used in indirect questions.
negō, āre, āvī, ātum, *say no, deny, refuse.*
negōtium, ī, n. (nec + ōtium, *leisure*), *occupation, employment, business;* tibi negōtium dō, *I employ you.*
nēmō, m. and f. (nē + homō), *no man, no one, nobody.* The gen. and abl. are borrowed from nullus.
neque (or nec), conj. and adv. (nē + que), *and not;* neque ... neque, *neither ... nor.*
nēquis (or nēquī), nēqua, nēquid (or nēquod), indef. pron., *lest any.* See N. 52, b.

neuter, tra, trum (nē + uter), gen. neutrīus, *neither* (of two); (plur.) *neither party.*
niger, gra, grum, *black, dark.*
nihil, n. indecl., *nothing;* used as adv., *not at all, in no respect.*
nihilō, adv. (abl. of nihilum, *nothing*), *in no respect;* with comp. as deg. of diff., nihilō minus, *nevertheless, none the less.*
nītor, ī, nīsus, or nixus sum, dep., *strive, attempt.*
nōbilis, e (noscō), *famous, noble.*
nōbilitās, ātis, f. (nōbilis), *nobility* (of rank); as a coll. noun, *the nobility, the nobles.*
noceō, ēre, uī, itum, *harm, injure.*
noctū, f., only in abl. (nox), *by night.*
nōlō, nolle, nōluī, irr. (nōn + volō), *be unwilling, wish not, refuse.*
nōmen, inis, n. (noscō), *name.*
nōminātim, adv. (nōminō, *name*), *by name, expressly.*
nōn, adv. (nē + ūnum), *not, by no means.*
Nōnae, ārum (nōnus, *ninth* [day before the Ides]), f. plur., *Nones,* the 7th of March, May, July, October, and the 5th of other months.
nondum, adv. (nōn + dum), *not yet.*
nonne, interrog. particle (nōn + ne), expecting the answer *Yes;* nonne vēnit, *has n't he come?*
nonnullī, ae, a (nōn + nullus), *some, several.*
nonnunquam, adv. (nōn + nunquam), *sometimes, at times.*
Nōrēia, ae, f., *Noreia,* capital of the Taurisci, a German people of Noricum.
Nōricus, a, um, *Noric,* pertaining to Noricum.
noscō, ere, nōvī, nōtum, *become acquainted with, learn;* in perf.-stem tenses, *know;* nōvī, *I know.* N. 91, Rem.
noster, tra, trum, poss. pron. (nōs), *our, ours;* as noun, nostrī, m.,

our men (soldiers, friends), **nostra,** n., *our possessions* (goods).

Noviodūnum, I, n., *Noviodūnum,* name of three towns in Gaul.

novissimus, a, um (novus), *newest* (that is, of soldiers, the *latest* or *last*), *hindmost, in the rear;* **agmen novissimum,** *the rear.*

novus, a, um, *new, strange, unusual;* **rēs novae,** *revolution.*

nox, noctis, f., *night;* **multā nocte,** *late at night.*

nūbēs, is, f., *cloud.*

nūdō, āre, āvī, ātum (**nūdus,** *bare*), *strip, deprive.*

nullus, a, um (nē + ullus), gen. **nullīus,** *no, none, not any.*

num, interrog. particle; in direct questions, not translated, and expects answer *No;* in indirect questions, *Whether.*

numerus, ī, m., *number, quantity, multitude.*

nunc, adv., *now, at present.*

nunquam, adv. (nē + unquam), *never.*

nuntiō (or nunciō), āre, āvī, ātum (**nuntius**), *announce, report, bring news.*

nuntius, ī, m., *messenger, message, news.*

nūper. adv. (for **noviper,** from **novus**), *newly, lately, recently.*

O.

ob, prep. with acc., *on account of, for.*

obaerātus, ī, m. (ob + aes, *money*), *debtor.*

objiciō, ere, jēcī, jectum (ob + **jaciō**), *throw against, throw up, oppose, expose.*

oblītus, a, um (oblīviscor), *forgetful.*

oblīviscor, ī, oblītus sum, dep., *forget.*

obses, idis, m. and f., *hostage, pledge, security.*

obstrictus, part. of **obstringō,** *bound, attached.*

obstringō, ere, strinxī, strictum (ob + **stringō,** *bind*), *bind close, pledge.*

obtineō, ēre, uī, tentum (ob + **teneō**), *hold, possess, gain, obtain.*

occāsus, ūs, m. (**occidō**), *fall, setting;* **occāsus sōlis,** *sunset, the west.*

occidō, ere, cidī, cāsum (ob + **cadō**), *fall down, fall, perish.*

occīdō, ere, cīdī, cīsum (ob + **caedō**), *cut down, kill, slay.*

occīsus, part. of **occīdō,** *slain.*

occupō, āre, āvī, ātum (ob + **capiō**), *seize, occupy.*

occurrō, ere, currī and **cucurrī, cursum** (ob + **currō**), *run towards, meet with, encounter.*

Oceanus, ī, m., *ocean,* the Atlantic.

Ocelum, ī, n., *Ocelum,* a Gallic town.

oculus, ī, m., *eye, sight.*

ōdī, ōdisse, def., *hate.* N. 91, 2.

offendō, ere, fendī, fensum, *offend, displease.*

omnīnō, adv. (**omnis**), *wholly, altogether, in all, at all.*

omnis, e, *all, every.*

onus, eris, n., *load, burden.*

oportet, ēre, uit, impers., *it is necessary, ought, must.*

oppidum, ī, n., *town* (walled).

oppugnātiō, ōnis, f. (**oppugnō**), *siege, assault, attack.*

oppugnō, āre, āvī, ātum (ob + **pugnō**), *attack, assault, besiege, storm.*

optimus, sup. of **bonus.**

opus, eris, n., *work, task, fortifications* or "*works.*"

opus, n. indecl., *need;* **opus est,** *there is need, it is necessary.*

ōrātiō, ōnis, f. (**ōrō,** *speak*), *speech, oration, words.*

Orgetorix, igis, m., *Orgetorix,* a chief of the Helvetii.

oriens, tis, part. of **orior,** *rising;* **sōl oriens,** *the rising sun, the east.*

orior, īrī, ortus sum, dep., *rise, arise, begin, spring from, descend.*

ortus, part. of orior, *descended, born.*
ostendō, ere, dī, sum and tum (ob, *towards* + tendō, *stretch*), *show, declare.*

P.

pābulum, ī, n. (pascō, *feed*), *food, fodder.*
pācō, āre, āvī, ātum (pax), *pacify, subdue.*
paene, adv., *almost, nearly.*
pāgus, ī, m., *district, canton.*
pār, paris, *equal, like, a match for.*
parātus, a, um (parō), *ready, equipped.*
pāreō, ēre, uī, itum, *obey.*
parō, āre, āvī, ātum, *prepare, get ready, provide, procure.*
pars, partis, f., *part, share, portion, direction, side.*
parum, adv. (parvus), *too little, not enough.*
parvus, a, um (comp. minor; sup. minimus), *small, little.*
passus, part. of patior.
passus, ūs, m., *pace* (five Roman feet); mille passūs, *a mile;* duo millia passuum, *two miles.*
patefaciō, ere, fēcī, factum (pateō + faciō), *throw open, open, expose;* pass., patefīō.
patens, tis (pateō), *open, wide.*
pateō, ēre, uī, *lie open, extend.*
pater, tris, m., *father, ancestor.*
patior, patī, passus sum, dep., *suffer, allow, permit.*
patria, ae, f. (pater), *native land, fatherland.*
paucī, ae, a, *few.*
paulō, adv. (abl. of paulus, as deg. of diff.), *by a little, a little.*
paulum, adv. (acc. neut. of paulus), *little, somewhat.*
paulus, a, um, *little, small.*
pax, pācis, f., *peace, quiet.*
pecūnia, ae, f. (pecus, *cattle*), *money;* literally, *wealth estimated in cattle.*

pedes, itis, m. (pēs), *foot-soldier;* (plur.) *infantry.*
pējor, us, comp. of malus, *worse;* pējus as noun, *a worse thing.*
pellō, ere, pepulī, pulsum, *drive, conquer, rout.*
pendō, ere, pependī, pensum, *weigh, pay.*
per, prep. with acc., *through, throughout, by;* in compounds, *through, thoroughly, very.*
perdūcō, ere, xī, ctum (per + dūcō), *bring through* or *all the way, lead, conduct, extend, construct.*
perfacilis, e (per + facilis), *very easy.*
perficiō, ere, fēcī, fectum (per + faciō), *finish, accomplish, bring about.*
perīculōsus, a, um (perīculum), *perilous, dangerous.*
perīculum, ī, n. (root in experior, *try*), *trial, risk, danger, peril.*
perlegō, ere, lēgī, lectum (per + legō), *read through.*
permoveō, ēre, mōvī, mōtum (per + moveō), *move thoroughly, arouse, excite.*
permultī, ae, a (per + multus), *very many.*
perpaucī, ae, a (per + paucī), *very few.*
perrumpō, ere, rūpī, ruptum (per + rumpō), *break through, force a passage.*
persequor, ī, cūtus sum, dep. (per + sequor), *follow persistently, pursue, take vengeance on.*
persevērō, āre, āvī, ātum, *persist, persevere.*
persolvō, ere, solvī, solūtum (per + solvō, *release, pay*), *pay* (in full).
persuādeō, ēre, sī, sum (per + suādeō, *advise*), *persuade, convince, prevail upon.*
perterreō, ēre, uī, itum (per + terreō), *frighten thoroughly, terrify.*
pertineō, ēre, uī (per + teneō), *reach, extend to, relate* or *pertain to, tend to.*

perveniō, īre, vēnī, ventum (per + veniō), *come (through) to, arrive at, reach.*
pēs, pedis, m., *foot.*
pessimus, sup. of malus, *worst.*
petō, ere, īvī (iī), ītum, *seek, ask, strive after.*
pīlum, ī, n., *heavy javelin, javelin.*
pirus, ī, f., *pear-tree.*
Pīsō, ōnis, m., *Piso,* a Roman name.
placeō, ēre, uī, itum, *please, satisfy, seem good.*
plānitiēs, ēī, f. (plānus, *level), level ground, plain.*
plebs, plēbis, f., *the common people, the multitude.*
plēnus, a, um (root in compleō), *full, complete.*
plērumque, adv. (acc. neut. of plērusque), *for the most part, mostly.*
plērusque, aque, umque; usually in the plur., plērīque, aeque, aque, *very many, the most, most.*
plūrimum, adv. (acc. neut. of plūrimus), *very much, exceedingly;* plūrimum posse, *to be very powerful.*
plūrimus, sup. of multus; usually in plur., plūrimī, ae, a, *very many, most;* quam plūrimī, *as many as possible.*
plūs, plūris, comp. of multus; in the sing., a neuter noun (N. 27), *more;* plūs audāciae, *more (of) boldness;* in the plur., an adj., *more, several.*
plūs, adv. (acc. neut. of plūs, above), *more;* plūs posse, *to have more power.*
poena, ae, f., *penalty, punishment.*
poēta, ae, m., *poet.*
polliceor, ērī, itus sum, dep., *promise, offer.*
Pompēius, ī, m., *Pompey,* a famous Roman general, rival of Caesar.
pōnō, ere, posuī, positum, *put, place, station;* castra pōnere, *pitch a camp.*
pons, pontis, m., *bridge.*

poposcī, perf. of poscō.
populor, ārī, ātus sum, dep. (populus), *lay waste, ravage, devastate, depopulate.*
populus, ī, m., *people, nation, tribe.*
porta, ae, f., *gate, entrance, door.*
portō, āre, āvī, ātum, *carry, bear, convey.*
poscō, ere, poposcī, *ask for, demand.*
possessiō, ōnis, f., *possession, estate, property.*
possum, posse, potuī, irr. (potis, *able* + sum), *be able, can, have influence or power;* plūs (plūrimum) posse, *to have more (very great) power.*
post, prep. with acc., *after, behind.*
post, adv., *after, afterwards.*
posteā, adv. (post + is), *after this, afterwards.*
posteāquam, conj. (posteā + quam), *after (that), after.*
posterus, a, um (post), comp. posterior; sup. postrēmus and postumus, *following, next.*
postquam, conj. (post + quam) *after (that), after, when, as soon as.*
postrēmus, sup. of posterus, *latest, last, in the rear.*
postrīdiē, adv. (posterō + diē), *on the following day;* p. ējus diēī, *on the day after that day.*
postulō, āre, āvī, ātum (poscō), *ask, demand.*
potens, tis, part. of possum as adj., *able, powerful, influential.*
potentātus, ūs, m. (potens), *power, dominion, rule.*
potestās, ātis, f. (possum), *power, ability, opportunity, right;* potestātem facere, *to give an opportunity.*
potior, īrī, ītus sum, dep. (potis, *able), get possession of, obtain, become master of.*
prae, prep. with abl., *before, in front of, in comparison with.*
praebeō, ēre, uī, itum (prae + habeō), *furnish, offer, show.*

GENERAL VOCABULARY. 287

praecēdō, ere, cessī, cessum (prae + cēdō, go), go before, surpass, excel.

praeceps, cipitis (prae + caput), headlong, hasty, steep.

praedor, ārī, ātus sum, dep. (praeda, prey), plunder, rob, make booty.

praeficiō, ere, fēcī, fectum (prae + faciō), set over, place in command of.

praemittō, ere, mīsī, missum (prae + mittō), send before or ahead, send in advance.

praemium, I, n., reward.

praescrībō, ere, psī, ptum (prae + scrībō), dictate, command, prescribe, appoint.

praescriptum, I, n. (praescrībō), command, order, direction.

praesidium, I, n., defence, guard, protection, garrison, aid.

praestō, āre, stitī, stitum (prae + stō), surpass, excel, show; impers., praestat, it is better.

praesum, esse, fuī, irr. (prae + sum), be in command of, have charge of.

praeter, prep. with acc. (prae), beyond, except, besides, contrary to.

praetereā, adv. (praeter + is), besides this, besides, moreover.

praeterquam, adv. (praeter + quam), besides, except.

premō, ere, pressī, pressum, press, press hard or hard press.

pretium, I, n., price, value, pay.

prīmō, adv. (abl. of prīmus), at first.

prīmum, adv. (acc. of prīmus), first, in the first place; quam prīmum, as soon as possible; quum prīmum, as soon as.

prīmus, a, um, sup. of prior, first, foremost, principal; prīmum agmen, the van; prīmā lūce, at daybreak.

princeps, cipis (prīmus + capiō), first, chief; as a noun, m. and f., leader, leading man, chief.

principātus, ūs, m. (princeps), first rank or place, chief position, leadership.

prior, us (no pos., sup. prīmus), former, previous, superior.

pristinus, a, um, former, early, original.

priusquam, conj. (prius + quam), before, sooner than.

prīvātus, a, um, private, one's own.

prō, prep. with abl., before, in front of, in behalf of or for, instead of, in proportion to, considering.

probō, āre, āvī, ātum, try, approve, show, prove.

prōcēdō, ere, cessī, cessum (prō + cēdō, go), advance, proceed.

prōcurrō, ere, currī or cucurrī, cursum (prō + currō), run forward, rush forth.

prōdō, ere, didī, ditum (prō + dō), give forth, hand down (to posterity), deliver, betray.

proelium, I, n., battle, combat.

profectiō, ōnis, f. (proficiscor), departure, setting out.

profectus, part. of proficiscor.

proficiscor, I, profectus sum, dep. (prō + faciō, that is, put one's self forward), set out, go, march.

prōfugiō, ere, fūgī, fugitum (prō + fugiō), escape, flee, flee for refuge.

prōgredior, I, gressus sum, dep. (prō + gradior, go), go forward, advance, proceed.

prohibeō, ēre, uī, itum (prō + habeō), hold back or off, check, restrain, keep from.

prōjiciō, ere, jēcī, jectum (prō + jaciō), throw forth or forward, prostrate.

prope, adv. (comp. propius; sup. proximē), near, almost.

prope, prep. with acc., near, close to.

propior, us (no pos.; sup. proximus), nearer.

propter, prep. with acc., on account of, by reason of.

proptereā, adv. (propter + is), *for this reason, on that account;* with **quod,** *because that.*
prōsum, prōdesse, prōfuī, irr. (prō + sum), *be helpful, benefit.*
prōvideō, ēre, vīdī, vīsum (prō + videō), *foresee, provide for, care for.*
prōvincia, ae, f. (prō + vincō), *subdued region, province.*
proximē, adv. (prope), *next, very recently, last.*
proximus, sup. of propior, *nearest, next, following;* with iter, *shortest road.*
publicus, a, um, *of the state, public.*
puella, ae, f., *girl.*
puer, ī, m., *boy, child.*
pugna, ae, f., *fight, combat, battle.*
pugnō, āre, āvī, ātum (pugna), *fight, contend.*
pulcher, chra, chrum, *beautiful, handsome, noble.*
pulsus, part. of pellō.
pūniō, īre, īvī, ītum (poena), *punish.*
putō, āre, āvī, ātum, *think, suppose, reckon, judge.*
Pȳrēnaeus, a, um; as a noun, **Pȳrēnaeī (montēs),** *the Pyrenees,* a mountain range between Gaul and Spain.

Q.

quā, adv. (abl. of quī, viā understood), *by which way, where.*
quaerō, ere, quaesīvī (iī), quaesītum, *seek, ask, inquire.*
quālis, e, (1) interrog. adj. (quis), *of what nature* or *kind, of what sort, what kind of;* (2) rel. adj. (quī), *as;* tālis . . . quālis, *such . . . as.*
quam, adv. (acc. of quis), *how, how much, as, than;* with superlative, *as possible;* quam prīmum, *as soon as possible.*
quamobrem, adv. (quam + ob + rem), *for what reason, wherefore, why, on this account.*

quantus, a, um (quam), *how great, how much;* as a correlative to tantus, *as;* as an abl. of deg. of diff., quantō . . . tantō, *the . . . the.*
quārē, adv. (quā + rē), *for what cause* or *reason, why, wherefore, therefore.*
-que, enclitic conj., *and.*
quemadmodum, adv. (ad + quem + modum), *after what manner, how.*
queror, ī, questus sum, dep., *complain, lament.*
quī, quae, quod, rel. pron., *who, which, what, that.*
quīdam, quaedam, quoddam or **quiddam,** indef. pron., *a certain one, a certain, some one, somebody, something.*
quidem, adv., *indeed, certainly, at least;* nē . . . quidem, *not even.*
quīn, conj. (quī + nē), *that not, but that, that;* quīn īrem, *from going.*
quis (or **quī**), **quae, quid** (or **quod**), interrog. pron., *who? which? what?*
quisquam, quaequam, quidquam or **quicquam,** indef. pron., *any, some, any one, something.*
quisque, quaeque, quidque or **quodque,** indef. pron., *each, every, any;* quisque dītissimus, *all the wealthiest men.*
quō, adv. (abl. of quī), *whither, where, why, wherefore;* with comparatives, as deg. of diff., quō . . . eō, *the . . . the.*
quō, conj. (abl. of quī), *in order that, that* (regularly with comparatives).
quod, conj. (acc. of quī), *in that, that, because, as to the fact that;* quod sī, *now if, but if.*
quōminus (or quō minus), conj., *by which the less, so that not, lest.*
quoniam, conj. (quum + jam), *since now, because, since.*
quoque, conj., *also, too.*

quot, indecl. adj., *how many, as many, as;* **tot ... quot,** *as many ... as.*
quotīdiānus, a, um (**quotīdiē,** *daily*), *every day, daily, ordinary.*
quum (or **cum**), conj., *when, after, while, since, because, although;* **quum ... tum,** *not only ... but also;* **quum prīmum,** *as soon as.*

R.

ratis, is, f., *float, raft.*
Rauracī, ōrum, m., *the Rauraci, a Gallic people, on the Rhine.*
recens, tis, *fresh, new, recent.*
recipiō, ere, cēpī, ceptum (**re + capiō**), *take back, recover, receive,* **sē recipere,** *withdraw, betake one's self.*
reddō, ere, didī, ditum (**re + dō**), *give back, restore, return, give up.*
redeō, īre, īvī (iī), itum, irr. (**re + eō**), *go back, return.*
reditiō, ōnis, f. (**redeō**), *returning, return.*
redūcō, ere, xī, ctum (**re + dūcō**), *lead back, bring back.*
referō, ferre, tulī, lātum, irr. (**re + ferō**), *bring back, carry back, pay back, announce, report.*
regnum, I, n. (**rex**), *sovereignty, rule, authority, kingdom.*
regō, ere, xī, ctum, *rule, govern, guide, direct.*
rējiciō, ere, jēcī, jectum (**re + jaciō**), *cast, hurl* or *throw back, throw away, drive back.*
relictus, part. of **relinquō.**
relinquō, ere, līquī, lictum (**re + linquō,** *leave*), *leave behind, leave, abandon.*
reliquus, a, um (**relinquō**), *remaining, rest of, future;* **reliquī Gallī,** *the rest of the Gauls;* **nihil est reliquī,** *there is nothing left;* **in reliquum tempus,** *for the future.*

reminiscor, I, dep. (**re +** root of **meminī**), *recall to mind, recollect, remember.*
remittō, ere, mīsī, missum (**re + mittō**), *send back, hurl back, give back, restore.*
removeō, ēre, mōvī, mōtum (**re + moveō**), *move back, take away, remove.*
Rēmus, I, m., *one of the Remi;* (plur.) **Rēmī, ōrum,** *the Remi, a Gallic people.*
renūtiō, āre, āvī, ātum (**re + nūtiō**), *bring back word* or *news, report.*
repellō, ere, pulī, pulsum (**re + pellō**), *drive back, repel, repulse, drive away.*
repentīnus, a, um, *sudden, unexpected.*
reperiō, īre, perī, pertum, *find, discover, learn, ascertain.*
repetō, ere, īvī, ītum (**re + petō**), *seek* or *ask again, demand back, claim.*
reprehendō, ere, dī, sum, *blame, rebuke, reprove.*
rēs, reī, f., *thing, affair, fact, event, circumstance, property;* **rēs familiāris,** *private property;* **rēs frūmentāria,** *provisions, corn-supply;* **respublica** (or **rēs publica**), *the state;* **rēs novae,** *revolution.*
rescindō, ere, scidī, scissum (**re + scindō,** *cut*), *cut down, break down, destroy.*
resistō, ere, stitī (**re + sistō,** *place*), *withstand, resist, oppose.*
respiciō, ere, spexī, spectum (**re + speciō,** *look*), *look back, look behind, consider.*
respondeō, ēre, dī, sum, *answer, reply, respond.*
responsum, I, n. (**respondeō**), *answer, reply.*
respublica (or **rēs publica**), **reīpublicae,** f., *republic, state, commonwealth.*
restō, āre, stitī (**re + stō**), *stay behind, remain;* impers., **restat,** *it remains.*

retineō, ēre, uī, tentum (re + teneō), *hold back, retain, keep, check, restrain.*
revertō, ere, tī, sum, and revertor, ī, sus sum, dep. (re + vertō, *turn*), *turn back, return;* the perfect-stem tenses are from the active forms; the others are from the deponent.
rex, rēgis, m. (regō), *king.*
Rhēnus, ī, m., *the Rhine,* eastern boundary of Gaul.
Rhodanus, ī, m., *the Rhone,* a large river of S. E. Gaul.
rīpa, ae, f., *bank* (of a river).
rogō, āre, āvī, ātum, *ask, request, beg.*
Rōma, ae, f., *Rome,* a city of Italy, capital of the Roman Empire.
Rōmānus, a, um (Rōma), *Roman;* as a noun, *a Roman, the Romans.*
rosa, ae, f., *rose.*
rursus, adv. (reversus), *back, again.*
rūs, rūris, n., *the country;* rūrī, *in the country.*

S.

Sabīnus, ī, m., *Sabinus,* one of Caesar's lieutenants.
saepe, adv. (comp. saepius; sup. saepissimē), *often, frequently;* minimē saepe, *very seldom.*
salūs, ūtis, f., *safety, security, place of safety.*
Santonī, ōrum (or Santonēs, um), m., *the Santones,* a Gallic people.
sapiens, tis, *wise, discreet.*
sapienter, adv. (sapiens), *wisely, prudently.*
sarcina, ae, f., *pack, burden;* especially in plural, sarcinae, *baggage* (carried by each soldier), *light baggage.*
Sardēs, ium, f., *Sardis,* capital of Lydia.
satis, (1) indecl. adj. ; (2) indecl. noun; (3) adv., *enough, sufficient, sufficiently, quite.*

satisfaciō, ere, fēcī, factum (satis + faciō), *give satisfaction, satisfy, apologize.*
sciō, īre, īvī (iī), ītum, *know, understand.*
scrībō, ere, psī, ptum, *write.*
secūtus, part. of sequor.
sed, conj., *but, but yet.*
sēdēs, is, f. (sedeō, *sit*), *seat, residence, abode.*
Segusiāvī, ōrum, m., *the Segusiāvi,* a Gallic people.
sēmentis, is, f., *a sowing.*
semper, adv., *always, ever.*
senātus, ūs, m. (senex, *old*), *council of elders, senate.*
sententia, ae, f., *opinion, thought, purpose, decision.*
septentriōnēs, um, m. (literally, *the seven plough-oxen*), *the north ;* the seven stars forming the constellation called the *Great Bear.*
Sēquana, ae, m., *the Seine,* a river in Gaul.
Sēquanus, a, um, *of the Sequani, Sequanian;* as a noun (masc. plur.), *the Sequani,* a Gallic people.
sequor, ī, cūtus sum, dep., *follow, pursue.*
sermō, ōnis, m., *discourse, conversation.*
servīlis, e (servus), *of a slave, servile.*
serviō, īre, īvī (iī), ītum (servus), *be a slave to, serve.*
servitūs, ūtis, f. (servus), *slavery, servitude.*
servō, āre, āvī, ātum, *preserve, save, keep, guard;* fidem servāre, *to keep one's word.*
servus, ī, m., *slave, servant.*
sestertius, ī, m., *a sestertius or sesterce,* coin worth about five cents.
sī, conj., *if;* in ind. quest., *whether.*
sīc, adv., *thus, so.*
signum, ī, n., *mark, sign, signal, standard;* signa inferre, *to march to the attack, attack;* signa convertere, *face about.*
silva, ae, f., *forest, wood.*
similis, e, *like, similar.*

sīn, conj. (sī + nē), *but if, if however.*
sine, prep. with abl., *without.*
singulī, ae, a, distrib. adj., *single, one by one.*
sinister, tra, trum, *left, on the left, unfavorable.*
sīquis (sīquī), sīqua, sīquid (sīquod), indef. pron. (also written separately), *if any, if any one, whoever, whatever.*
sīve, conj. (sī + ve), also written seu, *or if, whether;* sīve ... sīve, *whether ... or.*
socer, erī, m., *father-in-law.*
socius, I, m., *companion, ally.*
sōl, sōlis, m., *sun.*
soleō, ēre, itus sum, semi-dep., *be wont, be accustomed.*
solum, I, n., *ground, soil, land.*
sōlum, adv. (acc. of sōlus), *only, merely.*
sōlus, a, um (gen. īus), *alone, only, merely.*
soror, ōris, f., *sister.*
spatium, I, n., *space, distance, extent, period* (of time), *opportunity.*
spectō, āre, āvī, ātum (speciō, *look*), *look at, observe,* (of territory) *face, lie towards.*
spērō, āre, āvī, ātum (spēs), *hope, expect, long for.*
spēs, eī, f., *hope, expectation.*
spolium, I, n., *spoil, plunder.*
sponte, f. abl. (only other case in use, gen. spontis), *of one's own free will* or *accord, by one's self, without aid.*
statuō, ere, uī, ūtum, *set up, establish, determine, decide.*
stella, ae, f., *star.*
stīpendium, I, n., *tax, tribute, pay.*
stō, stāre, stetī, statum, *stand, stand firm* or *fast, persist, cost.*
studeō, ēre, uī, *be eager for, favor, desire, study.*
sub, prep. with acc. or abl. (N. 95, c), *under, beneath, at the foot of, towards;* sub monte, *at the foot of the mountain;* sub vesperum, *towards evening.*

subeō, īre, īvī (iī), itum (sub + eō), *go under, approach, undergo, encounter.*
sublātus, part. of tollō.
subsidium, I, n., *relief, reserve, help, protection.*
Suēvus, a, um, *of the Suevi,* Suevian; as a noun (plur.), *the Suevi,* a very powerful people of Germany.
suī, sibi, sē (sēsē), refl. pron. 3d pers., *of* (*to,* etc.) *himself, herself, itself, themselves.*
sum, esse, fuī, irr., *be, stay, belong, serve;* vōbīs est in animō, *you intend;* praesidiō urbī esse, *to serve as a protection to the city.*
summus, sup. of superus, *highest, chief, greatest, most important, top of;* rēs summae, *most important subjects;* summā vī, *with all their might;* summus mons, *top of the mountain.*
sūmō, ere, sumpsī, sumptum, *take, assume, claim, undertake;* supplicium dē tē sūmere, *to inflict punishment on you.*
superior, us, comp. of superus, *higher, upper, former, superior, greater.*
superō, āre, āvī, ātum (super, *above, over*), *overcome, surpass, excel, survive.*
supersum, esse, fuī (super, *over* + sum), *be over and above, be left, survive.*
superus, a, um, comp. superior; sup. suprēmus or summus (super, *above*), *upper, above.* See summus.
suppetō, ere, īvī (iī), ītum (sub + petō), *be at hand, be in store.*
supplicium, I, n., *punishment, penalty, torture.*
suprā, prep. with acc. or adv., *above, before, previously.*
suscipiō, ere, cēpī, ceptum (sub + capiō), *take up, undertake;* sibi suscipere, *to take upon one's self, undertake.*
suspiciō, ōnis, f., *suspicion, distrust.*

suspicor, ārī, ātus sum, dep., *suspect, distrust, mistrust.*
sustineō, ēre, uī, tentum (sub + teneō), *sustain, bear, endure, withstand.*
suus, a, um, poss. and refl. pron. (suī), *his, her, its, their;* masc. plur. suī, *one's friends, soldiers,* etc.; neut. plur. sua, *one's property, possessions.*

T.

tālis, e, *such* (in quality), *of such a kind.*
tam, adv., *so, so very.*
tamen, conj., *yet, nevertheless, still.*
tametsī, conj. (tamen + etsī), *although, notwithstanding.*
tangō, ere, tetigī, tactum, *touch, reach, border on.*
tantum, adv. (acc. neut. of tantus), *so much, so far, only.*
tantus, a, um (tam), *so great, such* (in size), *so much, so many;* tantō, abl. of deg. of diff., *by so much, the.*
tardō, āre, āvī, ātum (tardus), *delay, check, hinder.*
tardus, a, um, *slow, sluggish, tardy.*
tegō, ere, xī, ctum, *cover, hide, defend.*
tēlum, ī, n., *weapon* (thrown from a distance), *spear, javelin.*
temperō, āre, āvī, ātum, *restrain, govern, refrain, abstain.*
templum, ī, n., *temple.*
tempus, oris, n., *time, season, occasion;* in reliquum tempus, *for the future.*
teneō, ēre, uī, tentum, *hold, keep, occupy, possess, bind.*
terreō, ēre, uī, itum, *frighten, alarm, terrify.*
testis, is, m. and f., *witness.*
Tigurīnus, a, um, *of the Tigurīni;* as a noun (masc. plur.), *the Tigurini,* a Helvetian tribe.
timeō, ēre, uī, *fear, be afraid of.*

timidus, a, um (timeō), *timid, afraid, cowardly.*
timor, ōris, m. (timeō), *fear, alarm.*
Titus, ī, m., *Titus,* a Roman personal name.
tollō, ere, sustulī, sublātum, *raise, take away, remove, destroy, be elated* (pass.).
Tolōsātēs, ium, m., *the Tolosates,* inhabitants of Tolōsa (modern Toulouse).
tot, indecl. adj., *so many.*
tōtus, a, um (gen. īus), *all, the whole, entire.*
trādō, ere, didī, ditum (trans + dō), *give over, give up, surrender.*
trādūcō, see transdūcō.
trans, prep. with acc., *across, beyond, over, on the farther side of.*
Transalpīnus, a, um (trans + Alpēs), *situated beyond the Alps, Transalpine.*
transdūcō (or trādūcō), ere, xī, ctum (trans + dūcō), *lead across or over, bring over, transport.*
transeō, īre, īvī (iī), itum (trans + eō), *go over, pass over, cross.*
trēs, tria, num. adj., *three.*
tribuō, ere, uī, ūtum, *impart, render, attribute, ascribe.*
trīduum, ī, n. (trēs + diēs), *space of three days, three days.*
triplex, icis, *threefold, triple.*
tristis, e, *sad, gloomy, sorrowful.*
tū, tuī, pers. pron., *thou, you.*
tuba, ae, f., *trumpet.*
Tulingī, ōrum, m., *the Tulingi,* a Gallic people.
turris, is, f., *tower.*
tuus, a, um, poss. pron. (tū), *thy, your.*

U.

ubi, adv. and conj., *where, when, after.*
ulciscor, ī, ultus sum, dep., *take vengeance on, avenge, punish.*
ullus, a, um (gen. īus), *any, any one.*

GENERAL VOCABULARY. 293

ulterior, us (ultrā, *beyond*), sup.
ultimus, *farther, ulterior, more remote.*
ultimus, a, um (sup. of **ulterior**), *farthest, most distant, last.*
ūnā, adv. (abl. of **ūnus**, **viā** understood), *at one* or *the same time, together;* with **cum**, *together with.*
unde, adv., *whence, from which place.*
undique, adv. (**unde** + **que**), *from all sides, on all sides, everywhere.*
unquam, adv. (for **ūnumquam**), *at any time, ever.*
ūnus, a, um (gen. **ius**), num. adj., *one, only, alone;* (plur.) **ūnī**, *alone.*
urbs, urbis, f., *city,* the *city* (Rome).
urgeō, ēre, ursī, *press, press hard, crowd, oppress.*
ūsus, ūs, m. (**ūtor**), *use, practice, service, advantage.*
ut, conj., *that, in order that, so that,* (with verbs of fearing) *that not;* as an adv., *how, as.*
uter, tra, trum (gen. utrīus), *which* (of two).
uterque, traque, trumque (**uter** + **que**), *each* (of two), *both.*
utī = **ut.**
ūtilis, e (**ūtor**), *useful, serviceable, advantageous.*
utinam, adv. (in clauses expressing wish), *would that! O that!*
ūtor, I, ūsus sum, dep., *use, make use of, employ, adopt, enjoy.*
utrum, adv., used in double questions (**uter**); in direct questions, not translated; in indirect questions, *whether.*

V.

vacō, āre, āvī, ātum, *be empty, be unoccupied.*
vadum, I, n., *ford, shoal.*
vagor, ārī, ātus sum, dep., *wander about, roam.*
vallum, I, n., *wall, rampart, intrenchment.*

vastō, āre, āvī, ātum, *lay waste, ravage, devastate, destroy.*
vectīgal, ālis, n., *tax, revenue.*
vel, conj., *or, even;* **vel ... vel,** *either ... or.*
vendō, ere, didī, ditum, *sell, offer for sale.*
Venetī, ōrum, m., *the Veneti,* a Gallic people.
veniō, īre, vēnī, ventum, *come.*
verbum, I, n., *word;* (plur.) *words, language, conversation.*
vereor, ērī, itus sum, dep., *fear, dread, be afraid of.*
vergō, ere, *incline, lie towards, be situated towards.*
vērō, adv. (abl. of **vērus,** *true*), *in truth, truly, but, indeed.*
versor, ārī, ātus sum, dep. (**vertō,** *turn*), *move about, be busy, dwell, be.*
Verudoctius, I, m., *Verudoctius,* a Helvetian.
Vesontiō, ōnis, m., *Vesontio,* a town of the Sequani.
vesper, erī, m., *evening;* **sub vesperum,** *towards evening.*
vester, tra, trum, poss. pron. (**vōs**), *your, yours.*
vetus, eris, *old, ancient.*
via, ae, f., *way, road, journey, march.*
viātor, ōris, m. (**via**), *wayfarer, traveller.*
victor, ōris, m. (**vincō**), *conqueror, victor;* as an adj., *victorious.*
victōria, ae, f. (**victor**), *victory.*
victus, part. of **vincō;** as a noun, **victī,** *the conquered, vanquished.*
vīcus, I, m., *village.*
videō, ēre, vīdī, vīsum, *see, behold, perceive.*
videor, ērī, vīsus sum, dep. (pass. of **videō**), *seem, appear, seem good.*
vigilia, ae, f. (literally, *a watching, watch*), *a watch,* a fourth part of the night. The night was divided into four **vigiliae,** or *watches,* extending from sunset to sunrise. The third watch began at midnight. The length of each watch depended, of course, on the season of the year.

vincō, ere, vīcī, victum, *conquer, overcome, subdue.*
vinculum, ī, n. (vinciō, *bind*), *bond, fetters, chain;* ex vinculīs, *in chains.*
vir, virī, m., *man, brave man, hero;* homō means *man* or *woman, human being,* (in plur.) *mankind.*
virgō, inis, f., *maiden, maid, virgin.*
virtūs, ūtis, f. (vir), *manliness, courage, bravery, worth, ability.*
vīs, vīs, f., *force, power, violence;* (plur.) vīrēs, ium, *strength, power;* vim facere, *to use violence.*
vīta, ae, f. (vīvō), *life.*
vītō, āre, āvī, ātum, *avoid, shun, escape.*

vīvō, ere, vixī, victum, *live, dwell, live* or *subsist on.*
vix, adv., *with difficulty, scarcely, hardly.*
vocō, āre, āvī, ātum (vox), *call, summon, invite, name.*
Vocontiī, ōrum, m., *the Vocontii,* a Gallic people.
volō, velle, voluī, irr., *wish, desire.*
voluntās, ātis, f. (volō), *wish, will, consent, good-will.*
vox, vōcis, f., *voice, sound, word.*
vulgus, ī, n., *common people, crowd.*
vulnerō, āre, āvī, ātum (vulnus), *wound, hurt.*
vulnus, eris, n., *wound, injury.*

English - Latin.

A.

able (*to be*), **possum.**
about (= *concerning*), **dē.**
about, adv. with num. adj., **circiter, ad.**
about to, use the 1st Periphrastic Conj.
abundance, **cōpia.**
accuse, **accūsō.**
accustomed (*to be*), **consuēvī, soleō.**
across, **trans.**
active, **alacer.**
advance, **prōgredior.**
advise, **moneō.**
after, (conj.) **postquam**; (prep. or adv.) **post.**
against, **contrā, in.**
ago, **ante.**
aid, **auxilium.**
alarm, **commoveō.**
all, **omnis.**
allow, **patior.**
ally, **socius.**
alone, **sōlus.**
Alps, **Alpēs.**
although, **quum, etsī, tametsī.**
always, **semper.**
ambassador, **lēgātus.**
among, **inter, apud, in.**
and, **et, que, atque** (*and also*).
animal, **animal.**
announce, **nuntiō.**
another, **alius.**
any, **ullus**; *any one, anything*, **aliquis, aliquid**; *if any*, **sīquis.**
arms, **arma.**
army, **exercitus.**
arrival, **adventus.**
arrive, **perveniō.**
ascertain, **cognoscō.**
ask (N. 199, 4), **rogō, petō, quaerō.**
attack, **impetus**: *to attack*, **oppugnō, impetum in** (+ acc.) **facere.**
attempt, **cōnor.**
attentive, **attentus.**
auxiliaries, **auxilia.**
away from, **ā, ab.**

B.

bad, **malus.**
baggage (*heavy*), **impedīmenta**; (*light*) **sarcinae.**
barbarian, **barbarus.**
battle, **proelium.**
be, **sum**; *be distant*, **absum.**
bear, **ferō.**
beautiful, **pulcher.**
because, **quod.**
before, **ante.**
begin, **coepī, incipiō** (for pres.-stem tenses).
beginning, **initium.**
behind, **post.**
believe, **crēdō.**
besiege, **oppugnō.**
best, **optimus.**
between, **inter.**
black, **niger.**
body, **corpus.**
bold, **audax.**
boldly, **audacter.**
book, **liber.**
born (*to be*), **nascor.**
both . . . and, **et . . . et.**
boy, **puer.**
brave, **fortis.**
bravery, **virtūs.**
break up camp, **castra movēre.**
bridge, **pons.**
brief, **brevis.**
bright, **clārus.**
bring, **ferō, afferō.**
bring back word, **renuntiō.**
broad, **lātus.**
brother, **frāter.**
build, **aedificō.**

building, aedificium.
burden, onus.
burn, burn up, exūrō, combūrō.
but, sed.
by, ā, ab.

C.

call, vocō; *call together,* convocō.
camp, castra.
can, could, possum.
capture, capiō, expugnō.
careful, dīligens.
carry, portō, ferō.
carry on war, bellum gerō.
Carthage, Karthāgō.
cause, causa.
cavalry, equitātus, equitēs.
certain (a), quīdam.
chief, princeps.
choose, dēligō.
Cicero, Cicerō.
citadel, arx.
citizen, cīvis.
city, urbs.
close, claudō.
cloud, nūbēs.
cohort, cohors.
collect, conferō, cōgō.
come, veniō.
command, jubeō, imperō; *to be in command of,* praesum.
commander, imperātor.
compel, cōgō.
commonwealth, respublica.
concerning, dē.
congratulate, grātulor.
conquer, vincō.
conspire, conjūrō.
consul, consul.
contest, see *fight.*
corn, frūmentum.
council, concilium.
country, fīnēs, patria *(native land),* rūs.
courage, virtūs.
cowardly, ignāvus.
cross, transeō.
custom, mōs.

D.

danger, perīculum.
dare, audeō.
daughter, fīlia.
day, diēs; *at day-break,* prīmā lūce.
dear, cārus.
death, mors.
deep, altus.
defend, dēfendō.
delay, moror.
demand, postulō.
deny, negō.
depart, discēdō.
depth, altitūdō.
deserve, mereor.
desirous, cupidus.
destroy, dēleō.
determine, constituō.
die, morior.
differ, differō.
difficult, difficilis; *very difficult,* perdifficilis.
direction, pars.
dismiss, dīmittō.
do, faciō, agō.
door, porta.
doubt (to), dubitō; *there is no doubt that,* nōn est dubium quīn.
draw up, instruō.
drive back, rējiciō.
duty, see N. 126, *a.*
dwell, incolō.

E.

each, quisque.
eager, alacer.
easy, facilis; *very easy,* perfacilis.
easily, facile.
elect, creō.
embassy, lēgātiō.
empire, imperium.
encounter, subeō, occurrō.
encourage, hortor, cohortor.
end, fīnis.
enemy, hostis; *the enemy,* hostēs.
enlist, conscrībō.
equal, pār.

GENERAL VOCABULARY.

every, quisque, omnis.
example, exemplum.
exhort, hortor, cohortor.
exile, exsilium.
extend, pertineō.
eye, oculus.

F.

fact, rēs.
fall, cadō.
far, by far, longē.
farmer, agricola.
father, pater.
fear, timor, metus.
fear (to), vereor, timeō.
few, paucī.
field, ager.
fierce, ferox.
fight (to), pugnō; *the fight (contest) is carried on,* pugnātur.
fill, compleō.
find, inveniō, reperiō.
find out, cognoscō.
fire, ignis.
flee, fugiō.
flourishing, flōrens.
flower, flōs.
follow, sequor.
following, posterus.
foot, pēs; *at the foot of the mountain,* sub monte.
for (= towards), ad.
forces, cōpiae.
forest, silva.
forget, oblīviscor.
fortify, mūniō.
free, līber.
free (to), līberō.
friend, amīcus; *friendly,* amīcus.
frighten, terreō, perterreō.
from, ā, ab *(away from),* ē, ex *(out of); from each other,* inter nōs, sē, etc.

G.

gate, porta.
Gaul, Gallia; *a Gaul,* Gallus.
general, imperātor.
German, Germānus.

get possession of, potior.
gift, dōnum.
girl, puella.
give, dō; *give back,* reddō.
glory, glōria.
go, eō; *go out,* exeō; *go back,* redeō.
god, deus.
goddess, dea.
going to, use 1st Periphrastic Conj.
good, bonus.
government, imperium.
great, magnus; *so great,* tantus; *how great,* quantus.
greatness, magnitūdō.
guard, custōs, praesidium.

H.

hand, manus.
happen, accidō.
happy, beātus, fēlix.
harm, noceō; *harm is done,* nocētur.
hasten, mātūrō, contendō.
have, habeō.
head, caput.
hear, audiō.
heavy, gravis.
height, altitūdō.
hesitate, dubitō.
high, altus.
hill, collis.
hinder, impediō.
hither, hūc.
hold, teneō; *hold in possession,* obtineō.
home, domus.
honor, honor.
hope, spēs.
hope (to), spērō.
horse, equus.
horseman, eques.
hostage, obses.
hour, hōra.
house, domus.
how, quam, quemadmodum.
how great, quantus.
huge, ingens.
hurl, conjiciō.

I.

impose, impōnō.
in, in.
infantry, peditēs, peditātus.
influence, auctōritās; (*to*), addūcō.
inform, certiōrem (ēs) facere.
injury, injūria.
intend to, 1st Periphrastic Conj.
into, in.
invite, invītō.
island, insula.
Italy, Italia.

J.

join (*to*), jungō, conjungō.
join battle, proelium committere.
journey, iter.
judge, jūdex.
judge (*to*), jūdicō.
just, justus.

K.

keep from, prohibeō.
keeper, custōs.
king, rex.
kill, interficiō.
know, sciō.

L.

lake, lacus.
language, lingua.
large, magnus.
last part of, extrēmus; as, extrēmā hieme.
lay waste, vastō.
lead, dūcō; *lead across*, transdūcō, *lead back*, redūcō; *lead out*, ēdūcō.
leader, dux.
leave, relinquō.
legate, lēgātus.
legion, legiō.
length, longitūdō.
less, minus.
lest, nē.

letter, (of the alphabet) littera; (an epistle) litterae; epistola.
lieutenant, lēgātus.
life, vīta.
light, lux.
light, levis; *light baggage*, sarcinae.
like, similis.
limit (*to*), fīniō.
line of battle, aciēs; *line of march*, agmen.
lion, leō.
lofty, altus.
long, longus.
lose, āmittō.
love (*to*), amō.
lower, inferior.
Lyons, Lugdūnum.

M.

magistrate, magistrātus.
maiden, virgō.
make, faciō; *make war upon*, bellum inferō.
man, vir, homō.
many, multī; *very many*, permultī.
march, iter; *to march*, iter facere.
master (*teacher*), magister.
memory, memoria.
message, nuntius.
messenger, nuntius.
midnight, media nox.
mile, mille passūs; *miles*, millia passuum.
military science, rēs mīlitāris.
mind, animus, mens.
mindful, memor.
money, pecūnia.
more, plūs, amplius.
mortal, mortālis.
mother, māter.
mountain, mons; *mountain-top*, summus mons.
move, moveō.
much, multus; adv., multō (with comp.).
must, oportet or gerundive.
my, mine, meus.

GENERAL VOCABULARY.   299

N.

name, nōmen.
nature, nātūra.
near, prope.
neighbors, fīnitimī.
neighborhood of (in the), ad, circum.
neither, neque (nec).
new, novus.
night, nox.
no, nullus.
noble, nōbilis.
noon, merīdiēs.
nor, neque (nec).
not, nōn; in negative commands and wishes, nē.
nothing, nihil.
number, numerus.

O.

oath, jusjūrandum.
obey, pāreō.
obtain possession of, potior.
often, saepe.
one, ūnus; one... another, alius ... alius; the one... the other, alter... alter.
only, sōlus; adv., sōlum; not only, nōn sōlum.
opinion, sententia.
opportunity, potestās, facultās.
or, aut, vel; in double questions, an; or not, (direct questions) annōn, (indirect questions) necne.
order, jubeō (with acc.), imperō (with dat.).
other, alius; the other (of two), alter.
ought, oportet, dēbeō.
out of, ē (ex).
overcome, superō.

P.

pain, dolor.
part, pars.
pass the winter, hiemō.
pay, mercēs, pretium.

peace, pax.
people, populus.
peril, perīculum.
persuade, persuādeō.
pitch camp, castra pōnere.
place, locus; places, loca.
plan, consilium.
poet, poëta.
point out, monstrō, dēmonstrō.
Pompey, Pompēius.
possession (get or obtain), pŏtior.
possible (as), quam + superlative.
powerful, potens; to be more (or very) powerful, plūs (or plūrimum) posse.
praise (to), laudō.
praise, laus.
prefer, mālō.
price, pretium.
promise, polliceor.
protect, servō; esse praesidiō (+ dat. of advantage).
province, prōvincia.
punish, pūniō, animadvertō.

Q.

quick, celer.

R.

rampart, vallum.
read, legō.
reason, causa; for this reason, proptereā.
receive, accipiō, recipiō.
recent, recens.
rejoice, laetor, gaudeō.
release, līberō.
remain, maneō.
reply (to), respondeō.
reply, responsum.
republic, respublica.
resist, resistō.
respecting, dē.
rest of, reliquus.
restrain, retineō; restrain from, retinēre quīn.
return, revertor, redeō.

revolution, rēs novae.
reward, praemium.
Rhine, Rhēnus.
Rhone, Rhodanus.
rich, dīves.
right, jūs.
river, flūmen.
road, via, iter.
Roman, Rōmānus.
Rome, Rōma.
rose, rosa.
route, iter.
rule, regō.

S.

sad, tristis.
sailor, nauta.
sake of (for the), causā.
same, īdem.
satisfy, satisfaciō.
save, servō.
say, dīcō ; *he says*, dīcit.
science (military), rēs mīlitāris.
sea, mare.
see, videō.
seek, petō.
seize, occupō.
seem, videor.
self, ipse.
sell, vendō.
senate, senātus.
send, mittō ; *send ahead* or *forward*, praemittō ; *send back*, remittō.
serve (as), sum, with dat. of purpose.
sesterce or *sestertius*, sestertius.
set fire to, incendō.
set out, proficiscor.
severe, gravis.
ship, nāvis ; *ship of war*, n. longa.
short, brevis.
show, monstrō.
sick, aeger.
side of (on this), cis, citrā.
signal, signum.
since, quum.
sister, soror.
size, magnitūdō.
skilled, perītus.

slave, servus.
slavery, servitūs.
small, parvus.
so, ita, tam ; *so many*, tot.
soldier, mīles.
some . . . others, aliī . . . aliī.
some one, something, aliquis, aliquid.
son, fīlius.
sort (of such a), ējusmodī.
speak, dīcō, loquor.
speech, ōrātiō.
spur, calcar.
star, stella.
state, cīvitās, respublica.
stone, lapis.
storm, take by storm, expugnō.
story, fābula.
strength, vīs.
summon, vocō, convocō.
sunset, occāsus sōlis.
supplies, commeātus, cōpiae.
suppose, putō.
surpass, praestō (with dat.), praecēdō (with acc.).
surrender, dēdō.
suspect, suspicor.
sustain, sustineō.
sword, gladius.

T.

table, mensa.
take, capiō ; *take by storm*, expugnō.
tall, altus.
tax, vectīgal, stīpendium.
teach, doceō.
teacher, magister.
tell, dīcō, narrō.
temple, templum.
terrify, terreō, perterreō.
territory, fīnēs, ager.
than, quam.
that, conj., ut ; dem. pron., is, ille ; rel. pron., quī.
that not, (purpose) nē, (result) ut nōn.
thing, rēs or the neuter form of an adj. or pron.
think, putō, existimō.

GENERAL VOCABULARY. 301

this, hīc.
through, per.
throw, jaciō.
till (to), colō.
time, tempus.
timid, timidus.
to, ad.
tongue, lingua.
top of, summus.
towards, ad, sub (of time).
tower, turris.
town, oppidum.
tribute, stīpendium.
troops, cōpiae.
trumpet, tuba.
try, cōnor.

U.

uncertain, incertus.
under, sub.
undergo, subeō.
understand, intelligō.
unfriendly, inimīcus.
unhappy, infēlix.
unjust, injustus.
unlike, dissimilis.
until, dum.
unwilling (to be), nōlō.
upper, superior.
urge, hortor, cohortor.
use, ūtor.
useful, ūtilis.

V.

very, (1) sup. of adj. or adv.; (2) per as a prefix.
vicinity of (in the), ad, circum; *from the vicinity of*, ā, ab.
victor, victor.
victory, victōria.
violence, vīs.
voice, vox.

W.

wait, exspectō.
wall, mūrus; *walls of a city*, moenia; as a *rampart*, vallum.
wander about, vagor.
war, bellum.
watch, vigilia.
way, via, iter.
weapon, tēlum.
weep, fleō.
well, bene.
what, interrog., quis (quī); rel., quī.
when, quum, ubi.
whether, utrum, num.
which, (of two) uter, (of several) quis (quī).
while, dum; *a little while*, paulisper; *a little while ago*, paulo ante.
white, albus.
who, interrog., quis (quī); rel., quī.
whole, tōtus.
why, cūr, quāre.
wicked, malus.
wide, lātus.
width, lātitūdō.
wing (of an army), cornū.
winter (to pass the), hiemō; *winter-quarters*, hīberna.
wise, sapiens.
wish, volō.
with, cum.
without, sine.
woods, silva.
word, verbum.
work, opus.
worthy, dignus.
wound, vulnus; *to wound*, vulnerō.
wretched, miser.
write, scrībō.

Y.

yet, tamen.
yoke, jugum.
your, yours, tuus, vester.

INDEX.

In this Index N. stands for NOTE, L. for LESSON, and A. for APPENDIX. The significance of other abbreviations is evident, and needs no explanation.

a, final, long in Abl. sing., N. 8 (8), 9, d.
a (ab), how used, N. 95, a; how diff. from
e (ex), N. 95, b; with Abl. of Agent, N.
151, CAUTION; as prefix, N. 99, 1.
Ablative Case, pl. ending in -abus, N. 9, e;
ending in -i, or -e or -i, N. 17, b, 26, 28;
position, N. 193, 5. *Use* (general), 20 (page
24), N. 146; used Adverbially, N. 39, a, 94,
1, 2, 146; with e (ex) or de, instead of
Part. Gen., N. 123, a, L. xlvi; with peto,
postulo, quaero, N. 141, n. 2, 199, 4;
of Separation, N. 147, L. xxliii (but see N.
131, c); with opus and usus, N. 147, a;
of Source, Birth, etc., N. 148; of Cause, N.
149, L. xl; of Manner, N. 150, L. xlix; of Accompaniment, N. 150, a, L. xlix; of Means
and Agent, N. 151, L. xxii, xliii; with utor,
etc., N. 151, a, L. xlii, with Adj. (fretus,
etc.), N. 151, b, L. lxx, — (dignus, etc.) N.
156, L. lxx; of Price, N. 151, c, L. lxx; of
Quality, N. 152, L. lxx; of Respect, N. 153,
191, b, L. xlix; with Comparatives, N. 154, L.
lxviii; of Measure of Diff., N. 155, L. lxviii;
Ablative Absolute, N.157, L. lix; of Place, N.
158, 159, L. xxxix, lv; of Time, N. 160, L. xlv.
Abstract Nouns, page 44 (* at bottom of page).
ac (atque), N. 96, a.
Accent, 18 (page 21); of Gen. and Voc. in
-i (for -ii and -ie), N. 10, d, e; as affected
by an Enclitic, 18* (page 21), N. 195, 4.
accidit, inflection, A. 47.
Accompaniment, how expr., N. 150, a, L. xlix.
Accusative Case, 20 (page 24); in -im, N.
17, c; in -Is (pl.), N. 17, d, 18, 26; as Direct
Object, N. 102, R., 139, L. iii; Cognate,
N. 140; two Acc., N. 141, and c, L. xxxiii;
used Adverbially [54 (page 15)], expr. Time,
Distance, Degree, etc., N. 39, a, 94, 1, 142,
L. xlv-xlvii; with Prep., N. 95, L. xxxix;
of Place *to which*, N. 158, 159, b, L. xxxix,
lv; with Inf., N. 143, 166, 199, 3, L. xx;
with propior and proximus, N. 132, a;
position, N. 193, 3.

Active Voice, 14 (page 3).
Adjectives, 9 (page 2), N. 24-43; A. 10-20;
position, 193, 1. *Use* (general), 47 (page
13), N. 108; Attrib. and Pred., N. 108, 1-
5; used as Nouns, N. 109, L. xii; agreeing
with Inf. or Clause, N. 109, b, 126, a, R.,
L. lvi; connected by et or -que, N. 195,
6; special uses, N. 110. [See also *Declensions of Adjectives, Comparison, Numeral Adj.*, etc.]
Adjective Clause, 42, b (page 12).
Adjective Element, 38, a (page 11).
Adverbial Accusative, see *Accusative*.
Adverbial Clause, 42, c (page 12).
Adverbial Element, 38, c (page 11); position,
N. 193, 5.
Adverbs, 28 (page 9); position, N. 193, 5;
formation, N. 88, a, b, 89 (bene, magnopere, facile), 94; Comparison, N. 88, c,
d; Numeral Adverbs, N. 44. *Use*, N. 94,
L. xxix; Relative Adv. for a Relative Phrase,
N. 115, e.
Agent, expr. by Abl., N. 151, CAUTION, L. xxii;
expr. by Dat., N. 136, L. lx; indirect (with
per), N. 151, CAUTION.
alienus, alter, alius, N. 195, 7.
aliquis, N. 52, and a, c; L. liv; A. 27.
alius, N. 43, b; L. xlii; A. 11; alius . . .
alius, N. 195, 8, 9; L. xlviii; alius,
alter, alienus, diff. in meaning, N.
195, 7.
Alphabet (Latin), page 17.
alter, N. 43, b; L. xlii; A. 11; alter . . .
alter, N. 195, 8; L. xlviii.
ambo, how declined, N. 43, R.
amo, inflection, A. 28, 29.
an, see *Double Questions*.
Analysis of Sentences, 34 (page 9), N. 194.
Antecedent, 11, b (page 3); omitted, N. 115, a.
Antepenult, and its accent, 13, b and R. 3
(page 21).
antequam and priusquam, with Indic.
and Subj., N. 184, c; L. lxxii.

INDEX.   303

Aorist, N 62, 171.
Apodosis, N. 174.
APPENDIX, pages 235-258.
Apposition, 38, a (page 11), 46 (page 13); N. 106, L. v; in such phrases as *the city of Rome*, N. 119, CAUTION; expr. by Clause of Result, N. 181, e.
as, a Rel. Pron., N. 115, *f*; *as possible*, how expressed, N. 40, c.
Asking (verbs of), constr. with rogo, peto, postulo, quaero, N. 199, 4.
Assimilation, N. 1 (6).
"Attraction," Subj. of, N. 185.
Attributive Adjectives, N. 108, 1, 2.
audeo, N. 81; A. 38.
audio, inflection, A. 35, 36.
aut . . . aut, N. 195, 8.
Auxiliary Verbs, 25 (page 8).
ave, Imperative, N. 91, 2, b.

bene, how compared, N. 39.
bonus, N. 33, A. 17, a.
bos, how declined, A. 7.

c and g (with s, forming x), N. 1 (3), 12, 2.
Caesar's "Gallic War," — Bk. I., chap. 1-13, pages 136-142; NOTES on the same, pages 143-148.
can, how expressed, N. 197, 3.
capio, inflection, A. 34. [See *Verbs in* -io.]
Cardinal Adjectives, 9, b (page 2), N. 41; how declined, N. 42, c, 43. [See under unus, duo, tres, mille.]
Case, 8 (page 2), 15, a, b (page 22); Table of Latin Cases, 20 (page 24); Case-endings, N. 6; formation of cases, N. 7.
causā, with Genitive, N. 128, 149, a.
Cause, expr. by Ablative, N. 149, L. xl; by Indic. and Subj. Modes, N. 182, L. lxix.
celo, with two Accusatives, N. 141, R. 1.
certiorem facio, with Acc. and Inf., N. 199 3.
citerior, etc., N. 34, L. xxxiv, A. 17, b.
Clauses, 41 (page 12); as modifiers, 42 (page 12), N. 104; as Subject, 36, d (page 10); as Object, 42, a (page 12). [See *Causal, Concessive*, and *Temporal Clauses*.]
coepi, N. 91, 1, L. lxiii, A. 46.
cogo, with Acc. and Inf., N. 197, 8.
Collective Nouns, 3, d (page 1); with pl. verb, 51, b (page 14), N. 117, c.
Commands, Direct, N. 163, 178, CAUTION 2, L. xl; Indirect, N. 164, c, 178; Negative, N. 178, CAUTION 2.
Comparative Degree, 10 (page 2); how declined in Latin, N. 26, d, A. 15; plus, N.

27, A. 15, a; translated *rather, too, quite*, N. 40, a; with Abl., N. 154, L. lxviii.
Comparison of Adjectives, 10 (page 2), N. 29; Regular, N. 30, L. xxviii, A. 16; Irregular, N. 31-36, L. xxix, xxxiv [see under *Irregular Comparison*]; by magis and maxime, N. 37; of Participles, N. 30, a.
Comparison of Adverbs, N. 38, 39.
Complement, 37, a (page 10), 46, a (page 13), N. 55, 103, L. vi.
Complementary Infinitive, N. 165, b, L. xix.
Complex Sentence, 40, c (page 12), N. 105.
Compound (1) Nouns, N. 23, L. xxxvi; (2) Words, N. 99; (3) Sentences, 40, b (page 12), N. 105.
con (com, etc.), as prefix, N. 99, 1.
Concession, how expressed, N. 183, L. lxxi.
Conditional Sentences, N. 174, 175, L. xxi, lviii.
Conjugation, 15 a (page 22); the Four Conjugations, general statement, N. 54, 65 [See under *First, Second, Third,* and *Fourth Conjugations; Verbs in* -io; *Periphrastic Conjugations, Deponent, Semi-Deponent, Irregular, Defective,* and *Impersonal Verbs*]; peculiarities of the Four Conjugations, N. 79.
Conjunctions, 30 (page 9), N. 96; omitted, N. 96, b. [See et, -que, atque.]
Consonants, 3 (page 17); Consonant Changes, N. 1, 79, 8; Double Consonants, 4, c (page 17); Consonant Stems (Third Dec.), N. 11, a, 15.
constat, inflection, A. 47.
consuevi, with Pres. meaning, N. 91, R., A. 46.†
Contracted Syllables (length of), 11, e (page 21), N. 7, 20, c.
Copula (*to be*) and Copulative Verbs, 87 (page 10), N. 55, 103, L. vi.
Correlatives, N. 195, 8, L. xlviii.
cum (prep.), with Abl., N. 150, a, L. xlix; omitted, N. 150, R.; Enclitic, N. 53, a, 195, 3.
cum (quum), with Indic. and Subj., N. 182, b, 183, a, 184, a, ·L. lxix, lxxi, lxxii.

d and t, before s, N. 1 (4), 12, b.
Dates, N. 161.
Dative Case, 20 (page 24); how formed, N. 7; plural form in declension, N. 8 (5); ending in -i, see -ius *in Gen. Sing.*; ending in -abus, N. 9, e, L. viii; ending in -ubus, N. 20, R.; of Indirect Object, N. 129, L. ix; when *to* must be trans. by ad, N. 129, a; when *for* must be trans. by pro, N. 129, b;

with Intrans. Verbs, N. 130, (in the Passive) 131, *a*, CAUTION, 134, L. lxvi; of Advantage or Disadvantage, N. 131, L. lxvi; with Adjectives, N. 131, *b*, 132, L. xxxiv; for Abl. of Separation, N. 131, *c*; with Compound Verbs containing Prepositions, N. 133, L. lvii; denoting Possession, N. 135, L. lxvii; of Agent, N. 136, L. lx; two Datives, N. 137, L. lxvii; for Genitive, N. 138; position, N. 193, 3.
de, as a prefix, N. 99, 1; with Abl., instead of Part. Gen., N. 123, *a*
dea, N. 6, 9, *e*, L. viii.
Declaratory Sentences, 44, *a* (page 13), N. 100; in Indirect Discourse, N. 187.
Declension, 15, *a* (page 22); general laws, N. 8; Declensions of Nouns (how distinguished), 21 (page 25). [See under the different *Declensions of Nouns* and *Adjectives*.]
Defective Verbs, 27 (page 8), N. 91, L. lxiii, A. 46.
[See coepi, memini, odi, inquam, salve, ave.]
Degree, expr. by Obj. or Acc., 54, 6 (page 15), N. 142, L. xlvii; Degree of Difference, 54, 7 (page 15), N. 155, L. lxviii.
Demonstrative Pronouns, N. 49; as Adj., N. 114, 1; as Pers. Pron., N. 114, 2, L. li, A. 24; position, N. 193, 4.
Dependent Clauses, 41 (page 12).
Deponent Verbs, N. 80; Inflection, A. 37; with Abl., N. 151, *a*, L. xlii. [See under the different *Conjugations of Verbs*.]
Derived Words, N. 98. [See *Endings*.]
deus, N. 6, 10, *f*; L. xlii.
dic, duc, fac, fer, N. 79, 5.
dies, N. 22, *b-d*, A. 9. [See *Fifth Declension*.]
dignus, with Abl., N. 156, L. lxx.
Diminutives, N. 98, *b*.
Diphthongs, 5 (page 18); quantity, 11, *a* (page 20).
Direct Object, 39, *a* (page 11), 49 (page 14), N. 102, R., 139 L. iii; position, N. 193, 3.
Direct Questions, see *Questions*.
dis (di), as a prefix, N. 99, 2.
Distributive Adjectives, N. 41, *a*; how declined, N. 42, *b*.
diu, compared, N. 89, *b*.
dives, compared, N. 86, *a*; declined, A. 14, *a*.
domus, N. 21, *b*; expr. Place, N. 159, L. xxxv, A. 8, *a*.
Double Questions, see *Questions*.
dubito, with Subj. and Inf., N. 181, *d*, and CAUTIONS, 199, 1.

dubius, with Subj., N. 181, *d*, 199, 1.
dum, (*while*) with Hist. Pres., N. 168, R., L. lxvi; (*until*) N. 184, *b*, L. lxxii; (*provided*) N. 183, *d*, L. lxxii.
dummodo, with Subj., N. 183, *d*.
duo, N. 43, *c*, L. xlv, A. 20, *b*.

e, final, quantity in declension, N. 8 (9); *long before* i, N. 6, 22, *d*; -e, -al, -ar, with Abl. in -i, N. 16, R., 26, *b*.
e (ex), N. 95, *a*; how diff. from a (ab), N. 95, *b*; with Abl. instead of Part. Gen., N. 123, *a*.
ego, N. 46, L. 1, A. 21.
ejusmodi, meaning and use, N. 121.
Enclitics, N. 53, *a*, 195, 3; as affecting accent of a word, N. 195, 4.
Endings with *special meaning*: — Nouns (-or, -ulus), N. 98, *a*, *b*; Adjectives (-ulus, -osus), N. 98, *b*, *c*; Verbs (-sco, -to), N. 98, *d*, *e*; -que (as in quisque), N. 53, *c*; -vis (as in quivis), N. 52, *d*.
ENGLISH GRAMMAR REVIEWED, pages 1–16.
English Method of Pronunciation, 9 (page 19).
eo, N. 87, L. lviii, A. 43; compounds often *transitive*, N. 87, R.
eo ... quo, N. 195, 8.
esse omitted, N. 199, 2.
est, sunt (*there is, there are*), N. 193, 6.
et ... et, N. 195, 8.
et, -que, atque, N. 96, *a*; omitted, N. 96, *b*.
etsi in Concessions, N. 183, CAUTION.
Etymology, defined, 1 (page 1).
Euphonic Changes, N. 1, 2.
Exclamatory Sentences, 44, *d* (page 13), N. 100.
Expletives (*it, there*), 55 (page 15).
Extent of Space, 54, 3 (page 15), N. 142, *b*, L. xlvi; of Time, 54, 4 (page 15), N. 142, *a*, 160, L. xlv.
exterus, N. 85, L. xxxiv, A. 17, *c*.

facile, for faciliter, N. 89.
facilis, etc., N. 31, *b*, L. xxix, A. 16, *b*.
facio and its compounds, N. 88, R.; Imper. fac, N. 79, 5. [See flo.]
Fearing, verbs of, with Subj., N. 179, *e*.
fero, N. 86, L. lvi, A. 42.
fido, N. 81, A. 38.
Fifth Declension, N. 22, L. xxxvi, A. 9.
filia, N. 9, *e*, L. viii.
filius, how declined, N. 10, *d*, L. xi.
Finite Verbs, 15, *e* (page 4), 51 (page 14), 56, *a* (page 16), N. 117.
flo, N. 88, L. lxi, A. 44.

First Conjugation, N. 65-78; Synopsis, N. 78, L. vii-xxv, A. 28, 29; Deponent Verbs, L. xxxii, A. 37; First Periphrastic Conj., N. 82, a, L. lx, A. 39, a.
First Declension of Nouns, N. 9, L. i, viii, A. 1.
First and Second Declensions of Adjectives, N. 24, a, L. iv, A. 10, 11.
for, expr. by Dative, N. 129; by pro, N. 129, b.
fore and forem for futurus esse and essem, N. 84, d; fore ut with Subj. for Fut. Inf. Pass., N. 181, a, R.
Fourth Conjugation, N. 65-77, L. xli, A. 85, 36; Deponent Verbs, L. xlii, A. 37.
Fourth Declension, N. 20, 21, L. xxxv, A. 8.
Frequentative Verbs, N. 98, e.
fretus, with Abl., N. 151, b.
fruor, with Abl., N. 151, a.
fungor, with Abl., N. 151, a.
Future Tense, 17, a (page 4); *Indicative*, N. 60, 61, 1, 68, c, 73, c; trans. by Present *form*, N. 168, a; *Imperative*, N. 70, 75, b, c; *Infinitive*, N. 71, c, 76, c, 191, R.; substitute for Fut. Inf. Pass., N. 76, c, 181, a, R.; Fut. Inf. Act. without esse, N. 189, e, 199, 2; Fut. Inf. in Deponent Verbs, N. 80, a; Fut. Participle, (*active*) N. 58, a, 72, b; (*passive*) N. 58, b, 77, b.
Future Perfect Tense, 17, a (page 4), N. 60, 61, 1, 68, f, 73, d; trans. by Present *form*, N. 168, a.

g (with s, forming x), N. 1 (3), 6, 12, a.
gaudeo, N. 81, A. 38.
Gender, 5 (page 1); general rules, (*by meaning*) 18, 19 (page 23), N. 3; (*by ending*) N. 4. EXCEPTIONS (*by ending*),— First Dec., N. 9, c; Second Dec., N. 10, g; Third Dec., N. 19, a, b; Fourth Dec., N. 20*; Fifth Dec., N. 22, b. Gender of an Infinitive, Phrase, or Clause, 36 (page 10), 19, c, 2 (page 23); of an Indeclinable Noun, 19, c, 1 (page 23).
GENERAL FACTS AND USEFUL HINTS, N. 195-199.
Genitive, 20 (page 24); endings in the Five Declensions, N. 6; ending in -ii or -i, N. 10, e; general use, N. 119, L. v; of Possesion, N. 120, L. v; of Quality, N. 121, L. lxx; of Value, N. 121, a; Partitive, N. 122, 123; Subjective and Objective, N. 123, b, 124, L. lxiii; with Adjectives, N. 124, L. lxiii; with Verbs of *remembering* and *forgetting*, N. 125, L. lxiii; after sum, limited noun omitted, N. 126, a, L. lvi; expr. by Neuter of Poss. Pron., N. 126, R.; equivalent to Eng. *composed of*, N. 126, b, L. lvi; with Impersonal Verbs, N. 127; with causā or

gratiā, N. 128, L. xl; with pridie and postridie, N. 128, R.; with potior, N. 151, a, R.; position, N. 193, 2.
genius, how declined, N. 10, d.
Gerund, N. 59, a, 72, c, 190; L. lxxiii.
Gerundive, N. 58, b, 77, b; uses, N. 189, f, 190, a, L. lxxiii; without esse, N. 199, 2.
gratiā, with Genitive, N. 128.

h, a breathing, 4, b (page 17), 11, b, R., c, R. (page 20), N. 95, a.
hic, N. 49 and R. 1, 114, c, L. li, A. 24.
Hints on Translation, N. 200.
Historical Tenses, N. 171; Present, N. 168, b, L. lxvi; Perf., N. 61, b; Historical Infinitive, N. 167, L. lxxi.
Hortatory Subjunctive, see *Subjunctive*.
hortor, inflection, A. 87. [See *Deponent Verbs*.]

i final, quantity, N. 8 (7); i *short* in Supine. of eo, N. 87, a; -i in Abl., N. 17, b, 26; -i or -e in Abl., N. 17, b, 26, c, d, 28.
ibi . . . ubi, N. 195, 8.
idem, N. 49, L. li, A. 24.
Idus, N. 20*, 161, 3.
ille, N. 49, and R. 1, 114, b, L. li, A. 24.
-im in Acc. Sing., N. 17, c.
Imperative Mode, 15, d (page 4), 20 (page 7), N. 57, c, 163; Tenses, N. 63, c, 169; formation, N. 70, 75; dic, duc, fac, fer, N. 79, 5; Imperative Sentences, 44, c (page 13), N. 100. [See *Commands*.]
Imperfect Tense, N. 60, 61, 2; formation, (Indicative) N. 68, b, 73, b, (Subjunctive) 69, b, 74, a.
impero, with Dat., N. 131, b, CAUTION, 197, 1, L. lxvi; with Subj., N. 179, d; L. lxvi.
Impersonal Verbs and Verbs used Impersonally, 26 (page 8), N. 92, 93, L. lxiv; examples, N. 198; inflection, A. 47; used with the Gen., N. 127; used with the Dat., N. 134, L. lxiv, lxvi; with Clause as Subject, N. 188, L. lxiv, lxv. [See licet and oportet.]
in, as prefix, N. 99, 1, 2; with Acc. and Abl., N. 95, c, L. xxxix.
Inceptive Verbs, N. 98, d.
incipio, as Pres. of coepi, N. 91, 1.
inde . . . unde, N. 195, 8.
Indeclinable Adjectives, N. 42, c, 43, e.
Indeclinable Nouns, gender of, 19, c, 1 (page 23), N. 3.
Indefinite Pronouns, N. 52, 116, L. liv, A. 27. [See under aliquis, siquis, nequis, etc.]

306 INDEX.

Independent Case, 8, *d* (page 2), 52 (page 14).
Indicative Mode, 15, *a* (page 3), N. 57, *a*, 162; Tenses, 17 (page 4), N. 60, 61, 63, *a*; formation of tenses, N. 68, 73; special force of Fut., Fut. Perf., and Pres. (Historical), N. 168; in Conditional Sentences, N. 174, 175; in Indirect Discourse, N. 187, R. 2.
Indirect Discourse, N. 166, 186, 187, L. lxxv-lxxviii; laws of Modes and Tenses, N. 187, L. lxxvi; general practice, L. lxxvii, lxxviii.
Indirect Object, 39, *b* (page 11), N. 129, L. ix, lxvi; position, N. 193, 3.
Indirect Questions, N. 177, *b–d*, L. lxxv.
inferus, N. 35, L. xxxiv, A. 17, *c*.
Infinitive Mode, 15, *e* (page 4), 56 (page 16), N. 57, *d*; Tenses, N. 63, *d*, 71, 76; time denoted, N. 173, L. xliii; Fut. Inf. in Deponent Verbs, N. 80, *a*. Use, as Subject or Object, 36, *c* (page 10), 53 (page 15), N. 57, *d*, 165, L. lvi; modified by Neut. Adj., N. 109, *b*, 126, *a*, R.; Complementary, N. 165, *b*, L. xix; with Objective as Subject, 56, *b* (page 16); with Accusative as Subject, N. 166, L. xx; not used after verbs of *asking*, *urging*, etc., N. 166, CAUTION; Historical Inf., N. 167, L. lxxi; in Indirect Discourse, N. 166, 186, 187, L. xx, lxxv–lxxviii.
Inflection, 15 (page 22).
inquam, N. 91, 2, *a*; position, N. 193, 6.
inter nos, se, etc., N. 53, *d*, 112, *b*.
interest, with Gen., N. 127, *b*.
interior, N. 34, L. xxxiv, A. 17, *b*.
Interjections, 31 (page 9), N. 97.
Interrogative Pronouns, 11, *c* (page 8), N. 51, 116, L. liii; position, N. 193, 4.
Interrogative Sentences, 44, *b* (page 13), N. 100, 101. [See *Questions*.]
Intransitive Verbs, 12 (page 3); used in the *passive*, N. 93, 2, 134, L. lxvi; becoming *trans.* in compounds, N. 87, R., 139, *a*.
INTRODUCTION TO LATIN LESSONS, pages 17–25.
ipse, N. 49 and R. 3, 114, *a*, L. li, A. 24.
Irregular Comparison of Adjectives, L. xxix, xxxiv; ending in -er, N. 31, *a*, A. 16, *a*; ending in -lis (six), N. 31, *b*, A. 16, *b*; ending in -dicus, -ficus, -volus, N. 32, A. 16, *c*; bonus, etc., N. 33, A. 17, *a*; citerior, etc., N. 34, A. 17, *b*; exterus, etc., N. 35, A. 17, *c*; dives, juvenis, senex, N. 36.
Irregular Verbs, N. 83–90, A. 40–45. [See sum, possum, prosum, fero, eo, fio, volo, nolo, malo.]
-is, in Acc. pl., N. 6, 17, *d*, 18, 26.
is, ea, id, L. li, A. 24; as Dem. Pron., N. 49 and R. 2; as Pers. Pron., N. 46.
iste, N. 49 and R. 1, L. li, A. 24.

it, not expressed, 26 (page 8), 55 (page 15), N. 92, L. lxiv.
i'taque and ita'que, N. 195, 5.
-ius, in Gen. Sing., N. 43, *a*, *b*, 49, L. xlii. li, A. 11, 24.

j, consonant form of i, 3 (page 17).
jubeo and impero, difference in construction, N. 131, *b*, CAUTION, 197, 1, 8, L. lxvi.
Jupiter, declined, A. 7.
jusjurandum, N. 23, *b*.
juvenis, how compared, N. 36, *b*.
juvo, with Acc., N. 131, *b*, CAUTION.

k, rare in Latin, 2 (page 17).

Latin Language, 1 (page 17).
LATIN LESSONS, pages 27–148.
let, as a sign of a Command, etc., 20 (page 7), N. 164, *c*.
libet, with Dat., N. 134, R.
licet, N. 93, 1, *c*; with Dat., N. 134, R., 197 2, 3, L. lxiv; inflection, A. 47.
Liquids, 4, *a* (page 17).
Locative Case, 20, R. (page 24), N. 159.

m changed to n, N. 1 (5).
magis, N. 87, 39; in malo, N. 90, A. 45.
magnopere, compared, N. 39.
major natu, N. 36, *b*, L. xlix.
malo, irr. verb, N. 90, L. lxii, A. 45.
malus, N. 33, A. 17, *a*.
Manner, how expressed, N. 150, L. xlix.
maxime, N. 87, 39.
may, how expr. in Latin, N. 197, 2, 3, L. lxiv.
memini, N. 91, 2; with Gen., N. 125, L. lxii, A. 46.
meridies, N. 4, R. 5, 22, *b*.
meus, N. 48, L. xl, A. 23.
mille, N. 43, *e*, 123, *c*, L. xlvi, A. 20, *c*.
minor natu, N. 36, *b*, L. xlix.
miseret, with Gen., N. 125, L. lxii.
Mixed Stems (Third Dec.), N. 18, L. xvii, A. 6.
Mode, defined, 15 (page 3). [See under *Indicative*, *Subjunctive*, etc.]
modo, *provided*, with Subj., N. 183, *d*.
moneo, inflection, A. 30, 31.
Months (names of), really Adjectives, N. 161, *a*.
multum, multo, as Adverbs, N. 39, *a*.
multus, N. 33, A. 17, *a*.
must, how expr. in Latin, N. 82, *b*, 197, 2, 3, L. lx, lxiv.
Mutes, 4, *d* and R. (page 17).

INDEX. 807

natu, N. 36, b, L. xlix.
ne, in negative Wishes, N. 176, CAUTION; in neg. Commands, N. 178, 1, 2; in neg. Purposes, N. 179.
-ne, in Questions (single), N. 101, a, 195, 3, L. liii; -ne ... an, N. 101, b, 177, d.
ne ... quidem, N. 198, 5, 195, 2.
nego, for dico non, N. 199, 5.
neque (nec) ... neque (nec), N. 195, 8.
nequis, N. 52, b, c, L. liv, A. 27.
neuter, N. 43, b, L. xiii, A. 11.
Neuter Nouns, general law of decl., N. 8 (3); ending in -e, -al, -ar, N. 16, R., 17, b.
no, how expr. in Latin, N. 101, R.
nocetur, inflection, A. 47.
noli, in neg. Commands, N. 178, 2, b.
nolo, N. 90, L. lxii, A. 45.
Nominative, 8, a (page 2), 45 (page 13), 20 (page 24), N. 102, a, 118; how formed in the Five Declensions, N. 7; variety in formation in Third Dec., N. 12-15, b, 16, a, b, R.
nonne, use, N. 101, a, L. liii.
non solum ... sed etiam, N. 195, 8.
nos, for ego ("editor'r we"), N. 111, a.
noster, N. 48, L. 1, A. 23.
nostrum, nostri (Gen. pr.), diff. in use, N. 123, b.
NOTES, on Latin Etymology, pages 149-187; on Latin Syntax, pages 188-233.
novi, with Pres. meaning, N. 91, R., A. 46†.
Nouns, 3 (page 1), N. 3 23. [See under *First, Second*, etc., *Declensions*.]
nullus, N. 43, b, L. xiii, A. 11.
num, use, N. 101, a, 177, d, L. liii, lxxv.
Number, of Nouns and Verbs, 7 (page 1), 22 (page 7), 51 (page 14).
Numeral Adjectives [see also *Cardinal, Ordinal*, and *Distributive Adjectives*, and unus, duo, tres, mille], 9, b (page 2), N. 41, 42, 43, L. xlv, A. 19, 20; *do not take Part. Gen.*, N. 123, a.
Numeral Adverbs, N. 44, A. 19.

o final, quantity in decl., N. 8 (7).
ob, as prefix, N. 99, 1.
Object, Direct and Indirect, 39 (page 11).
Objective, 8, c (page 2); as Adv., 54 (page 15); as Subject of Infin., 56, b (page 16); Objective Genitive, N. 124, L. lxiii.
obliviscor, with Gen., N. 125, L. lxiii.
odi, N 91. 2, L. lxiii, A. 46.
oportet, N. 92, CAUTION, 93, 1, c, 197, 2, 3, L. lxiv.
opus, with Abl., N. 147, a.
Oratio Obliqua, see *Indirect Discourse.*

Order of words in a Latin Sentence, N 198, 193.
Ordinal Adjectives, 9, b (page 2), N. 41, 42, a, L. xlv, A. 19.
O si, use, N. 176.
ought, how expr. in Latin, N. 82, b, 197, 3.

par, inflection, A. 14, a.
Participles, 23 (page 7), 47 (page 13), N. 58, 108, 189, L. xliv; *time denoted*, 23, R. (page 8), N. 189, a; formation, N. 72, 77; how compared, N. 80, a; of Deponent Verbs, N. 80, b, L. xliv; how best trans., N. 189, d; in Abl. Abs., N. 157, L. lix.
Partitive Genitive, N. 122, 123, L. xlvi; how to express *all of us, the top of the mountain*, etc., N. 123, d, e.
Parts of Speech, 2 (page 1), 14 (page 22).
parvus, N. 33, A. 17, a.
Passive Voice, 14 (page 3), 46, c (page 13).
Past Tense, 17, a (page 4).
paterfamilias, etc., N. 23, c.
patior, with Acc. and Inf., N. 197, 8.
pelagus, gender, N. 4, R. 3.
Penult, and its accent, 13, a, b, and R. 2 (page 21).
per, as prefix, N. 40, d, 99, 1; with Acc. of Indirect Agent, N. 151, CAUTION.
Perfect Tense, 17, a (page 4); Stem, N. 67, 79; Definite and Aorist, N. 61, 3, 62; formation, (*Indicative*) N. 68, d, 73, d, (*Subjunctive*) N. 69, c, 74, b, (*Infinitive*) N. 71, b, 76, b; v dropped, N. 79, 4; Reduplicated, N. 79, 6; of lego, verto, etc., N. 79, 7; with Pres. meaning, N. 91, 2 and R.; Participle, N. 58, b, 77, a, 80, R. 1, 157, R. 1, (in Deponents) with *active meaning*, N. 80, R. 1, 157, R. 1, 189, c.
Periphrastic Conjugations, N. 82, L. lx, A. 39.
Person, 6 (page 1), 22 (page 7), 51 (page 14), N. 117, d.
Personal Endings, N. 54, 2, 64.
Personal Pronouns, 11 (page 3), N. 46, L. 1, A. 21; usually omitted, N. 111; Third Person, how supplied, N. 46, 114, 2; position, N. 193, 8.
peto, with a (ab), and Abl., N. 141, R. 2, 199, 4.
Phrase, 43 (page 12), N. 104; as Subject, 36, e (page 10).
Place, N. 158, 159, L. xxxix, lv.
Pluperfect Tense (in Eng., *Past Perfect*, 17, a, page 4), N. 60, 61, 4, 68, e, 69, d, 73, d, 74, b.
plus, N. 27, 122. b, L. xlvii, A. 15, a; plus, minus, etc, with other cases instead of Abl., N. 154. b.

poenitet, with Gen., N. 127, *a*.
Positive Degree, defined, 10 (page 2).
Possession, how expr., 48 (page 13), 20 (page 24); by Gen., N. 120, L. v; by Dative, N. 135, L. lxvii.
Possessive Pronouns, N. 48, 113, L. 1, A. 23; used as Nouns, N. 113, *a*, 126, *a*, R.
possum, N. 85, 1, L. xix, A. 41.
posterus, N. 35, A. 17, *c*.
postquam, posteaquam, with Indic., N. 184, CAUTION.
postridie, with Gen., N. 128, R.
postulo, with a (ab) and Abl., N. 141, R. 2, 199, 4.
Potential Mode, 15, *b* (page 3), 18 (page 5).
potior, inflected, A. 37; with Abl., N. 151, *a*, L. xlii; with Gen., N. 151, *a*, R.
Predicate, 35, *b*, 37 (page 10), N. 102, *b*, 103; Pred. Noun and Adj., 37, R. and *d* (page 11), 46, *a*, *b*, (page 13), N. 107 and R., 108, L. vi.
Prefixes, N. 40, *d*, 99.
Prepositions, 29 (page 9); with Acc. and Abl., N. 95, L xxxix; as Adverbs, 29, R. (page 9), N. 95; cum omitted, N. 150, *a*, R.; frequent position, N. 193, 7; in and sub, N. 95, *c*, L. xxxix.
Present Tense, 17, *a* (page 4), N. 60, 61, 1; Stem, N. 54, 1, 65, 67; formation of the Present, (*Indic.*) N. 54, 3, 68, *a*, 73, *a*; (*Subj.*) N. 69, *a*, 74, *a*; (*Imper.*) N. 70, 75, *a*; (*Inf.*) N. 71, *a*, 76, *a*; time expr. by Pres. *Inf.*, N. 173; Pres. Participle, N. 58, *a*, 72, *a*; no Pres. Partic. in sum, N. 84, *c*, 157; Historical Present, N. 168, *b*, L. lxvi.
Preteritive Verbs, A. 46†.
Price, how expr., 54, 9 (page 15); N. 151, *c*.
Principal Clauses, 41 (page 12).
pridie, with Gen., N. 128, R.
Primary, or Principal Tenses, N. 171.
Principal Parts of Verbs, N. 66; of Impersonal Verbs, A. 47.
prior, N. 34, L. xxxiv, A. 17, *b*.
priusquam, with Indic. and Subj., N. 184, *c*, L. lxxii.
pro (or prod), as prefix, see prosum.
Prohibitions, how expr., N. 178, CAUTION 2.
Pronominal Adjectives, 9, *a* (page 2).
Pronouns, 11 (page 3), N. 45-53, 111-116, L. l-liv; position, N. 193, 4. [See the various classes of Pronouns, — *Personal, Relative*, etc.]
Pronunciation of Latin, 7-9 (pages 18, 19).
propior, N. 34, L. xxxiv, A. 17, *b*; with Dat. or Acc., N. 132, *a*.
prosum, N. 85, 2, A. 41, *a*.
Protasis, N. 174.
pugnatur, inflection, A. 47.

Purpose, expr. by Dat, N. 137, L lxvii; by a Phrase, N. 137, *a*; by the Subj., N. 164, *d*, 179, L. xl, xlviii; expr. in *five ways*, N. 180, L. lxxiv.

qu = c, N. 1 (1).
qua, as an Adverb, N. 94, 2.
quaero, with a (ab), de, e (ex), and Abl., N. 141, R. 2, 199, 4.
Quality, expr. by Gen., N. 121, 152, *a*; by Abl., N. 152 and *a*, L. lxx.
quam with Superlative, N. 40, *c*; omitted (Abl. with Comparatives), N. 154, L. lxviii.
quamquam, with Indic., N. 183, CAUTION.
quamvis, with Subj., N. 183, *c*.
Quantity, 10 (page 20); Rules, 11, 12 (pages 20, 21). [See also *Vowels, long* and *short*.]
-que, Enclitic, N. 195, 3; force in quisque, etc., N. 53, *c*.
Questions (*single* and *double*), Direct, N. 101, *a*, *b*, L. liii, liv, lxxv; Indirect, N. 177, *d*, N. lxxv; implying a *doubt*, N. 164, *b*, 177, *a*.
qui (Relative), N. 50, L. lii, A. 25.
qui in clauses of *Purpose, Result, Cause*, and *Concession*, N. 179, *a*, 181, *c*, 182, *c*, 183, *b*, 197, 6, L. lii, lxv, lxix, lxxi.
quia, with Indic., N. 182, *a*.
quicumque, N. 52, *d*.
quidam, N. 52, *d*.
quin, with Subj., N. 181, *d*, 199, 1, L. lxv.
quis (qui), Interrogative, N. 51, L. liii, A. 26; Indefinite, N. 52, L. liv, A. 27; how diff. from uter, N. 51, CAUTION, 195, 7.
quisque, N. 52, *d*; with Superlatives, N. 53, *b*, L. liv.
quivis, N. 52, *d*.
quo for ut, N. 179, *b*.
quo ... eo, *the* ... *the*, N. 155, *b*.
quod, with Indic., N. 182, *a*, *d*; with Subj., N. 187, *f*.
quod (id quod, quae res), N. 115, *b*.
quominus, N. 179, *c*, 196.
quoniam, with Indic., N. 182, *a*.
quum (cum), with Indic. and Subj., (*since*) N. 182, *b*, L. lxix; (*although*) N. 183, *a*, L. lxxi; (*when*) N. 184, *a*, L. lxxii; quum ... tamen, N. 195, 8; quum ... tum, N. 195, 8.

re (red), as prefix, N. 85, 2, 99, 2.
Reduplication, N. 79, 6.
refert, with Gen., N. 127, *b*.
Reflexive Pronouns, N. 47, 112, L. l, A. 22.
rego, inflection, A. 32, 33. [See *Third Conjugation*.]
Relative Clauses of Purpose, etc., see qui.

INDEX. 309

Relative Pronouns, 11, *b* (page 3), 50 (page 14), N. 50, 115, L. lii, A. 25; *not omitted in Latin*, N. 115, *c*; at the beginning of a sentence, N. 115, *d*; trans. *as*, N. 115, *f*; position, N. 193, 4.
Respect, or Specification, see *Ablative*.
respublica, N. 23, *a*.
Result, how expr., N. 181; Result Clauses as Subject, Object, or Appositive, N. 181, *a*, *b*, *e*, L. lxv.
Regular Comparison, see *Comparison*.
rogo, peto, postulo, quaero, used with what cases, N. 199, 4.
Roman Method of Pronunciation, 8 (page 18).
rus, in expressions of Place, N. 159.

s changed to r, N. 1 (2), 13, R., 84, *b*.
salve, Imperative, N. 91, 2, *b*.
-sco, Verb-ending, see *Inceptive Verbs*.
se, as prefix, N. 99, 2.
Second Conjugation, N. 65-77, L. xxx, A. 30, 31; peculiarities of Perfect and Supine, N. 79, 1; Deponent Verbs, L. xxxii, A. 37; Second Periphrastic Conj., N. 82, *b*, A. 39, *b*.
Second Declension of Nouns, N. 10, L. iii, iv, xl, xlii, A. 2.
Secondary Tenses, N. 171. [See *Sequence of Tenses*.]
Semi-Deponent Verbs, N. 81, L. lxvii, A. 38.
senex, declined, A. 7; compared, N. 36, *b*.
Sentences, definition, 38 (page 9); Simple, Complex, Compound, 40 (page 11), N. 105; Declaratory, Interrogative, Imperative, 44 (page 13), N. 100; MISCELLANEOUS SENTENCES FOR TRANSLATION INTO LATIN, pages 132-135.
Separation, see under *Ablative* and *Dative*.
Sequence of Tenses, N. 172, L. xl, lxvi.
sequor, A. 37. [See *Deponent Verbs*.]
should, how expr. in Latin, N. 197, 3.
si, in Conditions, N. 174, 175; for num, N. 177, R. 1.
Simple Sentences, 40, *a* (page 12).
Single Questions, see *Questions*.
siquis, N. 52, and *b*, *c*, L. liv, A. 27.
soleo, N. 81, A. 38.
solus, N. 43, *b*, L. xlii, A. 11.
Stem, definition, 16 (page 22); Stem-Endings of Nouns, N. 5; Stems of Verbs, N. 54, 1, 67. [See also *Present*, *Perfect*, and *Supine Stems*.]
sub, with Acc. and Abl., N. 95, *c*, L. xxxix.
Subject, 35, *a*, 36 (page 10), 45 (page 13), N. 102; its modifiers, 88 (page 11); when omitted, N. 111; *Subject of an Impersonal Verb*, 26 (page 8), N. 92 and CAUTION, 93; Subject of the Infinitive, 56 (page 16), N. 106.

Subjective Genitive, N. 124.
Subjunctive, (Eng.) 15, *c* (page 4), 19 (page 6), (Lat.) N. 57, *b*, 164; Tenses, N. 63, *b*, 69, 74, 170. USES, — Expressing: *Condition*, N. 164, *a*, 174, 175, L. xxi, xxiv, lviii; *Wish*, N. 176, L. lxi; *Question* (implying *doubt*), N. 164, *b*, 177, *a*, (*Indirect*) N. 164, *b*, 177, *b*, *c*, *d*, L. lxxv; *Command*, *Exhortation*, etc., N. 164, *c*, 178, L. xxvii, xlviii, lxxvi; *Purpose*, N. 164, *d*, 166, CAUTION, 179, L. xl, xlviii; *Result*, N. 181, L. lxv; *Cause*, N. 182, 187, *f*, L. lxix; *Concession*, N. 183, L. lxxi; *Time*, N. 184, L. lxxii; *Indirect Discourse*, N. 186, 187, L. lxxv-lxxviii; "*Attraction*," N. 185.
Substantive Clauses, 42, *a* (page 12), N. 188, L. lxv.
sui and suus, N. 47, 48 and CAUTION, 112, *a*, L. l, A. 22, 23.
sum, inflection, A. 40; as Copula, N. 55, 103, L. vi, xviii; peculiarities, N. 84; with Pred. Gen., N. 126, L. lvi; with Dat. of Poss., N. 135, L. lxvii; Compounds, with Dat., N. 135, *a*.
sunt, *there are*, N. 193, 6.
Superlative Degree, 10 (page 2); trans. by *very*, N. 40, *b*, *as possible*, N. 40, *c*; with quisque, N. 53, *b*.
superus, N. 35, L. xxxiv, A. 17, *c*.
Supine N. 21, *a*, 59, *b*, 72, *d*; stem, N. 67, 79, and 1, 2; Use, N. 153, R., 191, L. lxxiv; in Fut. Inf. Pass., N. 191, R.
Syllables, 6 (page 18); *long* and *short*, 10, 11, 12 (pages 20, 21); contracted, 11, *c* (page 21), N. 7, 20, *c*.
Synopsis of Verb, N. 78.
Syntax, definition, 32 (page 9); LATIN SYNTAX, pages 188-232.

t before s, N. 1 (4), 12, *b*; in possum, N. 85, 1, A. 41.
talis . . . qualis, N. 195, 8.
tametsi, see *Concession*; tametsi . tamen, N. 195, 8.
tantus . . . quantus, N. 195, 8.
Temporal Clauses, see *Time*.
Tense, definition, 16 (page 4); not always accurately indicating *time* in Eng. Verbs, 17, NOTE, 18, 19 (pages 5, 6), N. 168, *a*; names and uses of the tenses, (Eng.) 17-21 (pages 4-7), (Latin) N. 60-63, 168-173; of Participles, 23, R. (page 8), N. 189, *a* [see also *Present*, *Imperfect*, etc.]; formation, N. 68-76. [See *Secondary Tenses*, and *Sequence of Tenses*.]
there is, *there are*, 55 page 15), N. 193, 6.
Third Conjugation, N. 65-77, L. xxxvii,

xxxviii, A. 32, 33; variety of forms, N. 79, 2-8; Verbs in -io, N. 79, 3, L. xliii, A. 34; Deponent Verbs, L. xl, A. 37.
Third Declension of Adjectives, N. 24, b-28; L. xxvi-xxviii, A. 12-15.
Third Declension of Nouns (three classes of nouns), N. 11, 18; L. xiv-xvii, A. 3-7; Nom. how formed, N. 12, 13, 14, 15, b, 16, a, b; Gender, N. 4, 19, a, b.
Time, (*how long*) 54, 4 (page 15), N. 142, a, 160, L. xlv; (*when*) 54, 5 (page 15), N. 160, L. xlv; Dates, N. 161; Temporal Clauses, N. 184, L. lxxii.
to, omitted with Eng. Inf., 56, R. (page 16); when rendered by Dat., N. 129; by ad, N. 129, a.
-to, Verb-ending, see *Frequentative Verbs.*
tot . . . quot, N. 195, 8.
totus, N. 43, b, L. xiii, A 11.
transduco, -mitto, etc., with two Acc., N. 141, c.
Transitive Verbs, definition, 12 (page 3).
Translation, Hints and Rules, N. 200, 201.
tres, N. 43, d, L. xlv, A. 20, b.
-trix, Noun-ending, N. 98, a.
tu, N. 46, L. l, A. 21.
tum . . . quum, N. 195, 8.
tuus, N. 48, L. l, A. 23.
Two Adjectives, connected by et or -que, N. 195, 6.
Two Negatives = an Affirmative, N. 195, 1.

u final, quantity, N. 8 (7).
ubi, with Indicative, N. 184, CAUTION.
-ubus in Dat. and Abl., N. 20, R.
ullus, N. 43, b, L. xiii. A. 11.
ulterior, N. 34, L. xxxiv, A. 17, b
Ultima, 13, R. 1 (page 22).
-ulus, as ending, see *Diminutives.*
una, as Adverb, N. 94, 2.
unus, N. 43, a, L. xlv, A. 11.
usus (Noun), with Abl., N. 147, a.
ut, in Purpose clauses, N. 179; = *that not*, N. 179, e; in Result clauses, N. 181; = *as*, N. 197, 5; = *how*, N. 177, R. 2; omitted, N. 179, f.
uter, N. 43, b, L. xiii, A. 11; how diff. from quis, N. 51, CAUTION, 195, 7, L. liii.
utinam, use, see *Wish.*
utor, fruor, etc., with Abl., N. 151, a, L. xlii.
utrum . . . an, see *Questions.*

v, cons. form of u, 3 (page 17); dropped in Perf. Stem, N. 79, 4.
Value, how expressed, N. 121, a.
vel . . . vel, N. 195, 8.
Verbal Nouns, 3, c (page 1), 53 (page 15), N. 57, d, 59. [See *Infinitive, Gerund*, and *Supine.*]
Verbs, see under *Transitive; Intransitive; Voice; Mode; Tense; Person; Number; Principal Parts; Stems; Conjugations* (First, Second, Third, Fourth); *Synopsis; Participles; Gerund; Supine; Verbs in -io; Deponent Verbs; Semi-Deponent Verbs; Irregular Verbs; Defective Verbs; Impersonal Verbs.*
vereor, inflection, A. 37.
vescor, with Abl., N. 151, a.
vester, N. 48, L. l, A. 23.
vestrum, vestri (Gen. pl.), how diff. in use, N. 123, b.
veto, with Acc. and Inf., N. 197, 8.
vetus, N. 26, c, A. 14, a.
virus, gender, N. 4, R. 3.
vis, inflection, A. 7; -vis, as ending, N. 52, d.
vivo, with Abl., N. 151, a.
VOCABULARY, — Latin-English, pages 269-294; English-Latin, pages 295-301; Special Vocabularies and Examples, pages 259-267.
Vocative (Eng. *Independent Case*, 8, d, page 2), 20 (page 24); law of form, N. 8 (1); EXCEPTIONS, N. 10, c, d (fīlius, etc.), f (deus), A. 23 (meus); use, N. 145, L. xi.
Voice, 14 (page 3), N. 56.
volo, N. 89, L. lxii, E. 45.
Vowels, pronunciation (Roman and English Methods), 8, 9 (pages 18, 19); quantity, 11, 12 (pages 20, 21); vowel long before another vowel (diēi, etc.) N. 22, d, (unĭus, etc.) N. 23, A. 11, (illīus, etc.) A. 24; vowel changes, N. 2, (Third Dec.) N. 13, 14, (Fourth Dec.) N. 20, d; vowel stems (Third Dec. of Nouns and Adj.), N. 11, b, 16-18, 26, a, b, c.
vulgus, gender, N. 10, g.

w, not in Latin, 2 (page 17).
Wish, how expr., N. 176, L. lxi.
with, when expr. by cum, N. 150, a, L. xlix.

yes, how expr. in Latin, N. 101, R.

www.ingramcontent.com/pod-product-compliance
Lightning Source LLC
Chambersburg PA
CBHW022019240426
43667CB00042B/943